Benchmark Series

Levels 1 & 2

Microsoft® Excel 2010

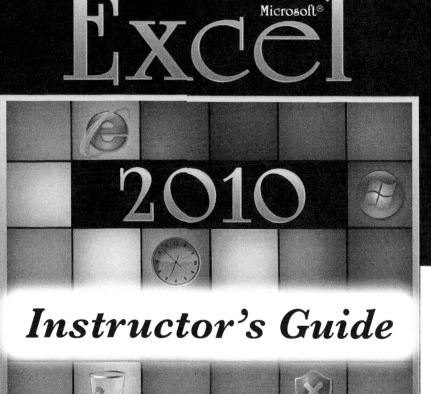

Instructor's Guide

Nita Rutkosky
Pierce College at Puyallup
Puyallup, Washington

Denise Seguin
Fanshawe College
London, Ontario

Audrey Rutkosky Roggenkamp
Pierce College at Puyallup
Puyallup, Washington

Paradigm PUBLISHING
St. Paul • Indianapolis

Developmental Editor: Christine Hurney
Production Editor: Donna Mears
Cover Designer: Leslie Anderson
Production Specialist: Desktop Solutions

Care has been taken to verify the accuracy of information presented in this book. However, the authors, editors, and publisher cannot accept responsibility for Web, email, newsgroup, or chat room subject matter or content, or for consequences from application of the information in this book, and make no warranty, expressed or implied, with respect to its content.

Trademarks: Some of the product names and company names included in this book have been used for identification purposes only and may be trademarks or registered trade names of their respective manufacturers and sellers. The authors, editors, and publisher disclaim any affiliation, association, or connection with, or sponsorship or endorsement by, such owners.

We have made every effort to trace the ownership of all copyrighted material and to secure permission from copyright holders. In the event of any question arising as to the use of any material, we will be pleased to make the necessary corrections in future printings. Thanks are due to the aforementioned authors, publishers, and agents for permission to use the materials indicated.

ISBN 978-0-76383-900-0 (Text + DVD)
ISBN 978-0-76383-899-7 (Text)

© Paradigm Publishing, Inc.
875 Montreal Way
St. Paul, MN 55102
Email: educate@emcp.com
Website: www.emcp.com

Printed in the United States of America

20 19 18 17 16 15 14 13 12   4 5 6 7 8 9 10

Contents

PLANNING *Guidelines for Choosing Outcomes, Instructional Approach, Resources, and Assessments*

Note: Lesson Blueprints providing detailed lesson plans for a 16-week course are provided on the Instructor disc and on the Internet Resource Center.

ASSESSMENT *Resources for Evaluating Student Achievement*

Note: Project Model Answers are provided in the student textbook at the beginning of each chapter.

Planning the Course

Most educators would agree that the key to teaching a successful course is careful, thorough planning. And, as noted in *Exceptional Teaching: Ideas in Action*, published by Paradigm Publishing, "Instructors assess, plan, implement, and evaluate . . . repeatedly. They do this based on many of the factors that make teaching learner-centered and on several other variables. Before students even think about entering or logging into the classroom, instructors make decisions about the course. These begin with identifying the heart of the course. That is, what, exactly, are the most important outcomes that students should achieve? And what plan of action can the instructor devise that will help ensure those outcomes?" Thinking through a course action plan typically includes four phases:

1. Developing course outcomes
2. Determining the course delivery mode and structure (dividing the course into parts, each with outcomes)
3. Selecting the instructional approach, resources, and activities of the course
4. Developing an assessment strategy

Developing Course Outcomes

In developing course outcomes, some of the key issues to consider are the following:

- When this course is complete, in what ways will the learner be permanently changed? Should instruction result in
    - building knowledge?
    - developing higher-order thinking?
    - developing independent learning skills?
    - developing technical literacy?
- What problems are encountered that are related to course content?
    - What must be communicated?
    - How will the learner find out whether the work is satisfactory?
    - How will the learner receive feedback?

Considering these questions, a set of end-of-course outcomes for a one-semester course on Microsoft Excel 2010 could include the following items, stated as performances objectives.

At course conclusion, the student will be able to:

- Create and edit spreadsheets of varying complexity
- Format cells, columns, and rows as well as entire workbooks in a uniform, attractive style
- Analyze numerical data and project outcomes to make informed decisions
- Plan, research, create, revise and publish worksheets and workbooks to meet specific communication needs
- Given a workplace scenario requiring a numbers-based solution, assess the information requirements and then prepare the materials that achieve the goal efficiently and effectively

Determining the Course Delivery Mode and Structure

Frequently, the course structure has been determined in advance by your department. However, if you are in a position to develop a plan or modify an existing structure, consider these questions:

- What topics in each subject area are essential for demonstrating the course outcomes?
- Is this the only course that will address this subject and skill set?
- What do students already know about each subject? What can they learn on their own without your direct instruction?
- Where in each subject will the instruction begin and end?

Your answers to these questions will help you divide the course content into parts and identify the associated learning outcomes (also called performance objectives). Note that course outcomes are marked by higher and more challenging skill sets and typically require the integration of many skills, while unit or part outcomes are more narrowly defined and focused.

Course Delivery: Traditional Classroom, Online (Distance Learning), or Hybrid?

While the core considerations are the same whether you are planning a traditional on-campus course, an online course (also called a distance learning course), or a hybrid of the two, the instructional delivery differences create distinct needs you must address in the planning stage.

A critical challenge in teaching online courses is the issue of interacting with students. How will you communicate with them? How will they submit assignments and tests? How will you deliver feedback? How will you get to know your students? Here are some additional questions to consider when planning an online or hybrid course:

- What course management system will you use: Blackboard or some other platform?
- Will students work independently offline? How will they use the course management system to review course outcomes, the syllabus, and assignment due dates? How will they communicate with you, take online quizzes, transmit completed work, and participate in chat sessions?
- Will you be able to offer an on-campus orientation meeting for students at the beginning of the course? If so, how will you prepare to answer the questions students will likely have?
- Will students come to the campus or school to take exams? If not, will students be directed to offsite locations where exams can be administered to verify that the person taking the exam is indeed the person getting credit for the course?
- What hardware configuration and/or software requirements must a student have to participate in your course?

Both the student and instructor resources offered with *Benchmark Microsoft Excel 2010, Levels 1 & 2* can be adapted for use in an online learning environment or a hybrid of traditional and online learning contexts. The SNAP Training and Assessment product, in particular, is well suited for these course delivery modes, and these online files are also designed for distance-learning situations.

The Syllabus

A comprehensive syllabus will help you and your students prepare for each part of the course. A well-planned syllabus is useful for traditional, on-campus courses as well as for courses that are delivered online. A syllabus normally includes:

1. Course-identifying data
2. Prerequisites
3. Instructor contact information
4. Course outcomes
5. Required course resources
6. Major assignments
7. Grade composition
8. Class structure
9. Course schedule
10. College/school requirements

Figure 1 shows a traditional, on-campus course syllabus for a 16-week course that meets three times a week and uses *Benchmark Excel 2010, Levels 1 & 2* as the core courseware. Lesson plans are referenced in the sample syllabus and are available on the Instructor Resources DVD as well as on the password-protected part of the Internet Resource Center (IRC) for *Benchmark Excel 2010* at www.emcp.net/BenchmarkExcel10.

FIGURE 1   Traditional 16-Week Semester Syllabus Example
Using Benchmark Excel 2010 Levels 1 & 2

Course Description
This course prepares students to work with Microsoft Excel 2010 in a career setting or for personal use. Using courseware that incorporates a step-by-step, project-based approach, students develop a mastery-level competency in Excel 2010 and explore the essential features of Windows 7 and Internet Explorer 8.0. Students also develop an understanding of fundamental computer hardware and software concepts.

Prerequisites: None

Instructor Contact Information

Name:	Office Location:
Office Phone:	Office Hours:
Office Email:	

Required Course Resources
Benchmark Series Microsoft Excel 2010, Levels 1 & 2
        by Rutkosky, Seguin, and Rutkosky Roggenkamp, © Paradigm Publishing, Inc.
Student Resources CD (provided with textbook)

Internet Resource Center, www.emcp.net/BenchmarkExcel10
USB flash drive or other storage medium

Computer Time
Approximately six to eight hours per week of computer time outside of class is recommended for successful completion of course requirements.

Grading
Final grades will be calculated as an average of all of the following assignments:
- Concepts Check   5%
- Skills Check   15%
- Visual Benchmark   15%
- Case Study   20%
- Unit Performance Assessment   25%
- Exams   20%

College and Course Policy Information
This college conforms to the provisions of the Americans with Disabilities Act. You are invited to report any special needs to your instructor.
- Your attendance is expected at all class sessions.
- We subscribe to the college policy on academic honesty found in the school catalog.

Course Schedule—Benchmark Excel 2010
16-week semester, three 1-hour classes per week

Week	Class	Chapter	Lesson Plan File	Description	Text Pages
1	Class 1	Getting Started/ Windows 7	BM-Excel2010-L1-Session01	Intro to course, Getting Started, Using Windows 7	1–28
	Class 2	Windows 7/ Internet Explorer	BM-Excel2010-L1-Session02	Finish Windows 7, Internet Explorer, Working with Data Files	28–48
	Class 3	Level 1, Ch 1	BM-Excel2010-L1-Session03	Preparing an Excel Worksheet	3–18
2	Class 4	Level 1, Ch 1	BM-Excel2010-L1-Session04	Preparing an Excel Worksheet	18–36
	Class 5	Level 1, Ch 2	BM-Excel2010-L1-Session05	Inserting Formulas in a Worksheet	37–45
	Class 6	Level 1, Ch 2	BM-Excel2010-L1-Session06	Inserting Formulas in a Worksheet	45–54
3	Class 7	Level 1, Ch 2	BM-Excel2010-L1-Session07	Inserting Formulas in a Worksheet	54–68
	Class 8	Level 1, Ch 3	BM-Excel2010-L1-Session08	Formatting an Excel Worksheet	69–80
	Class 9	Level 1, Ch 3	BM-Excel2010-L1-Session09	Formatting an Excel Worksheet	81–106
4	Class 10	Level 1, Ch 4	BM-Excel2010-L1-Session10	Enhancing a Worksheet	107–128
	Class 11	Level 1, Ch 4	BM-Excel2010-L1-Session11	Enhancing a Worksheet	126–148
	Class 12	**Level 1, U1**	BM-Excel2010-L1-Session12	**Level 1, U1 Performance Assessments**	149–154
5	Class 13	Level 1, Ch 5	BM-Excel2010-L1-Session13	Moving Data Within and Between Workbooks	155–178
	Class 14	Level 1, Ch 5	BM-Excel2010-L1-Session14	Moving Data Within and Between Workbooks	178–196
	Class 15	Level 1, Ch 6	BM-Excel2010-L1-Session15	Maintaining Workbooks	197–213
6	Class 16	Level 1, Ch 6	BM-Excel2010-L1-Session16	Maintaining Workbooks	213–238
	Class 17	Level 1, Ch 7	BM-Excel2010-L1-Session17	Creating a Chart in Excel	239–250
	Class 18	Level 1, Ch 7	BM-Excel2010-L1-Session18	Creating a Chart in Excel	251–270
7	Class 19	Level 1, Ch 8	BM-Excel2010-L1-Session19	Adding Visual Interest to Workbooks	271–281
	Class 20	Level 1, Ch 8	BM-Excel2010-L1-Session20	Adding Visual Interest to Workbooks	281–286
	Class 21	Level 1, Ch 8	BM-Excel2010-L1-Session21	Adding Visual Interest to Workbooks	286–304

Week	Class	Chapter	Lesson Plan File	Description	Text Pages
8	Class 22	**Level 1, U2**	BM-Excel2010-L1-Session22	**Level 1, U2 Performance Assessments**	**305–312**
	Class 23	**TEST**	BM-Excel2010-L1-Session23	**Excel Level 1 Test**	
	Class 24	Level 2, Ch 1	BM-Excel2010-L2-Session24	Advanced Formatting Techniques	3–16
9	Class 25	Level 2, Ch 1	BM-Excel2010-L2-Session25	Advanced Formatting Techniques	16–22
	Class 26	Level 2, Ch 1	BM-Excel2010-L2-Session26	Advanced Formatting Techniques	23–34
	Class 27	Level 2, Ch 2	BM-Excel2010-L2-Session27	Advanced Functions and Formulas	35–49
10	Class 28	Level 2, Ch 2	BM-Excel2010-L2-Session28	Advanced Functions and Formulas	49–70
	Class 29	Level 2, Ch 3	BM-Excel2010-L2-Session29	Working with Tables and Data Features	71–87
	Class 30	Level 2, Ch 3	BM-Excel2010-L2-Session30	Working with Tables and Data Features	87–102
11	Class 31	Level 2, Ch 4	BM-Excel2010-L2-Session31	Summarizing and Consolidating Data	103–114
	Class 32	Level 2, Ch 4	BM-Excel2010-L2-Session32	Summarizing and Consolidating Data	114–123
	Class 33	Level 2, Ch 4	BM-Excel2010-L2-Session33	Summarizing and Consolidating Data	123–138
12	Class 34	**Level 2, U1**	BM-Excel2010-L2-Session34	**Level 2, U1 Performance Assessments**	139–146
	Class 35	Level 2, Ch 5	BM-Excel2010-L2-Session35	Using Data Analysis Features	149–157
	Class 36	Level 2, Ch 5	BM-Excel2010-L2-Session36	Using Data Analysis Features	157–163
13	Class 37	Level 2, Ch 5	BM-Excel2010-L2-Session37	Using Data Analysis Features	164–180
	Class 38	Level 2, Ch 6	BM-Excel2010-L2-Session38	Protecting and Sharing Workbooks	181–194
	Class 39	Level 2, Ch 6	BM-Excel2010-L2-Session39	Protecting and Sharing Workbooks	194–214
14	Class 40	Level 2, Ch 7	BM-Excel2010-L2-Session40	Automating Repetitive Tasks and Customizing Excel	215–225
	Class 41	Level 2, Ch 7	BM-Excel2010-L2-Session41	Automating Repetitive Tasks and Customizing Excel	225–256
	Class 42	Level 2, Ch 8	BM-Excel2010-L2-Session42	Importing, Exporting and Distributing Data	257–267
15	Class 43	Level 2, Ch 8	BM-Excel2010-L2-Session43	Importing, Exporting and Distributing Data	267–278
	Class 44	Level 2, Ch 8	BM-Excel2010-L2-Session44	Importing, Exporting and Distributing Data	278–306
	Class 45	**Level 2, U2**	BM-Excel2010-L2-Session45	**Level 2, U2 Performance Assessments**	307–314
16	Class 46	**TEST**	BM-Excel2010-L2-Session46	**Excel Level 2 Test**	

Selecting the Instructional Approach, Resources, and Activities

After the course outcomes and structure are determined, it is important to plan the main content of the course. This includes selecting courseware, identifying resources for English language learners, considering instructional support materials, and reviewing other resources.

Student Courseware

Selecting high-quality student courseware is an important step in the planning process. Learning materials should be engaging and accessible. The Benchmark Series offers several valuable learning tools to support course performance objectives.

- *Benchmark Excel 2010, Levels 1 & 2* textbook with Student Resources CD
- eBook

- Student Internet Resource Center at www.emcp.net/BenchmarkExcel10
- SNAP Training and Assessment software
- SNAP Tutorials CD
- Blackboard cartridge

Textbook Structure and Features

Benchmark Excel 2010 prepares students to work with Microsoft Excel 2010 in business and academic settings, and also for personal use. Incorporating a project-based approach that organizes instruction and guided exercises around related program features, this text builds student competency in the 2010 version of Excel and the essential features of Windows 7 and Internet Explorer 8.0.

The *Excel 2010 Levels 1 & 2* text is just one book in the Benchmark Series. The Benchmark Series contains the following eleven textbooks:
- *Benchmark Series Microsoft Office 2010*
  - Getting Started (essential computer hardware and software concepts)
  - Windows 7
  - Internet Explorer 8.0
  - Word 2010 (8 chapters)
  - Excel 2010 (8 chapters)
  - Access 2010 (8 chapters)
  - PowerPoint 2010 (8 chapters)
  - Integrating Office 2010 Programs
- *Benchmark Series Microsoft Word 2010 Levels 1 and 2*
  - Getting Started
  - Windows 7
  - Internet Explorer 8.0
  - Word 2010 Level 1 (8 chapters)
  - Word 2010 Level 2 (8 chapters)
- *Benchmark Series Microsoft Word 2010 Level 1*
  - Getting Started
  - Windows 7
  - Internet Explorer 8.0
  - Word 2010 Level 1 (8 chapters)
- *Benchmark Series Microsoft Word 2010 Level 2*
  - Word 2010 Level 2 (8 chapters)
- *Benchmark Series Microsoft Excel 2010 Levels 1 and 2*
  - Getting Started
  - Windows 7
  - Internet Explorer 8.0
  - Excel 2010 Level 1 (8 chapters)
  - Excel 2010 Level 2 (8 chapters)
- *Benchmark Series Microsoft Excel 2010 Level 1*
  - Getting Started

- o Windows 7
- o Internet Explorer 8.0
- o Excel 2010 Level 1 (8 chapters)
- *Benchmark Series Microsoft Excel 2010 Level 2*
  - o Excel 2010 Level 2 (8 chapters)
- *Benchmark Series Microsoft Access 2010 Levels 1 and 2*
  - o Getting Started
  - o Windows 7
  - o Internet Explorer 8.0
  - o Access 2010 Level 1 (8 chapters)
  - o Access 2010 Level 2 (8 chapters)
- *Benchmark Series Microsoft Access 2010 Level 1*
  - o Getting Started
  - o Windows 7
  - o Internet Explorer 8.0
  - o Access 2010 Level 1 (8 chapters)
- *Benchmark Series Microsoft Access 2010 Level 2*
  - o Access 2010 Level 2 (8 chapters)
- *Benchmark Series Microsoft PowerPoint 2010*
  - o Getting Started
  - o Windows 7
  - o Internet Explorer 8.0
  - o PowerPoint 2010 (8 chapters)

The main Microsoft application sections of each book in the Benchmark Series contain eight chapters, split into two units. The opening page of a unit lists the four chapter titles included in the unit. Each chapter opener presents the chapter's Performance Objectives, an overview of the skills taught in the chapter, a listing of the SNAP tutorials that support the chapter content, and a CD icon and text identifying a folder of data files to be copied to the student's storage medium. These files are used to complete chapter projects and end-of-chapter activities. Following the opening page, the chapter begins with model answers of the chapter projects that students can reference to confirm they have completed the chapter projects correctly.

Skills instruction in the text is organized around projects that require using a group of related features to complete a document or build a file. A project overview, which lists the project number and title, identifies tasks to accomplish and the features to use in completing the work. The project overview also identifies the number of parts that make up the project. Following each project part (identified with the project number and letter), the text presents instruction on the features and skills necessary to accomplish the next section of the project. Typically, a file remains open throughout all parts of the project. Students save their work incrementally and usually print only at the end of the entire project. Instructors have access to the live project model answer files for the completed project as well as the project parts on the Instructor Resources DVD and on the password-protected Instructor section of www.emcp.net/BenchmarkExcel10.

Page margins include the following elements:

- Quick Steps—brief feature summaries for reference and review
- Hint boxes—trouble-shooting ideas and additional useful information
- Button graphics

Each chapter ends with the following review elements and exercises:

- Chapter Summary—A bulleted list captures the purpose and execution of key features.
- Commands Review—Commands taught in the chapter are listed with button, ribbon tab, and keyboard actions.
- Concepts Check—Short-answer questions allow students to test their comprehension and recall of program features, terminology, and functions. Printouts of the Concepts Check answer keys are provided in the print *Instructors Guide* and electronic files are available on the Instructor Resources DVD and on the password-protected Instructor section of www.emcp.net/ BenchmarkExcel10.
- Skills Check—Semi-guided exercises ask students to demonstrate their mastery of the major features and program skills taught in the chapter. The *Instructor's Guide* includes printed versions of the Skills Check model answers along with rubrics to assess student work. In addition, rubric Word documents, PDF files of the model answers, and live file model answers are available for instructors on the Instructor Resources DVD and on the password-protected Instructor section of www.emcp.net/BenchmarkExcel10.
- Visual Benchmark—With limited guidance, students are challenged to use their problem-solving skills and mastery of program features to build a file that matches a shown sample file.
- Case Study—Framed in a workplace project perspective, these less-guided assessments evaluate students' abilities to apply chapter skills and concepts in solving realistic problems. Case Study activities require demonstrating program skills as well as decision-making skills and include Help and Internet-based activities. Rubrics are provided in the *Instructor's Guide* for assessing student work. Electronic copies of the rubrics are available on the Instructor Resources DVD and on the password-protected Instructor section of www.emcp.net/BenchmarkExcel10.

Unit Performance Assessments follow each set of four chapters and offer opportunities for cross-disciplinary, comprehensive evaluation. There are four types of Unit Performance Assessments. Assessing Proficiency is a group of gently guided exercises. Writing Activities involve applying program skills in a communication context. An Internet Research project reinforces research, writing, and program skills. A Job Study activity in the Unit 2 Performance Assessment presents a capstone assessment requiring critical thinking and problem solving. Printouts of the model answers and rubrics for evaluating student work are included in the *Instructor's Guide*. The instructor Resources DVD and the password-protected Instructor section of www.emcp.net/BenchmarkExcel10 include live file model answers and rubric Word document files for these assessments.

Student Resources CD

Files that serve as a starting point for completing many of the project and end-of-chapter exercises are included on the CD that accompanies the student text. Typically, students are directed to open one of these files, save the file with a new name, and then edit and print the file. Some chapter work requires the students to start an activity from a blank file. As students begin a chapter, they should copy the folder of files for the chapter exercises to the storage medium of their choice. This folder name is displayed next to a CD icon on the first page of the chapter.

eBook

For student who prefer studying with an eBook, the texts in the Benchmark Series are available in an electronic form. The web-based, password-protected eBooks feature dynamic navigation tools, including bookmarking, a linked table of contents, and the ability to jump to a specific page. The eBook format also supports helpful study tools, such as highlighting and note taking.

Benchmark Excel 2010 Internet Resource Center

The Benchmark Excel 2010 Resource Center at www.emcp.net/BenchmarkExcel10 offers valuable information for both instructors and students. For students, the Internet Resource Center includes quick access to the student data files, informational Web links, study aids such as online quizzes, and more. All instructor resources posted on the website are password protected and are not accessible by students.

SNAP Training and Assessment

SNAP is a web-based training and assessment program designed to optimize skill-based learning for Excel with Windows and Internet Explorer. SNAP creates a virtual classroom on the Web, allowing instructors to employ an electronic gradebook and schedule tutorials, skill and concept exams, document assessments, and textbook assignments.
    SNAP contains:
- interactive, multimedia tutorials, aligned to textbook chapters, that can be used for direct instruction or remediation (See Table 1 for a listing of the SNAP tutorials for that are available for Benchmark Excel 2010.)
- a bank of performance skill items in which students perform tasks in Microsoft Excel 2010 that are reported in the learning management system; instructors can assign pre-defined skills exams or create their own
- a bank of 875 concept items that can be used to monitor student understanding of computer literacy and technical knowledge; instructors can assign pre-defined concepts exams or create their own
- a document checker that will download, collect, correct, and score selected Excel assessments taken directly from the textbook

TABLE 1   Benchmark SNAP Tutorials Correlation

Benchmark Excel Level 1 SNAP Tutorials

Chapter	Tutorial	Tutorial Title
1	1.1	Creating and Saving a Workbook
1	1.2	Editing Cells and Using Proofing Tools
1	1.3	Displaying Formulas and Navigating a Worksheet
1	1.4	Applying Basic Formatting
1	1.5	Applying Formatting; Using Undo and Redo; Changing Alignment
2	2.1	Performing Calculations Using Formulas
2	2.2	Writing Formulas in Excel
2	2.3	Copying and Testing Formulas
2	2.4	Creating Formulas with Absolute Addressing
2	2.5	Using Financial Functions
2	2.6	Writing Formulas with the FV Function
2	2.7	Using the Logical IF Function
3	3.1	Inserting, Adjusting, and Deleting Rows and Columns
3	3.2	Using Cell Styles and Themes
3	3.3	Formatting Numbers
3	3.4	Adding Borders and Shading; Copying Formats with Format Painter
3	3.5	Hiding and Unhiding Rows and Columns
4	4.1	Changing Page Margins and Layout Options
4	4.2	Formatting and Printing Options
4	4.3	Inserting a Page Break
4	4.4	Formatting a Worksheet Page
4	4.5	Adding Headers and Footers
4	4.6	Using Undo and Redo
4	4.7	Using Find and Replace
4	4.8	Sorting Data and Using Help
4	4.9	Using the Sort Feature in Tables
4	4.10	Filtering a Table
5	5.1	Moving and Copying Cells
5	5.2	Inserting, Moving, Renaming, and Hiding a Worksheet
5	5.3	Formatting Multiple Worksheets
5	5.4	Setting a Print Area and Printing Multiple Worksheets
5	5.5	Splitting a Worksheet into Windows
5	5.6	Freezing Panes and Changing the Zoom
5	5.7	Naming and Using a Range
5	5.8	Working with Windows
5	5.9	Linking Data and Using 3-D References
5	5.10	Copying and Pasting Data between Programs
6	6.1	Maintaining Workbooks
6	6.2	Managing Folders
6	6.3	Managing the Recent List
6	6.4	Managing Worksheets
6	6.5	Formatting with Cell Styles
6	6.6	Inserting Hyperlinks
6	6.7	Using Templates
7	7.1	Creating Charts in Excel
7	7.2	Editing Chart Data
7	7.3	Changing the Chart Design
7	7.4	Changing a Chart Type
7	7.5	Inserting Shapes and Images
7	7.6	Changing the Chart Formatting
8	8.1	Inserting Symbols and Special Characters
8	8.2	Inserting Pictures and Clip Art
8	8.3	Creating Screenshots
8	8.4	Inserting a Picture as a Watermark
8	8.5	Inserting and Formatting a SmartArt Diagram
8	8.6	Creating WordArt

Benchmark Excel Level 2 SNAP Tutorials

Chapter	Tutorial	Tutorial Title
1	1.1	Applying Conditional Formatting
1	1.2	Applying Conditional Formatting Using Icon Sets
1	1.3	Applying Conditional Formatting Using Data Bars and Color Scales
1	1.4	Applying Conditional Formatting Using a Formula
1	1.5	Using Fraction, Scientific, and Special Numbers Formatting
1	1.6	Creating a Custom Number Format
1	1.7	Wrapping and Shrinking Text to Fit within a Cell
1	1.8	Filtering a Worksheet Using a Custom AutoFilter
1	1.9	Filtering and Sorting Data Using Conditional Formatting and Cell Attributes
2	2.1	Creating and Managing Range Names
2	2.2	Using Statistical Functions: Count Functions
2	2.3	Using Statistical Functions: AVERAGEIF and AVERAGEIFS
2	2.4	Using Math and Trigonometry Functions
2	2.5	Using Lookup Functions
2	2.6	Using the PPMT Function
2	2.7	Using Logical Functions
2	2.8	Using Text Functions
3	3.1	Creating and Modifying Tables
3	3.2	Adding Rows to a Table
3	3.3	Formatting Data as a Table
3	3.4	Using Data Tools
3	3.5	Removing Duplicate Records
3	3.6	Validating and Restricting Data Entry
3	3.7	Converting a Table to a Normal Range; Subtotalling Related Data
3	3.8	Grouping and Ungrouping Data
4	4.1	Summarizing Data in Multiple Worksheets Using Range Names and 3-D References
4	4.2	Summarizing Data by Linking Ranges in Other Worksheets or Workbooks
4	4.3	Summarizing Data Using the Consolidate Feature
4	4.4	Creating a PivotTable Report
4	4.5	Filtering a PivotTable Using Slicers
4	4.6	Creating a PivotChart
4	4.7	Summarizing Data with Sparklines
5	5.1	Pasting Data Using Paste Special Options
5	5.2	Using Goal Seek to Populate a Cell
5	5.3	Using Scenario Manager
5	5.4	Performing What-If Analysis Using Data Tables
5	5.5	Using Auditing Tools
5	5.6	Circling Invalid Data and Watching Formulas
6	6.1	Inserting and Editing Comments
6	6.2	Adding Workbook Properties
6	6.3	Printing and Editing Comments
6	6.4	Sharing a Workbook
6	6.5	Resolving Conflicts in a Shared Workbook
6	6.6	Protecting and Unprotecting Worksheets
6	6.7	Protecting and Unprotecting Workbook Structure
6	6.8	Adding Password Protection to a Workbook
6	6.9	Tracking Changes
7	7.1	Using Macros
7	7.2	Managing Macros
7	7.3	Editing a Macro
7	7.4	Pinning Workbooks to the Recent Workbooks List
7	7.5	Customizing the Quick Access Toolbar
7	7.6	Customizing the Work Area
7	7.7	Customizing the Ribbon
7	7.8	Using Custom Templates
8	8.1	Importing Data from Access, a Text File, or a Website

Benchmark Excel Level 2 SNAP Tutorials

SNAP Tutorials CD

A CD of tutorials teaching Excel, Windows, and Internet Explorer skills is also available if instructors wish to assign SNAP tutorial work without using the web-based SNAP program.

Blackboard Cartridge

This set of files allows instructors to create a personalized website for their course and provides course content, tests, and the mechanisms for establishing communication via e-discussions and online group conferences. Available content includes a syllabus, test banks, PowerPoint presentations with audio support, and supplementary course materials. Upon request, the files can be available within 24–48 hours. Hosting the site is the responsibility of the educational institution.

Resources for English Language Learners[1]

One of the fastest growing groups of students in higher education is comprised of students whose first language is not English and whose English is not yet equivalent to that of native English speakers in lexicon and syntax. The wide differences in fluency among limited English speakers makes planning for meeting their needs somewhat more complex—and very important.

Many instructors find that they must meet the needs of students who are learning English and who need additional help. Because your goal is to help *all* the students in your course meet the intended outcomes, plan how you're going to assist students with limited English skills.

Begin by assessing the language abilities of your students:

1. One method is a "one-minute preview." Provide sheets of paper and ask students two questions. Give them one minute or so to write their answers. The questions could be about their language skills, but it might be better to ask about something else. That way you get a short writing sample plus information about something, such as why they are taking the course, what they would like to learn, the types of activities they enjoy, or what they are most worried about in the course. You will be able to see which students will need additional help.

2. If your class is small, conduct a discussion early in the course. Make sure you hear each student answer a question or ask one.

---

[1] Excerpted from *Exceptional Teaching: Ideas in Action,* published by EMC Corporation.

3. If you are conducting a pretest for the course, include some questions that ask students if they need to improve their English or writing skills.
4. Tell students to email you if they think they will need language help or extra exam time for reading assignments or tests.

In addition to the suggestions above, consider preparing a list of terms for each session that might be difficult for English language learners. You can suggest that students arrange for tutors to assist them with completing the unguided assessments. You may also want to dedicate a session (or part of one) to instruction on how to prepare the work you expect.

To help English language learners learn computer concept terminology, the Benchmark Excel 2010 Internet Resource Center at www.emcp.net/BenchmarkExcel10 includes a link an English and Spanish computer concepts glossary. This resource, found in the Technology Tools section of the website, provides computer concepts, terms, and definitions in both English and Spanish, with English audio support.

Instructor Resources

Along with the *Instructor's Guide*, instructional materials available with *Benchmark Excel 2010, Levels 1 & 2* include:

- Instructor Resources DVD with electronic files for all resources included in the *Instructor's Guide*. The DVD also offers the model answer files, PowerPoint presentations with lecture notes, and detailed lesson plans, which include lecture/demonstration notes, discussion topics, tips for students, and possible work for advanced students.
- Instructor resources available at the Internet Resource Center at www.emcp.net/BenchmarkExcel10, which includes all of the materials in the print *Instructor's Guide* and on the Instructor Resources DVD.
- **EXAM**VIEW® computerized test generator with approximately 875 multiple-choice items to create customized web-based or print tests.

Information about Microsoft Office 2010

Microsoft Office 2010 operates on the Windows 7 operating system, as well as on Vista and Windows XP.

e-Training on the Changes in Office 2010

At its website (www.microsoft.com), Microsoft offers online training in the new interface at http://office.microsoft.com/en-us/support/getting-started-with-office-2010-FX101822272.aspx?CTT=97.

What's New in Office 2010 Video

Microsoft Corporation offers a downloadable video presentation on the new features in Office 2010 at http://office.microsoft.com/en-us/products/cool-things-you-can-do-with-office-2010-VA101842280.aspx.

Command Reference Guides

Microsoft also provides interactive guides to show you where your favorite menu and toolbar commands are located in Office 2010 at http://office.microsoft.com/en-us/outlook-help/learn-where-menu-and-toolbar-commands-are-in-office-2010-HA101794130.aspx.

Certification: Microsoft Office Specialist

With the release of Office 2010, Microsoft has developed a new set of certification objectives, which are available at http://www.microsoft.com/learning/en/us/certification/mos.aspx#mos2010. The following books in the Benchmark Series have been validated and approved as courseware covering the Core-level objectives in the Microsoft Office Specialist Certification exam.

- *Benchmark Series Microsoft Word 2010 Levels 1 & 2*
- *Benchmark Series Microsoft Excel 2010 Levels 1 & 2*
- *Benchmark Series Microsoft Access 2010 Levels 1 & 2*
- *Benchmark Series Microsoft PowerPoint 2010*

Table 2 correlates the *Benchmark Excel 2010 Levels 1 & 2* text with the certification exam objectives.

TABLE 2   Benchmark Excel Levels 1 & 2 and Microsoft Office Specialist Certification Exam Correlation

Certification Exam Objective	Textbook Reference
1. Managing the Worksheet Environment	
1.1 Navigate through a worksheet	
1.1.1 Use hot keys	Level 1, Chapter 1, Page 21 Level 1, Chapter 4, Page 140
1.1.2 Use the name box	Level 1, Chapter 1, Pages 5-6 Level 1, Chapter 5, Page 177
1.2 Print a worksheet or workbook.	
1.2.1 Print only selected worksheets	Level 1, Chapter 5, Pages 173, 178
1.2.2 Print an entire workbook	Level 1, Chapter 5, Page 173
1.2.3 Construct headers and footers	Level 1, Chapter 4, Pages 120-125
1.2.4 Apply printing options	
1.2.4.1 Scale	Level 1, Chapter 4, Page 116
1.2.4.2 Print titles	Level 1, Chapter 4, Pages 115-117
1.2.4.3 Page setup	Level 1, Chapter 4, Pages 109-112
1.2.4.4 Print area	Level 1, Chapter 4, Pages 118-119
1.2.4.5 Gridlines	Level 1, Chapter 4, Page 118
1.3 Personalize the environment by using Backstage.	
1.3.1 Manipulate the Quick Access Toolbar	Level 2, Chapter 7, Pages 227-229
1.3.2 Customize the ribbon	
1.3.2.1 Tabs	Level 2, Chapter 7, Pages 232-238
1.3.2.2 Groups	Level 2, Chapter 7, Pages 232-238
1.3.3 Manipulate Excel default settings (Excel Options)	Level 2, Chapter 7, Pages 230-232
1.3.4 Manipulate workbook properties (document panel)	Level 2, Chapter 6, Pages 182-185
1.3.5 Manipulate workbook files and folders	
1.3.5.1 Manage versions	Level 2, Chapter 7, Pages 244-247

Certification Exam Objective	Textbook Reference
1.3.5.2 AutoSave	Level 2, Chapter 7, Pages 244-247
2. Creating Cell Data	
2.1 Construct cell data.	
2.1.1 Use paste special	
2.1.1.1 Formats	Level 1, Chapter 5, Pages 163-165
2.1.1.2 Formulas	Level 1, Chapter 5, Pages 166-167
2.1.1.3 Values	Level 1, Chapter 5, Pages 166-167
2.1.1.4 Preview icons	Level 1, Chapter 5, Pages 164-165
2.1.1.5 Transpose rows	Level 2, Chapter 5, Pages 151-154
2.1.1.6 Transpose columns	Level 2, Chapter 5, Pages151-154
2.1.1.7 Operations	
2.1.1.7.1 Add	Level 2, Chapter 5, Pages 154-155 & Page 175
2.1.1.7.2 Divide	Level 2, Chapter 5, Pages 154-155 & Page 175
2.1.1.8 Comments	Level 2, Chapter 6, Page 186
2.1.1.9 Validation	Level 2, Chapter 5, Page 151, 155 & 176
2.1.1.10 Paste as a link	Level 2, Chapter 5, Page 110
2.1.2 Cut	Level 1, Chapter 5, Pages 161-163
2.1.3 Move	Level 1, Chapter 5, Pages 161-163
2.1.4 Select cell data	Level 1, Chapter 1, Pages 10, 19-20
2.2 Apply AutoFill.	
2.2.1 Copy data	Level 1, Chapter 1, Pages 15-16
2.2.2 Fill a series	Level 1, Chapter 1, Pages 15-16
2.2.3 Preserve cell format	Level 1, Chapter 1, Pages 15-16
2.3 Apply and manipulate hyperlinks.	
2.3.1 Create a hyperlink in a cell	Level 1, Chapter 6, Pages 222-227
2.3.2 Modify hyperlinks	Level 1, Chapter 6, Pages 226-227
2.3.3 Modify hyperlinked cell attributes	Level 1, Chapter 6, Pages 226-227
2.3.4 Remove a hyperlink	Level 1, Chapter 6, Pages 226-227
3. Formatting Cells and Worksheets	
3.1 Apply and modify cell formats.	
3.1.1 Align cell content	Level 1, Chapter 3, Pages 78-80
3.1.2 Apply a number format	Level 1, Chapter 3, Pages 82-86
3.1.3 Wrapping text in a cell	Level 1, Chapter 3, Page 79 Level 2, Chapter 1, Page 22
3.1.4 Use Format Painter	Level 1, Chapter 3, Page 94
3.2 Merge or split cells.	
3.2.1 Use Merge & Center	Level 1, Chapter 3, Pages 78-79
3.2.2 Merge Across	Level 1, Chapter 3, Pages 78-79
3.2.3 Merge cells	Level 1, Chapter 3, Pages 78-79
3.2.4 Unmerge Cells	Level 1, Chapter 3, Pages 78-79
3.3 Create row and column titles.	
3.3.1 Print row and column headings	Level 1, Chapter 4, Pages 115-116
3.3.2 Print rows to repeat with titles	Level 1, Chapter 4, Pages 115-116
3.3.3 Print columns to repeat with titles	Level 1, Chapter 4, Pages 115-116
3.3.4 Configure titles to print only on odd or even pages	Level 1, Chapter 4, Pages 123-125
3.3.5 Configure titles to skip the first worksheet page	Level 1, Chapter 4, Pages 123-125

Certification Exam Objective	Textbook Reference
3.4 Hide or unhide rows and columns.	
3.4.1 Hide or unhide a column	Level 1, Chapter 3, Pages 94-96
3.4.2 Hide or unhide a row	Level 1, Chapter 3, Pages 94-96
3.4.3 Hide a series of columns	Level 1, Chapter 3, Pages 94-96
3.4.4 Hide a series of rows	Level 1, Chapter 3, Pages 94-96
3.5 Manipulate Page Setup options for worksheets.	
3.5.1 Configure page orientation	Level 1, Chapter 4, Page 112
3.5.2 Manage page scaling	Level 1, Chapter 4, Pages 116-117
3.5.3 Configure page margins	Level 1, Chapter 4, Pages 109-111
3.5.4 Change header and footer size	Level 1, Chapter 4, Page 124
3.6 Create and apply cell styles.	
3.6.1 Apply cell styles	Level 1, Chapter 6, Pages 214-215
3.6.2 Construct new cell styles	Level 1, Chapter 6, Pages 215-218
4. Managing Worksheets and Workbooks	
4.1 Create and format worksheets.	
4.1.1 Insert worksheets	
4.1.1.1 Single	Level 1, Chapter 6, Pages 167, 169
4.1.1.2 Multiple	Level 1, Chapter 6, Pages 167, 169
4.1.2 Delete worksheets	
4.1.2.1 Single	Level 1, Chapter 6, Pages 167, 169
4.1.2.2 Multiple	Level 1, Chapter 6, Pages 167, 169
4.1.3 Reposition worksheets	Level 1, Chapter 6, Pages 169-171
4.1.4 Copy worksheets	Level 1, Chapter 6, Pages 169-171
4.1.5 Move worksheets	Level 1, Chapter 6, Pages 169-171
4.1.6 Rename worksheets	Level 1, Chapter 6, Pages 169-171
4.1.7 Group worksheets	Level 1, Chapter 6, Pages 171-172
4.1.8 Apply color to worksheet tabs	Level 1, Chapter 6, Pages 170-171
4.1.9 Hide worksheet tabs	Level 1, Chapter 6, Pages 171-172
4.1.10 Unhide worksheet tabs	Level 1, Chapter 6, Pages 171-172
4.2 Manipulate window views.	
4.2.1 Split window views	Level 1, Chapter 5, Pages 174-176
4.2.2 Arrange window views	Level 1, Chapter 5, Pages 179-181
4.2.3 Open a new window with contents from the current worksheet	Level 1, Chapter 6, Pages 179, 181
4.3 Manipulate workbook views.	
4.3.1 Use Normal workbook view	Level 1, Chapter 4, Pages 113, 115
4.3.2 Use Page Layout workbook view	Level 1, Chapter 4, Pages 120-121
4.3.3 Use Page Break workbook view	Level 1, Chapter 4, Pages 112-115
4.3.4 Create custom views	Level 2, Chapter 7, Pages 238-240
5. Applying Formulas and Functions	
5.1 Create formulas.	
5.1.1 Use basic operators	Level 1, Chapter 2, Pages 40-42
5.1.2 Revise formulas	Level 1, Chapter 2, Page 55
5.2 Enforce precedence.	
5.2.1 Order of evaluation	Level 1, Chapter 2, Page 40
5.2.2 Precedence using parentheses	Level 1, Chapter 2, Page 40
5.2.3 Precedence of operators for percent vs. exponentiation	Level 1, Chapter 2, Page 40

Certification Exam Objective	Textbook Reference
5.3 Apply cell references in formulas.	
5.3.1 Relative and absolute references	Level 1, Chapter 2, Pages 57-60
5.4 Apply conditional logic in a formula.	
5.4.1 Create a formula with values that match conditions	Level 2, Chapter 2, Pages 39-47
5.4.2 Edit defined conditions in a formula	Level 2, Chapter 2, Page 44
5.4.3 Use a series of conditional logic values in a formula	Level 2, Chapter 2, Pages 55-58
5.5 Apply named ranges in formulas.	
5.5.1 Define ranges in formulas	Level 2, Chapter 2, Pages 37-39
5.5.2 Edit ranges in formulas	Level 2, Chapter 2, Pages 48-49
5.5.3 Rename a named range	Level 2, Chapter 2, Pages 48-49
5.6 Apply cell ranges in formulas.	
5.6.1 Enter a cell range definition in the formula bar	Level 1, Chapter 5, Pages 177-178
5.6.2 Define a cell range	Level 1, Chapter 5, Pages 177-178
6. Presenting Data Visually	
6.1 Create charts based on worksheet data.	Level 1, Chapter 7, Pages 241-262
6.2 Apply and manipulate illustrations.	
6.2.1 Insert	Level 1, Chapter 8, Pages 275-276
6.2.2 Position	Level 1, Chapter 8, Pages 276-277
6.2.3 Size	Level 1, Chapter 8, Pages 276-277
6.2.4 Rotate	Level 1, Chapter 8, Page 284
6.2.5 Modify Clip Art SmartArt	Level 1, Chapter 8, Pages 278-279
6.2.6 Modify Shape	Level 1, Chapter 8, Pages 281-284
6.2.7 Modify Screenshots	Level 1, Chapter 8, Pages 279-281
6.3 Create and modify images by using the Image Editor.	
6.3.1 Make corrections to an image	
6.3.1.1 Sharpen or soften an image	Level 1, Chapter 8, Page 281
6.3.1.2 Change brightness	Level 1, Chapter 8, Page 277
6.3.1.3 Change contrast	Level 1, Chapter 8, Page 277
6.3.2 Use picture color tools	Level 1, Chapter 8, Page 277
6.3.3 Change artistic effects on an image	Level 1, Chapter 8, Page 277
6.4 Apply Sparklines.	
6.4.1 Use Line chart types	Level 2, Chapter 4, Pages 128-129
6.4.2 Use Column chart types	Level 2, Chapter 4, Pages 128-129
6.4.3 Use Win/Loss chart types	Level 2, Chapter 4, Pages 128-129
6.4.4 Create a Sparkline chart	Level 2, Chapter 4, Page 129
6.4.5 Customize a Sparkline	Level 2, Chapter 4, Pages 129-130
6.4.6 Format a Sparkline	Level 2, Chapter 4, Pages 129-130
6.4.7 Show or hiding data markers	Level 2, Chapter 4, Pages 129-130
7. Sharing Worksheet Data with other users	
7.1 Share spreadsheets by using Backstage.	
7.1.1 Send a worksheet via E-mail or Skydrive	Level 2, Chapter 8, Pages 292-296
7.1.2 Change the file type to a different version of Excel	Level 2, Chapter 8, Pages 284-285
7.1.3 Save as PDF or XPS	Level 2, Chapter 8, Pages 286-289
7.2 Manage comments.	
7.2.1 Insert	Level 2, Chapter 6, Pages 185-187
7.2.2 View	Level 2, Chapter 6, Pages 185-187
7.2.3 Edit	Level 2, Chapter 6, Pages 185-187

Certification Exam Objective	Textbook Reference
7.2.4 Delete comments	Level 2, Chapter 6, Pages 185-187
8. Analyzing and Organizing Data	
8.1 Filter data.	
8.1.1 Define a filter	Level 1, Chapter 4, Page 135
8.1.2 Apply a filter	Level 1, Chapter 4, Page 136
8.1.3 Remove a filter	Level 1, Chapter 4, Page 136
8.1.4 Filter lists using AutoFilter	Level 1, Chapter 4, Page 137
8.2 Sort data.	
8.2.1 Use sort options	Level 1, Chapter 4, Pages 133-135
8.2.1.1 Values	Level 1, Chapter 4, Pages 133-135
8.2.1.2 Font color	Level 2, Chapter 1, Page 24-27 & Pages 30-32
8.2.1.3 Cell color	Level 2, Chapter 1, Page 24-27, & Pages 30-32
8.3 Apply conditional formatting.	
8.3.1 Apply conditional formatting to cells	Level 2, Chapter 1, Pages 6-8
8.3.2 Use the Rule Manager to apply conditional formats	Level 2, Chapter 1, Pages 8-12
8.3.3 Use the IF function to apply conditional formatting	Level 2, Chapter 1, Pages 15-16
8.3.4 Clear rules	Level 2, Chapter 1, Page 11
8.3.5 Use icon sets	Level 2, Chapter 1, Pages 12-13
8.3.6 Use data bars	Level 2, Chapter 1, Page 14 & Page 32

Microsoft Office 2010 Product Editions

Microsoft Office 2010 is available in the following editions:
- Microsoft Office Starter
- Office Home and Student
- Office Home and Business
- Office Professional
- Microsoft Office Professional Plus
- Microsoft Office Standard
- Microsoft Office Professional Academic

The programs included in each edition at http://office.microsoft.com/en-us/products/FX101635841033.aspx.

Microsoft Office 2010 System Requirements

This interactive text is designed for the student to complete chapter work on a computer running a standard installation of Microsoft Office 2010, Office Professional edition, and the Microsoft Windows 7 operating system. To effectively run the Microsoft Office 2010 suite and operating system, your computer should be outfitted with the following:
- 1 gigahertz (GHz) processor or higher; 1 gigabyte (GB) of RAM
- DVD drive
- 15 GB of available hard-disk space
- Computer mouse or compatible pointing device

Office 2010 will also operate on computers running the Windows XP Service Pack 3 or the Windows Vista operating system.

Screen captures for the books in the Benchmark Series were created using a screen resolution display setting of 1280 × 800. Refer to the Customizing Settings section of Getting Started in Office 2010, which follows the textbook's preface for instructions on changing a monitor's resolution. Figure G.10 on page 10 of the textbook illustrates the Microsoft Office Word ribbon at three resolutions for comparison purposes. Choose the resolution that best matches your computer; however, be aware that using a resolution other than 1280 × 800 means that your screens may not match the illustrations in this book.

Developing an Assessment Strategy

The final major phase of planning a course is to develop an assessment strategy based on the purpose of evaluation and on your philosophy of what constitutes high-quality assessments. The obvious purpose of assessing students' learning is to determine whether students have achieved the goals of the course and, if they have, to what degree, resulting in a grade for credits earned. Other functions of evaluation include motivating students, determining the overall effectiveness of your teaching, and meeting accreditation requirements.

In developing your philosophy of assessment, consider these suggestions from Paradigm Publishing's *Exceptional Teaching.*

Assessments should:
- contribute to students' learning by asking them to apply their skills in out-of-school or workplace situations
- be planned as an integral part of the course design in terms of timing, content, and form
- have a clear purpose
- be appropriate for the purpose in terms of content and format
- be scored as consistently and objectively as possible
- provide students with feedback on their learning
- emphasize intellectual traits of value—analytical reading, thinking, decision making, and research skills along with individual creativity and intelligence
- be conducted at specific, planned checkpoints
- be conducted in a positive learning environment, with every effort made to lower students' test anxieties
- allow students to demonstrate their accomplishment of outcomes in various ways, including ways that fit their individual learning styles

Determining the Number, Level, and Type of Assessments

Formulate your evaluation and grading strategy by answering these course-level questions. Consider if you should include:
- a course pre-assessment?
- a course comprehensive assessment that will determine students' mastery of the major intended outcomes for the entire course?
- pre-assessments for each section?
- comprehensive assessments for each section that assess students' mastery of the major intended outcomes for that section?
- interim or checkpoint assessments that assess students' mastery of intended outcomes of learning within units? How many? How often?

Also ask yourself: once my system is in place, will my students know that I value *how* and *how well* they think?

These questions will help you establish approximately how many assessments you wish to include and their place in the course.

The next decisions concern which types of assessment to use: traditional cognitive (objective) tests and/or performance-based assessments. Each of these two major categories of tests has its merits. Traditional cognitive tests such as multiple-choice exams usually work best for testing information recall, comprehension, and analysis. They also are reliable and efficient, and relatively easy to score. On the down side, objective-type tests are criticized for not representing how students will use their new skills in an unfamiliar setting or in the real world of work. On the other hand, performance-based testing requires students to demonstrate what they have learned and to apply it in a realistic context that closely approximates an on-the-job situation. These tests measure how well students can do what the course intended to teach them. As emphasized in *Exceptional Teaching,* "Authentic, performance-based assessments ask students to integrate what they have learned and apply it to resolve an issue, solve a problem, create something new, work collaboratively, or use their written and oral communication skills. Authentic assessments stress the process of learning as well as the outcomes of learning."

Creating a Grading Plan

By choosing the types of assessments that will measure students' achievement of course and program outcomes, you will already have established a schema of the major grading components. The next step is to weight the scores before entering them into a grade calculation system, such as, an Excel spreadsheet.

Will you include other factors such as effort and attendance in students' grades? If so, consider how to measure those elements. While it is simple to track attendance, it is not as easy to objectively evaluate effort and attitude. Some experts recommend that teachers provide regular verbal and written feedback on these factors, but confine grades to academic achievement.

The following grading plan, which is part of the sample syllabus presented earlier in this section, offers a starting point as you develop your comprehensive grading strategy:

- Concepts Check assignments   5%
- Skills Check assignments   15%
- Visual Benchmark assignments   15%
- Case Study assignments   20%
- Unit Performance Assessments   25%
- Exams   20%

For More Information

Much of the content of this "Planning the Course" article is based on information found in *Exceptional Teaching: Ideas in Action.* To order a copy of this resource, please visit www.emcp.com or contact Customer Care at 800-535-6865 or educate@emcp.com.

Chapter Overviews

Using Windows 7

Performance Objectives

- Use desktop icons and the Taskbar to launch programs and open files or folders
- Add and remove gadgets
- Organize and manage data, including copying, moving, creating, and deleting files and folders; and create a shortcut
- Explore the Control Panel and personalize the desktop
- Use the Windows Help and Support features
- Use search tools

Projects

Project 1	Opening Programs, Switching between Programs, and Manipulating Windows
Project 2	Changing Taskbar Properties
Project 3	Adding and Removing Gadgets
Project 4	Copying a File and Folder and Deleting a File
Project 5	Copying and Deleting Files
Project 6	Creating a New Folder
Project 7	Deleting Files to and Restoring Files from the Recycle Bin
Project 8	Emptying the Recycle Bin
Project 9	Creating a Shortcut
Project 10	Changing the Desktop Theme
Project 11	Customizing the Mouse
Project 12	Customizing with a Shortcut Command
Project 13	Getting Help
Project 14	Searching for Programs and Files

Overview
Browsing the Internet Using Internet Explorer 8.0

Performance Objectives
- Navigate the Internet using URLs and hyperlinks
- Use search engines to locate information
- Download web pages and images

Projects

Overview
Excel 2010 Level 1, Chapter 1
Preparing an Excel Workbook

Performance Objectives
- Identify the various elements of an Excel workbook
- Create, save, and print a workbook
- Enter data in a workbook
- Edit data in a workbook
- Insert formula using the AutoSum button
- Apply basic formatting to cells in a workbook
- Use the Help feature

Projects
Project 1   Prepare a Worksheet with Employee Information
      1a   Creating and Saving a Document
      1b   Editing Data in a Cell
      1c   Inserting Data in Cells with AutoComplete
Project 2   Open and Format a Workbook and Insert Formulas
      2a   Inserting Data in Cells with the Fill Handle
      2b   Adding Values with the AutoSum Button
      2c   Inserting the AVERAGE Function and copying a Formula Relatively
Project 3   Format a Worksheet
      3a   Changing Column Width and Merging and Centering Cells
      3b   Formatting Numbers
Project 4   Use the Help Feature
      4a   Using the Help Feature
      4b   Getting Help in a Dialog Box and Backstage View
      4c   Customizing Help

End-of-Chapter Assessments

Concepts Check
Sixteen short answer questions

Skills Check
1. Create a Worksheet Using AutoComplete
2. Create and Format a Worksheet
3. Create a Worksheet Using the Fill Handle
4. Insert Formulas in a Worksheet

Visual Benchmark
Create, Format, and Insert Formulas in a Worksheet

Case Study
Office manager for Deering Industries
Part 1 Create a monthly calendar containing information on staff meetings, training, and due dates for time cards.
Part 2 Prepare a worksheet containing information on quarterly purchases.
Part 3 Prepare a note to the finances coordinator about the Purchasing Department expenditures you have created.
Part 4 Use the Internet to research information about three companies that sell copy machines.

Overview
Excel 2010 Level 1, Chapter 2
Inserting Formulas in a Worksheet

Performance Objectives
- Write formulas with mathematical operators
- Types a formula in the Formula bar
- Copy a formula
- Use the Insert Function feature to insert a formula in a cell
- Write formulas with the AVERAGE, MAX, MIN, COUNT, PMT, FV, DATE, NOW, and IF functions
- Create an absolute and mixed cell reference

Projects
Project 1 Insert Formulas in a Worksheet
    1a Finding Differences by Inserting and Copying a Formula
    1b Calculating Salary by Inserting and Copying a Formula with the Fill Handle
    1c Writing a Formula by Pointing that Calculates Percentage of Actual Budget
    1d Writing a Formula by Pointing That Calculates Percentage of Down Time
Project 2 Insert Formulas with Statistical Functions
    2a Averaging Test Scores in a Worksheet
    2b Finding Maximum and Minimum Values in a Worksheet
    2c Counting the Number of Students Taking Tests
    2d Displaying Formulas
Project 3 Insert Formulas with Financial and Date and Time Functions
    3a Calculating Payments
    3b Finding the Future Value of an Investment
    3c Using the DATE and NOW Functions

Project 4   Insert Formulas with the IF Logical Function
 4a   Writing a Formula with an IF Function and Editing the Formula
 4b   Writing IF Statements with Text
Project 5   Insert Formulas Using Absolute and Mixed Cell References
 5a   Inserting and Copying a Formula with an Absolute Cell Reference
 5b   Inserting and Copying a Formula with Multiple Absolute Cell References
 5c   Determining Payroll Using Formulas with Absolute and Mixed Cell References
 5d   Determining Simple Interest Using a Formula with Mixed Cell References

End-of-Chapter Assessments

Concepts Check
Twelve short answer questions

Skills Check
1. Insert AVERAGE, MAX, and MIN Functions
2. Insert PMT Function
3. Insert FV Function
4. Write IF Statement Formulas
5. Write Formulas with Absolute Cell References
6. Use Help to Learn about Excel Options

Visual Benchmark
Create a Worksheet and Insert Formulas

Case Study
Loan officer for Dollar Wise Financial Services, specializing in home loans
Part 1   Prepare a sample home mortgage worksheet to show prospective clients.
Part 2   Insert an IF statement to determine which home buyers require mortgage insurance.
Part 3   Using resources available to you determine a current interest rate in your area. Input the new rate in the worksheet.
Part 4   Use the Help feature to insert a hyperlink into the worksheet. Create a letter that contains a linked worksheet.

Overview
Excel 2010 Level 1, Chapter 3
Formatting an Excel Worksheet

Performance Objectives
- Change column widths
- Change row heights
- Insert row and columns in a worksheet
- Delete cells, rows, and columns in a worksheet
- Clear data in cells
- Apply formatting to data in cells
- Apply formatting to selected data using the Mini toolbar
- Preview a worksheet
- Apply a theme and customize the theme font and color
- Format numbers
- Repeat the last action
- Automate formatting with Format Painter
- Hide and unhide rows and columns

Projects
Project 1   Format a Product Pricing Worksheet
    1a   Changing Column Width Using a Column Boundary
    1b   Changing Column Width at the Column Width Dialog Box
    1c   Changing Row Height
    1d   Inserting Rows
    1e   Inserting a Column
    1f   Deleting and Clearing Rows in a Worksheet
    1g   Applying Font and Alignment Formatting
Project 2   Apply a Theme to a Payroll Worksheet
    2   Applying a Theme
Project 3   Format an Invoices Worksheet
    3a   Formatting Numbers with Buttons in the Number Group
    3b   Formatting Numbers at the Format Cells Dialog Box
Project 4   Format a Company Budget Worksheet
    4a   Aligning and Rotating Data in Cells
    4b   Applying Font Formatting at the Format Cells Dialog Box
    4c   Adding Borders to Cells
    4d   Adding Fill Color and Shading to Cells
    4e   Formatting with Format Painter
    4f   Hiding and Unhiding Columns and Rows

End-of-Chapter Assessments

Concepts Check
Fourteen short answer questions

Skills Check
1. Format a Sales and Bonuses Worksheet
2. Format an Overdue Accounts Worksheet
3. Format a Supplies and Equipment Worksheet
4. Format a Financial Analysis Worksheet

Visual Benchmark
Create a Worksheet and Insert Formulas

Case Study
Office manager for Health Wise Fitness Center
Part 1 Prepare an Excel worksheet that displays the various plans offered by the
health club, including the yearly and quarterly payments for each plan.
Part 2 Prepare a payroll sheet for the employees of the fitness center.
Part 3 Use the Internet to research information on models and prices for new
exercise equipment and prepare an Excel document with all the information.
Part 4 Create a letter template to send to prospective clients interested in joining
the health club including information about the fitness center, the plans
offered, and the dues amounts.

Overview
Excel 2010 Level 1, Chapter 4
Enhancing a Worksheet

Performance Objectives
- Change worksheet margins
- Center a worksheet horizontally and vertically on the page
- Insert a page break in a worksheet
- Print gridlines and row and column headings
- Set and clear a print area
- Insert headers and footers
- Customize print jobs
- Complete a spelling check on a worksheet
- Find and replace data and cell formatting in a worksheet
- Sort data in cells in ascending and descending order
- Filter a list using AutoFilter

Projects

Project 1 Format a Yearly Budget Worksheet
- 1a Changing Margins and Horizontally and Vertically Centering a Worksheet
- 1b Changing Page Orientation and Size
- 1c Inserting a Page Break in a Worksheet
- 1d Printing Column Titles on Each Page of a Worksheet
- 1e Scaling Data to Fit on One Page and Printing Row Titles on Each Page
- 1f Inserting a Background Picture
- 1g Printing Gridlines and Row and Column Headings
- 1h Printing Specific Areas
- 1i Inserting a Header in a Worksheet
- 1j Inserting a Footer and Modifying a Header in a Worksheet
- 1k Creating Different Odd and Even Page Headers and Footers and a Different First Page Header and Footer
- 1l Printing Specific Pages of a Worksheet

Project 2 Format a May Sales and Commissions Worksheet
- 2a Spell Checking and Formatting a Worksheet
- 2b Finding and Replacing Data
- 2c Finding and Replacing Cell Formatting

Project 3 Format a Billing Worksheet
- 3a Sorting Data
- 3b Sorting Data Using the Sort Dialog Box
- 3c Sorting Data in Two Columns
- 3d Filtering Data

End-of-Chapter Assessments

Concepts Check
Fifteen short answer questions

Skills Check
1. Format a Data Analysis Worksheet
2. Format a Test Results Worksheet
3. Format an Equipment Rental Worksheet
4. Format an Invoices Worksheet
5. Create a Worksheet Containing Keyboard Shortcuts

Visual Benchmark
Create and Format an Expense Worksheet

Case Study
Sales manager for Macadam Realty

Part 1 Create sample mortgage worksheets including numerous formulas and then format the document.

Part 2 Complete an Individual Retirement Account (IRA) worksheet using the formulas you have learned and then format the document.

Part 3 Use the Internet to search for the MS MoneyCentral Investor Currency Rates site and create and format a conversion worksheet for clients living in Canada who are interested in buying real estate in the United States.

Overview
Excel 2010 Level 1, Unit 1
Performance Assessment

Assessing Proficiency

1. Create Sales Bonuses Workbook
2. Format Equipment Purchase Plan Workbook
3. Format Accounts Due Workbook
4. Format First Quarter Sales Workbook
5. Format Weekly Payroll Workbook
6. Format Customer Sales Analysis Workbook
7. Format Invoices Workbook

Writing Activities

1. Plan and Prepare Orders Summary Workbook
2. Prepare Depreciation Workbook
3. Insert Straight-Line Depreciation Formula

Internet Research

Create a Travel Planning Worksheet

Overview
Excel 2010 Level 1, Chapter 5
Moving Data within and between Workbooks

Performance Objectives
- Create a workbook with multiple worksheets
- Move, copy, and paste cells within a worksheet
- Split a worksheet into windows and freeze panes
- Name a range of cells and use a range in a formula
- Open multiple workbooks
- Arrange, size, and move workbooks
- Copy and paste data between workbooks
- Link data between worksheets

Projects
Project 1   Manage Data in a Multiple-Worksheet Account Workbook
     1a   Displaying Worksheets in a Workbook
     1b   Moving Selected Cells
     1c   Copying Selected Cells in a Worksheet
     1d   Copying and Pasting Cells Using the Office Clipboard
     1e   Copying and Pasting Values
     1f   Inserting a Worksheet
     1g   Selecting, Moving, Renaming, and Changing the Color of Worksheet Tabs
     1h   Hiding a Worksheet and Formatting Multiple Worksheets
     1i   Printing All Worksheets in a Workbook
Project 2   Write Formulas Using Ranges in an Equipment Usage Workbook
     2a   Splitting Windows and Editing Cells
     2b   Naming a Range and Using a Range in a Formula
Project 3   Arrange, Size, and Copy Data between Workbooks
     3a   Opening, Arranging, and Hiding/Unhiding Workbooks
     3b   Minimizing, Maximizing, and Restoring Workbooks
     3c   Copying Selected Cells from One Open Worksheet to Another
Project 4   Linking and Copying Data within and between Worksheets and Word
     4a   Linking Cells between Worksheets
     4b   Copying and Pasting Excel Data into a Word Document

End-of-Chapter Assessments

Concepts Check
Fifteen short answer questions

Skills Check
1. Copy and Paste Data between Worksheets in a Sales Workbook

2. Copy, Paste, and Format Worksheets in an Income Statement Workbook
3. Freeze and Unfreeze Window Panes in a Test Scores Workbook
4. Create, Copy, Paste, and Format Cells in an Equipment Usage Workbook
5. Copying and Linking Data in a Word Document

Visual Benchmark
Create and format a sales worksheet using formulas.

Case Study
Administrator for Gateway Global, an electronics manufacturing corporation
Part 1 Create and format a workbook containing worksheet for monthly expenditures.
Part 2 Make changes to the softball team statistics workbook and use Help to learn how to apply conditional formatting to the data.
Part 3 Use the Internet to find conversion tables for length, weight, volume, and temperature and prepare a conversion chart in Excel.
Part 4 Create a letterhead document in Word containing the company name, address, and phone number and paste in the Fahrenheit conversion information from the conversion chart.

Overview
Excel 2010 Level 1, Chapter 6
Maintaining Workbooks

Performance Objectives
- Create and rename a folder
- Delete workbooks and folders
- Copy and move workbooks within and between folders
- Copy, move, and rename worksheets within a workbook
- Maintain consistent formatting with styles
- Insert, modify, and remove hyperlinks
- Create financial forms using templates

Projects
Project 1 Manage Workbooks
      1a Creating a Folder
      1b Renaming a Folder
      1c Selecting and Deleting Workbooks
      1d Saving a Copy of an Open Workbook
      1e Copying a Workbook at the Open Dialog Box
      1f Cutting and Pasting a Workbook

End-of-Chapter Assessments

Concepts Check
Fourteen short answer questions

Skills Check
1. Manage Workbooks
2. Move and Copy Worksheets between Sales Analysis Workbooks
3. Define and Apply Styles to a Projected Earnings Workbook
4. Insert Hyperlinks in a Book Store Workbook
5. Apply Conditional Formatting to a Sales Workbook

Visual Benchmark
Fill in an Expense Report Form

Case Study
Office manager for Leeward Marine
Part 1   Consolidate expense worksheets into one workbook and apply formatting and styles to data.
Part 2   Create a worksheet for the expense workbook that summarizes each category of the workbook.
Part 3   Go to the Microsoft online site and download the *Product price list* template, insert the company information into the template, and format the form.
Part 4   Use the letterhead you created in Word, copy the product list information from an Excel document, and format the document.

Overview
Excel 2010 Level 1, Chapter 7
Creating a Chart in Excel

Performance Objectives
- Create a chart with data in an Excel worksheet
- Size, move, and delete charts
- Print a selected chart and print a worksheet containing a chart
- Choose a chart style, layout, and formatting
- Change chart location
- Insert, move, size, and delete chart labels, shapes, and pictures

Projects

Project 1 Create a Quarterly Sales Column Chart
     1a Creating a Chart
     1b Printing the Chart
Project 2 Create a Technology Purchases Bar Chart and Column Chart
     2a Creating a Chart and Changing the Design
     2b Changing Chart Layout, Style, and Location
Project 3 Create a Population Comparison Bar Chart
     3a Creating a Chart and Changing Layout of Chart Labels
     3b Inserting and Customizing a Shape
     3c Inserting a Picture in a Chart
Project 4 Create a Costs Percentage Pie Chart
     4 Creating and Formatting a Pie Chart
Project 5 Create a Regional Sales Column Chart
     5 Changing the Height and Width of a Chart

End-of-Chapter Assessments

Concepts Check
Ten short answer questions

Skills Check
1. Create a Company Sales Column Chart
2. Create Quarterly Domestic and Foreign Sales Bar Chart
3. Create and Format a Corporate Sales Column Chart
4. Create a Funds Allocations Pie Chart
5. Create an Actual and Projected Sales Chart
6. Create a Stacked Cylinder Chart

Visual Benchmark
Create and Format a Pie Chart

Case Study
Administrator for Dollar Wise Financial Services
Part 1 Prepare two charts indicating home loan and commercial loan amounts for the past year.
Part 2 Convert the amounts given into percentages of the entire budget and then create a pie chart with that information.
Part 3 Use the Help feature to learn about stock charts and then create a stock chart with the information given.
Part 4 Use the Internet to search for historical data on the national average for mortgage rates and create a chart using this information.

Overview
Excel 2010 Level 1, Chapter 8
Adding Visual Interest to Workbooks

Performance Objectives
- Insert symbols and special characters
- Insert, size, move, and format a clip art image
- Insert a screenshot
- Draw, format, and copy shapes
- Insert, size, move, and format a picture image
- Insert, format, and type text in a text box
- Insert a picture image as a watermark
- Insert and format SmartArt diagrams
- Insert and format WordArt

Projects
Project 1   Insert a Clip Art Image and Shapes in a Financial Analysis Workbook
    1a   Inserting Symbols and Special Characters
    1b   Formatting an Image
    1c   Inserting and Formatting a Clip Art Image
    1d   Inserting and Formatting a Screenshot
    1e   Drawing Arrow Shapes
Project 2   Insert a Picture and Text Box in a Division Sales Workbook
    2a   Inserting and Customizing a Picture
    2b   Inserting and Formatting a Text Box
Project 3   Insert a Watermark in an Equipment Usage Workbook
    3   Inserting a Picture as a Watermark
Project 4   Insert and Format Diagrams in a Company Sales Workbook
    4a   Inserting a Diagram in a Worksheet
    4b   Changing the Diagram Design

4c Changing the Diagram Formatting
4d Inserting and Formatting WordArt

End-of-Chapter Assessments

Concepts Check
Eleven short answer questions

Skills Check
1. Insert a Clip Art Image and WordArt in an Equipment Purchase Workbook
2. Insert Formulas and Format a Travel Company Workbook
3. Insert and Format Shapes in a Company Sales Workbook
4. Insert and Format a SmartArt Diagram in a Sales Workbook
5. Create and Insert a Screenshot

Visual Benchmark
Insert Formulas, WordArt, and Clip Art in a Worksheet

Case Study
Office manager for Ocean Truck Sales
Part 1 Maintain a spreadsheet of the truck and SUV inventory, apply formatting, and insert one clip art image.
Part 2 Take the inventory workbook from Part 1, separate the vehicles onto different worksheets, and list them from most expensive to least expensive.
Part 3 Save the inventory worksheet as a single file web page for viewing online.
Part 4 Create a PowerPoint presentation of the incentive diagram.

Overview
Excel 2010 Level 1, Unit 2
Performance Assessment

Assessing Proficiency
1. Copy and Paste Data and Insert WordArt in a Training Scores Workbook
2. Manage Multiple Worksheets in a Projected Earnings Workbook
3. Create Charts in Worksheets in a Sales Totals Workbook
4. Create and Format a Line Chart
5. Create and Format a Pie Chart
6. Insert a Text Box in and Save a Travel Workbook as a Web Page
7. Insert Clip Art Image and SmartArt Diagram in a Projected Quotas Workbook
8. Insert Symbol, Clip Art, and Comments in a Sales Workbook
9. Insert and Format a Shape in a Budget Workbook

Writing Activities

1. Prepare a Projected Budget
2. Create a Travel Tours Bar Chart
3. Prepare a Ski Vacation Worksheet

Internet Research

Find Information on Excel Books and Present the Data in a Worksheet

Job Study

Create a Customized Time Card for a Landscaping Company

Overview
Excel 2010 Level 2, Chapter 1
Advanced Formatting Techniques

Performance Objectives
- Apply conditional formatting by entering parameters for a rule
- Apply conditional formatting using a predefined rule
- Create and apply a new rule for conditional formatting
- Edit, delete and clear conditional formatting
- Apply conditional formatting using an icon set, data bars, and color scale
- Apply conditional formatting using a formula
- Apply fraction and scientific formatting
- Apply a special format for a number
- Create a custom number format
- Apply wrap text and shrink to fit text control options
- Filter a worksheet using a custom AutoFilter
- Filter and sort a worksheet using conditional formatting or cell attributes

Projects
Project 1 Format Cells Based on Values
    1a Formatting Cells Based on a Value Comparison
    1b Formatting Cells Based on Top/Bottom Rules
Project 2 Apply Conditional Formatting to Insurance Policy Data
    2a Creating and Applying New Formatting Rules
    2b Creating, Editing, and Deleting a Formatting Rule
    2c Applying Conditional Formatting Using an Icon Set
    2d Applying Conditional Formatting Using a Formula
Project 3 Use Fraction and Scientific Formatting Options
    3 Applying Fraction and Scientific Formatting
Project 4 Apply Advanced Formatting Options
    4a Applying Special Formatting
    4b Creating a Custom Number Format
    4c Applying Wrap Text and Shrink to Fit Text Control Options
Project 5 Filter and Sort Data Based on Values, Icon Set, and Font Color
    5a Filtering Policy Information
    5b Filtering Data by Icon Set
    5c Filtering by Font Color
    5d Sorting by Cell Color

End-of-Chapter Assessments

Concepts Check
Thirteen short answer questions

Skills Check Assessments
1. Use Conditional and Fraction Formatting
2. Apply Custom Number Formatting
3. Use Custom AutoFilter; Filter and Sort by Color
4. Create, Edit, and Delete Formatting Rules

Visual Benchmark
Format a Billing Summary

Case Study
Market research assistant for NuTrends Market Research
- Format a worksheet containing median annual income obtained from the U.S. Census Bureau. Use different colors to focus on significant data.
- Sort and filter the worksheet from Part 1 and then set up a contact telephone reference list.
- Apply color gradation to illustrate data in two-color and three-color scales with conditional formatting.
- Go to the U.S. Census Bureau website and gather facts about the history of the Census Bureau.

Overview
Excel 2010 Level 2, Chapter 2
Advanced Functions and Formulas

Performance Objectives
- Create and use named ranges in formulas
- Use functions COUNTA, COUNTIF, COUNTIFS
- Use functions AVERAGEIF, AVERAGEIFS
- Use functions SUMIF, SUMIFS
- Edit a named range
- Rename and delete a named range
- Look up data using the lookup functions VLOOKUP and HLOOKUP
- Analyze loan payments using PPMT
- Use conditional logic functions IF, AND, and OR
- Modify text using the text functions PROPER, UPPER, LOWER, and SUBSTITUTE

Projects

Project 1 Calculate Statistics and Sums Using Conditional Formulas
   1a Creating Range Names
   1b Creating COUNTIF Functions
   1c Creating COUNTIFS Functions
   1d Creating AVERAGEIF Functions
   1e Creating AVERAGEIFS Functions
   1f Creating SUMIF Functions
   1g Editing and Deleting a Range Name
Project 2 Populate Cells by Looking Up Data
   2 Creating a VLOOKUP Function
Project 3 Analyze an Expansion Project Loan
   3 Calculating Principal Portion of Loan Payments
Project 4 Calculate Benefit Costs Using Conditional Logic
   4a Calculating Pension Cost Using Nested IF and AND Functions
   4b Calculating Health and Dental Costs Using Nested IF and OR Functions
Project 5 Convert Text Using Text Functions
   5 Converting Text Using SUBSTITUTE and UPPER Text Functions

End-of-Chapter Assessments

Concepts Check
Fifteen short answer questions

Skill Check Assessments
1. Create Range Names and Use the LOOKUP Function
2. Use Conditional Statistical and Math Functions
3. Use Financial Functions PMT and PPMT
4. Use Logical Functions
5. Work with the HLOOKUP Function

Visual Benchmark
1. Use LOOKUP, Statistical, and Math Functions in a Billing Summary
2. Use LOOKUP and Logical Functions to Calculate Cardiology Costs

Case Study
Market research assistant for NuTrends Market Research
- Extract statistics and calculate payments in a workbook for a new client, Pizza by Mario.
- Create formulas to calculate the royalty percentage and royalty payment for each Pizza by Mario store.
- Use the Help feature to learn about the MEDIAN and STDEV functions.
- Use the Internet to research statistics on two states in close proximity to Michigan, Ohio, Wisconsin, and Iowa for a new marketing plan for Pizza by Mario.

Overview
Excel 2010 Level 2, Chapter 3
Working with Tables and Data Features

Performance Objectives
- Create a table in a worksheet
- Expand a table to include new rows and columns
- Add a calculated column in a table
- Format a table by applying table styles and table style options
- Add a total row to a table and add formulas to total cells
- Sort and filter a table
- Split contents of a cell into separate columns
- Remove duplicate records
- Restrict data entry by creating validation criteria
- Convert a table to a normal range
- Create subtotals in groups of related data
- Group and ungroup data

Projects
Project 1		Create and Modify a Table
	1a	Converting a Range to a Table
	1b	Adding a Row and a Calculated Column to a Table
	1c	Formatting a Table and Adding a Total Row
	1d	Sorting and Filtering a Table
Project 2		Use Data Tools to Split Data and Ensure Data Integrity
	2a	Separating Attorney Names into Two Columns
	2b	Removing Duplicate Rows
	2c	Restricting Data Entry to Dates Within a Range
	2d	Restricting Data Entry to Values Within a List
	2e	Ensuring Data Entered Is a Specified Text Length
Project 3		Group and Subtotal Related Records
	3a	Converting a Table to a Range and Creating Subtotals
	3b	Modifying Subtotals
	3c	Grouping and Ungrouping Data

End-of-Chapter Assessments

Concepts Check
Fifteen short answer questions

Skills Check Assessments
1. Create and Format a Table

2. Use Data Tools
3. Subtotal Records

Visual Benchmark
1. Using Table and Data Tools in a Call List
2. Using Subtotals in a Call List

Case Study
Market research assistant of NuTrends Market Research
- Improve and format a marketing plan for three marketing consultants.
- Add statistics for each consultant including total marketing plan value managed by each consultant and planned expenditures by month to the workbook from Part 1.
- Use the Help feature to research how to filter a range of cells using the Advanced Filter button and use that information to copy rows and filter the list for a new marketing plan.
- Use the Internet to find information on current salary ranges for a market researcher in the U.S. and create a workbook summarizing this information.

Overview
Excel 2010 Level 2, Chapter 4
Summarizing and Consolidating Data

Performance Objectives
- Summarize data by creating formulas with range names that reference other worksheets
- Modify the range assigned to a range name
- Summarize data by creating 3-D formulas
- Create formulas that link to a source worksheets or workbooks
- Edit a link to a source workbook
- Break a link to an external reference
- Use the Consolidate feature to summarize data in multiple worksheets
- Create, edit, and format a PivotTable
- Filter a PivotTable using Slicers
- Create and format a PivotChart
- Create and format Sparklines

Projects
Project 1 Calculate Park Attendance Totals
      1a Summarizing Data in Multiple Worksheets by Creating and Modifying Range Names

End-of-Chapter Assessments

Concepts Check
Fifteen short answer questions

Skills Check Assessments
1. Summarize Data in Multiple Worksheets Using Range Names
2. Summarize Data Using Linked External References
3. Break Linked References
4. Summarize Data Using 3-D References
5. Summarize Data in a PivotTable and PivotChart
6. Filter a PivotTable Using Slicers
7. Creating and Customizing Sparklines

Visual Benchmark
Summarizing Real Estate Sales and Commission Data

Case Study
Marketing research assistant for NuTrends Market Research
• Create a PivotTable that provides the average gross sales and average net income by city by state for Pizza by Mario and apply formatting to improve the appearance.
• Using the PivotTable from Part 1, create a PivotChart that summarizes the Net Income data for the state of Michigan only.
• Use the Help feature to learn how to modify a numeric field setting to show values as ranked numbers from largest to smallest. Change the display of the Pivot Table as requested.

* Use the Internet to research the sales and net income information of a pizza franchise with which you are familiar and create a workbook comparing that information with information about Pizza by Mario.

Overview
Excel 2010 Level 2, Unit 1
Performance Assessment

Assessing Proficiency
1. Conditionally Format and Filter a Help Desk Worksheet
2. Use Conditional Logic Formulas in a Help Desk Worksheet
3. Use Table and Data Management Features in a Help Desk Worksheet
4. Add Subtotals and Outline a Help Desk Worksheet
5. Use Financial and Text Functions to Analyze Data for a Project
6. Analyze Sales Using a PivotTable, a PivotChart, and Sparklines
7. Link to an External Data Source and Calculate Distributor Payments

Writing Activities
1. Create a Worksheet to Track Video Rental Memberships
2. Create a Worksheet to Log Hours Walked in a Company Fitness Contest

Internet Research
Create a Worksheet to Compare Online Auction Listing Fees

Overview
Excel 2010 Level 2, Chapter 5
Using Data Analysis Features

Performance Objectives
* Switch data arranged in columns to rows and vice versa
* Perform a mathematical operation during a paste routine
* Populate a cell using Goal Seek
* Save and display various worksheet models using Scenario Manager
* Create a scenario summary report
* Create a one-variable data table to analyze various outcomes
* Create a two-variable data table to analyze various outcomes

- View relationships between cells in formulas
- Identify Excel error codes and troubleshoot a formula using formula auditing tools
- Circle invalid data
- Use the Watch Window to track a value

Projects

Project 1   Analyze Data from a Request for Proposal
       1a   Converting Data from Rows to Columns
       1b   Multiplying the Source Cells by the Destination Cells
Project 2   Calculate a Target Test Score
       2   Using Goal Seek to Return a Target Value
Project 3   Forecast a Budget Based on Various Inflation Rates
       3a   Adding Scenarios to a Worksheet Model
       3b   Applying a Scenario's Values to the Worksheet
       3c   Generating a Scenario Summary Report
Project 4   Compare Impact of Various Inputs Related to Cost and Sales Pricing
       4a   Creating a One-Variable Data Table
       4b   Creating a Two-Variable Data Table
Project 5   Audit a Worksheet to View and Troubleshoot Formulas
       5a   Viewing Relationships between Cells and Formulas
       5b   Troubleshooting Formulas
       5c   Circling Invalid Data and Watching a Formula Cell

End-of-Chapter Assessments

Concepts Check
Fifteen short answer questions

Skills Check Assessments
1. Convert Columns to Rows; Add Source Cells to Destination Cells; Filter
2. Use Goal Seek
3. Use Scenario Manager
4. Create a Two-Variable Data Table
5. Find and Correct Formula Errors

Visual Benchmark
1. Find the Base Hourly Rate for Drum Lessons
2. Create Scenarios for Drum Lesson Revenue

Case Study
Market research assistant NuTrends Market Research
- In a workbook for prospective new franchise owners, apply a what-if analysis to find out how much a franchise has to make in its first year of sales in order to pay back the initial investment in 12 months.

- Create a report that shows the input variables for each model shown and the impact of each on the number of months to recoup the initial investment.
- Use the Help feature to find out how to select cells that contain formulas and use that information to review the formulas in the worksheet to ensure they are logically correct.
- Search the Internet for current lending rates for secured credit lines at the bank which you have an account and use that information to create a workbook , adding two percentage points to the bank's lending rate; create a linked cell to a new worksheet which calculates the monthly loan payment for a term of five years.

Overview
Excel 2010 Level 2, Chapter 6
Protecting and Sharing Workbooks

Performance Objectives
- Add information to a workbook's properties
- Add comments containing additional information or other notes to the reader
- Share a workbook with other people and view other users who have the shared workbook open at the same time
- Edit a shared workbook and resolve conflicts with changes
- Print a history of changes made to a shared workbook
- Stop sharing a workbook
- Protect cells within a worksheet to prevent changes
- Add a password to open a workbook
- Track changes made to a workbook
- Modify and resolve tracked changes

Projects
Project 1 Add Workbook Properties, Insert Comments, and Share a Workbook
    1a Adding Information to Workbook Properties
    1b Inserting, Editing, Pasting, Viewing, and Deleting Comments
    1c Sharing a Workbook
    1d Changing the User Name and Editing a Shared Workbook
    1e Viewing Other Users of a Shared Workbook
    1f Resolving Conflicts in a Shared Workbook
    1g Printing the History Sheet and Removing Shared Access to a Workbook
Project 2 Lock and Unlock a Workbook, a Worksheet, and Ranges
    2a Protecting an Entire Worksheet
    2b Unlocking Cells and Protecting a Worksheet

2c Protecting the Structure of a Workbook
　　2c Protecting the Structure of a Workbook
　　2d Adding a Password to Open a Workbook
Project 3 Track and Resolve Changes Made to a Workbook
　　3a Tacking Changes Made to a Workbook
　　3b Editing a Tracked Workbook
　　3c Highlighting and Reviewing Tracked Changes

End-of-Chapter Assessments

Concepts Check
Fifteen short answer questions

Skills Check Assessments
1. Enter and Display Workbook Properties; Insert Comments
2. Share a Workbook; Edit a Shared Workbook; Print a History Sheet
3. Remove Shared Access
4. Protect an Entire Worksheet; Add a Password to a Workbook
5. Unlock Cells and Protect a Worksheet; Protect Workbook Structure
6. Track Changes; Accept/Reject Changes; Print a History Sheet

Visual Benchmark
Track Changes; Insert Comments

Case Study
Market research assistant for NuTrends Market Research
- Add comments and protect a workbook for Pizza by Mario to ensure there are no accidental modifications when the workbook is shared with others. Password protect the workbook.
- Make some changes to the data in the workbook and create a History sheet.
- Unprotect the worksheet and remove the passwords. Add the comments. Print the worksheet with the comments.
- Research on the Internet the guidelines for creating strong passwords and create a table in Word of the dos and don'ts for creating strong passwords in a user-friendly format.

Overview
Excel 2010 Level 2, Chapter 7
Automating Repetitive Tasks and Customizing Excel

Performance Objectives
- Record and run and edit a macro
- Save a workbook containing macros as a macro-enabled workbook
- Create a macro that is run using a shortcut key combination
- Pin and unpin a frequently used file to the Recent Documents list
- Add and remove buttons for frequently-used commands to the Quick Access toolbar
- Hide the ribbon to increase space in the work area
- Customize the display options for Excel
- Customize the ribbon by creating a custom tab and adding buttons
- Create and apply custom views
- Create and use a template
- Customize save options for AutoRecover files

Projects

Project 1 Create Macros
  1a Creating a Macro and Saving a Workbook as a Macro-Enabled Workbook
  1b Running a Macro
  1c Creating and Running a Macro Using a Shortcut Key
  1d Editing a Macro
Project 2 Customize the Excel Work Environment
  2a Pinning a Frequently Used Workbook to the Recent Workbooks List
  2b Adding Commands to the Quick Access Toolbar
  2c Removing Buttons from the Quick Access Toolbar
  2d Customizing Display Options and Minimizing the Ribbon
  2e Restoring Default Display Options
  2f Customizing the Ribbon
  2g Restoring the Ribbon
  2h Creating and Applying Custom Views
Project 3 Save a Workbook as a Template
  3a Saving a Workbook as a Template
  3b Using a Custom Template
  3c Deleting a Custom Template
Project 4 Manage Excel's Save Options
  4a Customizing Save Options
  4b Recovering a Workbook

End-of-Chapter Assessments

Concepts Check
Thirteen short answer questions

Skills Check Assessments
1. Create Macros
2. Run Macros
3. Create Macros; Save as a Macro-Enabled Workbook
4. Print Macros
5. Customize the Excel Environment
6. Create Custom Views
7. Create and Use a Template

Visual Benchmark
1. Customize the Ribbon
2. Create a Custom Template

Case Study
Market research assistant for NuTrends Market Research
- Create macros for the list of tasks and then document the name of the macro, the shortcut key, and a description of the action.
- Use the macros created in Part 1 and format the new franchise workbook.
- Use the Help feature to learn how to add a button to the Quick Access toolbar directly from the ribbon and test the information by adding two buttons to the Quick Access toolbar. Prepare a memo that describes the steps.
- Prepare a memo to explain why the task pane named Document Recovery sometimes appears and what should be done when it appears.

Overview
Excel 2010 Level 2, Chapter 8
Importing, Exporting, and Distributing Data

Performance Objectives
- Import data from an Access table, a website, and a text file
- Append data from an Excel worksheet to an Access table
- Embed and link data in an Excel worksheet to a Word document
- Copy and paste data in an Excel worksheet to a PowerPoint presentation
- Export data as a text file
- Scan and remove private or confidential information from a workbook

- Mark a workbook as final
- Check a workbook for features incompatible with earlier versions of Excel
- Save an Excel worksheet as a PDF or XPS file
- Save an Excel worksheet as a web page
- Send an Excel worksheet via an email message
- Save an Excel worksheet to a SkyDrive

Projects

Project 1 Import Data from Eternal Sources to Excel
    1a Importing Data from an Access Database
    1b Importing a Table from a Web Page
    1c Importing Data from a Comma Separated Text File
Project 2 Export Data in Excel
    2a Copying and Pasting Excel Data to an Access Datasheet
    2b Embedding Excel Data in a Word Document
    2c Linking Excel Data in a Word Document
    2d Breaking a Link
    2e Embedding Excel Data in a PowerPoint Presentation
    2f Exporting a Worksheet as a Text File
Project 3 Prepare a Workbook for Distribution
    3a Removing Private and Confidential Data from a Workbook
    3b Marking a Workbook as Final
    3c Checking a Workbook for Compatibility with Earlier Versions of Excel
Project 4 Distribute Workbooks
    4a Publishing a Worksheet as a PDF Document
    4b Publishing a Worksheet as an XPS Document
    4c Publishing a Worksheet as a Web Page
    4d Sending a Workbook via Email
    4e Saving a Workbook to Windows Live SkyDrive

End-of-Chapter Assessments

Concepts Check
Fifteen short answer questions

Skills Check Assessments
1. Import Data from Access and a Text File
2. Link Data to a Word Document
3. Embed Data in a PowerPoint Presentation
4. Export Data as a Text File
5. Prepare a Workbook for Distribution
6. Prepare and Distribute a Workbook

Visual Benchmark
Import, Analyze, and Export Population Data

Case Study
Market research assistant for NuTrends Market Research
- Start a new workbook and set up three worksheet for each of the states listed and using the New Web Query feature display the Census Bureau web page and import the People Quickfacts table for the state. Modify the workbook as indicated.
- Copy selected information from each state from Part 1 to a Word document.
- Use the Help feature to learn how to manage connections to external data using the Workbook Connections dialog box and create a memo with information you have learned.
- Research in Help how to use the Internet Fax feature and prepare a memo that explains how to use this feature. Include the URL of two fax service providers.

Overview
Excel 2010 Level 2, Unit 2
Performance Assessment

Assessing Proficiency
1. Use Goal Seek and Scenario Manager to Calculate Investment Proposals
2. Calculate Investment Outcomes for a Portfolio Using a Two-Variable Data Table
3. Solve an Error and Check for Accuracy in Investment Commission Formulas
4. Document and Share a Workbook and Manage Changes in an Investment Portfolio Worksheet
5. Insert Comments and Protect a Confidential Investment Portfolio Workbook
6. Automate and Customize an Investment Portfolio Workbook
7. Create and Use an Investment Planner Template
8. Export a Chart and Prepare and Distribute an Investment Portfolio Worksheet

Writing Activities
Create a Computer Maintenance Template

Internet Research
Apply What-If Analysis to a Planned Move
Research and Compare Smartphones

Job Study
Prepare a Wages Budget and Link the Budget to a Word Document

Overview of Assessment Venues

Several venues of different types are available for assessing student achievement in your course.

Comprehension-Based Assessments

- Concepts Check questions appear at the end of each chapter. These short-answer questions test student comprehension and recall of program features, terminology, and functions. Answer keys are included in the *Instructor's Guide*, on the Instructor Resources DVD, and on the password-protected Instructor section of the Internet Resource Center.
- **EXAM**VIEW® test generating software and test banks include multiple-choice items for each chapter of the text. Use **EXAM**VIEW® to create web-based or print tests.
- SNAP web-based assessments include multiple-choice items for each chapter of the text (prepared from the **EXAM**VIEW® test banks). Instructors can assign pre-designed concepts exams or create their own.
- Quizzes of multiple-choice items for each chapter of the text (different from the items in the **EXAM**VIEW® test banks) are available on the Internet Resource Center. Students can take quizzes in either practice mode with immediate feedback or in scores-reported mode with results emailed to the instructor.

Performance-Based Assessments

- End-of-chapter assessments are provided to assess student understanding of major features and program skills taught in the chapter. Instructor support for these assessments is included in the *Instructor's Guide*, on the Instructor Resources DVD, and on the password-protected Instructor section of the Internet Resource Center.
  - Skills Check assessments include some guidance, but less than the chapter projects.
  - Visual Benchmark activities provide limited guidance and challenge students to use their problem-solving skills and mastery of program features to build a file that matches a document or file displayed with the exercise.
  - Case Studies offer realistic scenarios that require taking initiative and determining solutions using skills developed throughout the chapter. Students search the Internet or the program's Help feature to find the additional information they need to create final documents and files.
- Unit Performance Assessments are separate sections at the end of each group of four chapters that include a range of activities to evaluate student achievement.
  - Assessing Proficiency exercises involve using program features to create a variety of documents, all with little or no assistance.
  - Writing Activities stress the vital cross-disciplinary skill of writing clearly during the course of preparing specific documents.

- o Internet Research is a scenario-based activity requiring Internet navigation and searching plus information analysis and presentation.
- o Job Study is a culminating case study exercise that simulates workplace tasks and challenges. This Performance Assessment activity is found in Unit 2 Performance Assessments.
- Supplemental activities are provided for use in evaluating student comprehension of program skills. Resources for these assessments are included in the *Instructor's Guide*, on the Instructor Resources DVD, and on the Instructor section of the Internet Resources Center.
  - o Supplemental Skills Assessments are similar in format to the end-of-chapter Skills Check or Visual Benchmark assessments, and are supported with data files, model answer files, and rubrics. There is one Supplemental Skills Assessment for each unit, or two for each level.
  - o Final Case Studies are similar in format to the end-of-chapter Case Studies and are supported with data files, model answer files, and rubrics. There is one Final Case Study for each application level.
- SNAP Skill Assessments are available to evaluate students' mastery of Microsoft application skills. For these assessments, students perform tasks in the Microsoft application and the results are reported in the learning management system. Instructors can assign predefined skills exams or create their own.

Grading Sheet

Benchmark Office Microsoft Excel 2010 Level 1

Assignment	Title	Start from Scratch	Date Due	Grade
Unit 1: Preparing and Formatting a Worksheet				
Chapter 1 Preparing an Excel Workbook				
Concepts Check				
Skills Check Assessment 1	Create a Worksheet Using AutoComplete	✓		
Skills Check Assessment 2	Create and Format a Worksheet	✓		
Skills Check Assessment 3	Create a Worksheet Using the Fill Handle	✓		
Skills Check Assessment 4	Insert Formulas in a Worksheet			
Visual Benchmark	Create, Format, and Insert Formulas in a Worksheet	✓		
Case Study Part 1	Deering Industries: Calendar			
Case Study Part 2	Deering Industries: Quarterly Purchases			
Case Study Part 3	Deering Industries: Expenditures Memo			
Case Study Part 4	Deering Industries: Copy Machines (Internet)	✓		
SNAP Tutorial 1.1	Creating and Saving a Workbook			
SNAP Tutorial 1.2	Editing Cells and Using Proofing Tools			
SNAP Tutorial 1.3	Displaying Formulas and Navigating a Worksheet			
SNAP Tutorial 1.4	Applying Basic Formatting			
SNAP Tutorial 1.5	Applying Formatting; Using Undo and Redo; Changing Alignment			
Chapter 2 Inserting Formulas in a Worksheet				
Concepts Check				
Skills Check Assessment 1	Insert AVERAGE, MAX, and MIN Functions			
Skills Check Assessment 2	Insert PMT Function			
Skills Check Assessment 3	Insert FV Function			
Skills Check Assessment 4	Write IF Statement Formulas			

Assignment	Title	Start from Scratch	Date Due	Grade
Skills Check Assessment 5	Write Formulas with Absolute Cell References			
Skills Check Assessment 6	Use Help to Learn About Excel Options	✓		
Visual Benchmark	Create a Worksheet and Insert Formulas	✓		
Case Study Part 1	Dollar Wise Financial Services: Home Mortgage Worksheet			
Case Study Part 2	Dollar Wise Financial Services: IF Statement			
Case Study Part 3	Dollar Wise Financial Services: Interest Rates (Internet)			
Case Study Part 4	Dollar Wise Financial Services: Mortgage Insurance (Help, Internet)			
SNAP Tutorial 2.1	Performing Calculations Using Formulas			
SNAP Tutorial 2.2	Writing Formulas in Excel			
SNAP Tutorial 2.3	Copying and Testing Formulas			
SNAP Tutorial 2.4	Creating Formulas with Absolute Addressing			
SNAP Tutorial 2.5	Using Financial Functions			
SNAP Tutorial 2.6	Writing Formulas with the FV Function			
SNAP Tutorial 2.7	Using the Logical IF Function			

Chapter 3 Formatting an Excel Worksheet

Assignment	Title	Start from Scratch	Date Due	Grade
Concepts Check				
Skills Check Assessment 1	Format a Sales and Bonuses Worksheet			
Skills Check Assessment 2	Format an Overdue Accounts Worksheet			
Skills Check Assessment 3	Format a Supplies and Equipment Worksheet			
Skills Check Assessment 4	Format a Financial Analysis Worksheet			
Visual Benchmark	Create a Worksheet and Insert Formulas	✓		
Case Study Part 1	HealthWise Fitness Center: Dues			
Case Study Part 2	HealthWise Fitness Center: Payroll Sheet	✓		
Case Study Part 3	HealthWise Fitness Center: New Equipment (Internet)	✓		
Case Study Part 4	HealthWise Fitness Center: Prospective Clients	✓		
SNAP Tutorial 3.1	Inserting, Adjusting, and Deleting Rows and Columns			
SNAP Tutorial 3.2	Using Cell Styles and Themes			
SNAP Tutorial 3.3	Formatting Numbers			

Assignment	Title	Start from Scratch	Date Due	Grade
SNAP Tutorial 3.4	Adding Borders and Shading; Copying Formats with Format Painter			
SNAP Tutorial 3.5	Hiding and Unhiding Rows and Columns			

Chapter 4 Enhancing a Worksheet

Assignment	Title	Start from Scratch	Date Due	Grade
Concepts Check				
Skills Check Assessment 1	Format a Data Analysis Worksheet			
Skills Check Assessment 2	Format a Test Results Worksheet			
Skills Check Assessment 3	Format an Equipment Rental Worksheet			
Skills Check Assessment 4	Format an Invoices Worksheet			
Skills Check Assessment 5	Create a Worksheet Containing Keyboard Shortcuts (Help)	✓		
Visual Benchmark	Create and Format an Expense Worksheet	✓		
Case Study Part 1	Macadam Realty: Sample Mortgages			
Case Study Part 2	Macadam Realty: IRAs	✓		
Case Study Part 3	Macadam Realty: Conversion Worksheet (Internet)	✓		
SNAP Tutorial 4.1	Changing Page Margins and Layout Options			
SNAP Tutorial 4.2	Formatting and Printing Options			
SNAP Tutorial 4.3	Inserting a Page Break			
SNAP Tutorial 4.4	Formatting a Worksheet Page			
SNAP Tutorial 4.5	Adding Headers and Footers			
SNAP Tutorial 4.6	Using Undo and Redo			
SNAP Tutorial 4.7	Using Find and Replace			
SNAP Tutorial 4.8	Sorting Data and Using Help			
SNAP Tutorial 4.9	Using the Sort Feature in Tables			
SNAP Tutorial 4.10	Filtering a Table			

Unit 1 Performance Assessments

Assignment	Title	Start from Scratch	Date Due	Grade
Assessment 1	Create Sales Bonuses Workbook	✓		
Assessment 2	Format Equipment Purchase Plan Workbook			
Assessment 3	Format Accounts Due Workbook			
Assessment 4	Format First Quarter Sales Workbook			
Assessment 5	Format Weekly Payroll Workbook			
Assessment 6	Format Customer Sales Analysis Workbook			

Assignment	Title	Start from Scratch	Date Due	Grade
Assessment 7	Format Invoices Workbook			
Writing Activity 1	Plan and Prepare Orders Summary Workbook	✓		
Writing Activity 2	Prepare Depreciation Workbook	✓		
Writing Activity 3	Insert Straight-Line Depreciation Formula			
Internet Research	Create a Travel Planning Worksheet	✓		
Supplemental Assessment 1	Doctor Visits	✓		
Supplemental Assessment 2	Doctor Visits	✓		

Unit 2: Enhancing the Display of Workbooks

Chapter 5 Moving Data within and between Workbooks

Concepts Check				
Skills Check Assessment 1	Copy and Paste Data Between Worksheets in a Sales Workbook			
Skills Check Assessment 2	Copy, Paste, and Format Worksheets in an Income Statement Workbook			
Skills Check Assessment 3	Freeze and Unfreeze Window Panes in a Test Scores Workbook			
Skills Check Assessment 4	Create, Copy, Paste, and Format Cells in an Equipment Usage Workbook	✓		
Skills Check Assessment 5	Copying and Linking Data in a Word Document			
Visual Benchmark	Create and Format a Sales Worksheet Using Formulas	✓		
Case Study Part 1	Gateway Global: Supplies and Equipment Purchases	✓		
Case Study Part 2	Gateway Global: Softball Statistics (Help)	✓		
Case Study Part 3	Gateway Global: Length, Weight, and Volume Conversions (Internet)	✓		
Case Study Part 4	Gateway Global: Placing an Excel Image in a Letter	✓		
SNAP Tutorial 5.1	Moving and Copying Cells			
SNAP Tutorial 5.2	Inserting, Moving, Renaming, and Hiding a Worksheet			
SNAP Tutorial 5.3	Formatting Multiple Worksheets			
SNAP Tutorial 5.4	Setting a Print Area and Printing Multiple Worksheets			
SNAP Tutorial 5.5	Splitting a Worksheet into Windows			
SNAP Tutorial 5.6	Freezing Panes and Changing the Zoom			

Assignment	Title	Start from Scratch	Date Due	Grade
SNAP Tutorial 5.7	Naming and Using a Range			
SNAP Tutorial 5.8	Working with Windows			
SNAP Tutorial 5.9	Linking Data and Using 3-D References			
SNAP Tutorial 5.10	Copying and Pasting Data between Programs			

Chapter 6 Maintaining Workbooks

Assignment	Title	Start from Scratch	Date Due	Grade
Concepts Check				
Skills Check Assessment 1	Manage Workbooks			
Skills Check Assessment 2	Move and Copy Worksheets Between Sales Analysis Workbooks			
Skills Check Assessment 3	Define and Apply Styles to a Projected Earnings Workbook	✓		
Skills Check Assessment 4	Insert Hyperlinks in a Book Store Workbook			
Skills Check Assessment 5	Apply Conditional Formatting to a Sales Workbook (Help)	✓		
Visual Benchmark	Fill in an Expense Report Form	✓		
Case Study Part 1	Leeward Marine: Expenses Summary			
Case Study Part 2	Leeward Marine: Estimated Expenses			
Case Study Part 3	Leeward Marine: Products List	✓		
Case Study Part 4	Leeward Marine: Product List	✓		
SNAP Tutorial 6.1	Maintaining Workbooks			
SNAP Tutorial 6.2	Managing Folders			
SNAP Tutorial 6.3	Managing the Recent List			
SNAP Tutorial 6.4	Managing Worksheets			
SNAP Tutorial 6.5	Formatting with Cell Styles			
SNAP Tutorial 6.6	Inserting Hyperlinks			
SNAP Tutorial 6.7	Using Templates			

Chapter 7 Creating a Chart in Excel

Assignment	Title	Start from Scratch	Date Due	Grade
Concepts Check				
Skills Check Assessment 1	Create a Company Sales Column Chart			
Skills Check Assessment 2	Create a Quarterly Domestic and Foreign Sales Bar Chart			
Skills Check Assessment 3	Create and Format a Corporate Sales Column Chart			
Skills Check Assessment 4	Create a Fund Allocations Pie Chart	✓		

Assignment	Title	Start from Scratch	Date Due	Grade
Skills Check Assessment 5	Create an Actual and Projected Sales Chart			
Skills Check Assessment 6	Create a Stacked Cylinder Chart (Help)	✓		
Visual Benchmark	Create and Format a Pie Chart	✓		
Case Study Part 1	Dollar Wise Financial Services: Loan Amounts	✓		
Case Study Part 2	Dollar Wise Financial Services: Budget	✓		
Case Study Part 3	Dollar Wise Financial Services: Stock Prices (Help)	✓		
Case Study Part 4	Dollar Wise Financial Services: Mortgage Rates (Internet)	✓		
SNAP Tutorial 7.1	Creating Charts in Excel			
SNAP Tutorial 7.2	Editing Chart Data			
SNAP Tutorial 7.3	Changing the Chart Design			
SNAP Tutorial 7.4	Changing a Chart Type			
SNAP Tutorial 7.5	Inserting Shapes and Images			
SNAP Tutorial 7.6	Changing the Chart Formatting			

Chapter 8 Adding Visual Interest to Workbooks

Assignment	Title	Start from Scratch	Date Due	Grade
Concepts Check				
Skills Check Assessment 1	Insert a Clip Art Image and WordArt in an Equipment Purchase Workbook			
Skills Check Assessment 2	Insert Formulas and Format a Travel Company Workbook			
Skills Check Assessment 3	Insert and Format Shapes in a Company Sales Workbook			
Skills Check Assessment 4	Insert and Format a SmartArt Diagram in a Sales Workbook			
Skills Check Assessment 5	Create and Insert a Screenshot			
Visual Benchmark	Insert Formulas, WordArt and Clip Art in a Worksheet			
Case Study Part 1	Ocean Truck Sales: Truck and SUV Inventory			
Case Study Part 2	Ocean Truck Sales: Truck and SUV Inventory			
Case Study Part 3	Ocean Truck Sales: Posting to a Web Page			
Case Study Part 4	Ocean Truck Sales: Incentive Diagram in PowerPoint			
SNAP Tutorial 8.1	Inserting Symbols and Special Characters			
SNAP Tutorial 8.2	Inserting Pictures and Clip Art			
SNAP Tutorial 8.3	Creating Screenshots			

Assignment	Title	Start from Scratch	Date Due	Grade
SNAP Tutorial 8.4	Inserting a Picture as a Watermark			
SNAP Tutorial 8.5	Inserting and Formatting a SmartArt Diagram			
SNAP Tutorial 8.6	Creating WordArt			

Unit 2 Performance Assessments

Assignment	Title	Start from Scratch	Date Due	Grade
Assessment 1	Copy and paste Data and Insert WordArt in a Training Scores Workbook			
Assessment 2	Manage Multiple Worksheets in a Projected Earnings Workbook			
Assessment 3	Create Charts in Worksheets in a Sales Totals Workbook			
Assessment 4	Create and Format a Line Chart	✓		
Assessment 5	Create and Format a Pie Chart			
Assessment 6	Insert a Text Box in and Save a Travel Workbook as a Web Page			
Assessment 7	Insert Clip art Image and SmartArt Diagram in a Projected Quotes Workbook			
Assessment 8	Insert Symbol, Clip Art, and Comments in a Sales Workbook			
Assessment 9	Insert and Format a Shape in a Budget Workbook			
Writing Activity 1	Prepare a Projected Budget	✓		
Writing Activity 2	Create a Travel Tours Bar Chart	✓		
Writing Activity 3	Prepare a Ski Vacation Worksheet	✓		
Internet Research	Find Information on Excel Books and Present the Data in a Worksheet	✓		
Job Study	Create a Customized Time			
Supplemental Assessment 1	Stock Portfolio	✓		
Supplemental Assessment 2	Roller Coaster Statistics	✓		
Final Case Study	Body Mechanics & Rehabilitation			

Grading Sheet

Benchmark Office Microsoft Excel 2010 Level 2

Assignment	Title	Start from Scratch	Date Due	Grade
Unit 1: Advanced Formatting, Formulas and Data Management				
Chapter 1 Advanced Formatting Techniques				
Concepts Check				
Skills Check Assessment 1	Use Conditional and Fraction Formatting			
Skills Check Assessment 2	Apply Custom Number Formatting			
Skills Check Assessment 3	Use Custom AutoFilter; Filter and Sort by Color			
Skills Check Assessment 4	Create, Edit, and Delete Formatting Rules			
Visual Benchmark	Format a Billing Summary			
Case Study Part 1	NuTrends Market Research: Income Statistics			
Case Study Part 2	NuTrends Market Research: Income Statistics			
Case Study Part 3	NuTrends Market Research: Income Statistics			
Case Study Part 4	NuTrends Market Research: Income Statistics (Internet)	✓		
SNAP Tutorial 1.1	Applying Conditional Formatting			
SNAP Tutorial 1.2	Applying Conditional Formatting Using Icon Sets			
SNAP Tutorial 1.3	Applying Conditional Formatting Using Data Bars and Color Scales			
SNAP Tutorial 1.4	Applying Conditional Formatting Using a Formula			
SNAP Tutorial 1.5	Using Fraction, Scientific, and Special Numbers Formatting			
SNAP Tutorial 1.6	Creating a Custom Number Format			
SNAP Tutorial 1.7	Wrapping and Shrinking Text to Fit within a Cell			
SNAP Tutorial 1.8	Filtering a Worksheet Using a Custom AutoFilter			
SNAP Tutorial 1.9	Filtering and Sorting Data Using Conditional Formatting and Cell Attributes			

Assignment	Title	Start from Scratch	Date Due	Grade
Chapter 2 Advanced Functions and Formulas				
Concepts Check				
Skills Check Assessment 1	Create Range Names and use the Lookup Function			
Skills Check Assessment 2	Use Conditional Statistical and Math Functions			
Skills Check Assessment 3	Use Financial Functions and PMT and PPMT			
Skills Check Assessment 4	Use Logical Functions			
Skills Check Assessment 5	Use the HLOOKUP Function			
Visual Benchmark 1	Use Lookup, Statistical, and Math Functions in a Billing Summary			
Visual Benchmark 2	Use Lookup and Logical Functions to Calculate Cardiology Costs			
Case Study Part 1	NuTrends Market Research: Pizza by Mario Sales			
Case Study Part 2	NuTrends Market Research: Pizza by Mario Sales	✓		
Case Study Part 3	NuTrends Market Research: Pizza by Mario Sales (Help)	✓		
Case Study Part 4	NuTrends Market Research: Pizza by Mario Sales (Internet)	✓		
SNAP Tutorial 2.1	Creating and Managing Range Names			
SNAP Tutorial 2.2	Using Statistical Functions: Count Functions			
SNAP Tutorial 2.3	Using Statistical Functions: AVERAGEIF and AVERAGEIFS			
SNAP Tutorial 2.4	Using Math and Trigonometry Functions			
SNAP Tutorial 2.5	Using Lookup Functions			
SNAP Tutorial 2.6	Using the PPMT Function			
SNAP Tutorial 2.7	Using Logical Functions			
SNAP Tutorial 2.8	Using Text Functions			
Chapter 3 Working with Tables and Data Features				
Concepts Check				
Skills Check Assessment 1	Create and Format a Table			
Skills Check Assessment 2	Use Data Tools			

Assignment	Title	Start from Scratch	Date Due	Grade
Skills Check Assessment 3	Subtotal Records			
Visual Benchmark 1	Using Table and Data Tools in a Call List			
Visual Benchmark 2	Using Subtotals in a Call List			
Case Study Part 1	NuTrends Market Research: Marketing Plans			
Case Study Part 2	NuTrends Market Research: Marketing Plans			
Case Study Part 3	NuTrends Market Research: Marketing Plans (Help)			
Case Study Part 4	NuTrends Market Research: Marketing Plans (Internet)	✓		
SNAP Tutorial 3.1	Creating and Modifying Tables			
SNAP Tutorial 3.2	Adding Rows to a Table			
SNAP Tutorial 3.3	Formatting Data as a Table			
SNAP Tutorial 3.4	Using Data Tools			
SNAP Tutorial 3.5	Removing Duplicate Records			
SNAP Tutorial 3.6	Validating and Restricting Data Entry			
SNAP Tutorial 3.7	Converting a Table to a Normal Range; Subtotalling Related Data			
SNAP Tutorial 3.8	Grouping and Ungrouping Data			

Chapter 4 Summarizing and Consolidating Data

Assignment	Title	Start from Scratch	Date Due	Grade
Concepts Check				
Skills Check Assessment 1	Summarize Data in Multiple Worksheets using Range Names			
Skills Check Assessment 2	Summarize Data Using Linked External References			
Skills Check Assessment 3	Break Linked References			
Skills Check Assessment 4	Summarize Data Using 3-D References			
Skills Check Assessment 5	Summarize Data in a PivotTable and PivotChart			
Skills Check Assessment 6	Filtering a PivotTable Using Slicers			
Skills Check Assessment 7	Creating and Customizing Sparklines			
Visual Benchmark	Summarizing Real Estate Sale and Commission Data			
Case Study Part 1	NutTrends Market Research: Pizza by Mario			
Case Study Part 2	NutTrends Market Research: Pizza by Mario			

Assignment	Title	Start from Scratch	Date Due	Grade
Case Study Part 3	NutTrends Market Research: Pizza by Mario (Help)			
Case Study Part 4	NutTrends Market Research: Franchise Comparison (Interent)			
SNAP Tutorial 4.1	Summarizing Data in Multiple Worksheets Using Range Names and 3-D References			
SNAP Tutorial 4.2	Summarizing Data by Linking Ranges in Other Worksheets or Workbooks			
SNAP Tutorial 4.3	Summarizing Data Using the Consolidate Feature			
SNAP Tutorial 4.4	Creating a PivotTable Report			
SNAP Tutorial 4.5	Filtering a PivotTable Using Slicers			
SNAP Tutorial 4.6	Creating a PivotChart			
SNAP Tutorial 4.7	Summarizing Data with Sparklines			

Unit 1 Performance Assessments

Assignment	Title	Start from Scratch	Date Due	Grade
Assessment 1	Conditionally Format and Filter a Help Desk Worksheet			
Assessment 2	Use Conditional Logic Formulas in a Help Desk Worksheet			
Assessment 3	Use Table and Data Management Features in a Help Desk Worksheet			
Assessment 4	Add Subtotals and Outline a Help Desk Worksheet			
Assessment 5	Use Financial and Text Functions to Analyze Data for a Project			
Assessment 6	Analyze Sales Using a PivotTable, a PivotChart, and Sparklines			
Assessment 7	Link to External Data source and Calculate Distractor Payments			
Writing Activity 1	Create a Worksheet to Track Video Rental Memberships	✓		
Writing Activity 2	Create a Worksheet to Log Hours Walked in a Company Fitness Contents	✓		
Internet Research	Create a Worksheet to Compare Online Auction Listing Fees	✓		
Supplemental Assessment 1	Gradebook	✓		
Supplemental Assessment 2	Lab Revenue			

Assignment	Title	Start from Scratch	Date Due	Grade
Unit 2: Managing and Integrating Data and the Excel Environment				
Chapter 5 Using Data Analysis Features				
Concepts Check				
Skills Check Assessment 1	Convert Columns to Rows; Add Source Cells to Destination Cells; Filter			
Skills Check Assessment 2	Use Goal Seek			
Skills Check Assessment 3	Use Scenario Manager			
Skills Check Assessment 4	Create a Two-Variable Data Table			
Skills Check Assessment 5	Find and Correct Formula Errors			
Visual Benchmark 1	Find the Base Hourly Rate for Drum Lessons			
Visual Benchmark 2	Create Scenarios for Drum Lesson Review			
Case Study Part 1	NuTrends Market Research: Pizza by Mario Startup			
Case Study Part 2	NuTrends Market Research: Pizza by Mario Startup			
Case Study Part 3	NuTrends Market Research: Pizza by Mario Startup (Help)			
Case Study Part 4	NuTrends Market Research: Pizza by Mario Startup (Internet)			
SNAP Tutorial 5.1	Pasting Data Using Paste Special Options			
SNAP Tutorial 5.2	Using Goal Seek to Populate a Cell			
SNAP Tutorial 5.3	Using Scenario Manager			
SNAP Tutorial 5.4	Performing What-If Analysis Using Data Tables			
SNAP Tutorial 5.5	Using Auditing Tools			
SNAP Tutorial 5.6	Circling Invalid Data and Watching Formulas			
Chapter 6 Protecting and Sharing Workbooks				
Concepts Check				
Skills Check Assessment 1	Enter and Display Workbook Properties; Insert Comments			
Skills Check Assessment 2	Share a Workbook; Edit a Shared Workbook; Print a History Sheet			
Skills Check Assessment 3	Remove Shared Access			

Assignment	Title	Start from Scratch	Date Due	Grade
Skills Check Assessment 4	Protect an Entire Worksheet; Add a Password to a Workbook			
Skills Check Assessment 5	Unlock Cells and Protect a Worksheet; Protect Workbook Structure			
Skills Check Assessment 6	Track Changes; Accept/Reject Changes; Print a History Sheet			
Visual Benchmark	Track Changes; Insert Comments			
Case Study Part 1	NuTrends Market Research: Pizza by Mario New Franchises			
Case Study Part 2	NuTrends Market Research: Pizza by Mario New Franchises			
Case Study Part 3	NuTrends Market Research: Pizza by Mario New Franchises			
Case Study Part 4	NuTrends Market Research: Pizza by Mario New Franchises (Internet)			
SNAP Tutorial 6.1	Inserting and Editing Comments			
SNAP Tutorial 6.2	Adding Workbook Properties			
SNAP Tutorial 6.3	Printing and Editing Comments			
SNAP Tutorial 6.4	Sharing a Workbook			
SNAP Tutorial 6.5	Resolving Conflicts in a Shared Workbook			
SNAP Tutorial 6.6	Protecting and Unprotecting Worksheets			
SNAP Tutorial 6.7	Protecting and Unprotecting Workbook Structure			
SNAP Tutorial 6.8	Adding Password Protection to a Workbook			
SNAP Tutorial 6.9	Tracking Changes			

Chapter 7 Automating Repetitive Tasks and Customizing Excel

Assignment	Title	Start from Scratch	Date Due	Grade
Concepts Check				
Skills Check Assessment 1	Create Macros	✓		
Skills Check Assessment 2	Run Macros			
Skills Check Assessment 3	Create Macros; Save as a Macro-Enabled Workbook			
Skills Check Assessment 4	Print Macros			
Skills Check Assessment 5	Customize the Excel Environment			
Skills Check Assessment 6	Create Custom Views			
Skills Check Assessment 7	Create and Use a Template			

Assignment	Title	Start from Scratch	Date Due	Grade
Visual Benchmark 1	Customize the Ribbon	✓		
Visual Benchmark 2	Create a Custom Template	✓		
Case Study Part 1	NuTrends Market Research: Macros			
Case Study Part 2	NuTrends Market Research: Pizza by Mario Macros			
Case Study Part 3	NuTrends Market Research: Quick Access Toolbar (Help)	✓		
Case Study Part 4	NuTrends Market Research: Document Recovery	✓		
SNAP Tutorial 7.1	Using Macros			
SNAP Tutorial 7.2	Managing Macros			
SNAP Tutorial 7.3	Editing a Macro			
SNAP Tutorial 7.4	Pinning Workbooks to the Recent Workbooks List			
SNAP Tutorial 7.5	Customizing the Quick Access Toolbar			
SNAP Tutorial 7.6	Customizing the Work Area			
SNAP Tutorial 7.7	Customizing the Ribbon			
SNAP Tutorial 7.8	Using Custom Templates			

Chapter 8 Importing, Exporting, and Distributing Data

Assignment	Title	Start from Scratch	Date Due	Grade
Concepts Check				
Skills Check Assessment 1	Import Data from Access and a Text File			
Skills Check Assessment 2	Link Data to a Word Document			
Skills Check Assessment 3	Embed Data in a PowerPoint Presentation			
Skills Check Assessment 4	Export Data as a Text File			
Skills Check Assessment 5	Prepare a Workbook for Distribution			
Skills Check Assessment 6	Prepare and Distribute a Workbook			
Visual Benchmark	Import, Analyze, and Export Population Data			
Case Study Part 1	NuTrends Market Research: Pizza by Mario Research Data			
Case Study Part 2	NuTrends Market Research: Pizza by Mario Expansion Research			
Case Study Part 3	NuTrends Market Research: Research Data (Help)			
Case Study Part 4	NuTrends Market Research: Internet Fax Memo (Internet)			

Assignment	Title	Start from Scratch	Date Due	Grade
SNAP Tutorial 8.1	Importing Data from Access, a Text File, or a Website			
SNAP Tutorial 8.2	Exporting Data from Excel			
SNAP Tutorial 8.3	Copying and Pasting Worksheet Data between Programs			
SNAP Tutorial 8.4	Copying and Pasting Worksheet Data to a Word Document			
SNAP Tutorial 8.5	Exporting Data as a Text File			
SNAP Tutorial 8.6	Preparing a Worksheet for Distribution			
SNAP Tutorial 8.7	Converting a Workbook to a Different Format			
SNAP Tutorial 8.8	Creating a PDF/XPS Copy of a Worksheet			
SNAP Tutorial 8.9	Publishing a Worksheet as a Web Page			
SNAP Tutorial 8.10	Sending a Workbook via Email; Saving a Workbook to Windows Live SkyDrive			

Unit 2 Performance Assessments

Assignment	Title	Start from Scratch	Date Due	Grade
Assessment 1	Use Goal Seek and Scenario Manager to Calculate Investment Proposals			
Assessment 2	Calculate Investment Outcomes for a Portfolio Using a Two-Variable Data Table			
Assessment 3	Solve and Error and Check for Accuracy in Investment Commission Formulas			
Assessment 4	Document and Share a Workbook and Manage Changes in an Investment Portfolio Worksheet			
Assessment 5	Insert Comments and Protect a Confidential Investment Portfolio Workbook			
Assessment 6	Automate and Customize and Investment Portfolio Workbook			
Assessment 7	Create and Use an Investment Planner Template			
Assessment 8	Export a Chart and Prepare and Distribute and Investment Portfolio Workbook			
Writing Activity	Create a Computer Maintenance Template	✓		
Internet Research 1	Apply What-If Analysis to a Planned Move	✓		
Internet Research 2	Research and Compare Smartphones	✓		
Job Study	Prepare a Wages Budget and Link the Budget to a Word Document			
Supplemental Assessment 1	Calculate Monthly House Payments	✓		
Supplemental Assessment 2	Travel Routes Mileage Spreadsheet and Memo			
Final Case Study	Worldwide Enterprises Human Resources			

Concepts Check Answer Key
Benchmark Excel 2010, Level 1, Chapter 1

1.	The horizontal and vertical lines that define the cells in a worksheet area are referred to as this.	gridlines	page 7
2.	Columns in a worksheet are labeled with these.	letters	page 7
3.	Rows in a worksheet are labeled with these.	numbers	page 7
4.	Press this key on the keyboard to move the insertion point to the next cell.	Tab	page 7 (Table 1.2)
5.	Press these keys on the keyboard to move the insertion point to the previous cell.	Shift + Tab	page 7 (Table 1.2)
6.	Data being typed in a cell displays in the cell as well as here.	Formula bar	page 7
7.	If a number entered in a cell is too long to fit inside the cell, the number is changed to this.	number symbols (###)	page 8
8.	This feature will automatically insert words, numbers, or formulas in a series.	AutoFill	page 13
9.	This is the name of the small black square that displays in the bottom right corner of the active cell.	AutoFill fill handle	page 15
10.	Use this button in the Editing group in the Home tab to insert a formula in a cell.	AutoSum	page 17
11.	With this function, a range of cells is added together and then divided by the number of cell entries.	AVERAGE	page 18
12.	To select nonadjacent columns using the mouse, hold down this key on the keyboard while clicking the column headers.	Ctrl	page 20 (Table 1.4)
13.	Click this button in the worksheet area to select all of the cells in the table.	Select All	page 20 (Table 1.4)
14.	Click this button to merge selected cells and center data within the merged cells.	Merge & Center	page 21
15.	The Accounting Number Format button is located in this group in the Home tab.	Number	page 22
16.	Press this function key to display the Excel Help window.	F1	page 24

Concepts Check Answer Key
Benchmark Excel 2010, Level 1, Chapter 2

1.	When typing a formula, begin the formula with this sign.	equals	page 40
2.	This is the operator for division that is used when writing a formula.	/ (forward slash)	page 41 (Table 2.1)
3.	This is the operator for multiplication that is used when writing a formula.	* (asterisk)	page 41 (Table 2.1)
4.	As an alternative to the fill handle, use this button to copy a formula relatively in a worksheet.	Fill	page 41
5.	A function operates on this, which may consist of a constant, a cell reference, or other function.	argument	page 45
6.	This function returns the largest value in a set of values.	MAX	page 47
7.	This is the keyboard shortcut to display formulas in a worksheet.	Ctrl + ` (grave accent)	page 51
8.	This function finds the periodic payment for a loan based on constant payments and a constant interest rate.	PMT	page 51
9.	This function returns the serial number of the current date and time.	NOW	page 53
10.	This function is considered a conditional function.	IF	page 54
11.	Suppose cell B2 contains the total sales amount. Write a formula that would insert the word *BONUS* in cell C2 if the sales amount was greater than $99,999 and inserts the words *NO BONUS* if the sales amount is not greater than $99,999.	IF(B2>99999, "BONUS","NO BONUS")	page 55
12.	To identify an absolute cell reference, type this symbol before the column and row.	$	page 57

Concepts Check Answer Key
Benchmark Excel 2010, Level 1, Chapter 3

1.	By default, a column is inserted in this direction from the column containing the active cell.	left	page 75
2.	To delete a row, select the row and then click the Delete button in this group in the Home tab.	Cells	page 76
3.	With the options at this button's drop-down list, you can clear the contents of the cell or selected cells.	Clear	page 77
4.	Use this button to insert color in the active cell or selected cells.	Fill Color	page 78
5.	Select data in a cell and this displays in a dimmed fashion above the selected text.	Mini toolbar	page 78
6.	By default, numbers are aligned at this side of a cell.	right	page 78
7.	Click this button in the Alignment group in the Home tab to rotate data in a cell.	Orientation	page 79
8.	The Themes button is located in this tab.	Page Layout	page 81
9.	If you type a number with a dollar sign, such as $50.25, Excel automatically applies this formatting to the number.	Currency	page 82
10.	If you type a number with a percent sign, such as 25%, Excel automatically applies this formatting to the number.	Percent	page 82
11.	Align and indent data in cells using buttons in the Alignment group in the Home tab or with options at this dialog box with the Alignment tab selected.	Format Cells	page 86
12.	You can repeat the last action performed with the command Ctrl + Y or by pressing this function key.	F4	page 92
13.	The Format Painter button is located in this group in the Home tab.	Clipboard	page 94
14.	To hide a column, select the column, click this button in the Cells group in the Home tab, point to *Hide & Unhide*, and then click *Hide Columns*.	Format	page 94

Concepts Check Answer Key
Benchmark Excel 2010, Level 1, Chapter 4

1.	This is the default left and right margin measurement.	0.7 inch	page 109
2.	This is the default top and bottom margin measurement.	0.75 inch	page 109
3.	The Margins button is located in this tab.	Page Layout	page 109
4.	By default, a worksheet prints in this orientation on a page.	Portrait	page 112
5.	Click the Print Titles button in the Page Setup group in the Page Layout tab and the Page Setup dialog box displays with this tab selected.	Sheet	page 115
6.	Use options in this group in the Page Layout tab to adjust the printed output by a percentage to fit the number of pages specified.	Scale to Fit	page 116
7.	Use this button in the Page Setup group in the Page Layout tab to select and print specific areas in a worksheet.	Print Area	page 118
8.	Click the Header & Footer button in the Text group in the Insert tab and the worksheet displays in this view.	Page Layout	page 120
9.	This tab contains options for formatting and customizing a header and/or footer.	Header & Footer Tools Design	page 120
10.	Click this tab to display the Spelling button.	Review	page 126
11.	The Undo and Redo buttons are located on this toolbar.	Quick Access	page 126
12.	Click this button in the Find and Replace dialog box to expand the dialog box.	Options	page 129
13.	Use these two buttons at the expanded Find and Replace dialog box to search for specific cell formatting and replace with other formatting.	Format	page 131
14.	Use this button in the Editing group in the Home tab to sort data in a worksheet.	Sort & Filter	page 133
15.	Use this feature to temporarily isolate specific data in a worksheet.	filter	page 135

Concepts Check Answer Key
Benchmark Excel 2010, Level 1, Chapter 5

1.	By default, a workbook contains this number of worksheets.	three	page 161
2.	The Cut, Copy, and Paste buttons are located in this group in the Home tab.	Clipboard	page 161
3.	To copy selected cells with the mouse, hold down this key while dragging the outline of the selected cells to the desired location.	Ctrl	page 163
4.	This button displays in the lower right corner of pasted cells.	Paste Options	page 163
5.	Use this task pane to collect and paste multiple items.	Clipboard	page 165
6.	Click this tab to insert a new worksheet.	Insert Worksheet	page 167
7.	Click this option at the sheet tab shortcut menu to apply a color to a worksheet tab.	*Tab Color*	page 170
8.	To select adjacent worksheet tabs, click the first tab, hold down this key, and then click the last tab.	Shift	page 171
9.	To select nonadjacent worksheet tabs, click the first tab, hold down this key, and then click any other tabs you want selected.	Ctrl	page 171
10.	To print all worksheets in a workbook, display the Print tab Backstage view, click the first gallery in the Settings category, and then click this option at the drop-down list.	*Print Entire Workbook*	page 173
11.	The Split button is located in this tab.	View	page 174
12.	Display the Arrange Windows dialog box by clicking this button in the Window group in the View tab.	Arrange All	page 179
13.	Click this button to make the active workbook expand to fill the screen.	Maximize	page 182
14.	Click this button to reduce the active workbook to a layer behind the Excel button on the Taskbar.	Minimize	page 182
15.	When linking data between worksheets, the worksheet containing the original data is called this.	source	page 184

1.	Perform file management tasks such as copying, moving, or deleting workbooks with options at the Open dialog box or this dialog box.	Save As	page 200
2.	At the Open dialog box, a list of folders and files displays in this pane.	Content pane	page 201
3.	Rename a folder or file at the Open dialog box using a shortcut menu or this button.	Organize	page 202
4.	At the Open dialog box, hold down this key while selecting nonadjacent workbooks.	Ctrl	page 202
5.	Workbooks deleted from the hard drive are automatically sent to this location.	Windows Recycle Bin	page 203
6.	Insert a check mark in this check box at the Recent tab Backstage view and the four most recently opened workbook names display in the Backstage navigation bar.	*Quickly access this number of Recent Workbooks*	page 208
7.	Do this to a workbook name you want to remain at the top of the *Recent Workbooks* list at the Recent tab Backstage view.	pin the workbook	page 208
8.	If you close a workbook without saving it, you can recover it with this option at the Recent tab Backstage view.	*Recover Unsaved Workbooks*	page 209
9.	The Cell Styles button is located in this group in the Home tab.	Styles	page 214
10.	Click the *New Cell Style* option at the Cell Styles button drop-down gallery and this dialog box displays.	Style	page 215
11.	A style you create displays in this section of the Cell Styles button drop-down gallery.	*Custom*	page 215
12.	Copy styles from one workbook to another with options at this dialog box.	Merge Styles	page 220
13.	To link a workbook to another workbook, click this button in the Link to group in the Insert Hyperlink dialog box.	Existing File or Web Page	page 223
14.	Display installed templates by clicking this button in the Available Templates category at the New tab Backstage view.	Sample templates	page 227

Concepts Check Answer Key
Benchmark Excel 2010, Level 1, Chapter 7

1.	This is the keyboard shortcut to create a chart with the default chart type in the active worksheet.	Alt + F1	page 241
2.	The Charts group contains buttons for creating charts and is located in this tab.	Insert	page 241
3.	This type of chart shows proportions and relationships of parts to the whole.	pie	page 242 (Table 7.1)
4.	When you create a chart, the chart is inserted in this location by default.	worksheet containing data or same worksheet as selected cells	page 242
5.	Select a chart in a worksheet, display the Print tab Backstage view, and the first gallery in the Settings category is automatically changed to this option.	*Print Selected Chart*	page 245
6.	Use buttons in the Insert group in this tab to insert shapes or pictures.	Chart Tools Layout	page 255
7.	When Excel creates a chart, the data in the first row (except the first cell) is used to create this.	legend	page 247
8.	Click this option at the Move Chart dialog box to move the chart to a separate sheet.	*New sheet*	page 248
9.	Click the Picture button in the Chart Tools Layout tab and this dialog box displays.	Insert Picture	page 257
10.	Change the chart size by entering measurements in these measurement boxes in the Size group in the Chart Tools Format tab.	*Shape Height* and *Shape Width*	page 261

Concepts Check Answer Key
Benchmark Excel 2010, Level 1, Chapter 8

1.	The Symbol button is located in this tab.	Insert	page 273
2.	The *Font* option is available at the Symbol dialog box with this tab selected.	Symbols	page 273
3.	Insert a picture, clip art image, screenshot, shape, or SmartArt diagram with buttons in this group in the Insert tab.	Illustrations	page 275
4.	When you insert a picture or clip art image in a worksheet, this tab is active.	Picture Tools Format	page 275
5.	Maintain the proportions of the image by holding down this key while dragging a sizing handle.	Shift	page 276
6.	To move an image, position the mouse pointer on the image border until the mouse pointer displays with this attached and then drag the image to the desired location.	four-headed arrow	page 276
7.	To capture a portion of a screen, click the Screenshot button and then click this option at the drop-down list.	*Screen Clipping*	page 280
8.	To copy a shape, hold down this key while dragging the shape.	Ctrl	page 281
9.	When you draw a text box in a worksheet and then release the mouse button, this tab is active.	Drawing Tools Format	page 285
10.	This term refers to a lightened image that displays behind data in a file.	watermark	page 287
11.	Click the SmartArt button in the Illustrations group in the Insert tab and this dialog box displays.	Choose a SmartArt Graphic	page 288

Concepts Check Answer Key
Benchmark Excel 2010, Level 2, Chapter 1

1.	Point to this option from the Conditional Formatting drop-down list to format cells based on a comparison operator such as *Greater Than*.	*Highlight Cells Rules*	page 7 (Figure 1.1)
2.	To conditionally format a range using the Above Average condition, click this option from the Conditional Formatting drop-down list.	*Top/Bottom Rules*	page 8
3.	Open this dialog box to create, edit, or delete a conditional formatting rule.	Conditional Formatting Rules Manager	page 10
4.	Excel uses threshold values to classify data into three to five categories when conditionally formatting by this option.	*Icon Sets*	page 12
5.	Select this option in the *Select a Rule Type* section of the New Formatting Rule dialog box to create a rule that conditionally formats cells based on the value(s) in another cell.	*Use a formula to determine which cells to format*	page 15
6.	Open this dialog box to format a selected range using a fraction and select the type of fraction to display.	Format Cells with Number tab active	page 16
7.	Scientific formatting is used by scientists or others who need to write very large numbers using this notation.	exponential	page 16
8.	The special number format options displayed in the *Type* list box are dependent on this other setting.	country and language at *Locale* option	page 18
9.	What would display in a cell in which you typed *156.3568* for which the custom number format code ###.## applied?	156.36	page 20 (Table 1.1)
10.	Use either of these two text control options to format a long label within the existing column width.	*Wrap text* or *Shrink to Fit*	page 22
11.	Open this dialog box to filter by more than one criterion using a comparison operator.	Custom AutoFilter	page 23
12.	A worksheet can be filtered by a cell color that has been applied manually or by this feature.	conditional formatting	page 24
13.	Open this dialog box to arrange cells in a worksheet by more than one color.	Sort	page 27

Concepts Check Answer Key
Benchmark Excel 2010, Level 2, Chapter 2

1.	Assign a name to a selected range by typing the desired name in this text box.	Name	page 38
2.	A range name can be a combination of letters, numbers, underscore characters, and this punctuation character.	period	page 38
3.	This COUNTIF function would count the number of cells in a range named *sales* where the values are greater than $50 thousand.	=COUNTIF(sales,">50000")	page 40
4.	Use this statistical function to find the mean of a range based on two criteria.	AVERAGEIFS	page 43
5.	SUMIF is found in this function category.	Math & Trig	page 46
6.	Open this dialog box to delete a range name.	Name Manager	page 48
7.	Use this lookup function to look up a value in a reference table where the comparison data in the table is arranged in rows.	HLOOKUP	page 52
8.	This financial function returns the principal portion of a specified loan payment.	PPMT	page 53
9.	The IF function is accessed from this button in the Function Library group of the Formulas tab.	Logical	page 55
10.	This term refers to a formula where one function is created inside of another function.	nested function	page 55
11.	Excel's AND and OR functions use this type of logic to construct a conditional test.	Boolean	page 56
12.	When would Excel return False for an OR function?	when all conditions are false	page 56 (Table 2.3)
13.	This text function can be used to capitalize the first letter of each word in a cell.	PROPER	page 59
14.	This formula converts text typed in lowercase within a cell to all uppercase characters.	=UPPER	page 59 (Table 2.4)
15.	Use this text function to change a text string in the source cell to new text in the formula cell.	SUBSTITUTE	page 59

Concepts Check Answer Key
Benchmark Excel 2010, Level 2, Chapter 3

1.	The first row of a table that contains the column headings is called the field names row or this row.	header	page 74
2.	Typing a formula in the first row of a column in a table causes Excel to define the field as this type of column.	calculated	page 75
3.	This is the term that describes the formatting feature in a table in which even rows are formatted differently than odd rows.	banded	page 76
4.	Change the visual appearance of a table using this gallery in the Table Tools Design tab.	Table Styles	page 76
5.	Clicking this button causes the Convert Text to Columns wizard to appear.	Text to Columns	page 80
6.	Open this dialog box to instruct Excel to compare the entries in the columns you specify and automatically delete rows that contain repeated data.	Remove Duplicates	page 81
7.	Open this dialog box to restrict entries in a cell to those that you set up in a drop-down list.	Data Validation	page 83
8.	This option in the *Allow* list box is used to force data entered into a cell to be a specific number of characters.	*Text length*	page 83 (Figure 3.5)
9.	This is the default error alert style that prevents invalid data from being entered into a cell.	Stop	page 84 (Table 3.1)
10.	The Convert to Range button is found in this tab.	Table Tools Design	page 88
11.	Prior to creating subtotals using the Subtotal button in the Outline group of the Data tab, arrange the data in this order.	sort by fields to group records	page 88
12.	In a worksheet with subtotal rows only displayed, click this button next to a subtotal row in order to view the grouped rows.	Show Detail	page 88
13.	Click this button in an outlined worksheet to collapse the rows for a group.	Hide Detail	page 88
14.	In an outlined worksheet, this button collapses all records and displays only the Grand Total row.	level 1	page 91
15.	Clicking this button in an outlined worksheet will cause the Hide Detail button for the selected rows to be removed.	Ungroup	page 92

Concepts Check Answer Key
Benchmark Excel 2010, Level 2, Chapter 4

1.	This symbol separates a worksheet reference from a cell reference.	exclamation point	page 106
2.	This term describes a formula that references the same cell in a range that spans two or more worksheets.	3-D reference	page 106
3.	Assume a workbook contains the following defined range names that reference cells in four worksheets: Qtr1, Qtr2, Qtr3, and Qtr4. Provide the *Sum* formula to add the data in the four ranges.	=Qtr1+Qtr2+Qtr3+Qtr4 or =Sum(Qtr1,Qtr2,Qtr3,Qtr4)	page 106 or 108
4.	This would be the formula entry to link to an external reference C12 in a worksheet named Summary in a workbook named QtrlySales.	=[QtrlySales.xlsx]Summary!C12	page 110
5.	Open this dialog box to change the source of a linked external reference if you moved the source workbook to another folder.	Edit Links	page 111
6.	Click this button to permanently remove a linked external reference and convert the linked cells to their existing values.	Break Link	page 111
7.	This is the default function active when you open the Consolidate dialog box.	Sum	page 115
8.	Add fields to a PivotTable report by clicking the field check box in this pane.	PivotTable Field List	page 117
9.	The PivotTable Styles gallery is accessible from this tab.	PivotTable Tools Design	page 119
10.	Insert this type of pane to filter a PivotTable with one mouse click.	Slicer	page 121
11.	Change the summary function for a PivotTable numeric field by clicking this button in the PivotTable Tools Options tab.	Field Settings	page 123
12.	A PivotChart visually displays the data from this source.	PivotTable	page 123
13.	Buttons to filter a PivotChart are found here.	within PivotChart chart area	page 124
14.	This is the first step to complete to add Sparklines in a worksheet.	select empty range to insert Sparklines into	page 128
15.	Click this tab to customize Sparklines.	Sparkline Tools Design	page 129

Concepts Check Answer Key
Benchmark Excel 2010, Level 2, Chapter 5

1.	This option from the Paste drop-down menu will convert columns to rows and rows to columns.	*Transpose*	page 152
2.	Open this dialog box to perform a mathematical operation while pasting the copied range to the destination cells.	Paste Special	page 154
3.	Use this feature if you know the end result you want to obtain but are not sure what input value you need to achieve the end value.	Goal Seek	page 155
4.	This feature allows you to store various sets of data for specified cells under a name.	Scenario Manager	page 157
5.	This report compares various saved data sets side-by-side so you can view all of the results in one page.	Scenario Summary	page 160
6.	A one-variable data table requires the formula to be entered at this location within the data table range.	one cell above and one column right of input values	page 163
7.	In a two-variable data table, the source formula is entered at this location within the data table range.	top left cell	page 164
8.	The Data Table feature is accessed from this button.	What-If Analysis	page 163
9.	Click this button to draw arrows to cells that feed data into the active cell.	Trace Precedents	page 166
10.	Click this button to draw arrows to cells that use the data in the active cell.	Trace Dependents	page 166
11.	This button in the Formula Auditing group can be used to assist with locating the source cell that is causing an error code.	Error Checking	page 166
12.	This error code indicates that a value needed to calculate the formula result is not available.	*#N/A*	page 168
13.	This type of error occurs when the formula has correct syntax but is not correct for the data or the situation.	logic	page 167
14.	This type of formula is entered outside the main worksheet area and is used to check key figures within the worksheet.	proof formula	page 167
15.	Use this feature to test existing data in a worksheet that has had a new data validation rule created.	Circle Invalid Data	page 170

Concepts Check Answer Key
Benchmark Excel 2010, Level 2, Chapter 6

1.	Open this view to add descriptive information about a workbook such as a title or subject heading.	Info tab Backstage view	page 182
2.	This panel displays the workbook's properties between the ribbon and the worksheet.	Document Information Panel	page 183
3.	A diagonal red triangle in the upper right corner of a cell indicates this box will pop up when the mouse pointer rests on the cell.	comment	page 185
4.	Open this dialog box to turn on the feature that allows changes by more than one user at the same time.	Share Workbook	page 188
5.	Change the user name for the computer that you are using by opening this dialog box.	Excel Options	page 189
6.	When two users have the same workbook open at the same time and each makes a change to the same cell, this dialog box appears when the second person saves the workbook.	Resolve Conflicts	page 191
7.	Open this dialog box to create a History sheet that includes a record of all changes made to a shared workbook.	Highlight Changes	page 192
8.	Add a password that is required to unprotect a worksheet at this dialog box.	Protect Sheet	page 194
9.	Select a cell that you want to allow changes to and then click this button and menu option to unlock the cell before protecting the worksheet.	Format, *Lock Cell*	page 194
10.	Prevent users from inserting or deleting worksheets in a workbook by opening this dialog box.	Protect Structure and Windows	page 197
11.	Click this option from the Protect Workbook drop-down list at the Info tab Backstage view to assign a password to open a workbook.	*Encrypt with Password*	page 198
12.	Turn this feature on and Excel automatically changes the workbook to a shared workbook if it is not already shared.	Track Changes	page 201
13.	Excel applies this formatting to cells in a shared workbook that have been modified in order to make the revised cells stand out.	Colored border; each user's changes are in a different color	page 201
14.	Use this option to navigate to each changed cell in a shared workbook and decide whether to keep the change or restore the cell back to its previous value.	*Accept/Reject Changes*	page 202
15.	This feature is not available to restore cells to their previous values after you have finished reviewing tracked changes.	Undo	page 202

Concepts Check Answer Key
Benchmark Excel 2010, Level 2, Chapter 7

1.	Macro names must begin with a letter and can contain a combination of letters, numbers, and this other character.	underscore character	page 217
2.	Click this button to indicate you have finished the tasks or keystrokes you want saved in the macro.	Stop Recording	page 218
3.	A workbook containing a macro is saved in this file format.	Excel Macro-Enabled Workbook (*.xlsm)	page 218
4.	A macro can be assigned to a shortcut key that is a combination of a lowercase or uppercase letter and this other key.	Ctrl	page 221
5.	Macro instructions are stored in this program code.	Visual Basic for Applications (VBA)	page 223
6.	A workbook that you use frequently can be permanently added to the *Recent Workbooks* list by clicking this icon next to the workbook name.	push pin	page 226
7.	Click this option at the Customize Quick Access Toolbar drop-down list to locate a feature to add to the toolbar from a commands list box.	*More Commands*	page 227
8.	Display options are shown in the Excel Options dialog box with this option selected in the left pane.	*Advanced*	page 230
9.	Click this button to minimize the ribbon to provide more space in the work area.	Minimize the Ribbon	page 230
10.	Click this option in the left pane at the Excel Options dialog box to create a custom ribbon tab.	*Customize Ribbon*	page 232
11.	Click this button at the Custom Views dialog box to create a new custom view that will save the current display settings for the active worksheet.	Add	page 238
12.	Change *Save as type* to this option at the Save As dialog box to save the current workbook as a standard workbook that can be opened from the New dialog box.	*Excel Template (*.xltx)*	page 241
13.	This task pane opens when Excel is restarted after the previous session ended abnormally.	Document Recovery	page 244

Concepts Check Answer Key
Benchmark Excel 2010, Level 2, Chapter 8

1.	This group in the Data tab contains buttons for importing data into Access from external sources.	Get External Data	page 260
2.	If the source database used to import data contains more than one table, this dialog box appears after you select the data source to allow you to choose the desired table.	Select Table	page 261
3.	To import tables from a web page, open this dialog box to browse to the website and click arrows next to tables on the page that you want to import.	New Web Query	page 262
4.	These are the two commonly used delimiter characters in delimited text file formats.	tab, comma	page 265
5.	To add to the bottom of the active Access datasheet cells that have been copied to the clipboard, click this option at the Paste button drop-down list.	*Paste Append*	page 268
6.	Choosing *Microsoft Excel Worksheet Object* at the Paste Special dialog box in a Word document and then clicking OK inserts the copied cells as this type of object.	embedded	page 270
7.	If the Excel data you are pasting into a Word document is likely to be updated in the future and you want the Word document to reflect the updated values, paste the data as this type of object.	linked	page 270
8.	A chart copied from Excel and pasted to a slide in a PowerPoint presentation is pasted as this type of object by default.	embedded	page 273
9.	Click this option in the *File Types* section of the Save & Send tab Backstage view to select the CSV file format in order to export the active worksheet as a text file.	*Change File Type*	page 276
10.	This feature scans the open workbook for personal and hidden information and provides you with the opportunity to remove the items.	Document Inspector	page 278
11.	A workbook that has been marked as final is changed to this type of workbook to prevent additions, deletions, and modifications to cells.	read-only	page 282
12.	Use this feature to check the current workbook for formatting or features used that are not available with earlier versions of Excel and that could cause loss of functionality if saved in the earlier file format.	Compatibility Checker	page 284
13.	Save a worksheet in either of these fixed-layout formats that preserve Excel's formatting and layout features while allowing you to distribute the file to others who may not have Excel installed on their computer.	PDF or XPS	page 286
14.	Click this button in the Save As dialog box once the *Save as type* option has been changed to a web page file format in order to type a page title.	Change Title	page 290
15.	This is the name of the free service from Microsoft which provides you with storage space on a Web server in order to save a workbook that you can share, edit, or download from any location with Internet access.	SkyDrive	page 293

Premiere Plan©

Plan A	Category
	Available
	Balance
Plan B	Category
	Available
	Balance

Construction Project

Expense	Original	Current
Material	$ 129,000	$ 153,000
Labor	97,000	98,500
Equipmental rental	14,500	11,750
Permits	1,200	1,350
Tax	1,950	2,145
Total	$ 243,650	$ 266,745

DEERING INDUSTRIES

SEMIANNUAL CUSTOMER SALES ANALYSIS

Salesperson	First Half	Second Half	Average
Johnson, Craig	$ 95,400	$ 120,380	$ 107,890
Rehberg, Robin	1,100,500	976,350	1,038,425
Singleton, Catherine	70,450	94,230	82,340
Im, Kwan	80,700	92,410	86,555
Hutchinson, Lee	1,500,750	1,482,404	1,491,577
Kulisek, Andre	1,014,505	999,080	1,006,793
Ludlow, William	79,525	64,230	71,878
Marshall, Isabelle	89,750	78,034	83,892
Newman, Jared	73,400	83,200	78,300
Ortega, Cecilia	1,250,770	1,304,290	1,277,530
Pascual, Maureen	1,535,075	1,599,520	1,567,298
Total	$ 6,890,825	$ 6,894,128	

CAPITAL INVESTMENTS

	Monday	Tuesday	Wednesday	Thursday	Friday	Total
Budget	$ 350.00	$ 350.00	$ 350.00	$ 350.00	$ 350.00	$ 1,750.00
Actual	$ 310.00	$ 425.00	$ 290.00	$ 375.00	$ 400.00	$ 1,800.00

Personal Expenses - July through December

Expense	July	August	September	October	November	December	Average
Rent	$ 850	$ 850	$ 850	$ 850	$ 850	$ 850	$ 850
Rental Insurance	55	55	55	55	55	55	55
Health Insurance	120	120	120	120	120	120	120
Electricity	129	135	110	151	168	173	144
Utilities	53	62	49	32	55	61	52
Telephone	73	81	67	80	82	75	76
Groceries	143	137	126	150	147	173	146
Gasoline	89	101	86	99	76	116	95
Total	$ 1,512	$ 1,541	$ 1,463	$ 1,537	$ 1,553	$ 1,623	$ 1,538

EL1-C1-VB-PersExps.xlsx

CLEARLINE MANUFACTURING
Refinance Plan

Lender	Amount	Interest Rate	Term Months	Monthly Payments	Total Payments	Total Interest
Keystone Mortgage	$ 125,000	7.50%	120	$1,483.77	$178,052.65	$ 53,052.65
Keystone Mortgage	300,000	7.20%	120	$3,514.26	$421,710.75	$ 121,710.75
Willows Credit Union	125,000	7.40%	96	$1,729.20	$166,003.52	$ 41,003.52
Willows Credit Union	300,000	7.10%	96	$4,105.06	$394,085.80	$ 94,085.80

DEERING INDUSTRIES
SEMIANNUAL CUSTOMER SALES ANALYSIS

Customer	January	February	March	April	May	June	Average
Lakeside Trucking	$ 89,450	$ 75,340	$ 98,224	$ 84,231	$ 73,455	$ 97,549	$ 86,375
Gresham Machines	45,210	28,340	53,400	33,199	40,390	50,112	41,775
Real Photography	30,219	28,590	34,264	30,891	35,489	36,400	32,642
Genesis Productions	65,290	51,390	79,334	72,190	75,390	83,219	71,136
Landower Company	12,168	19,355	45,209	22,188	14,228	38,766	25,319
Jewell Enterprises	44,329	21,809	33,490	19,764	50,801	32,188	33,730
Total	$ 286,666	$ 224,824	$ 343,921	$ 262,463	$ 289,753	$ 338,234	$ 290,977
Highest Total	$ 343,921						
Lowest Total	$ 224,824						

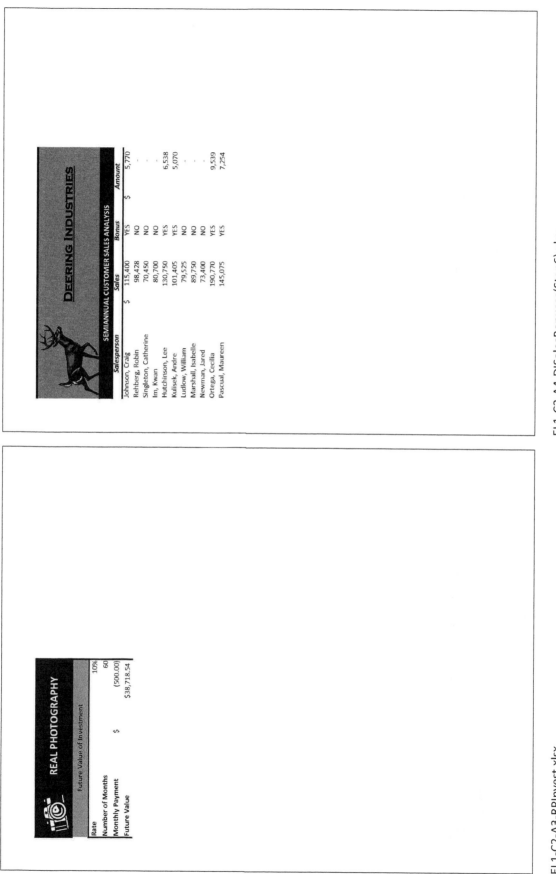

DEERING INDUSTRIES

SEMIANNUAL CUSTOMER SALES ANALYSIS

Salesperson	Sales	Bonus	Amount
Johnson, Craig	$ 115,400	YES	$ 5,770
Rehberg, Robin	98,428	NO	-
Singleton, Catherine	70,450	NO	-
Im, Kwan	80,700	NO	-
Hutchinson, Lee	130,750	YES	6,538
Kulisek, Andre	101,405	YES	5,070
Ludlow, William	79,525	NO	-
Marshall, Isabelle	89,750	NO	-
Newman, Jared	73,400	NO	-
Ortega, Cecilia	190,770	YES	9,539
Pascual, Maureen	145,075	YES	7,254

REAL PHOTOGRAPHY

Future Value of Investment	
Rate	10%
Number of Months	60
Monthly Payment	$ (500.00)
Future Value	$38,718.54

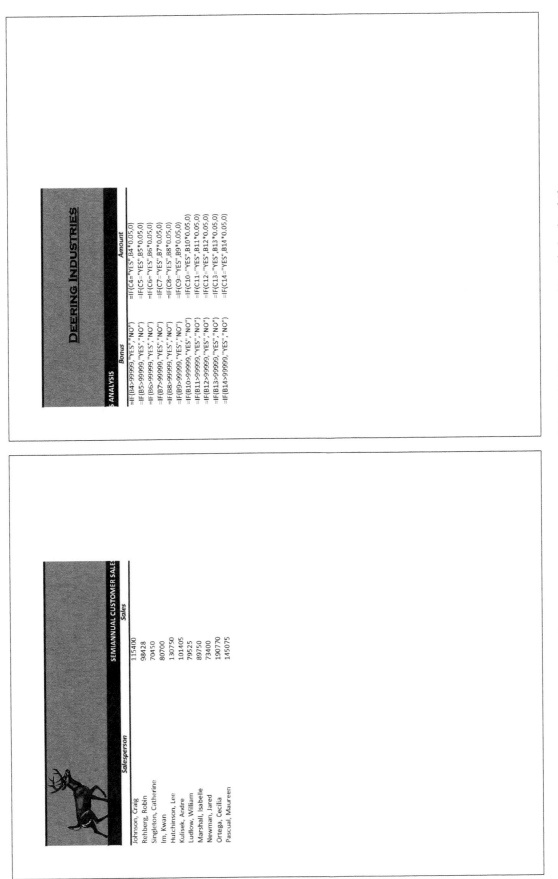

DEERING INDUSTRIES

	S ANALYSIS	
	Bonus	*Amount*
	=IF(B4>99999,"YES",,"NO")	=IF(C4="YES",B4*0.05,0)
	=IF(B5>99999,"YES","NO")	=IF(C5="YES",B5*0.05,0)
	=IF(B6>99999,"YES","NO")	=IF(C6="YES",B6*0.05,0)
	=IF(B7>99999,"YES","NO")	=IF(C7="YES",B7*0.05,0)
	=IF(B8>99999,"YES","NO")	=IF(C8="YES",B8*0.05,0)
	=IF(B9>99999,"YES","NO")	=IF(C9="YES",B9*0.05,0)
	=IF(B10>99999,"YES","NO")	=IF(C10="YES",B10*0.05,0)
	=IF(B11>99999,"YES","NO")	=IF(C11="YES",B11*0.05,0)
	=IF(B12>99999,"YES","NO")	=IF(C12="YES",B12*0.05,0)
	=IF(B13>99999,"YES","NO")	=IF(C13="YES",B13*0.05,0)
	=IF(B14>99999,"YES","NO")	=IF(C14="YES",B14*0.05,0)

EL1-C2-A4-DISalesBonuses(Step7).xlsx (2 of 2)

SEMIANNUAL CUSTOMER SALE	
Salesperson	*Sales*
Johnson, Craig	115400
Rehberg, Robin	98428
Singleton, Catherine	70450
Im, Kwan	80700
Hutchinson, Lee	130750
Kulisek, Andre	101405
Ludlow, William	79525
Marshall, Isabelle	89750
Newman, Jared	73400
Ortega, Cecilia	190770
Pascual, Maureen	145075

EL1-C2-A4-DISalesBonuses(Step7).xlsx (1 of 2)

Benchmark Excel 2010 Level 1 Model Answers

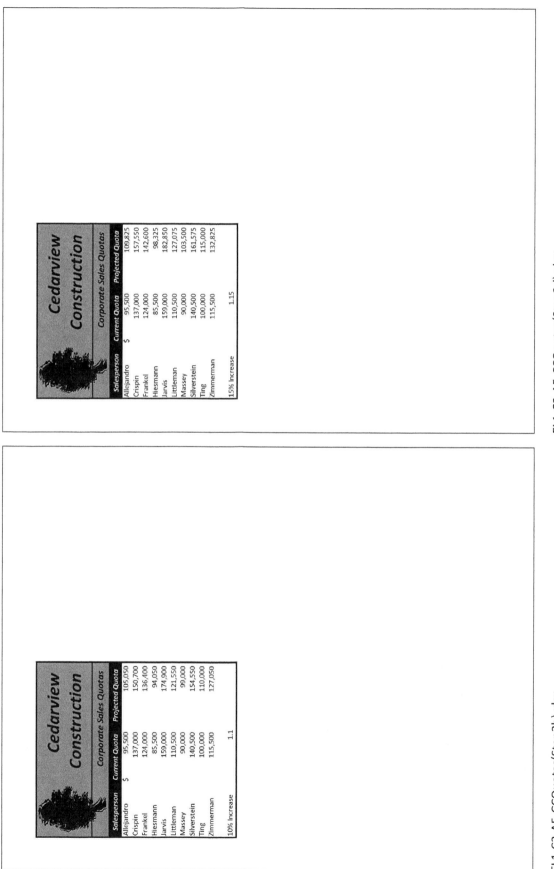

Cedarview Construction

Corporate Sales Quotas

Salesperson	Current Quota	Projected Quota
Allejandro	$ 95,500	109,825
Crispin	137,000	157,550
Frankel	124,000	142,600
Hiesmann	85,500	98,325
Jarvis	159,000	182,850
Littleman	110,500	127,075
Massey	90,000	103,500
Silverstein	140,500	161,575
Ting	100,000	115,000
Zimmerman	115,500	132,825
15% Increase	1.15	

Cedarview Construction

Corporate Sales Quotas

Salesperson	Current Quota	Projected Quota
Allejandro	$ 95,500	105,050
Crispin	137,000	150,700
Frankel	124,000	136,400
Hiesmann	85,500	94,050
Jarvis	159,000	174,900
Littleman	110,500	121,550
Massey	90,000	99,000
Silverstein	140,500	154,550
Ting	100,000	110,000
Zimmerman	115,500	127,050
10% Increase	1.1	

Cedarview Construction

Corporate Sales Quotas

Salesperson	Current Quota	Projected Quota
Allejandro	$95,500	$114,600
Crispin	137,000	164,400
Frankel	124,000	148,800
Hiesmann	85,500	102,600
Jarvis	159,000	190,800
Littleman	110,500	132,600
Massey	90,000	108,000
Silverstein	140,500	168,600
Ting	100,000	120,000
Zimmerman	115,500	138,600

20% Increase	1.2

EL1-C2-A5-CCQuotas(Step5).xlsx

Weekly Payroll

Employee	Hours	Rate	Salary
Alvarez, Rita	40	$22.50	$900.00
Campbell, Owen	15	22.50	337.50
Heitmann, Luanne	25	19.00	475.00
Malina, Susan	40	18.75	750.00
Parker, Kenneth	40	18.75	750.00
Reitz, Collette	20	15.00	300.00
Shepard, Gregory	15	12.00	180.00

Construction Projects

Project	Projected	Actual	Difference
South Cascade	$145,000	$141,597	$(3,403)
Rogue River Park	120,000	124,670	4,670
Meridian	120,500	99,450	(21,050)
Lowell Ridge	95,250	98,455	3,205
Walker Canyon	70,000	68,420	(1,580)
Nettleson Creek	52,000	49,517	(2,483)

Overdue Accounts

Client	Account #	Amount Due	Pur. Date	Terms	Due Date
Sunrise Marketing	120	$9,875	12/4/2012	15	12/19/2012
National Systems	398	8,525	12/7/2012	30	1/6/2013
First Street Signs	188	5,000	12/12/2012	15	12/27/2012
Valley Services	286	3,250	12/19/2012	30	1/18/2013

Test Scores

Employee	Test No. 1	Test No. 2	Test No. 3	Wgt. Avg.
Coffey, Annette	62%	64%	76%	70%
Halverson, Ted	88%	96%	90%	91%
Kohler, Jeremy	80%	76%	82%	80%
McKnight, Carol	68%	72%	78%	74%
Parkhurst, Jody	98%	96%	98%	98%
Test Averages	79%	81%	85%	
Test Weights	25%	25%	50%	

EL1-C2-VB-Formulas(Step4).xlsx

Salary
=C3*B3
=C4*B4
=C5*B5
=C6*B6
=C7*B7
=C8*B8
=C9*B9

Difference
=C14-B14
=C15-B15
=C16-B16
=C17-B17
=C18-B18
=C19-B19

Terms	Due Date
15	=D24+E24
30	=D25+E25
15	=D26+E26
30	=D27+E27

Pur. Date
=DATE(2012,12,4)
=DATE(2012,12,7)
=DATE(2012,12,12)
=DATE(2012,12,19)

Test No. 3	Wgt. Avg.
0.76	=$B$38*B32+$C$38*
0.9	=$B$38*B33+$C$38*
0.82	=$B$38*B34+$C$38*
0.78	=$B$38*B35+$C$38*
0.98	=$B$38*B36+$C$38*
=AVERAGE(D32:D36)	
0.5	

Weekly Payroll

Employee	Hours	Rate
Alvarez, Rita	40	22.5
Campbell, Owen	15	22.5
Heitmann, Luanne	25	19
Malina, Susan	40	18.75
Parker, Kenneth	40	18.75
Reitz, Collette	20	15
Shepard, Gregory	15	12

Construction Projects

Project	Projected	Actual
South Cascade	145000	141597
Rogue River Park	120000	124670
Meridian	120500	99450
Lowell Ridge	95250	98455
Walker Canyon	70000	68420
Nettleson Creek	52000	49517

Overdue Accounts

Client	Account #	Amount Due
Sunrise Marketing	120	9875
National Systems	398	8525
First Street Signs	188	5000
Valley Services	286	3250

Test Scores

Employee	Test No. 1	Test No. 2
Coffey, Annette	0.62	0.64
Halverson, Ted	0.88	0.96
Kohler, Jeremy	0.8	0.76
McKnight, Carol	0.68	0.72
Parkhurst, Jody	0.98	0.96
Test Averages	=AVERAGE(B32:B36)	=AVERAGE(C32:C36)
Test Weights	0.25	0.25

Northwest Supplies and Production
Sales Department

Salesperson	1st Half	2nd Half	Total	Average	Bonus
Martinez	$ 30,450	$ 52,100	$ 82,550	$ 41,275	No
Gallagher	75,000	84,650	159,650	79,825	Yes
Slattery	100,200	101,250	201,450	100,725	Yes
Timbrook	65,200	73,250	138,450	69,225	No
Wickstrom	42,500	28,450	70,950	35,475	No
Kuong	75,400	77,450	152,850	76,425	Yes
Bolton	34,500	29,450	63,950	31,975	No
Dearing	72,000	68,560	140,560	70,280	No

Northwest Supplies and Production
Sales Department

Salesperson	1st Half	2nd Half	Total	Average	Bonus
Martinez	$ 30,450	$ 52,100	$ 82,550	$ 41,275	No
Gallagher	75,000	84,650	159,650	79,825	Yes
Slattery	100,200	101,250	201,450	100,725	Yes
Timbrook	65,200	73,250	138,450	69,225	No
Wickstrom	42,500	28,450	70,950	35,475	No
Kuong	75,400	77,450	152,850	76,425	Yes
Bolton	34,500	29,450	63,950	31,975	No
Dearing	72,000	68,560	140,560	70,280	No

Compass Corporation
Overdue Accounts

Customer	Account #	Amount Due	Purchase Date	Terms	Due Date
Nelson Enterprises	9005	$ 5,403	10/1/2012	30	10/31/2012
Kaufer's Supplies	5042	9,085	10/3/2012	15	10/18/2012
Pioneer Products	6078	10,745	10/8/2012	15	10/23/2012
Meridian Restoration	7553	2,034	10/10/2012	30	11/9/2012
Alliance Equipment	5430	11,950	10/15/2012	30	11/14/2012
Liberty Corporation	6920	900	10/30/2012	15	11/14/2012
Douglas Technical	7844	355	11/6/2012	15	11/21/2012
Frontline Solutions	9331	12,350	11/13/2012	30	12/13/2012

EL1-C3-A2-CCorpAccts.xlsx

O'Rourke Enterprises
Supplies and Equipment Budget

Budget Amount	$750,000		
Research and Development			
	Supplies	3.5%	$26,250
	Equipment	22.0%	$165,000
Technical Support			
	Supplies	4.5%	$33,750
	Equipment	19.0%	$142,500
Sales and Marketing			
	Supplies	7.0%	$52,500
	Equipment	14.0%	$105,000
Human Resources			
	Supplies	5.5%	$41,250
	Equipment	10.0%	$75,000
Finances			
	Supplies	4.5%	$33,750
	Equipment	10.0%	$75,000

EL1-C3-A3-OEBudget.xlsx

Capstan Marine Products

Sales Department Bonuses

Salesperson	Sales	Bonus	Amount
Abrams, Warner	$ 130,490	Yes	$ 6,524.50
Allejandro, Elaine	95,500.00	No	-
Crispin, Nicolaus	137,000.00	Yes	6,850.00
Frankel, Maria	124,000.00	Yes	6,200.00
Hiesmann, Thomas	85,500.00	No	-
Jarvis, Lawrence	159,000.00	Yes	7,950.00
Littleman, Shirley	110,500.00	No	-
McBride, Leah	78,420.00	No	-
Ostlund, Sonya	101,435.00	No	-
Ryckman, Graham	83,255.00	No	-
Sharma, Anja	121,488.00	Yes	6,074.40

EL1-C3-VB-BonusAmounts(Step4).xlsx

ANALYSIS OF FINANCIAL CONDITION

	Actual	Planned	Prior
Stockholders' equity ratio	62%	60%	57%
Bond holders' equity ratio	45%	39%	41%
Liability liquidity ratio	122%	115%	120%
Fixed obligation security ratio	196%	190%	187%
Fixed interest ratio	23%	20%	28%
Earnings ratio	7%	6%	6%
Average	76%	72%	73%

EL1-C3-A4-FinAnalysis.xlsx

Capstan Marine Products

Sales Department Bonuses

Salesperson	Sales	Bonus	Amount
Abrams, Warner	130490	=IF(B4>114999,"Yes","No")	=IF(C4="Yes",B4*0.05,0)
Allejandro, Elaine	95500	=IF(B5>114999,"Yes","No")	=IF(C5="Yes",B5*0.05,0)
Crispin, Nicolaus	137000	=IF(B6>114999,"Yes","No")	=IF(C6="Yes",B6*0.05,0)
Frankel, Maria	124000	=IF(B7>114999,"Yes","No")	=IF(C7="Yes",B7*0.05,0)
Hiesmann, Thomas	85500	=IF(B8>114999,"Yes","No")	=IF(C8="Yes",B8*0.05,0)
Jarvis, Lawrence	159000	=IF(B9>114999,"Yes","No")	=IF(C9="Yes",B9*0.05,0)
Littleman, Shirley	110500	=IF(B10>114999,"Yes","No")	=IF(C10="Yes",B10*0.05,0)
McBride, Leah	78420	=IF(B11>114999,"Yes","No")	=IF(C11="Yes",B11*0.05,0)
Ostlund, Sonya	101435	=IF(B12>114999,"Yes","No")	=IF(C12="Yes",B12*0.05,0)
Ryckman, Graham	83255	=IF(B13>114999,"Yes","No")	=IF(C13="Yes",B13*0.05,0)
Sharma, Anja	121488	=IF(B14>114999,"Yes","No")	=IF(C14="Yes",B14*0.05,0)

EL1-C3-VB-BonusAmounts(Step5).xlsx (1 of 2)

EL1-C3-VB-BonusAmounts(Step5).xlsx (2 of 2)

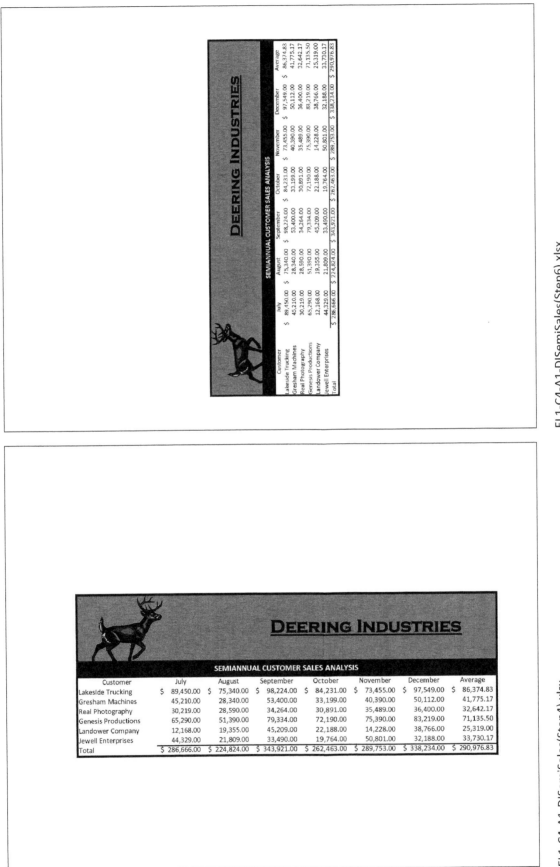

Benchmark Excel 2010 Level 1 Model Answers

...rfacturing

...fication

Name	Test 7	Test 8	Test 9	Test 10	Test 11	Test 12	Average
Morris, Eugene	78%	82%	60%	84%	64%	70%	73%
Jiang, Allison	86%	90%	100%	98%	89%	96%	93%
Callahan, Jerome	72%	62%	78%	64%	86%	92%	75%
Longren, Isabella	89%	91%	90%	93%	86%	80%	90%
Soulez, Monica	78%	75%	87%	88%	64%	69%	76%
White, Logan	92%	80%	93%	90%	86%	82%	91%
Howell, Angela	98%	94%	99%	89%	100%	90%	94%
Reed-Carter, Katie	55%	0%	42%	65%	72%	59%	43%
Compton, Aidan	78%	75%	87%	88%	64%	76%	76%
Acosta, Miguel	92%	80%	93%	90%	86%	84%	91%
Potter, Aaron	98%	94%	99%	89%	100%	93%	95%
Rhoden, Christopher	55%	0%	42%	65%	72%	40%	41%
Slater, Chad	78%	69%	83%	87%	84%	69%	80%
Tuell, Paulette	89%	93%	84%	100%	95%	92%	94%
Whitlow, Angelina	78%	73%	81%	82%	67%	69%	76%
Young, Lee	82%	89%	79%	74%	80%	82%	80%
Goldman, Shannon	89%	93%	100%	91%	86%	90%	92%
Bertram, Richard	58%	45%	63%	51%	60%	59%	57%
Average	80%	71%	81%	83%	80%	77%	79%

EL1-C4-A2-CMTests.xlsx

EL1-C4-A2-CMTests(Step9).xlsx (2 of 2)

Clearline Manu...

Software Certi...

Name	Test 1	Test 2	Test 3	Test 4	Test 5	Test 6
Morris, Eugene	78%	80%	68%	66%	82%	60%
Jiang, Allison	98%	86%	92%	96%	88%	92%
Callahan, Jerome	78%	65%	82%	68%	74%	80%
Longren, Isabella	84%	93%	95%	81%	96%	98%
Soulez, Monica	70%	67%	55%	87%	82%	88%
White, Logan	95%	100%	98%	88%	95%	89%
Howell, Angela	100%	95%	96%	91%	87%	94%
Reed-Carter, Katie	65%	0%	0%	48%	52%	56%
Compton, Aidan	70%	67%	55%	87%	82%	88%
Acosta, Miguel	95%	100%	98%	88%	95%	89%
Potter, Aaron	100%	95%	96%	91%	87%	94%
Rhoden, Christopher	65%	0%	0%	48%	52%	56%
Slater, Chad	80%	82%	88%	79%	83%	76%
Tuell, Paulette	95%	100%	89%	94%	98%	94%
Whitlow, Angelina	82%	72%	85%	83%	71%	73%
Young, Lee	86%	72%	74%	82%	76%	79%
Goldman, Shannon	88%	86%	100%	98%	90%	97%
Bertram, Richard	63%	52%	66%	67%	53%	49%
Average	83%	73%	74%	80%	80%	81%

EL1-C4-A2-CMTests.xlsx

EL1-C4-A2-CMTests(Step9).xlsx (1 of 2)

Clearline Manu

Software Certi

Name	Test 1	Test 2	Test 3	Test 4	Test 5	Test 6
Morris, Eugene	78%	80%	68%	66%	82%	60%
Jiang, Allison	98%	86%	92%	96%	88%	92%
Callahan, Jerome	78%	65%	82%	68%	74%	80%
Longren, Isabella	84%	93%	95%	81%	96%	98%
Soulez, Monica	70%	67%	55%	87%	82%	88%
White, Logan	95%	100%	98%	88%	95%	89%
Howell, Angela	100%	95%	96%	91%	87%	94%
Reed-Carter, Katie	65%	0%	0%	48%	52%	56%
Compton, Aidan	70%	67%	55%	87%	82%	88%
Acosta, Miguel	95%	100%	98%	88%	95%	89%
Potter, Aaron	100%	95%	96%	91%	87%	94%
Rhoden, Christopher	65%	0%	0%	48%	52%	56%
Slater, Chad	80%	82%	88%	79%	83%	76%
Tuell, Paulette	95%	100%	89%	94%	98%	94%
Whitlow, Angelina	82%	72%	85%	83%	71%	73%
Young, Lee	86%	72%	74%	82%	76%	79%
Goldman, Shannon	88%	86%	100%	98%	90%	97%
Bertram, Richard	63%	52%	66%	67%	53%	49%
Average	83%	73%	74%	80%	80%	81%

EL1-C4-A2-CMTests(Step12).xlsx (1 of 2)

Name	Average
Morris, Eugene	73%
Jiang, Allison	93%
Callahan, Jerome	75%
Longren, Isabella	90%
Soulez, Monica	76%
White, Logan	91%
Howell, Angela	94%
Reed-Carter, Katie	43%
Compton, Aidan	76%
Acosta, Miguel	91%
Potter, Aaron	95%
Rhoden, Christopher	41%
Slater, Chad	80%
Tuell, Paulette	94%
Whitlow, Angelina	76%
Young, Lee	80%
Goldman, Shannon	92%
Bertram, Richard	57%
Average	79%

EL1-C4-A2-CMTests(Step10).xlsx

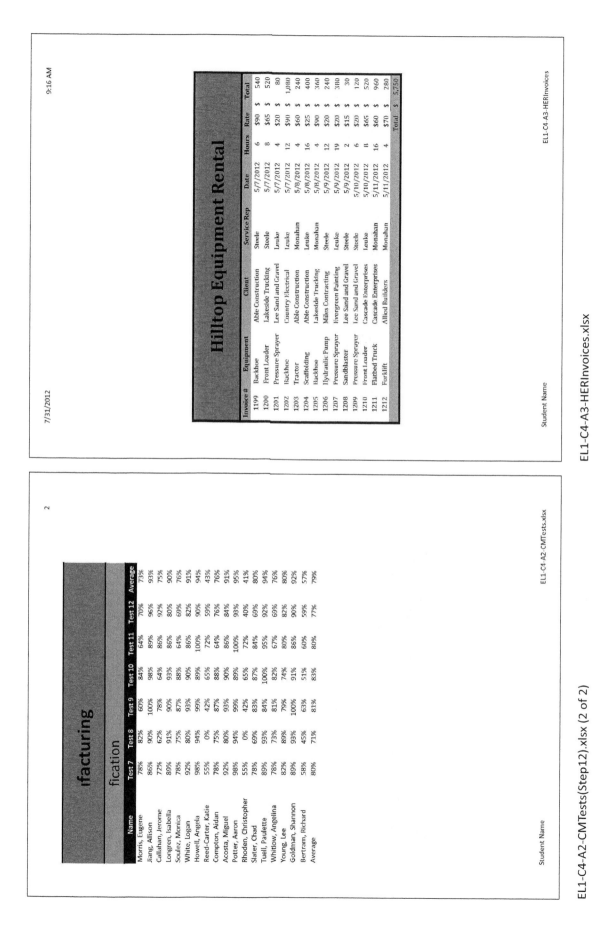

Hilltop Equipment Rental

Invoice #	Equipment	Client	Service Rep	Date	Hours	Rate	Total
1199	Backhoe	Able Construction	Steele	5/7/2012	6	$90	$ 540
1200	Front Loader	Lakeside Trucking	Steele	5/7/2012	8	$65	$ 520
1201	Pressure Sprayer	Lee Sand and Gravel	Leuke	5/7/2012	4	$20	$ 80
1202	Backhoe	Country Electrical	Leuke	5/7/2012	12	$90	$ 1,080
1203	Tractor	Able Construction	Monahan	5/8/2012	4	$60	$ 240
1204	Scaffolding	Lakeside Trucking	Leuke	5/8/2012	16	$25	$ 400
1205	Backhoe	Lakeside Trucking	Monahan	5/8/2012	4	$90	$ 360
1206	Hydraulic Pump	Miles Contracting	Steele	5/9/2012	12	$20	$ 240
1207	Pressure Sprayer	Evergreen Painting	Leuke	5/9/2012	19	$20	$ 380
1208	Sandblaster	Lee Sand and Gravel	Steele	5/9/2012	2	$15	$ 30
1209	Pressure Sprayer	Lee Sand and Gravel	Steele	5/10/2012	6	$20	$ 120
1210	Front Loader	Cascade Enterprises	Leuke	5/10/2012	8	$65	$ 520
1211	Flatbed Truck	Cascade Enterprises	Monahan	5/11/2012	16	$60	$ 960
1212	Forklift	Allied Builders	Monahan	5/11/2012	4	$70	$ 280
						Total:	$ 5,750

2

		ifacturing						
		fication						
Name	Test 7	Test 8	Test 9	Test 10	Test 11	Test 12	Average
Morris, Eugene	78%	82%	60%	84%	64%	70%	73%
Jiang, Allison	86%	90%	100%	98%	89%	96%	93%
Callahan, Jerome	72%	62%	78%	64%	86%	92%	75%
Longren, Isabella	89%	91%	90%	93%	86%	80%	90%
Soulez, Monica	78%	75%	87%	88%	64%	69%	76%
White, Logan	92%	80%	93%	90%	86%	82%	91%
Howell, Angela	98%	94%	99%	89%	100%	90%	94%
Reed-Carter, Katie	55%	0%	42%	65%	72%	59%	43%
Compton, Aidan	78%	75%	87%	88%	64%	76%	76%
Acosta, Miguel	92%	80%	93%	90%	86%	84%	91%
Potter, Aaron	98%	94%	99%	89%	100%	93%	95%
Rhoden, Christopher	55%	0%	42%	65%	72%	40%	41%
Slater, Chad	78%	69%	83%	87%	84%	69%	80%
Tuell, Paulette	89%	93%	84%	100%	95%	92%	94%
Whitlow, Angelina	78%	73%	81%	82%	67%	69%	76%
Young, Lee	82%	89%	79%	74%	80%	82%	80%
Goldman, Shannon	89%	93%	100%	91%	86%	90%	92%
Bertram, Richard	58%	45%	63%	51%	60%	59%	57%
Average	80%	71%	81%	83%	80%	77%	79%

Benchmark Excel 2010 Level 1 Model Answers   101

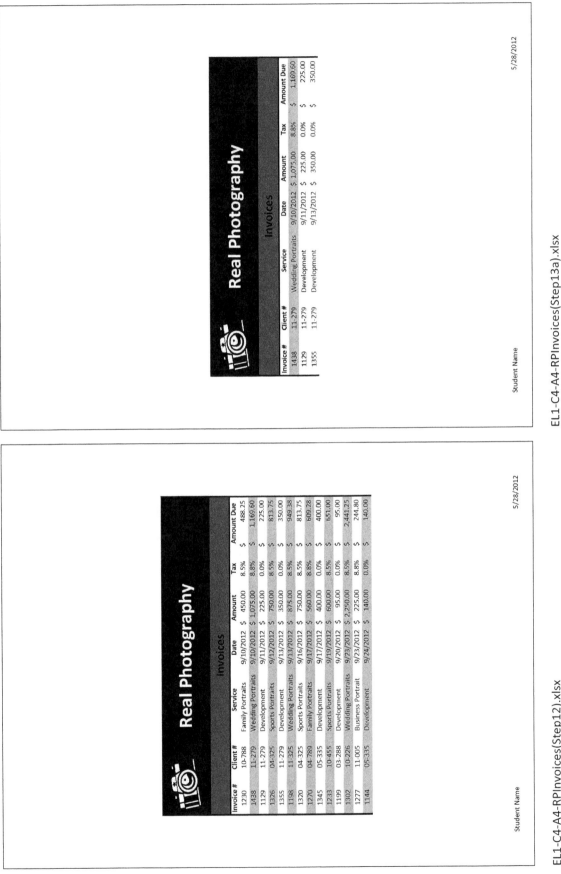

Real Photography — Invoices (EL1-C4-A4-RPInvoices(Step13a).xlsx)

Invoice #	Client #	Service	Date	Amount	Tax	Amount Due
1438	11-279	Wedding Portraits	9/10/2012	$ 1,075.00	8.8%	$ 1,169.60
1129	11-279	Development	9/11/2012	$ 225.00	0.0%	$ 225.00
1355	11-279	Development	9/13/2012	$ 350.00	0.0%	$ 350.00

Real Photography — Invoices (EL1-C4-A4-RPInvoices(Step12).xlsx)

Invoice #	Client #	Service	Date	Amount	Tax	Amount Due
1230	10-788	Family Portraits	9/10/2012	$ 450.00	8.5%	$ 488.25
1438	11-279	Wedding Portraits	9/10/2012	$ 1,075.00	8.8%	$ 1,169.60
1129	11-279	Development	9/11/2012	$ 225.00	0.0%	$ 225.00
1326	04-325	Sports Portraits	9/12/2012	$ 750.00	8.5%	$ 813.75
1355	11-279	Development	9/13/2012	$ 350.00	0.0%	$ 350.00
1198	11-325	Wedding Portraits	9/13/2012	$ 875.00	8.5%	$ 949.38
1320	04-325	Sports Portraits	9/16/2012	$ 750.00	8.5%	$ 813.75
1270	04-789	Family Portraits	9/17/2012	$ 560.00	8.8%	$ 609.28
1345	05-335	Development	9/17/2012	$ 400.00	0.0%	$ 400.00
1233	10-455	Sports Portraits	9/19/2012	$ 600.00	8.5%	$ 651.00
1199	03-288	Development	9/20/2012	$ 95.00	0.0%	$ 95.00
1302	10-226	Wedding Portraits	9/23/2012	$ 2,250.00	8.5%	$ 2,441.25
1277	11-005	Business Portrait	9/23/2012	$ 225.00	8.8%	$ 244.80
1144	05-335	Development	9/24/2012	$ 140.00	0.0%	$ 140.00

Student Name

5/28/2012

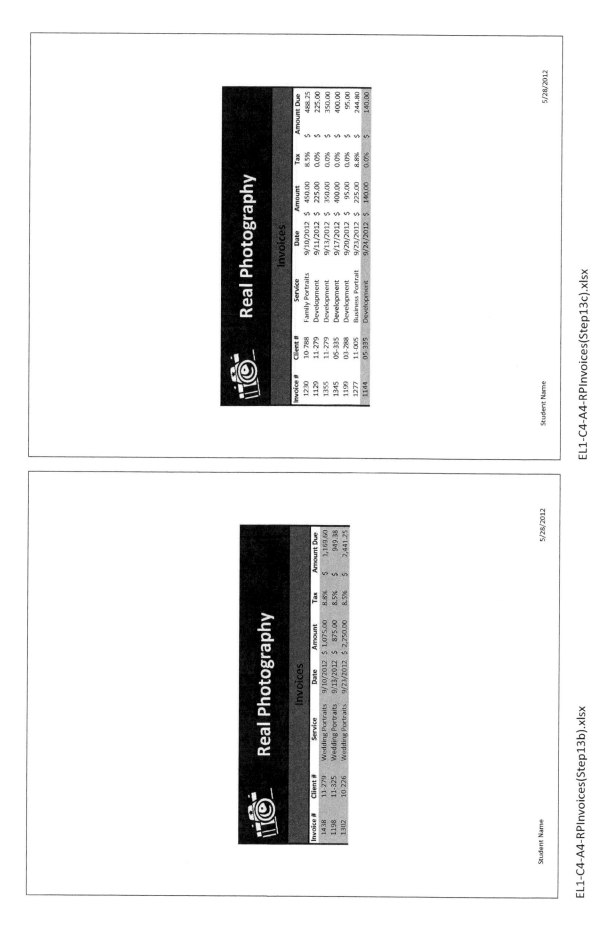

(Student Name)

nent Rental

Expenses	July	August	September	October	November	December	Total
Lease	$ 3,250	$ 3,250	$ 3,250	$ 3,250	$ 3,250	$ 3,250	$ 39,000
Utilities	1,845	1,555	1,890	2,451	2,899	3,005	29,380
Payroll	13,503	13,258	12,475	10,548	10,122	9,359	135,607
Insurance	895	895	895	895	895	895	10,740
Maintenance	2,479	3,100	1,870	6,105	4,220	3,544	40,086
Supplies	451	550	211	580	433	601	5,520
Total Expenses	$ 22,423	$ 22,608	$ 20,591	$ 23,829	$ 21,819	$ 20,654	$ 260,341

EL1-C4-VB-HERExpenses

(Student Name)

Hilltop Equip

Expenses	January	February	March	April	May	June
Lease	$ 3,250	$ 3,250	3,250	$ 3,250	$ 3,250	$ 3,250
Utilities	3,209	2,994	2,987	2,500	2,057	1,988
Payroll	10,545	9,533	11,512	10,548	11,199	12,675
Insurance	895	895	895	895	895	895
Maintenance	2,439	1,856	2,455	5,410	3,498	3,110
Supplies	341	580	457	330	675	319
Total Expenses	$ 20,679	$ 19,108	$ 21,556	$ 22,933	$ 21,874	$ 22,237

EL1-C4-VB-HERExpenses

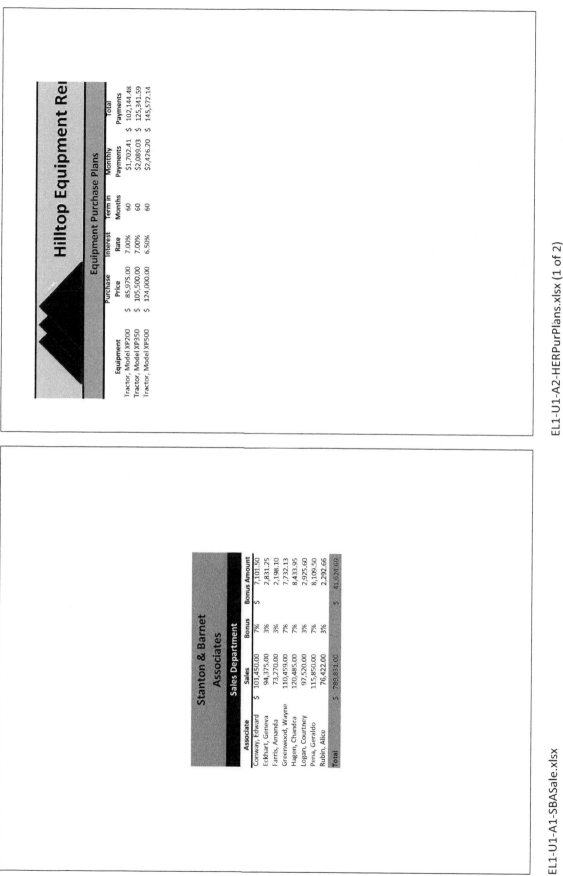

Hilltop Equipment Re...

Equipment Purchase Plans

Equipment	Purchase Price	Interest Rate	Term in Months	Monthly Payments	Total Payments
Tractor, Model XP200	$ 85,975.00	7.00%	60	$1,702.41	$ 102,144.48
Tractor, Model XP350	$ 105,500.00	7.00%	60	$2,089.03	$ 125,341.59
Tractor, Model XP500	$ 124,000.00	6.50%	60	$2,426.20	$ 145,572.14

Stanton & Barnet Associates

Sales Department

Associate	Sales	Bonus	Bonus Amount
Conway, Edward	$ 101,450.00	7%	$ 7,101.50
Eckhart, Geneva	94,375.00	3%	2,831.25
Farris, Amanda	73,270.00	3%	2,198.10
Greenwood, Wayne	110,459.00	7%	7,732.13
Hagen, Chandra	120,485.00	7%	8,433.95
Logan, Courtney	97,520.00	3%	2,925.60
Pena, Geraldo	115,850.00	7%	8,109.50
Rubin, Alice	76,422.00	3%	2,292.66
Total	$ 789,831.00		$ 41,624.69

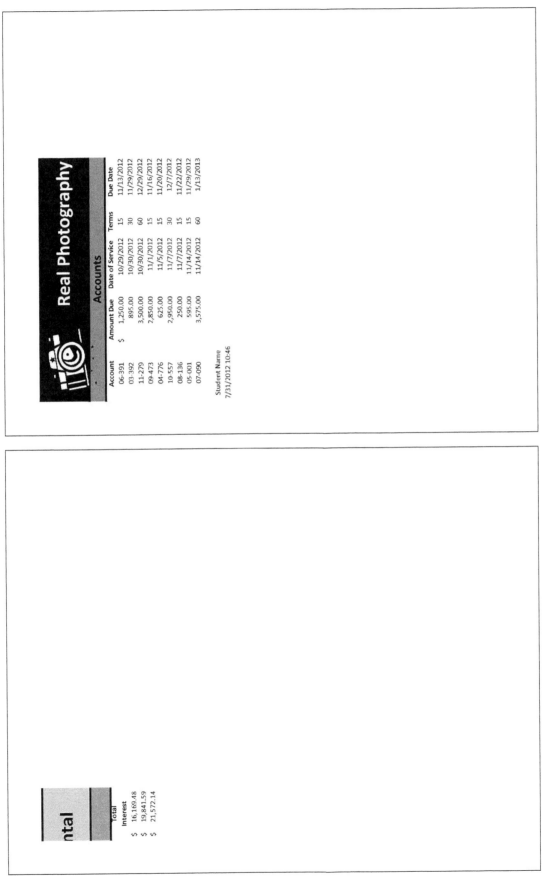

Cedarview Construction
Weekly Payroll

Employee	Hrly Rate	Hours	Overtime	Gross	W/H Tax	SS Tax	Net
Allesandro, Maria	$ 55.00	40	2	$ 2,365.00	$ 662.20	$ 180.92	$ 1,521.88
Bauman, Heather	$ 34.00	40	0	$ 1,360.00	$ 380.80	$ 104.04	875.16
Ellington, Troy	$ 52.50	40	4	$ 2,415.00	$ 676.20	$ 184.75	$ 1,554.05
Goodman, Matthew	$ 45.00	25	0	$ 1,125.00	$ 315.00	86.06	723.94
Holland, Charles	$ 55.00	40	0	$ 2,200.00	$ 616.00	$ 168.30	$ 1,415.70
Huntington, Ella	$ 34.00	40	0	$ 1,360.00	$ 380.80	$ 104.04	875.16
Kaplan-Downing, Eve	$ 23.50	25	5	763.75	$ 213.85	58.43	491.47
Larimore, Rebecca	$ 19.00	40	5	760.00	$ 212.80	58.14	489.06
McBride, Jennifer	$ 52.50	40	2	$ 2,257.50	$ 632.10	$ 172.70	$ 1,452.70
Powell, Caleb	$ 50.00	40	6	$ 2,450.00	$ 686.00	$ 187.43	$ 1,576.58
Washington, Keith	$ 45.00	30	5	$ 1,687.50	$ 472.50	$ 129.09	$ 1,085.91
Wilks, Aaron	$ 25.00	20	0	500.00	$ 140.00	38.25	321.75
Yu, Myong	$ 60.00	20	0	$ 1,200.00	$ 336.00	91.80	772.20
Zarelli, Sheila	$ 42.50	30	0	$ 1,275.00	$ 357.00	97.54	820.46

Overtime	1.5	W/H Rate	28%	SS Rate	7.65%

EL1-U1-A5-CCPayroll.xlsx

Pyramid Sales

FIRST-QUARTER SALES - 2012

Customer	January	February	March	Total	Discount
Landower Company	$ 22,542	$ 29,009	$ 11,340	$ 62,891	0%
Jewell Enterprises	32,397	41,265	48,975	122,637	5%
Genesis Productions	-	-	22,316	22,316	0%
Real Photography	10,563	22,168	15,653	48,384	0%
Westside Corporation	44,214	31,238	19,086	94,538	5%
Kaylor Manufacturing	54,388	49,876	55,437	159,701	5%
Moon Bay Products	19,203	23,310	8,349	50,862	0%
Crossroads Studios	5,640	4,392	-	10,032	0%
Royal Care	20,432	35,223	25,394	81,049	5%
Washburn Dynamics	20,192	33,278	43,110	96,580	5%
All West Transport	10,293	8,745	9,437	28,475	0%
Edgewood Distributors	22,394	13,920	19,994	56,308	0%
Superior Coating	5,604	3,908	4,432	13,944	0%
Parkland Associates	3,203	4,540	-	7,743	0%
Pioneer Securities	12,540	14,320	9,048	35,908	0%

EL1-U1-A4-PSQtrlySales.xlsx

Customer	November	December	Average
Lakeside Trucking	$ 45,200	$ 51,450	$ 76,587
Gresham Machines	19,300	18,435	38,996
Real Photography	41,395	32,120	35,244
Genesis Productions	58,250	42,300	70,197
Landower Company	39,625	41,760	30,180
Jewell Enterprises	15,445	12,500	28,429
Total	$ 219,215	$ 198,565	$ 279,634
Highest Total			
Lowest Total			

Student Name

DEERING INDUSTRIES

ANNUAL CUSTOMER SALES ANALYSIS

Customer	January	February	March	April	May	June	July	August	September	October
Lakeside Trucking	$ 89,450	$ 75,340	$ 98,224	$ 84,231	$ 73,455	$ 97,549	$ 69,340	$ 88,230	$ 91,235	$ 55,340
Gresham Machines	45,210	28,340	53,400	33,199	40,390	50,112	39,230	44,289	45,930	50,122
Real Photography	30,219	28,590	34,264	30,891	35,489	36,400	29,039	34,377	40,126	50,020
Genesis Productions	65,290	51,390	79,334	72,190	75,390	83,219	95,600	52,800	75,245	91,355
Landower Company	12,168	19,355	45,209	22,188	14,228	38,766	20,380	24,565	33,560	50,360
Jewell Enterprises	44,329	21,809	33,490	19,764	50,801	32,188	35,700	31,900	24,550	18,675
Total	$ 286,666	$ 224,824	$ 343,921	$ 262,463	$ 289,753	$ 338,234	$ 289,289	$ 276,161	$ 310,646	$ 315,872
Highest Total	$ 343,921									
Lowest Total	$ 198,565									

Student Name

Real Photography

Invoices

Invoice #	Client #	Service	Date	Amount	Tax	Amount Due
4930	03-392	Family Portraits	7/2/2012	$ 450.00	9.0%	$ 490.50
4942	02-498	Wedding Portraits	7/3/2012	1,075.00	8.8%	1,169.60
5002	10-005	Development	7/4/2012	225.00	0.0%	225.00
5007	04-325	Sports Portraits	7/4/2012	750.00	9.0%	817.50
5129	10-005	Development	7/6/2012	350.00	0.0%	350.00
2048	11-325	Wedding Portraits	7/9/2012	875.00	9.0%	953.75
2054	04-325	Sports Portraits	7/10/2012	750.00	9.0%	817.50
2064	05-665	Family Portraits	7/10/2012	560.00	8.8%	609.28
2077	10-005	Development	7/13/2012	400.00	0.0%	400.00
2079	04-325	Sports Portraits	7/16/2012	600.00	9.0%	654.00
1002	10-005	Development	7/18/2012	100.00	0.0%	100.00
2239	04-334	Sitting	7/19/2012	50.00	8.8%	54.40
4749	02-449	Wedding Portraits	7/23/2012	2,450.00	8.8%	2,665.60
1043	11-557	Development	7/24/2012	125.00	0.0%	125.00
5098	04-235	Sports Portraits	7/30/2012	500.00	9.0%	545.00

7/31/2012

Evergreen Products

2011 TOTAL SALES

Customer	First Half	Second Half	Total Sales
Harbor Manufacturing	$ 14,530	$ 15,365	$ 29,895
Timberlake Designs	20,412	18,368	38,780
Cascade Plastics	55,429	61,355	116,784
Avalon Clinic	105,300	105,300	210,600
Gravelly Lake Plumbing	175,257	180,552	355,809
Bavarian Productions	33,122	40,001	73,123
Stealth Media	5,300	2,950	8,250
Robinson Group	155,300	135,000	290,300
Lincoln Services	11,350	9,500	20,850
Danmark Contracting	45,750	50,250	96,000
Earthway Systems	31,230	28,525	59,755
Total Sales			$ 1,300,146

Student Name

7/31/2012

Evergreen Products

2010 TOTAL SALES

Customer	First Half	Second Half	Total Sales
Harbor Manufacturing	$ 32,500	$ 41,305	$ 73,805
Timberlake Designs	10,200	14,230	24,430
Cascade Plastics	64,230	50,304	114,534
Avalon Clinic	105,300	105,300	210,600
Gravelly Lake Plumbing	200,500	150,700	351,200
Bavarian Productions	45,890	29,405	75,295
Stealth Media	5,300	2,950	8,250
Robinson Group	136,492	144,366	280,858
Lincoln Services	21,890	18,445	40,335
Danmark Contracting	45,750	50,250	96,000
Earthway Systems	35,500	28,750	64,250
Total Sales			$ 1,339,557

Student Name

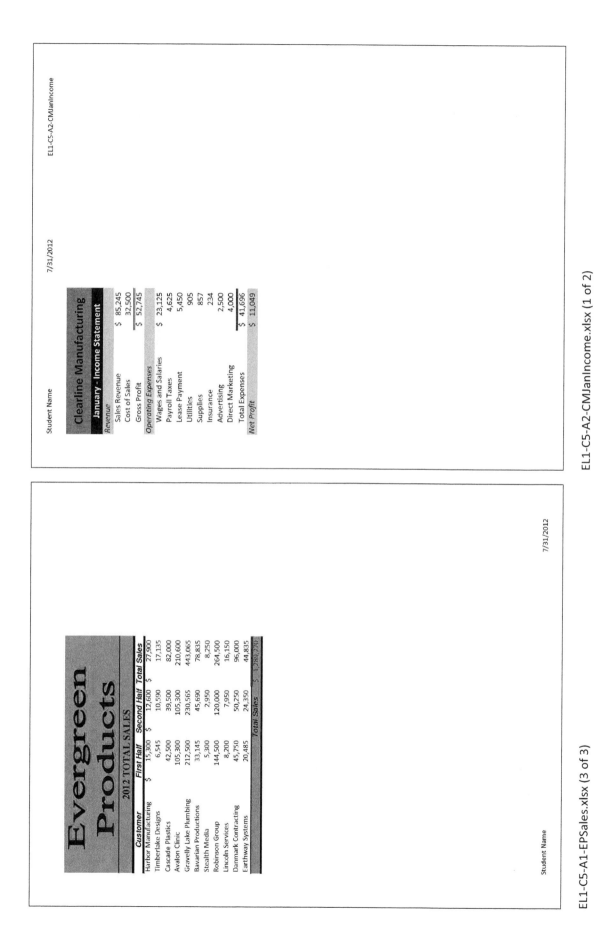

Clearline Manufacturing

January - Income Statement

Revenue		
Sales Revenue	$	85,245
Cost of Sales		32,500
Gross Profit	$	52,745
Operating Expenses		
Wages and Salaries	$	23,125
Payroll Taxes		4,625
Lease Payment		5,450
Utilities		905
Supplies		857
Insurance		234
Advertising		2,500
Direct Marketing		4,000
Total Expenses	$	41,696
Net Profit	$	11,049

EL1-C5-A2-CMJanIncome.xlsx (1 of 2)

Evergreen Products

2012 TOTAL SALES

Customer	First Half	Second Half	Total Sales
Harbor Manufacturing	$ 15,300	$ 12,600	$ 27,900
Timberlake Designs	6,545	10,590	17,135
Cascade Plastics	42,500	39,500	82,000
Avalon Clinic	105,300	105,300	210,600
Gravelly Lake Plumbing	212,500	230,565	443,065
Bavarian Productions	33,145	45,690	78,835
Stealth Media	5,300	2,950	8,250
Robinson Group	144,500	120,000	264,500
Lincoln Services	8,200	7,950	16,150
Danmark Contracting	45,750	50,250	96,000
Earthway Systems	20,485	24,350	44,835
Total Sales			$ 1,289,270

EL1-C5-A1-EPSales.xlsx (3 of 3)

| | | | | | | Clearline Manufacturing | | | | | | | |
| | | | | | | Software Certification | | | | | | | |
Name	Test 1	Test 2	Test 3	Test 4	Test 5	Test 6	Test 7	Test 8	Test 9	Test 10	Test 11	Test 12	Average
Amson, Patrick	89%	65%	76%	89%	98%	65%	76%	87%	55%	78%	67%	69%	76%
Barclay, Jeanine	78%	66%	87%	90%	92%	82%	100%	84%	67%	86%	82%	91%	84%
Calahan, Jack	65%	71%	64%	66%	70%	81%	64%	59%	76%	76%	45%	49%	66%
Cumpston, Kurt	89%	91%	90%	93%	86%	80%	84%	93%	95%	81%	96%	98%	90%
Dimmitt, Marian	78%	73%	81%	82%	67%	69%	82%	72%	85%	83%	71%	73%	76%
Donovan, Nancy	82%	89%	79%	74%	80%	82%	86%	72%	74%	82%	76%	79%	80%
Fisher-Edwards, Teri	89%	93%	100%	91%	86%	90%	88%	86%	100%	98%	90%	97%	92%
Flanery, Stephanie	58%	45%	63%	51%	60%	59%	63%	52%	66%	67%	53%	49%	57%
Heyrnan, Grover	78%	75%	87%	88%	64%	76%	70%	67%	55%	87%	82%	88%	76%
Herbertson, Wynn	92%	80%	93%	90%	86%	84%	95%	100%	98%	88%	95%	89%	91%
Jewett, Troy	98%	94%	99%	89%	100%	93%	100%	95%	96%	91%	87%	94%	95%
Kwieciak, Kathleen	55%	0%	42%	65%	72%	40%	65%	0%	0%	48%	52%	55%	41%
Leibrand, Maxine	78%	69%	83%	87%	84%	69%	80%	82%	88%	79%	83%	76%	80%
Markovits, Claude	89%	93%	84%	100%	95%	92%	95%	100%	89%	94%	98%	94%	94%
Moonstar, Siana	73%	87%	67%	83%	90%	84%	73%	81%	75%	65%	84%	88%	79%
Nauer, Sheryl	75%	83%	85%	78%	82%	80%	79%	82%	92%	90%	86%	84%	83%
Nunez, James	98%	96%	100%	90%	95%	93%	88%	91%	89%	100%	96%	98%	95%
Nyegaard, Curtis	90%	89%	84%	85%	93%	85%	100%	94%	98%	93%	100%	95%	92%
Oglesbee, Randy	65%	55%	73%	90%	87%	67%	85%	77%	85%	73%	78%	77%	76%
Pherson, Douglas	69%	82%	87%	74%	70%	82%	84%	85%	66%	77%	91%	86%	79%

Student Name

7/31/2012

EL1-C5-A2-CMJanIncome

Clearline Manufacturing
February - Income Statement

Revenue	
Sales Revenue	$ 97,655
Cost of Sales	39,558
Gross Profit	$ 58,097
Operating Expenses	
Wages and Salaries	$ 23,125
Payroll Taxes	4,625
Lease Payment	5,450
Utilities	1,105
Supplies	857
Insurance	234
Advertising	2,500
Direct Marketing	4,000
Total Expenses	$ 41,896
Net Profit	$ 16,201

Benchmark Excel 2010 Level 1 Model Answers

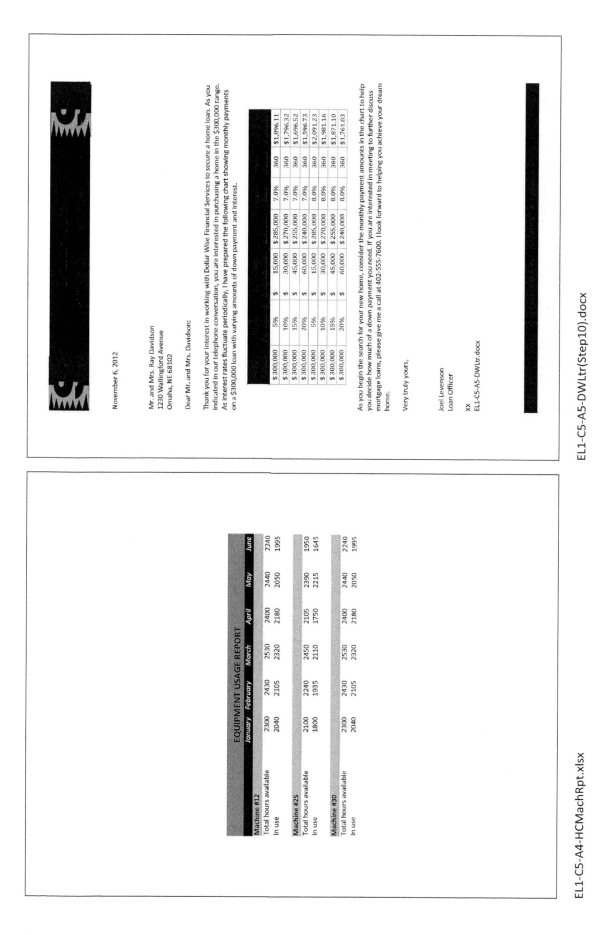

November 6, 2012

Mr. and Mrs. Ray Davidson
1230 Wallingford Avenue
Omaha, NE 68102

Dear Mr. and Mrs. Davidson:

Thank you for your interest in working with Dollar Wise Financial Services to secure a home loan. As you indicated in our telephone conversation, you are interested in purchasing a home in the $300,000 range. As interest rates fluctuate periodically, I have prepared the following chart showing monthly payments on a $300,000 loan with varying amounts of down payment and interest.

$300,000	5%	$ 15,000	$285,000	7.0%	360	$1,896.11
$300,000	10%	$ 30,000	$270,000	7.0%	360	$1,796.32
$300,000	15%	$ 45,000	$255,000	7.0%	360	$1,696.52
$300,000	20%	$ 60,000	$240,000	7.0%	360	$1,596.73
$300,000	5%	$ 15,000	$285,000	8.0%	360	$2,091.23
$300,000	10%	$ 30,000	$270,000	8.0%	360	$1,981.16
$300,000	15%	$ 45,000	$255,000	8.0%	360	$1,871.10
$300,000	20%	$ 60,000	$240,000	8.0%	360	$1,761.03

As you begin the search for your new home, consider the monthly payment amounts in the chart to help you decide how much of a down payment you need. If you are interested in meeting to further discuss mortgage loans, please give me a call at 402-555-7600. I look forward to helping you achieve your dream home.

Very truly yours,

Joel Levenson
Loan Officer

XX
EL1-C5-A5-DWLtr.docx

EL1-C5-A5-DWLtr(Step10).docx

EQUIPMENT USAGE REPORT						
	January	February	March	April	May	June
Machine #12						
Total hours available	2300	2430	2530	2400	2440	2240
In use	2040	2105	2320	2180	2050	1995
Machine #25						
Total hours available	2100	2240	2450	2105	2390	1950
In use	1800	1935	2110	1750	2215	1645
Machine #30						
Total hours available	2300	2430	2530	2400	2440	2240
In use	2040	2105	2320	2180	2050	1995

EL1-C5-A4-HCMachRpt.xlsx

November 6, 2012

Mr. and Mrs. Ray Davidson
1230 Wallingford Avenue
Omaha, NE 68102

Dear Mr. and Mrs. Davidson:

Thank you for your interest in working with Dollar Wise Financial Services to secure a home loan. As you indicated in our telephone conversation, you are interested in purchasing a home in the $300,000 range. As interest rates fluctuate periodically, I have prepared the following chart showing monthly payments on a $300,000 loan with varying amounts of down payment and interest.

$ 400,000	5%	$	20,000	$ 380,000	7.0%	360	$2,528.15
$ 400,000	10%	$	40,000	$ 360,000	7.0%	360	$2,395.09
$ 400,000	15%	$	60,000	$ 340,000	7.0%	360	$2,262.03
$ 400,000	20%	$	80,000	$ 320,000	7.0%	360	$2,128.97
$ 400,000	5%	$	20,000	$ 380,000	8.0%	360	$2,788.31
$ 400,000	10%	$	40,000	$ 360,000	8.0%	360	$2,641.55
$ 400,000	15%	$	60,000	$ 340,000	8.0%	360	$2,494.80
$ 400,000	20%	$	80,000	$ 320,000	8.0%	360	$2,348.05

As you begin the search for your new home, consider the monthly payment amounts in the chart to help you decide how much of a down payment you need. If you are interested in meeting to further discuss mortgage loans, please give me a call at 402-555-7600. I look forward to helping you achieve your dream home.

Very truly yours,

Joel Levenson
Loan Officer

XX
EL1-C5-A5-DWLtr.docx

EL1-C5-A5-DWLtr(Step16).docx

$ 400,000	5%	$	20,000	$ 380,000	7.0%	360	$2,528.15
$ 400,000	10%	$	40,000	$ 360,000	7.0%	360	$2,395.09
$ 400,000	15%	$	60,000	$ 340,000	7.0%	360	$2,262.03
$ 400,000	20%	$	80,000	$ 320,000	7.0%	360	$2,128.97
$ 400,000	5%	$	20,000	$ 380,000	8.0%	360	$2,788.31
$ 400,000	10%	$	40,000	$ 360,000	8.0%	360	$2,641.55
$ 400,000	15%	$	60,000	$ 340,000	8.0%	360	$2,494.80
$ 400,000	20%	$	80,000	$ 320,000	8.0%	360	$2,348.05

EL1-C5-A5-DWMortgages(Step13).xlsx

Clearline Manufacturing

SEMIANNUAL SALES - 2012

Customer	1st Half	2nd Half	Total
Lakeside Trucking	$ 84,300	$ 73,500	$ 157,800
Gresham Machines	33,000	40,500	73,500
Real Photography	20,750	15,790	36,540
Genesis Productions	51,270	68,195	119,465
Landower Company	22,000	15,000	37,000
Jewell Enterprises	14,470	33,770	48,240

Clearline Manufacturing

SEMIANNUAL SALES - 2011

Customer	1st Half	2nd Half	Total
Lakeside Trucking	$ 84,300	$ 73,500	$ 157,800
Gresham Machines	33,000	40,500	73,500
Real Photography	30,890	35,465	66,355
Genesis Productions	72,190	75,390	147,580
Landower Company	22,000	15,000	37,000
Jewell Enterprises	19,764	50,801	70,565

DEERING INDUSTRIES

SECOND QUARTER SALES ANALYSIS

Customer	April	May	June	Average
Lakeside Trucking	$ 92,450	$ 78,500	$ 71,250	$ 80,733
Gresham Machines	41,200	33,000	40,500	38,233
Real Photography	19,750	15,780	18,325	17,952
Genesis Productions	63,900	54,210	49,960	56,023
Landower Company	17,550	14,230	15,700	15,827
Jewell Enterprises	44,770	38,650	28,570	37,330
Total	$ 279,620	$ 234,370	$ 224,305	$ 246,098

Student Name

Page 2

7/31/2012

EL1-C6-A2-DISales.xlsx (2 of 4)

DEERING INDUSTRIES

FIRST QUARTER SALES ANALYSIS

Customer	January	February	March	Average
Lakeside Trucking	$ 78,450	$ 81,340	$ 75,224	$ 78,338
Gresham Machines	39,210	29,340	51,250	39,933
Real Photography	25,200	32,575	29,725	29,167
Genesis Productions	70,200	59,900	61,350	63,817
Landower Company	15,120	17,300	29,500	20,640
Jewell Enterprises	50,320	29,875	35,400	38,532
Total	$ 278,500	$ 250,330	$ 282,449	$ 270,426

Student Name

Page 1

7/31/2012

EL1-C6-A2-DISales.xlsx (1 of 4)

DEERING INDUSTRIES

FOURTH QUARTER SALES ANALYSIS

Customer	October	November	December	Average
Lakeside Trucking	$ 87,470	$ 73,405	$ 68,590	$ 76,488
Gresham Machines	41,300	34,500	42,300	39,367
Real Photography	19,450	21,700	20,525	20,558
Genesis Productions	70,200	52,500	48,750	57,150
Landower Company	10,500	12,525	14,525	12,517
Jewell Enterprises	33,500	42,100	35,400	37,000
Total	$ 262,420	$ 236,730	$ 230,090	$ 243,080

EL1-C6-A2-DISales.xlsx (4 of 4)

DEERING INDUSTRIES

THIRD QUARTER SALES ANALYSIS

Customer	July	August	September	Average
Lakeside Trucking	$ 50,400	$ 62,000	$ 48,650	$ 53,683
Gresham Machines	33,220	40,500	42,190	38,637
Real Photography	19,700	22,500	23,175	21,792
Genesis Productions	63,100	58,790	48,660	56,850
Landower Company	12,500	15,500	13,670	13,890
Jewell Enterprises	40,700	37,670	30,250	36,207
Total	$ 219,620	$ 236,960	$ 206,595	$ 221,058

EL1-C6-A2-DISales.xlsx (3 of 4)

ARMIN ASSOCIATES

Projected Annual Earnings

Projected Yearly Income $ 1,345,800

Month	Percentage	Earnings
January	8.80%	$ 118,430.40
February	8.30%	111,701.40
March	9.10%	122,467.80
April	8.50%	114,393.00
May	8.60%	115,738.80
June	7.40%	99,589.20
July	6.90%	92,860.20
August	7.80%	104,972.40
September	8.60%	115,738.80
October	9.10%	122,467.80
November	8.50%	114,393.00
December	8.40%	113,047.20

EL1-C6-A3-ProjEarnings(Step13).xlsx

ARMIN ASSOCIATES

Projected Annual Earnings

Projected Yearly Income $ 1,345,800

Month	Percentage	Earnings
January	8.80%	$ 118,430.40
February	8.30%	111,701.40
March	9.10%	122,467.80
April	8.50%	114,393.00
May	8.60%	115,738.80
June	7.40%	99,589.20
July	6.90%	92,860.20
August	7.80%	104,972.40
September	8.60%	115,738.80
October	9.10%	122,467.80
November	8.50%	114,393.00
December	8.40%	113,047.20

EL1-C6-A3-ProjEarnings(Step11).xlsx

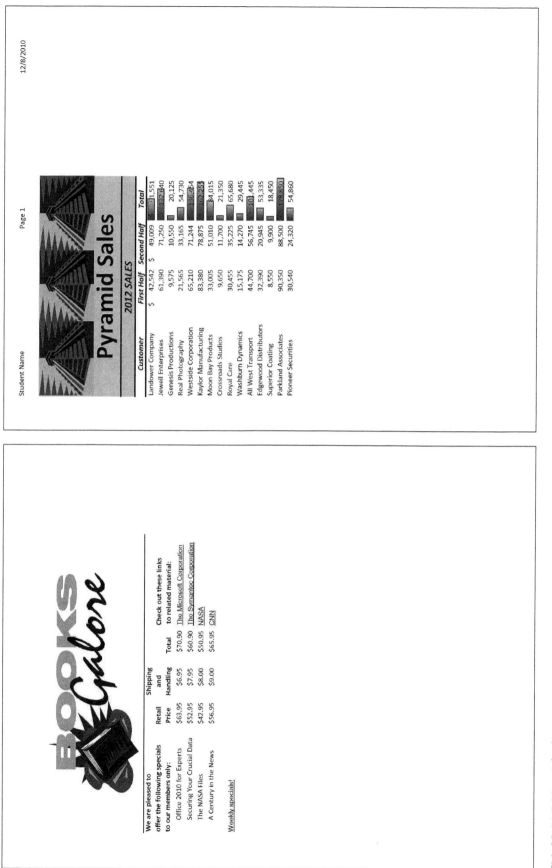

Pyramid Sales

Customer	2012 SALES		
	First Half	Second Half	Total
Landower Company	$ 42,542	$ 49,009	91,551
Jewell Enterprises	61,390	71,250	132,640
Genesis Productions	9,575	10,550	20,125
Real Photography	21,565	33,165	54,730
Westside Corporation	65,210	71,244	136,454
Kaylor Manufacturing	83,380	78,875	162,255
Moon Bay Products	33,005	51,010	84,015
Crossroads Studios	9,650	11,700	21,350
Royal Care	30,455	35,225	65,680
Washburn Dynamics	15,175	14,270	29,445
All West Transport	44,700	56,745	101,445
Edgewood Distributors	32,390	20,945	53,335
Superior Coating	8,550	9,900	18,450
Parkland Associates	90,350	88,500	178,850
Pioneer Securities	30,540	24,320	54,860

EL1-C6-A5-PSSales.xlsx

BOOKS Galore

We are pleased to offer the following specials to our members only:	Retail Price	Shipping and Handling	Total	Check out these links to related material:
Office 2010 for Experts	$63.95	$6.95	$70.90	The Microsoft Corporation
Securing Your Crucial Data	$52.95	$7.95	$60.90	The Symantec Corporation
The NASA Files	$42.95	$8.00	$50.95	NASA
A Century in the News	$56.95	$9.00	$65.95	CNN

Weekly specials!

EL1-C6-A4-BGSpecials.xlsx

O'Rourke Enterprises

For Office Use Only

Expense Report

PURPOSE: Advertising Media Conference

STATEMENT NUMBER: 2301

PAY PERIOD: From 10/16/2012 To 10/31/2012

EMPLOYEE INFORMATION:

Name Sophia Constanza   Position Manager   SSN N/A

Department Advertising   Manager Seth Morgenstern   Employee ID 34237

Date	Account	Description	Hotel	Transport	Fuel	Meals	Phone	Entertainment	Misc	Total
22-Oct-12	Advertising	Travel to conference	$ 210.00	$ 358.00		$ 38.75				$ 606.75
23-Oct-12	Advertising	Conference/dinner with client	$ 210.00			$ 53.29		$ 78.50		$ 341.79
24-Oct-12	Advertising	Conference	$ 210.00			$ 68.65				$ 278.65
25-Oct-12	Advertising	Conference	$ 210.00			$ 52.60				$ 262.60
26-Oct-12	Advertising	Conference				$ 40.55				$ 40.55
Total			$ 840.00	$ 358.00	$ -	$ 253.84	$ -	$ 78.50	$ -	$ 1,530.34

Subtotal $ 1,530.34
Cash Advances $ 500.00
Total $ 1,030.34

APPROVED: Approved by Seth Morgenstern on 10/31/2012

NOTES: Cash advance issued 10/19/2012

Page 1 of 1

EL1-C6-VB-OEExpRpt.xlsx

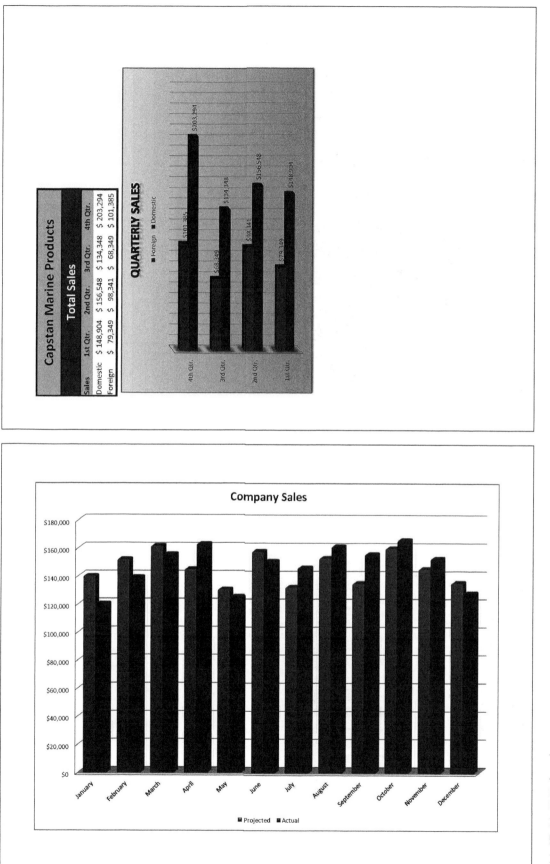

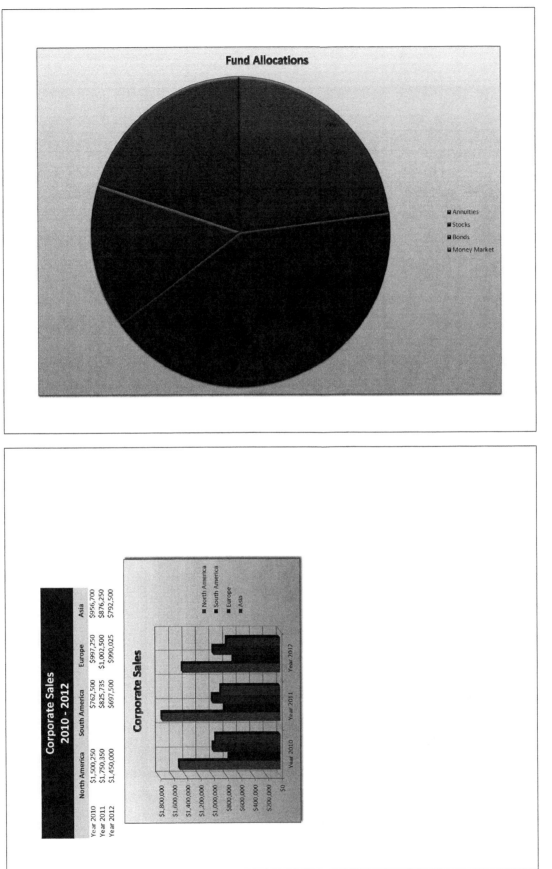

Benchmark Excel 2010 Level 1 Model Answers

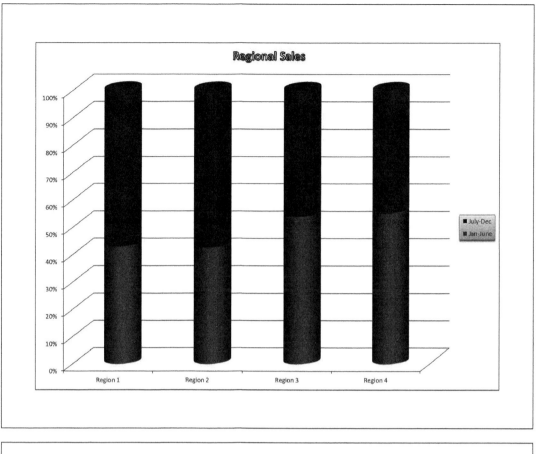

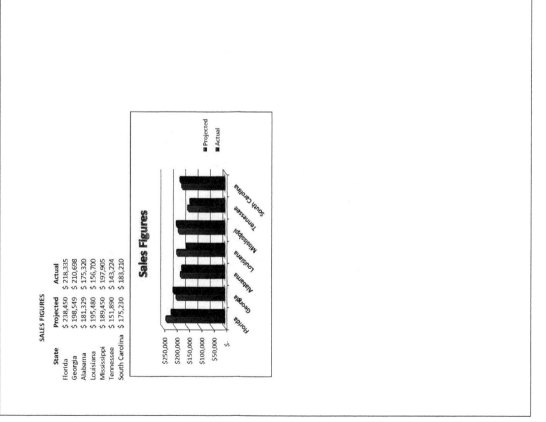

SALES FIGURES		
State	Projected	Actual
Florida	$ 238,450	$ 218,335
Georgia	$ 198,549	$ 210,698
Alabama	$ 181,329	$ 175,320
Louisiana	$ 195,480	$ 156,700
Mississippi	$ 189,450	$ 197,905
Tennessee	$ 151,890	$ 143,224
South Carolina	$ 175,230	$ 183,210

Clearline Manufacturing
February Expense Percentages

Expense	Percentage
Wages and salaries	55.72%
Lease payment	13.14%
Payroll taxes	9.14%
Utilities	4.27%
Supplies	2.06%
Advertising	6.03%
Direct marketing	9.64%

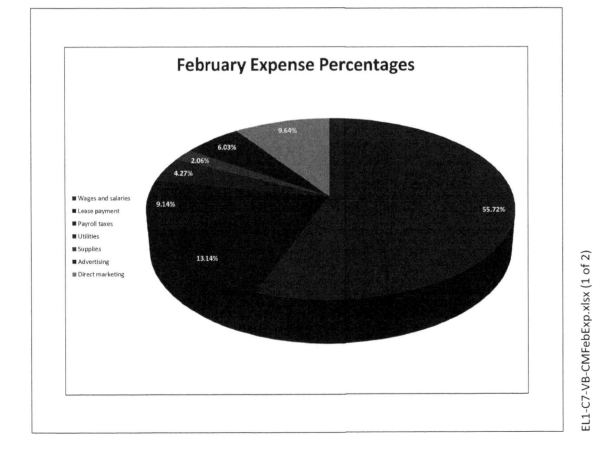

Travel Services

"Great Escape" Vacations

Seven-day Vacation Package	Price per Person*	Group of 4+ 10% discount	Group of 8+ 20% discount
Aspen, Colorado	$ 650	$ 585	$ 520
Orlando, Florida	895	806	716
New York, New York	950	855	760
Los Angeles, California	745	671	596
Honolulu, Hawaii	1,025	923	820

*Prices based on double occupancy and do not include airfare. Taxes extra.
A surcharge will apply for single occupancy.

Airfare from Portland, Oregon, as of today, June 2, 2010:

Portland to Aspen, Colorado: $239
Portland to Orlando, Florida: $445
Portland to New York, New York: $519
Portland to Los Angeles, California: $215
Portland to Honolulu, Hawaii: $575

AZURE STUDIOS

Equipment Purchase Plans

Equipment	Purchase Price	Interest Rate	Term in Months	Monthly Payments	Total Payments	Total Interest
Photocopier, Model C120	$8,500.00	8.80%	60	$175.62	$10,537.33	$2,037.33
Photocopier, Model C150	$12,750.00	8.80%	60	$263.43	$15,805.99	$3,055.99
Photocopier, Model C280	$19,250.00	8.80%	60	$397.73	$23,863.94	$4,613.94

Pyramid Sales

Second Quarter Sales - 2012

Customer	April	May	June	Total
Landower Company	$ 22,542	$ 26,505	$ 19,560	$ 68,607
Jewell Enterprises	$ 32,397	$ 41,265	$ 48,975	$ 122,637
Genesis Productions	$ 24,570	$ 18,900	$ 21,350	$ 64,820
Real Photography	$ 10,563	$ 22,168	$ 15,653	$ 48,384
Westside Corporation	$ 44,214	$ 31,238	$ 19,086	$ 94,538
Kaylor Manufacturing	$ 54,388	$ 49,876	$ 55,437	$ 159,701
Moon Bay Products	$ 19,203	$ 23,310	$ 8,349	$ 50,862
Crossroads Studios	$ 6,230	$ 5,250	$ 7,500	$ 18,980
Royal Care	$ 19,650	$ 32,825	$ 28,900	$ 81,375
Washburn Dynamics	$ 19,560	$ 25,675	$ 38,600	$ 83,835
All West Transport	$ 11,255	$ 9,670	$ 11,760	$ 32,685
Edgewood Distributors	$ 25,400	$ 29,575	$ 23,450	$ 78,425
Superior Coating	$ 6,230	$ 3,525	$ -	$ 9,755
Parkland Associates	$ 3,203	$ 1,500	$ -	$ 4,703
Pioneer Securities	$ 45,750	$ 38,560	$ 22,100	$ 106,410

Gold Level
$100,000+

Blue Level
$50,000 to $99,999

Mountain Systems

FIRST QUARTER SALES - 2012

Customer	January	February	March
Lakeside Trucking	$ 84,231	$ 73,455	$ 97,549
Gresham Machines	33,199	40,390	50,112
Real Photography	30,891	35,489	36,400
Genesis Productions	72,190	75,390	83,219
Landower Company	22,188	14,228	38,766
Jewell Enterprises	19,764	50,801	32,188
Total	$ 262,463	$ 289,753	$ 338,234

Largest Order

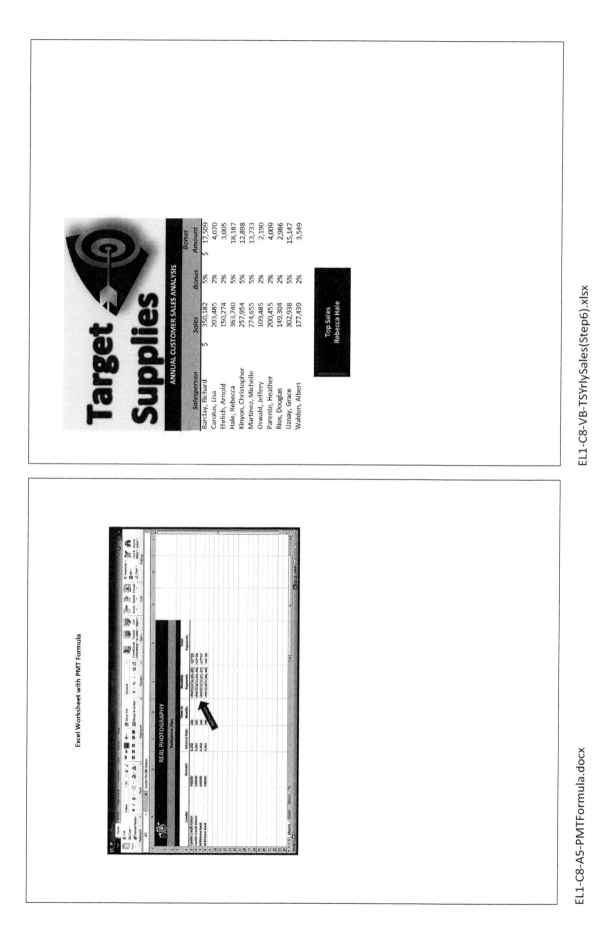

Excel Worksheet with PMT Formula

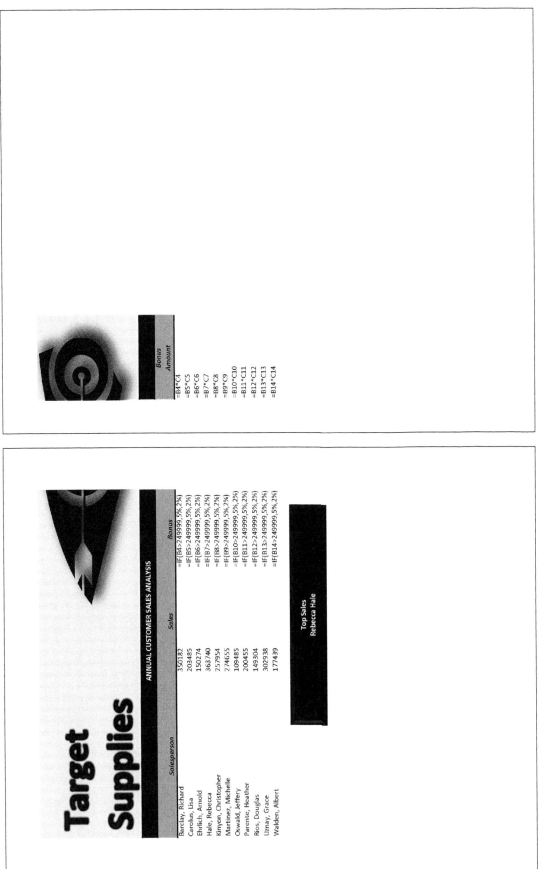

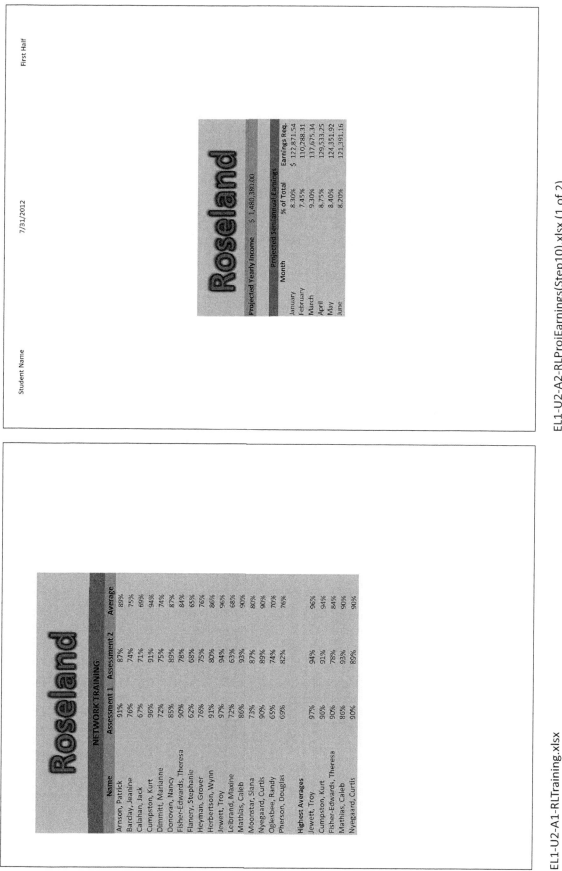

Benchmark Excel 2010 Level 1 Model Answers

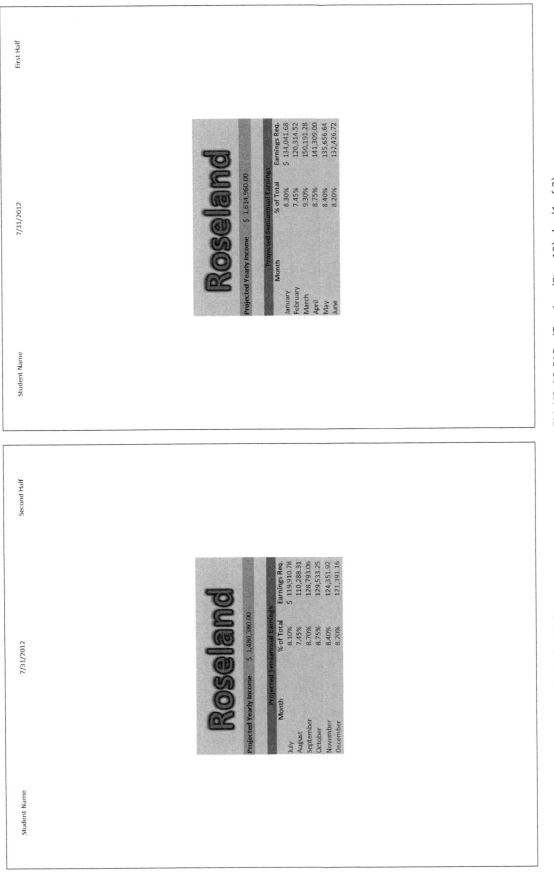

EL1-U2-A2-RLProjEarnings(Step12).xlsx (1 of 2)

EL1-U2-A2-RLProjEarnings(Step10).xlsx (2 of 2)

Benchmark Excel 2010 Level 1 Model Answers

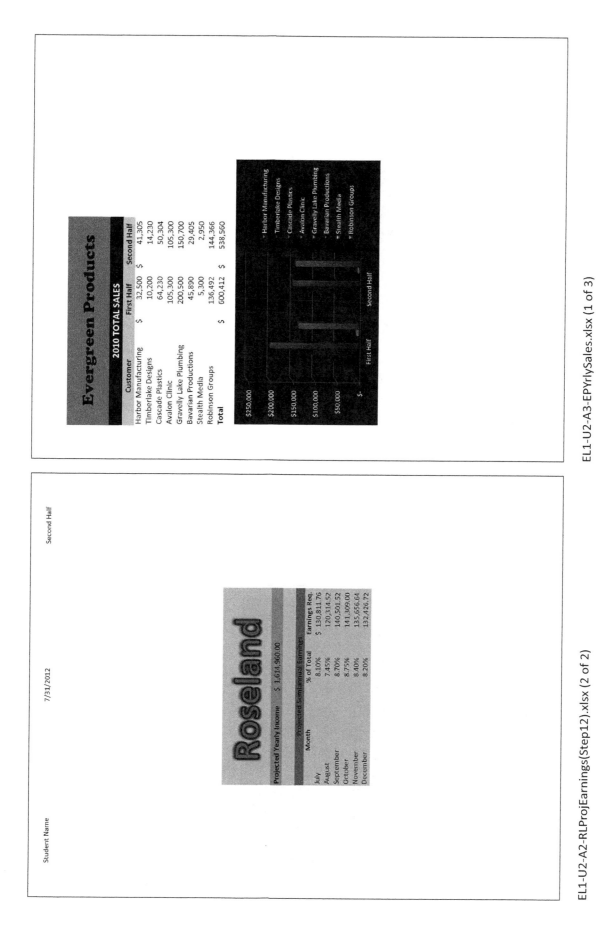

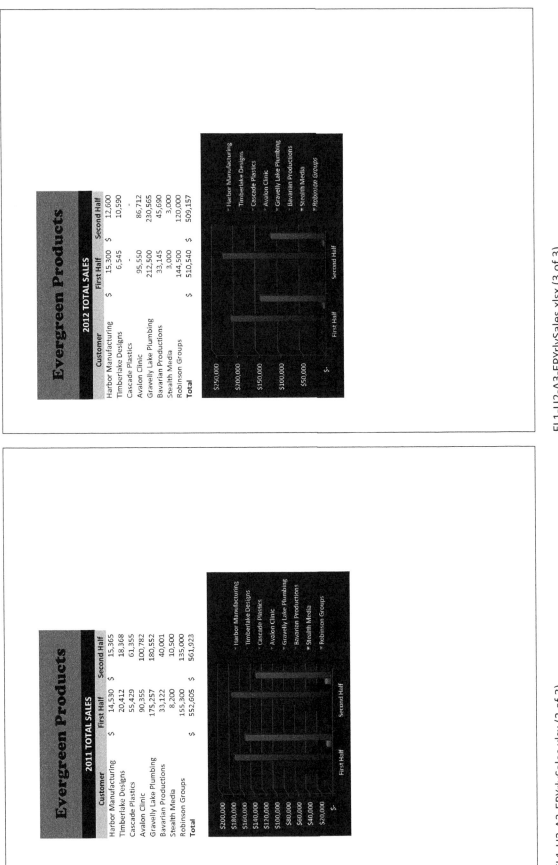

Evergreen Products

2011 TOTAL SALES		
Customer	**First Half**	**Second Half**
Harbor Manufacturing	$ 14,530	$ 15,365
Timberlake Designs	20,412	18,368
Cascade Plastics	55,429	61,355
Avalon Clinic	90,355	100,782
Gravelly Lake Plumbing	175,257	180,552
Bavarian Productions	33,122	40,001
Stealth Media	8,200	10,500
Robinson Groups	155,300	135,000
Total	$ 552,605	$ 561,923

Evergreen Products

2012 TOTAL SALES		
Customer	**First Half**	**Second Half**
Harbor Manufacturing	$ 15,300	$ 12,600
Timberlake Designs	6,545	10,590
Cascade Plastics		-
Avalon Clinic	95,550	86,712
Gravelly Lake Plumbing	212,500	230,565
Bavarian Productions	33,145	45,690
Stealth Media	3,000	3,000
Robinson Groups	144,500	120,000
Total	$ 510,540	$ 509,157

EL1-U2-A3-EPYrlySales.xlsx (3 of 3)

EL1-U2-A3-EPYrlySales.xlsx (2 of 3)

Benchmark Excel 2010 Level 1 Model Answers

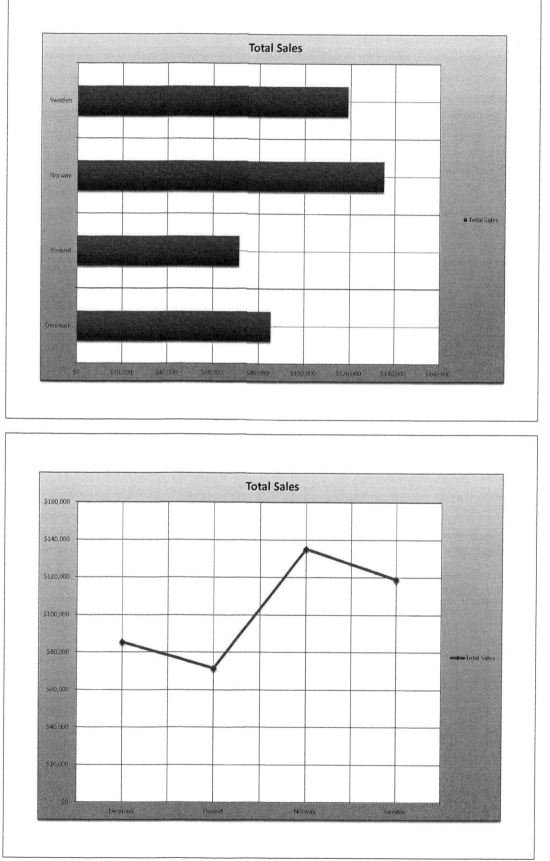

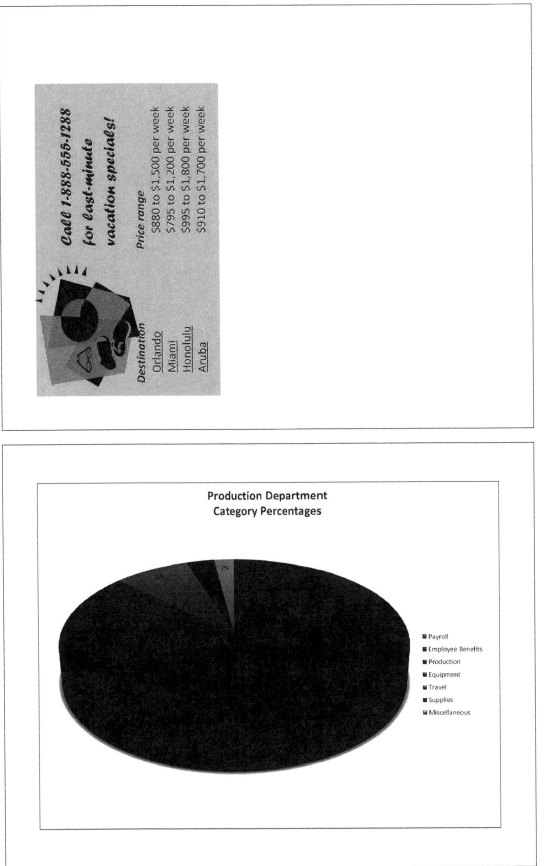

Production Department
Category Percentages

- Payroll
- Employee Benefits
- Production
- Equipment
- Travel
- Supplies
- Miscellaneous

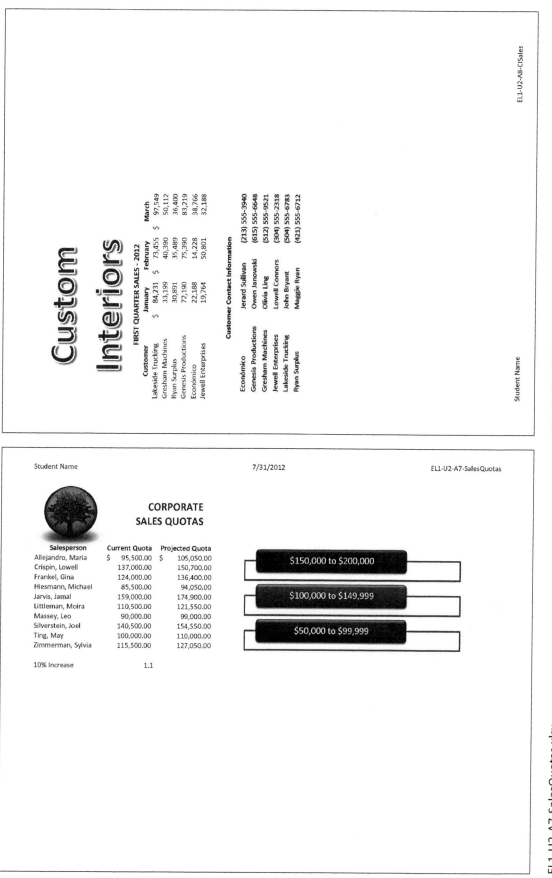

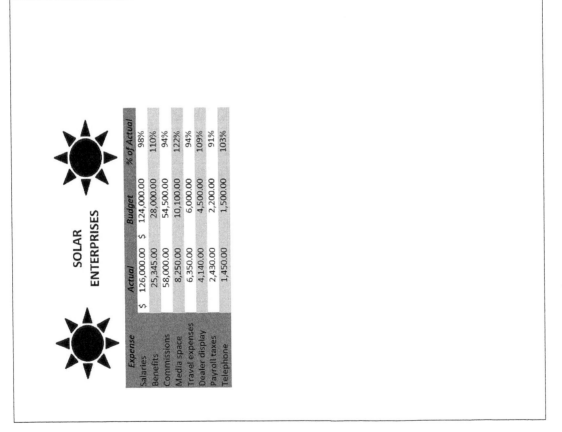

SOLAR ENTERPRISES

Expense	Actual	Budget	% of Actual
Salaries	$ 126,000.00	$ 124,000.00	98%
Benefits	25,345.00	28,000.00	110%
Commissions	58,000.00	54,500.00	94%
Media space	8,250.00	10,100.00	122%
Travel expenses	6,350.00	6,000.00	94%
Dealer display	4,140.00	4,500.00	109%
Payroll taxes	2,430.00	2,200.00	91%
Telephone	1,450.00	1,500.00	103%

EL1-U2-A9-SEExpenses.xlsx

RSR Computer Services
Service Division Report

Date	Work Order Number	Hours Billed	Rate Code	Extended Labor	Parts	Total Invoice
9/4/2012	RSR-65012	2 1/4 hrs	1	56.25	22.50	78.75
9/6/2012	RSR-65013	3 1/4 hrs	2	97.50	75.85	173.35
9/10/2012	RSR-65014	2 1/4 hrs	1	56.25	28.95	85.20
9/12/2012	RSR-65015	1 3/4 hrs	1	43.75	-	43.75
9/13/2012	RSR-65016	1 2/4 hrs	1	37.50	25.75	63.25
9/16/2012	RSR-65017	2 1/4 hrs	3	84.38	45.15	129.53
9/16/2012	RSR-65018	4 1/4 hrs	3	159.38	55.85	215.23
9/17/2012	RSR-65019	3 3/4 hrs	1	93.75	22.50	116.25
9/17/2012	RSR-65020	1 3/4 hrs	2	52.50	-	52.50
9/19/2012	RSR-65021	2 hrs	1	50.00	-	50.00
9/20/2012	RSR-65022	1 2/4 hrs	3	56.25	18.50	74.75
9/22/2012	RSR-65023	2 1/4 hrs	1	56.25	75.85	132.10
9/25/2012	RSR-65024	3 1/4 hrs	1	81.25	112.50	193.75
9/26/2012	RSR-65025	3 2/4 hrs	1	87.50	187.50	275.00
9/27/2012	RSR-65026	2 3/4 hrs	2	82.50	110.50	193.00
9/28/2012	RSR-65027	3 2/4 hrs	2	105.00	35.95	140.95
9/30/2012	RSR-65028	4 2/4 hrs	3	168.75	47.66	216.41
TOTAL SERVICE HOURS BILLED:		46 1/4 hrs		1,368.75	865.01	2,233.76

Rate Code Chart

Description	Code	Rate
Regular	1	$ 25.00
Evening	2	$ 30.00
Weekend	3	$ 37.50

RSR Computer Services
Service Division Report

Date	Work Order Number	Hours Billed	Rate Code	Extended Labor	Parts	Total Invoice
9/4/2012	65012	2 1/4	1	56.25	22.50	78.75
9/6/2012	65013	3 1/4	2	97.50	75.85	173.35
9/10/2012	65014	2 1/4	1	56.25	28.95	85.20
9/12/2012	65015	1 3/4	1	43.75	-	43.75
9/13/2012	65016	1 2/4	1	37.50	25.75	63.25
9/16/2012	65017	2 1/4	3	84.38	45.15	129.53
9/16/2012	65018	4 1/4	3	159.38	55.85	215.23
9/17/2012	65019	3 3/4	1	93.75	22.50	116.25
9/17/2012	65020	1 3/4	2	52.50	-	52.50
9/19/2012	65021	2	1	50.00	-	50.00
9/20/2012	65022	1 2/4	3	56.25	18.50	74.75
9/22/2012	65023	2 1/4	1	56.25	75.85	132.10
9/25/2012	65024	3 1/4	1	81.25	112.50	193.75
9/26/2012	65025	3 2/4	1	87.50	187.50	275.00
9/27/2012	65026	2 3/4	2	82.50	110.50	193.00
9/28/2012	65027	3 2/4	2	105.00	35.95	140.95
9/30/2012	65028	4 2/4	3	168.75	47.66	216.41
TOTAL SERVICE HOURS BILLED:		46 1/4		1,368.75	865.01	2,233.76

Rate Code Chart

Description	Code	Rate
Regular	1	$ 25.00
Evening	2	$ 30.00
Weekend	3	$ 37.50

RSR Computer Services
Service Division Report

Date	Work Order Number	Hours Billed	Rate Code	Extended Labor	Parts	Total Invoice
9/12/2012	RSR-65015	1 3/4 hrs	1	43.75	.	43.75
9/17/2012	RSR-65020	1 3/4 hrs	2	52.50		52.50
9/19/2012	RSR-65021	2 hrs	1	50.00		50.00

Rate Code Chart		
Weekend	3	$ 37.50

EL2-C1-A3-RSRServRpt(Step4e).xlsx

RSR Computer Services
Service Division Report

Date	Work Order Number	Hours Billed	Rate Code	Extended Labor	Parts	Total Invoice
9/4/2012	RSR-65012	2 1/4 hrs	1	56.25	22.50	78.75
9/6/2012	RSR-65013	3 1/4 hrs	2	97.50	75.85	173.35
9/10/2012	RSR-65014	2 1/4 hrs	1	56.25	28.95	85.20
9/12/2012	RSR-65015	1 3/4 hrs	1	43.75	.	43.75
9/16/2012	RSR-65017	2 1/4 hrs	3	84.38	45.15	129.53
9/17/2012	RSR-65019	3 3/4 hrs	1	93.75	22.50	116.25
9/17/2012	RSR-65020	1 3/4 hrs	2	52.50	.	52.50
9/19/2012	RSR-65021	2 hrs	1	50.00		50.00
9/22/2012	RSR-65023	2 1/4 hrs	1	56.25	75.85	132.10
9/25/2012	RSR-65024	3 1/4 hrs	1	81.25	112.50	193.75
9/26/2012	RSR-65025	3 2/4 hrs	1	87.50	187.50	275.00
9/27/2012	RSR-65026	2 3/4 hrs	2	82.50	110.50	193.00
9/28/2012	RSR-65027	3 2/4 hrs	2	105.00	35.95	140.95

Rate Code Chart		
Description	Code	Rate
Regular	1	$ 25.00
Evening	2	$ 30.00
Weekend	3	$ 37.50

EL2-C1-A3-RSRServRpt(Step4b).xlsx

138   *Benchmark Excel 2010 Level 2* Model Answers

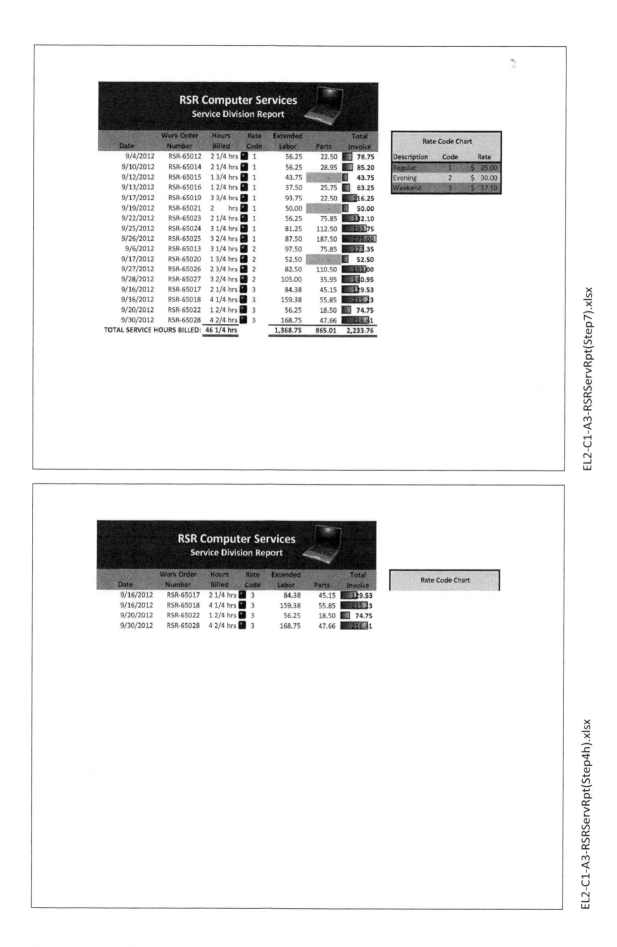

RSR Computer Services
Service Division Report

Date	Work Order Number	Hours Billed	Rate Code	Extended Labor	Parts	Total Invoice
9/4/2012	RSR-65012	2 1/4 hrs	1	56.25	22.50	78.75
9/10/2012	RSR-65014	2 1/4 hrs	1	56.25	28.95	85.20
9/12/2012	RSR-65015	1 3/4 hrs	1	43.75	-	43.75
9/13/2012	RSR-65016	1 2/4 hrs	1	37.50	25.75	63.25
9/17/2012	RSR-65019	3 3/4 hrs	1	93.75	22.50	116.25
9/19/2012	RSR-65021	2 hrs	1	50.00	-	50.00
9/22/2012	RSR-65023	2 1/4 hrs	1	56.25	75.85	132.10
9/25/2012	RSR-65024	3 1/4 hrs	1	81.25	112.50	193.75
9/26/2012	RSR-65025	3 2/4 hrs	1	87.50	187.50	275.00
9/6/2012	RSR-65013	3 1/4 hrs	2	97.50	75.85	173.35
9/17/2012	RSR-65020	1 3/4 hrs	2	52.50	-	52.50
9/27/2012	RSR-65026	2 3/4 hrs	2	82.50	110.50	193.00
9/28/2012	RSR-65027	3 2/4 hrs	2	105.00	35.95	140.95
9/16/2012	RSR-65017	2 1/4 hrs	3	84.38	45.15	129.53
9/16/2012	RSR-65018	4 1/4 hrs	3	159.38	55.85	215.23
9/20/2012	RSR-65022	1 2/4 hrs	3	56.25	18.50	74.75
9/30/2012	RSR-65028	4 2/4 hrs	3	168.75	47.66	216.41
TOTAL SERVICE HOURS BILLED:		46 1/4 hrs		1,368.75	865.01	2,233.76

Rate Code Chart

Description	Code	Rate
Regular	1	$ 25.00
Evening	2	$ 30.00
Weekend	3	$ 37.50

EL2-C1-A3-RSRServRpt(Step7).xlsx

RSR Computer Services
Service Division Report

Date	Work Order Number	Hours Billed	Rate Code	Extended Labor	Parts	Total Invoice
9/16/2012	RSR-65017	2 1/4 hrs	3	84.38	45.15	129.53
9/16/2012	RSR-65018	4 1/4 hrs	3	159.38	55.85	215.23
9/20/2012	RSR-65022	1 2/4 hrs	3	56.25	18.50	74.75
9/30/2012	RSR-65028	4 2/4 hrs	3	168.75	47.66	216.41

Rate Code Chart

EL2-C1-A3-RSRServRpt(Step4h).xlsx

Vantage Video Rentals
Payroll
Week Ended: October 27, 2012

First Name	Last Name	Sun	Mon	Tue	Wed	Thu	Fri	Sat	Total Hours	Overtime Hours	Pay Rate	Gross Pay
Alexis	Torres	-	5.0	7.0	8.0	8.0	9.0	9.5	46.5	6.5	7.75	**385.56**
Derrick	MacLean	8.0	-	6.5	8.0	8.0	8.5	9.0	48.0	8.0	7.35	**382.20**
Priya	Singh	8.0	-	4.0	8.0	8.0	8.5	6.5	43.0	3.0	7.35	**327.08**
Emil	Fedorov	8.0	8.0	8.0	5.5	8.0	-	8.0	45.5	5.5	7.75	**373.94**
Leslie	Sparling	-	6.0	7.5	8.0	8.0	-	8.0	37.5	-		305.63
Irene	O'Rourke	4.0	-	8.0	-	6.5	9.5	7.5	35.5	-		289.33
Ruthann	Goldstein	5.5	-	8.0	-	4.0	7.5	6.0	31.0	-	7.75	240.25
Stefan	Kominek	-	6.0	8.0	-	8.0	8.5	4.5	35.0	-	7.75	271.25
Alex	Spivak	-	5.0	8.0	8.5	7.5	8.0	8.0	45.0	5.0	7.75	**368.13**
Erica	Wilkins	-	7.0	-	6.0	-	6.0	6.4	25.4	-	7.35	186.69
Dana	Vanderhoek	8.0	7.0	-	8.0	-	5.5	5.0	33.5	-	7.35	246.23
Ashley	Castillo	4.0	8.0	-	7.5	8.0	4.0	8.5	40.0	-		326.00
Susan	Anez	-	3.0	5.5	-	-	7.0	7.0	22.5	-		183.38
Dana	Ivanowski	4.5	4.0	6.0	-	8.5	6.8	-	29.8	-	7.75	230.95
Maria	Alvarez	-	7.0	4.5	-	7.5	7.5	-	26.5	-	7.35	194.78
Xue	Chen	9.0	-	9.0	8.0	7.5	8.0	-	41.5	1.5	7.35	**310.54**
Annette	Fournier	8.0	-	-	6.5	5.0	7.5	7.0	34.0	-	7.35	249.90
Randy	Brown	6.5	-	-	5.5	4.0	6.0	4.0	26.0	-	7.35	191.10
TOTAL		73.5	66.0	90.0	87.5	106.5	117.8	104.9	646.2	29.5		5,062.90

Vantage Video Rentals
Payroll
Week Ended: October 27, 2012

First Name	Last Name	Sun	Mon	Tue	Wed	Thu	Fri	Sat	Total Hours	Overtime Hours	Pay Rate	Gross Pay
Alexis	Torres	-	5.0	7.0	8.0	8.0	9.0	9.5	46.5	6.5	7.75	**385.56**
Derrick	MacLean	8.0	-	6.5	8.0	8.0	8.5	9.0	48.0	8.0	7.35	**382.20**
Priya	Singh	8.0	-	4.0	8.0	8.0	8.5	6.5	43.0	3.0	7.35	**327.08**
Emil	Fedorov	8.0	8.0	8.0	5.5	8.0	-	8.0	45.5	5.5	7.75	**373.94**
Leslie	Sparling	-	6.0	7.5	8.0	8.0	-	8.0	37.5	-	8.15	305.63
Irene	O'Rourke	4.0	-	8.0	-	6.5	9.5	7.5	35.5	-	8.15	289.33
Ruthann	Goldstein	5.5	-	8.0	-	4.0	7.5	6.0	31.0	-	7.75	240.25
Stefan	Kominek	-	6.0	8.0	-	8.0	8.5	4.5	35.0	-	7.75	271.25
Alex	Spivak	-	5.0	8.0	8.5	7.5	8.0	8.0	45.0	5.0	7.75	**368.13**
Erica	Wilkins	-	7.0	-	6.0	-	6.0	6.4	25.4	-	7.35	186.69
Dana	Vanderhoek	8.0	7.0	-	8.0	-	5.5	5.0	33.5	-	7.35	246.23
Ashley	Castillo	4.0	8.0	-	7.5	8.0	4.0	8.5	40.0	-	8.15	326.00
Susan	Anez	-	3.0	5.5	-	-	7.0	7.0	22.5	-	8.15	183.38
Dana	Ivanowski	4.5	4.0	6.0	-	8.5	6.8	-	29.8	-	7.75	230.95
Maria	Alvarez	-	7.0	4.5	-	7.5	7.5	-	26.5	-	7.35	194.78
Xue	Chen	9.0	-	9.0	8.0	7.5	8.0	-	41.5	1.5	7.35	**310.54**
Annette	Fournier	8.0	-	-	6.5	5.0	7.5	7.0	34.0	-	7.35	249.90
Randy	Brown	6.5	-	-	5.5	4.0	6.0	4.0	26.0	-	7.35	191.10
TOTAL		73.5	66.0	90.0	87.5	106.5	117.8	104.9	646.2	29.5		5,062.90

Benchmark Excel 2010 Level 2 Model Answers

O'DONOVAN & SULLIVAN LAW ASSOCIATES
BILLING SUMMARY
OCTOBER 8 TO 12, 2012

File	Client	Date	Billing Code	Attorney Code	Legal Fees	Disbursements	Total Due		Billing Code Table	
EP-652	10106	10/8/2012	Amicus#-3	1	1,028.50	23.75	1,052.25	Code	Area of Practice	
EL-632	10225	10/9/2012	Amicus#-5	3	1,211.00	37.85	1,248.85	1	Corporate	
CL-501	10341	10/10/2012	Amicus#-1	2	1,143.75	55.24	1,198.99	2	Divorce & Separation	
IN-745	10210	10/11/2012	Amicus#-6	3	1,450.00	24.25	1,474.25	3	Wills & Estates	
CL-412	10125	10/12/2012	Amicus#-1	2	1,143.75	38.12	1,181.87	4	Real Estate	
IN-801	10346	10/12/2012	Amicus#-6	3	1,425.00	62.18	1,487.18	5	Employment Litigation	
RE-501	10384	10/12/2012	Amicus#-4	4	1,237.50	34.28	1,271.78	6	Insurance Personal Injury	
FL-325	10104	10/8/2012	Amicus#-2	1	1,273.75	95.10	2,368.85	7	Other	
CL-412	10125	10/8/2012	Amicus#-1	2	2,493.75	55.40	2,549.15			
IN-745	10210	10/9/2012	Amicus#-3	3	2,425.00	65.20	2,490.20		Attorney Code Table	
RE-475	10285	10/9/2012	Amicus#-4	4	3,807.00	48.96	3,855.96	Code	Attorney	
CL-521	10334	10/10/2012	Amicus#-1	2	1,518.75	27.85	1,546.60	1	Marty O'Donovan	
PL-348	10420	10/10/2012	Amicus#-7	3	2,500.00	34.95	2,534.95	2	Toni Sullivan	
RE-492	10425	10/10/2012	Amicus#-4	4	2,043.00	38.75	2,081.75	3	Rosa Martinez	
EL-632	10225	10/11/2012	Amicus#-5	3	2,300.00	42.15	2,342.15	4	Kyle Williams	
PL-512	10290	10/11/2012	Amicus#-7	3	1,620.00	65.15	1,685.15			
FL-385	10278	10/11/2012	Amicus#-2	1	2,040.00	85.47	2,125.47			
CL-450	10358	10/12/2012	Amicus#-1	2	1,762.50	55.24	1,817.74			
EP-685	10495	10/12/2012	Amicus#-3	3	2,375.00	94.55	2,469.55			

EL2-C1-VB-BillingsOct8to12.xlsx

RSR Computer Services
Labor Cost Report
In-Home Computer Service Billings

Date	Work Order Number	Hours Logged	Technician Code	Hourly Rate	WO Labor Cost
10/1/2012	IH-90010	2.25	1	12.50	28.13
10/3/2012	IH-90011	3.75	3	18.75	70.31
10/5/2012	IH-90012	1.50	1	12.50	18.75
10/8/2012	IH-90013	2.75	1	12.50	34.38
10/8/2012	IH-90014	3.00	3	18.75	56.25
10/9/2012	IH-90015	4.25	2	15.00	63.75
10/10/2012	IH-90016	3.75	2	15.00	56.25
10/11/2012	IH-90017	2.25	1	12.50	28.13
10/12/2012	IH-90018	1.50	2	15.00	22.50
10/18/2012	IH-90019	2.25	1	12.50	28.13
10/17/2012	IH-90020	2.75	3	18.75	51.56
10/22/2012	IH-90021	4.50	1	12.50	56.25
10/24/2012	IH-90022	5.25	1	12.50	65.63
10/26/2012	IH-90023	3.25	3	18.75	60.94
10/29/2012	IH-90024	2.75	3	18.75	51.56
10/30/2012	IH-90025	5.50	2	15.00	82.50
TOTAL LABOR COST		**51.25**			**775.00**

Hourly Rate Chart

Description	Code	Rate
Technician 1	1	$ 12.50
Technician 2	2	$ 15.00
Technician 3	3	$ 18.75

Labor Cost Statistics

By Technician Code	Calls Billed	Total Labor
Technician 1	7	259.38
Technician 2	4	225.00
Technician 3	5	290.63

Technician 3 calls over 3 hours		
Technician 3	2	131.25

By Technician Code		Average Labor
Technician 1		37.05
Technician 2		56.25
Technician 3		58.13

Calls billed in Oct.	16

RSR Computer Services
Labor Cost Report
In-Home Computer Service Billings

Date	Work Order Number	Hours Logged	Technician Code	Hourly Rate	WO Labor Cost
10/1/2012	IH-90010	2.25	1	12.50	28.13
10/3/2012	IH-90011	3.75	3	18.75	70.31
10/5/2012	IH-90012	1.50	1	12.50	18.75
10/8/2012	IH-90013	2.75	1	12.50	34.38
10/8/2012	IH-90014	3.00	3	18.75	56.25
10/9/2012	IH-90015	4.25	2	15.00	63.75
10/10/2012	IH-90016	3.75	2	15.00	56.25
10/11/2012	IH-90017	2.25	1	12.50	28.13
10/12/2012	IH-90018	1.50	2	15.00	22.50
10/18/2012	IH-90019	2.25	1	12.50	28.13
10/17/2012	IH-90020	2.75	3	18.75	51.56
10/22/2012	IH-90021	4.50	1	12.50	56.25
10/24/2012	IH-90022	5.25	1	12.50	65.63
10/26/2012	IH-90023	3.25	3	18.75	60.94
10/29/2012	IH-90024	2.75	3	18.75	51.56
10/30/2012	IH-90025	5.50	2	15.00	82.50
TOTAL LABOR COST		**51.25**			**775.00**

Hourly Rate Chart

Description	Code	Rate
Technician 1	1	$ 12.50
Technician 2	2	$ 15.00
Technician 3	3	$ 18.75

Labor Cost Statistics

By Technician Code	Calls Billed	Total Labor
Technician 1		
Technician 2		
Technician 3		

Technician 3 calls over 3 hours	
Technician 3	

By Technician Code		Average Labor
Technician 1		
Technician 2		
Technician 3		

Calls billed in Oct.

AllClaims Insurance Brokers
Insurance Policy Premium Review

Policy ID	Number of Claims	At Fault Claims	Current Rating	Deductible	Claims Cost Estimate	Increase Premium?	Increase Deductible?
6388569	3	1	2	500.00	16,300.00	No	Yes
4236512	2	1	2	750.00	6,524.00	No	Yes
6974583	1	0	3	1,000.00	10,500.00	No	No
2563845	0	0	4	1,000.00	-	No	No
2215473	0	0	2	250.00	-	No	Yes
6952384	2	1	4	500.00	7,275.00	No	Yes
4668457	4	2	3	1,000.00	18,562.00	Yes	Yes
8512475	3	3	5	2,000.00	21,475.00	Yes	Yes
6984563	2	1	5	1,000.00	10,500.00	No	No
4856972	2	1	4	2,500.00	16,741.00	No	No
6845962	1	1	3	500.00	6,475.00	No	Yes
8457326	1	1	2	1,000.00	8,752.00	No	No
4968532	1	0	2	250.00	3,150.00	No	Yes
5741356	0	0	1	250.00	-	No	Yes
2486597	0	0	3	750.00	-	No	Yes
7134586	0	0	2	500.00	-	No	Yes
4234875	3	2	4	1,000.00	14,755.00	Yes	Yes
3894124	0	3	4	2,000.00	-	Yes	No
6845216	2	1	2	250.00	19,855.00	No	Yes
8663418	0	0	1	500.00	-	No	Yes

Precision Design and Packaging
Proposed New Warehouse Construction

Financing through NewVentures Capital Inc.

Quoted interest rate per annum		7.75%
Amortization period in years		18
Principal amount to be borrowed	$	1,750,000
Monthly loan payment		($15,048.32)
Principal portion of first loan payment		($3,746.24)
Principal portion of last loan payment		($14,951.76)
Total cost of loan		($3,250,437.08)
Total interest paid		($1,500,437.08)

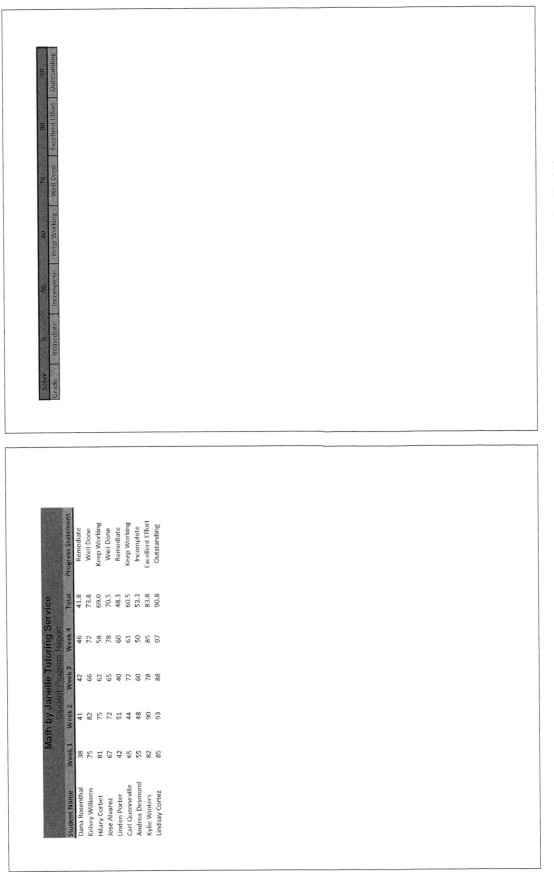

Score	0	50	60	70	80	90
Grade	Remediate	Incomplete	Keep Working	Well Done	Excellent Effort	Outstanding

Math by Janelle Tutoring Service
Student Progress Report

Student Name	Week 1	Week 2	Week 3	Week 4	Total	Progress Statement
Dana Rosenthal	38	41	42	46	41.8	Remediate
Kelsey Williams	75	82	66	72	73.8	Well Done
Hilary Corbet	81	75	62	58	69.0	Keep Working
Jose Alvarez	67	72	65	78	70.5	Well Done
Linden Porter	42	51	40	60	48.3	Remediate
Carl Quenneville	65	44	72	61	60.5	Keep Working
Andrea Desmond	55	48	60	50	53.3	Incomplete
Kylie Winters	82	90	78	85	83.8	Excellent Effort
Lindsay Cortez	85	93	88	97	90.8	Outstanding

Wellington Park Medical Center
Division of Cardiology
Adult Cardiac Surgery Costs

Month:	October	Surgeon:	Novak								

Patient No	Patient Last Name	Patient First Name	Surgery Code	Days in hospital	Surgery Fee		Valve Cost		Postoperative Hospital Cost		Total Cost
60334124	Wagner	Sara	MRP	7	$	5,325.00	$	-	$	6,317.50	$ 11,642.50
60334567	Gonzalez	Hector	ARP	10	$	4,876.00	$	-	$	9,025.00	$ 13,901.00
60398754	Vezina	Paula	ABP	5	$	4,820.00	$	-	$	4,512.50	$ 9,332.50
60347821	Dowling	Jager	MRT	11	$	6,240.00	$	775.00	$	9,927.50	$ 16,942.50
60328192	Ashman	Carl	ARP	4	$	4,876.00	$	-	$	3,610.00	$ 8,486.00
60321349	Kaiser	Lana	ART	12	$	6,190.00	$	775.00	$	10,830.00	$ 17,795.00
60398545	Van Bomm	Emile	ABP	7	$	4,820.00	$	-	$	6,317.50	$ 11,137.50
60342548	Youngblood	Frank	ABP	6	$	4,820.00	$	-	$	5,415.00	$ 10,235.00
60331569	Lorimar	Hannah	MRT	8	$	6,240.00	$	775.00	$	7,220.00	$ 14,235.00
60247859	Peterson	Mark	ART	9	$	6,190.00	$	775.00	$	8,122.50	$ 15,087.50
60158642	O'Connor	Terry	ABP	7	$	4,820.00	$	-	$	6,317.50	$ 11,137.50
60458962	Jenkins	Esther	MRP	9	$	5,325.00	$	-	$	8,122.50	$ 13,447.50
68521245	Norfolk	Leslie	ABP	8	$	4,820.00	$	-	$	7,220.00	$ 12,040.00
63552158	Adams-Wiley	Susan	MRT	6	$	6,240.00	$	775.00	$	5,415.00	$ 12,430.00
68451278	Estevez	Stefan	ARP	6	$	4,876.00	$	-	$	5,415.00	$ 10,291.00

Postoperative hospital cost per day: $ 902.50
Aortic or Mitral valve cost: $ 775.00

Total Cost: $ 80,478.00 $ 3,875.00 $ 103,787.50 $ 188,140.50

Surgery Code	Surgery Fee	Surgery Procedure
ABP	4,820	Artery Bypass
ARP	4,876	Aortic Valve Repair
ART	6,190	Aortic Valve Replacement
MRP	5,325	Mitral Valve Repair
MRT	6,240	Mitral Valve Replacement

EL2-C2-VB2-WPMCCardiologyCosts.xlsx

O'DONOVAN & SULLIVAN LAW ASSOCIATES
BILLING SUMMARY
OCTOBER 8 TO 12, 2012

File No	Client ID	Date	Attorney Code	Billable Hours	Hourly Rate	Legal Fees	Billing Statistics		
FL-325	10104	10/8/2012	1	26.75	85.00	2,273.75	**Total Legal Fees Billed by Attorney**		
EP-652	10106	10/8/2012	1	12.10	85.00	1,028.50	1	Marty O'Donovan	$ 5,342.25
CL-412	10125	10/8/2012	2	33.25	75.00	2,493.75	2	Toni Sullivan	$ 8,062.50
IN-745	10210	10/9/2012	3	24.25	100.00	2,425.00	3	Rosa Martinez	$ 15,306.00
EL-632	10225	10/9/2012	3	12.11	100.00	1,211.00	4	Kyle Williams	$ 7,087.50
RE-475	10285	10/9/2012	4	42.30	90.00	3,807.00		TOTAL	$ 35,798.25
CL-501	10341	10/10/2012	2	15.25	75.00	1,143.75			
CL-521	10334	10/10/2012	2	20.25	75.00	1,518.75	**Average Billable Hours by Attorney**		
PL-348	10420	10/10/2012	3	25.00	100.00	2,500.00	1	Marty O'Donovan	20.95
RE-492	10425	10/10/2012	4	22.70	90.00	2,043.00	2	Toni Sullivan	21.50
EL-632	10225	10/11/2012	3	23.00	100.00	2,300.00	3	Rosa Martinez	19.13
PL-512	10290	10/11/2012	3	16.20	100.00	1,620.00	4	Kyle Williams	26.25
IN-745	10210	10/11/2012	3	14.50	100.00	1,450.00			
FL-385	10278	10/11/2012	1	24.00	85.00	2,040.00			
CL-412	10125	10/12/2012	2	15.25	75.00	1,143.75	**Attorney Code Table**		
CL-450	10358	10/12/2012	2	23.50	75.00	1,762.50	Code	Attorney	Hourly Rate
IN-801	10346	10/12/2012	3	14.25	100.00	1,425.00	1	Marty O'Donovan	85.00
EP-685	10495	10/12/2012	3	23.75	100.00	2,375.00	2	Toni Sullivan	75.00
RE-501	10384	10/12/2012	4	13.75	90.00	1,237.50	3	Rosa Martinez	100.00
			TOTAL	402.16	TOTAL	$ 35,798.25	4	Kyle Williams	90.00

EL2-C2-VB1-BillableHrsOct8to12.xlsx

Benchmark Excel 2010 Level 2 Model Answers

145

Vantage Video Rentals
Classic Video Collection

Stock No.	Title	Year	Genre	Stock Date	Director FName	Director LName	Copies	VHS	DVD	Blu-ray	Category	Cost Price	Total Cost
CV-1001	Abbott & Costello Go to Mars	1953	Comedy	9/5/2006	Charles	Lamont	2	Yes	No	No	7-day rental	5.87	11.74
CV-1002	Miracle on 34th Street	1947	Family	9/15/2006	George	Seaton	8	Yes	No	Yes	2-day rental	7.55	60.40
CV-1003	Moby Dick	1956	Action	10/4/2006	John	Huston	3	No	Yes	No	7-day rental	8.10	24.30
CV-1004	Dial M for Murder	1954	Thriller	10/12/2006	Alfred	Hitchcock	5	No	Yes	Yes	7-day rental	6.54	32.70
CV-1005	Breakfast at Tiffany's	1961	Comedy	11/1/2006	Blake	Edwards	1	Yes	No	Yes	7-day rental	4.88	4.88
CV-1006	Gone with the Wind	1939	Drama	11/29/2006	Victor	Fleming	4	Yes	No	Yes	7-day rental	8.22	32.88
CV-1007	Doctor Zhivago	1965	Drama	12/6/2006	David	Lean	4	Yes	No	Yes	7-day rental	5.63	22.52
CV-1008	The Great Escape	1963	War	1/15/2007	John	Sturges	3	Yes	No	No	2-day rental	6.15	18.45
CV-1009	The Odd Couple	1968	Comedy	2/15/2007	Gene	Saks	4	Yes	Yes	No	2-day rental	4.95	19.80
CV-1010	The Sound of Music	1965	Musical	3/9/2007	Robert	Wise	5	Yes	Yes	Yes	2-day rental	5.12	25.60
CV-1011	A Christmas Carol	1951	Family	7/18/2007	Brian	Hurst	4	Yes	Yes	Yes	2-day rental	5.88	23.52
CV-1012	The Bridge on the River Kwai	1957	War	8/15/2007	David	Lean	2	Yes	No	Yes	2-day rental	6.32	12.64
CV-1013	Cool Hand Luke	1967	Drama	10/23/2007	Stuart	Rosenberg	5	Yes	Yes	Yes	2-day rental	5.42	27.10
CV-1014	Patton	1970	War	12/18/2007	Franklin	Schaffner	3	Yes	Yes	Yes	7-day rental	6.84	20.52
CV-1016	Psycho	1960	Horror	1/31/2008	Alfred	Hitchcock	2	Yes	No	Yes	2-day rental	7.54	15.08
CV-1017	The Longest Day	1962	War	2/5/2008	Ken	Annakin	5	Yes	Yes	No	7-day rental	6.51	32.55
CV-1018	To Kill a Mockingbird	1962	Drama	2/12/2008	Robert	Mulligan	2	Yes	No	Yes	2-day rental	8.40	16.80
CV-1019	Bonnie and Clyde	1967	Drama	3/15/2009	Arthur	Penn	3	Yes	Yes	Yes	2-day rental	8.95	26.85
CV-1020	The Maltese Falcon	1941	Drama	11/10/2009	John	Huston	1	No	No	Yes	7-day rental	12.15	12.15
CV-1022	The Wizard of Oz	1939	Musical	5/3/2010	Victor	Fleming	5	Yes	Yes	Yes	7-day rental	9.56	47.80
CV-1023	Rear Window	1954	Thriller	8/15/2010	Alfred	Hitchcock	3	Yes	Yes	Yes	2-day rental	8.55	25.65
CV-1024	Citizen Kane	1941	Drama	6/10/2011	Orson	Welles	2	No	Yes	Yes	2-day rental	9.85	19.70
CV-1025	Ben-Hur	1959	History	10/15/2011	William	Wyler	1	No	No	Yes	7-day rental	9.85	9.85
CV-1026	The Philadelphia Story	1940	Comedy	12/12/2011	George	Cukor	3	No	Yes	Yes	2-day rental	10.15	30.45
Total							3					7.46	573.93

EL2-C3-A2-VantageClassics.xlsx

Vantage Video Rentals
Classic Video Collection

Stock No.	Title	Year	Genre	Stock Date	Director	Copies	VHS	DVD	Blu-ray	Category	Cost Price	Total Cost
CV-1001	Abbott & Costello Go to Mars	1953	Comedy	9/5/2006	Charles Lamont	2	Yes	No	No	7-day rental	5.87	11.74
CV-1002	Miracle on 34th Street	1947	Family	9/15/2006	George Seaton	8	Yes	No	No	2-day rental	7.55	60.40
CV-1003	Moby Dick	1956	Action	10/4/2006	John Huston	3	No	Yes	No	7-day rental	8.10	24.30
CV-1004	Dial M for Murder	1954	Thriller	10/12/2006	Alfred Hitchcock	5	No	Yes	Yes	7-day rental	6.54	32.70
CV-1005	Breakfast at Tiffany's	1961	Comedy	11/1/2006	Blake Edwards	1	Yes	No	Yes	7-day rental	4.88	4.88
CV-1006	Gone with the Wind	1939	Drama	11/29/2006	Victor Fleming	4	Yes	No	Yes	7-day rental	8.22	32.88
CV-1007	Doctor Zhivago	1965	Drama	12/6/2006	David Lean	4	Yes	No	Yes	7-day rental	5.63	22.52
CV-1008	The Great Escape	1963	War	1/15/2007	John Sturges	3	Yes	No	No	2-day rental	6.15	18.45
CV-1009	The Odd Couple	1968	Comedy	2/15/2007	Gene Saks	4	Yes	Yes	No	2-day rental	4.95	19.80
CV-1010	The Sound of Music	1965	Musical	3/9/2007	Robert Wise	5	Yes	Yes	Yes	2-day rental	5.12	25.60
CV-1011	A Christmas Carol	1951	Family	7/18/2007	Brian Hurst	4	Yes	No	No	2-day rental	6.32	12.64
CV-1012	The Bridge on the River Kwai	1957	War	8/15/2007	David Lean	2	Yes	No	Yes	2-day rental	5.42	27.10
CV-1013	Cool Hand Luke	1967	Drama	10/23/2007	Stuart Rosenberg	5	Yes	Yes	Yes	2-day rental	6.84	20.52
CV-1014	Patton	1970	War	12/18/2007	Franklin Schaffner	3	Yes	No	Yes	2-day rental	7.54	15.08
CV-1016	Psycho	1960	Horror	1/31/2008	Alfred Hitchcock	2	Yes	Yes	No	7-day rental	6.51	32.55
CV-1017	The Longest Day	1962	War	2/5/2008	Ken Annakin	5	Yes	Yes	No	7-day rental	8.40	16.80
CV-1018	To Kill a Mockingbird	1962	Drama	2/12/2008	Robert Mulligan	2	Yes	No	Yes	2-day rental	8.95	26.85
CV-1019	Bonnie and Clyde	1967	Drama	3/15/2009	Arthur Penn	3	No	Yes	Yes	2-day rental	12.15	12.15
CV-1020	The Maltese Falcon	1941	Drama	11/10/2009	John Huston	1	Yes	No	Yes	7-day rental	5.63	22.52
CV-1007	Doctor Zhivago	1965	Drama	12/6/2006	David Lean	4	Yes	Yes	Yes	7-day rental	9.56	47.80
CV-1022	The Wizard of Oz	1939	Musical	5/3/2010	Victor Fleming	5	Yes	Yes	Yes	7-day rental	8.55	25.65
CV-1023	Rear Window	1954	Thriller	8/15/2010	Alfred Hitchcock	3	No	Yes	No	7-day rental	6.54	32.70
CV-1004	Dial M for Murder	1954	Thriller	10/12/2006	Alfred Hitchcock	5	No	Yes	Yes	2-day rental	9.85	19.70
CV-1024	Citizen Kane	1941	Drama	6/10/2011	Orson Welles	2	No	No	Yes	7-day rental	9.85	9.85
CV-1025	Ben-Hur	1959	History	10/15/2011	William Wyler	1					7.24	598.70
Total						3					7.24	598.70

EL2-C3-A1-VantageClassics.xlsx

Benchmark Excel 2010 Level 2 Model Answers

Wellington Park Medical Center
Nursing Division Casual Relief Call List

Payroll No	First Name	Last Name	Designation	Hire Date	Telephone	OR Exp?	Day Shift Only?	Night Shift Only?	Either Shift?	Hourly Rate	Shift Cost
78452	Terry	Mason	RN	5/3/1998	555-1279	Yes	No	Yes	No	38.50	308.00
19658	Paula	Sanderson	RN	4/28/2000	555-3485	No	No	No	Yes	38.50	308.00
38642	Tania	Ravi	RN	6/22/2002	555-6969	Yes	Yes	No	Weekends only	38.50	308.00
96523	Lynn	Pietre	RN	10/22/1998	555-2548	Yes	Yes	No	Weekends only	35.00	280.00
45968	David	Featherstone	RN	9/9/2001	555-5961	No	No	No	Yes	35.00	280.00
46956	Orlando	Zambian	RN	11/10/2001	555-1186	No	Yes	No	No	35.00	280.00
56983	Amanda	Sanchez	RN	4/27/1999	555-4896	Yes	No	Yes	No	33.00	264.00
68429	Rene	Quenneville	RN	8/15/2003	555-4663	Yes	Yes	No	Weekends only	22.50	180.00
69417	Denis	LaPierre	RN	8/23/2003	555-8643	No	No	Yes	No	22.50	180.00
37944	Fernando	Este	RN	7/18/2005	555-4545	No	No	No	Yes	22.50	180.00
78647	Jay	Bjorg	RN	5/14/2007	555-6598	No	No	No	Yes	22.50	180.00
95558	Sam	Vargas	RN	3/2/2009	555-4571	No	No	No	Yes	22.50	180.00
98731	Zail	Singh	RN	5/6/2011	555-3561	Yes	Yes	No	Yes	22.50	180.00
58612	Savana	Ruiz	RN	4/15/2012	555-8457	Yes	No	Yes	Weekends only	22.50	180.00
96721	Noreen	Kalir	RN	4/3/2009	555-1876	Yes	Yes	No	No	21.50	172.00
89367	Xiu	Zheng	LPN	4/23/2006	555-7383	Yes	Yes	No	No	18.75	150.00
14586	Alma	Fernandez	LPN	8/3/1997	555-7412	Yes	No	No	Yes	16.75	134.00
48652	Dana	Casselman	LPN	10/15/1997	555-6325	Yes	No	No	Yes	16.75	134.00
85412	Kelly	Lund	LPN	11/19/1998	555-3684	No	Yes	No	Weekends only	15.75	126.00
98364	Lana	Bourne	LPN	7/15/2008	555-9012	Yes	Yes	No	No	15.50	124.00
90467	Nadir	Abouzeen	LPN	8/12/2008	555-9023	No	No	No	Yes	14.50	116.00
68475	Kelly	O'Brien	LPN	1/20/2012	555-6344	No	Yes	No	Weekends only	13.75	110.00
								Average Hourly Rate and Shift Cost:		24.74	197.91

Vantage Video Rentals
Classic Video Collection

Stock No.	Title	Year	Genre	Stock Date	Director FName	Director LName	Copies	VHS	DVD	Blu-ray	Category	Cost Price	Total Cost
			Action Total										24.30
CV-1026	The Philadelphia Story	1940	Comedy	12/12/2011	George	Cukor	3	No	Yes	Yes	7-day rental	10.15	30.45
CV-1005	Breakfast at Tiffany's	1951	Comedy	11/1/2006	Blake	Edwards	1	Yes	No	Yes	7-day rental	4.88	4.88
CV-1001	Abbott & Costello Go to Mars	1953	Comedy	9/5/2006	Charles	Lamont	2	Yes	No	No	7-day rental	5.87	11.74
CV-1009	The Odd Couple	1968	Comedy	2/15/2007	Gene	Saks	4	Yes	Yes	No	2-day rental	4.95	19.80
			Comedy Average										16.72
			Comedy Total										66.87
CV-1006	Gone with the Wind	1939	Drama	11/29/2006	Victor	Fleming	4	Yes	No	Yes	7-day rental	8.22	32.88
CV-1020	The Maltese Falcon	1941	Drama	11/10/2009	John	Huston	1	No	No	Yes	2-day rental	12.15	12.15
CV-1007	Doctor Zhivago	1965	Drama	12/8/2006	David	Lean	4	Yes	No	Yes	7-day rental	5.63	22.52
CV-1018	To Kill a Mockingbird	1962	Drama	2/12/2008	Robert	Mulligan	2	Yes	No	Yes	2-day rental	8.40	16.80
CV-1019	Bonnie and Clyde	1967	Drama	3/15/2009	Arthur	Penn	3	Yes	Yes	Yes	2-day rental	8.95	26.85
CV-1013	Cool Hand Luke	1967	Drama	10/23/2007	Stuart	Rosenberg	5	Yes	Yes	Yes	2-day rental	5.42	27.10
CV-1024	Citizen Kane	1941	Drama	6/10/2011	Orson	Welles	2	No	Yes	Yes	2-day rental	9.85	19.70
			Drama Average										22.57
			Drama Total										158.00
CV-1011	A Christmas Carol	1951	Family	7/18/2007	Brian	Hurst	4	Yes	Yes	Yes	2-day rental	5.88	23.52
CV-1002	Miracle on 34th Street	1947	Family	9/15/2006	George	Seaton	8	Yes	No	Yes	2-day rental	7.55	60.40
			Family Average										41.96
			Family Total										83.92
			History Total										9.85
			Horror Total										15.08
			Musical Total										73.40
			Thriller Total										58.35
			War Total										84.16
			Grand Average										23.91
			Grand Total										573.93

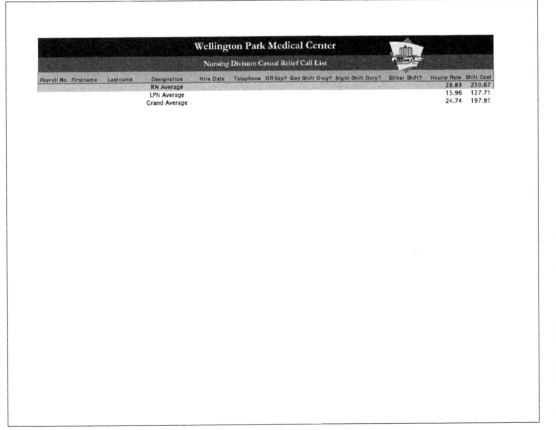

Payroll No	Firstname	Lastname	Designation	Hire Date	Telephone	OR Exp?	Day Shift Only?	Night Shift Only?	Either Shift?	Hourly Rate	Shift Cost
			RN Average							28.83	230.67
			LPN Average							15.96	127.71
			Grand Average							24.74	197.91

EL2-C3-VB2-WPMCNurseCallList.xlsx

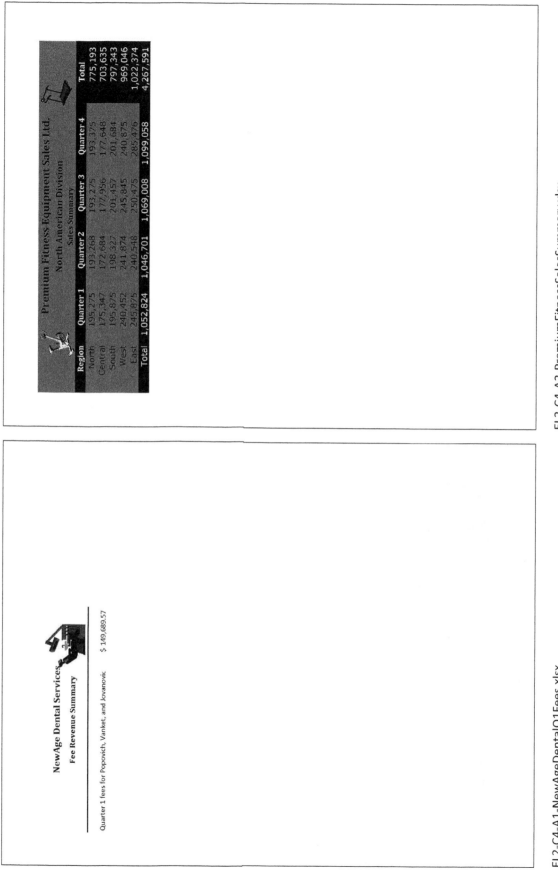

Premium Fitness Equipment Sales Ltd.
North American Division
Sales Summary

Region	Quarter 1	Quarter 2	Quarter 3	Quarter 4	Total
North	195,275	193,268	193,275	193,375	775,193
Central	175,347	172,684	177,956	177,648	703,635
South	195,875	198,327	201,457	201,684	797,343
West	240,452	241,874	245,845	240,875	969,046
East	245,875	240,548	250,475	285,476	1,022,374
Total	1,052,824	1,046,701	1,069,008	1,099,058	4,267,591

EL2-C4-A2-PremiumFitnessSalesSummary.xlsx

NewAge Dental Services
Fee Revenue Summary

Quarter 1 fees for Popovich, Vanket, and Jovanovic	$ 149,689.57

EL2-C4-A1-NewAgeDentalQ1Fees.xlsx

National Park Service
U.S. Department of the Interior
May 2012
Attendance Summary
Southwest Region, Zone C

Day	Entries	Day	Entries
1	271	17	314
2	270	18	306
3	240	19	314
4	277	20	389
5	286	21	323
6	246	22	384
7	204	23	356
8	237	24	385
9	281	25	384
10	263	26	430
11	257	27	469
12	299	28	518
13	225	29	588
14	253	30	538
15	235	31	620
16	298		

Total Vehicle and Individual Entrances   10,460

EL2-C4-A4-MayParkEntries.xlsx

Premium Fitness Equipment Sales Ltd.
North American Division
Sales Summary

Region	Quarter 1	Quarter 2	Quarter 3	Quarter 4	Total
North	195,275	193,268	193,275	193,375	775,193
Central	175,347	172,684	177,956	177,648	703,635
South	195,875	198,327	201,457	201,684	797,343
West	240,452	241,874	245,845	240,875	969,046
East	245,875	240,548	250,475	285,476	1,022,374
Total	1,052,824	1,046,701	1,069,008	1,099,058	4,267,591

EL2-C4-A3-PremiumFitnessSalesSummary.xlsx

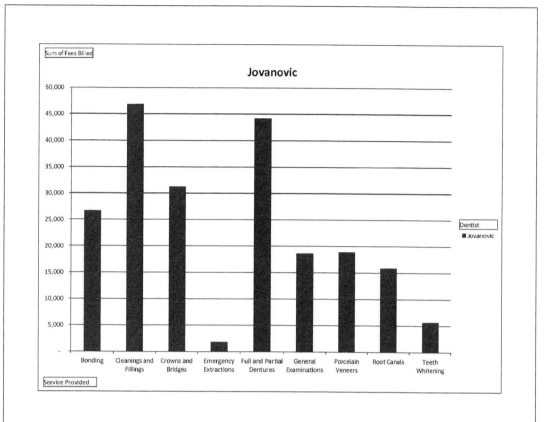

EL2-C4-A5-NewAgeDental2012Fees(PivotChart).xlsx

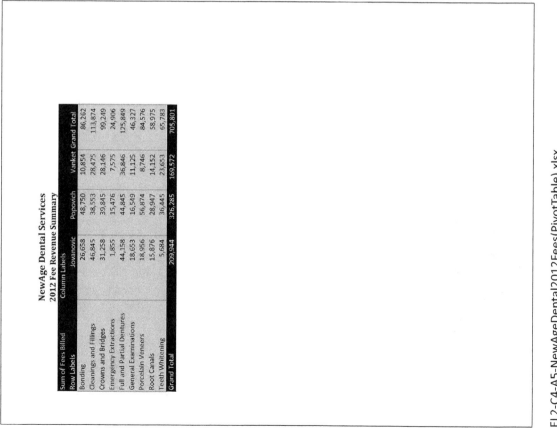

EL2-C4-A5-NewAgeDental2012Fees(PivotTable).xlsx

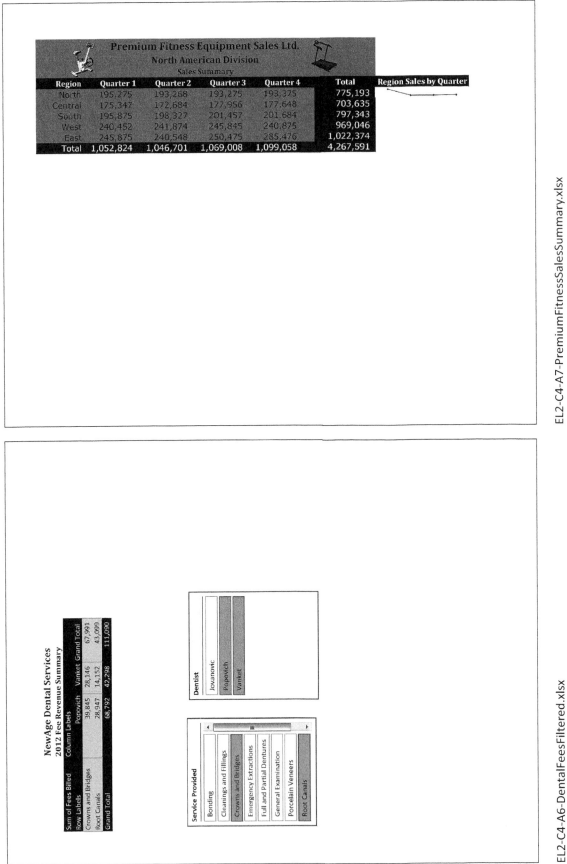

Premium Fitness Equipment Sales Ltd.
North American Division
Sales Summary

Region	Quarter 1	Quarter 2	Quarter 3	Quarter 4	Total	Region Sales by Quarter
North	195,275	193,268	193,275	193,375	775,193	
Central	175,347	172,684	177,956	177,648	703,635	
South	195,875	198,327	201,457	201,684	797,343	
West	240,452	241,874	245,845	240,875	969,046	
East	245,875	240,548	250,475	285,476	1,022,374	
Total	1,052,824	1,046,701	1,069,008	1,099,058	4,267,591	

EL2-C4-A7-PremiumFitnessSalesSummary.xlsx

NewAge Dental Services
2012 Fee Revenue Summary

Sum of Fees Billed	Column Labels		
Row Labels	Popovich	Vanket	Grand Total
Crowns and Bridges	39,845	28,146	67,991
Root Canals	28,947	14,152	43,099
Grand Total	68,792	42,298	111,090

Dentist

Jovanovic
Popovich
Vanket

Service Provided

Bonding
Cleanings and Fillings
Crowns and Bridges
Emergency Extractions
Full and Partial Dentures
General Examination
Porcelain Veneers
Root Canals

EL2-C4-A6-DentalFeesFiltered.xlsx

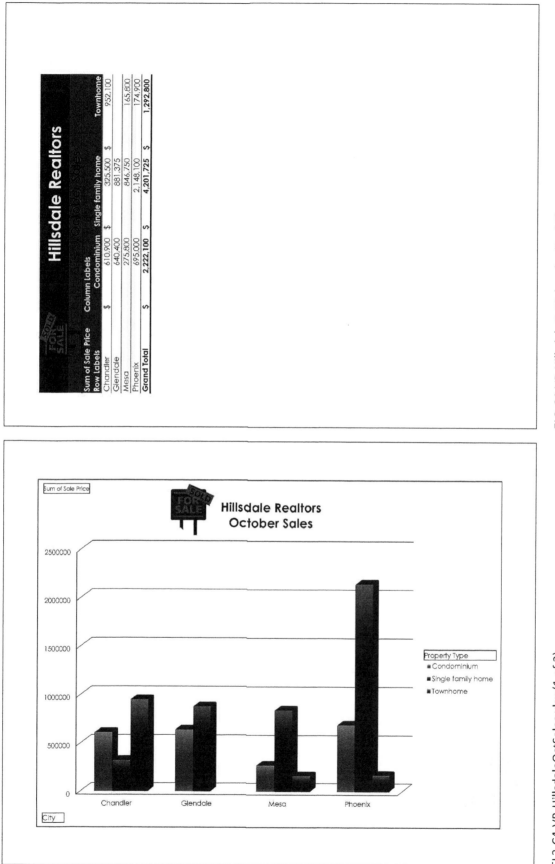

Hillsdale Realtors

Sum of Sale Price Row Labels	Column Labels Condominium	Single family home	Townhome
Chandler	$ 610,900	$ 325,500	$ 952,100
Glendale	640,400	881,375	
Mesa	275,800	846,750	165,800
Phoenix	695,000	2,148,100	174,900
Grand Total	$ 2,222,100	$ 4,201,725	1,292,800

	Grand Total
$	1,888,500
	1,521,775
	1,288,350
	3,018,000
$	**7,716,625**

EL2-C4-VB-HillsdaleOctSales.xlsx (3 of 3)

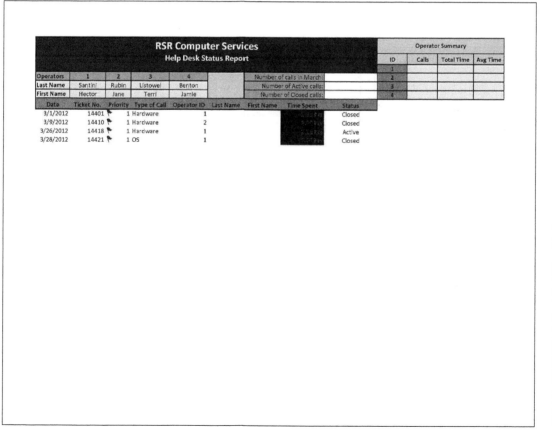

RSR Computer Services
Help Desk Status Report

					Operator Summary			
					ID	Calls	Total Time	Avg Time
					1			
Operators	1	2	3	4	Number of calls in March:	2		
Last Name	Santini	Rubin	Listowel	Benton	Number of Active calls:	3		
First Name	Hector	Jane	Terri	Jamie	Number of Closed calls:	4		

Date	Ticket No.	Priority	Type of Call	Operator ID	Last Name	First Name	Time Spent	Status
3/1/2012	14401	1	Hardware	1				Closed
3/1/2012	14402	1	Password	2			0.25 hrs	Closed
3/2/2012	14403	1	OS	2			0.50 hrs	Closed
3/2/2012	14404	2	Email	1			1.25 hrs	Closed
3/5/2012	14405	1	Password	3			0.25 hrs	Closed
3/5/2012	14406	2	Hardware	4			1.75 hrs	Active
3/6/2012	14407	2	Email	4			1.00 hrs	Closed
3/8/2012	14408	3	Internet	4			0.50 hrs	Closed
3/8/2012	14409	3	Internet	2			0.50 hrs	Closed
3/9/2012	14410	1	Hardware	2				Closed
3/9/2012	14411	3	Email	1			1.00 hrs	Closed
3/12/2012	14412	3	Email	1			0.50 hrs	Closed
3/13/2012	14413	2	Internet	3			0.75 hrs	Closed
3/15/2012	14414	2	Internet	3			1.25 hrs	Closed
3/20/2012	14415	3	Password	2			0.50 hrs	Closed
3/22/2012	14416	2	Email	2			0.75 hrs	Active
3/25/2012	14417	1	Email	1			1.25 hrs	Active
3/26/2012	14418	1	Hardware	1				Active
3/27/2012	14419	3	OS	4			1.75 hrs	Active
3/28/2012	14420	2	Hardware	3			1.25 hrs	Closed
3/28/2012	14421	1	OS	1				Closed
3/29/2012	14422	3	Internet	2			0.75 hrs	Active
3/29/2012	14423	1	Hardware	4			1.00 hrs	Active

RSR Computer Services
Help Desk Status Report

					Operator Summary			
					ID	Calls	Total Time	Avg Time
					1			
Operators	1	2	3	4	Number of calls in March:	2		
Last Name	Santini	Rubin	Listowel	Benton	Number of Active calls:	3		
First Name	Hector	Jane	Terri	Jamie	Number of Closed calls:	4		

Date	Ticket No.	Priority	Type of Call	Operator ID	Last Name	First Name	Time Spent	Status
3/1/2012	14401	1	Hardware	1				Closed
3/9/2012	14410	1	Hardware	2				Closed
3/26/2012	14418	1	Hardware	1				Active
3/28/2012	14421	1	OS	1				Closed

RSR Computer Services
Help Desk Status Report

Operator Summary

ID	Calls	Total Time	Avg Time
1	7	10.75	1.54
2	7	6.50	0.93
3	5	4.25	0.85
4	6	6.25	1.04

Operators	1	2	3	4		Number of calls in March:	25
Last Name	Santini	Rubin	Listowel	Benton		Number of Active calls:	8
First Name	Hector	Jane	Terri	Jamie		Number of Closed calls:	17

Date	Ticket No.	Priority	Type of Call	Operator ID	Last Name	First Name	Time Spent	Status	Cost
3/1/2012	14401	1	Hardware	1	Santini	Hector		Closed	33.75
3/1/2012	14402	1	Password	2	Rubin	Jane	0.25 hrs	Closed	3.75
3/2/2012	14403	1	OS	2	Rubin	Jane	0.50 hrs	Closed	7.50
3/2/2012	14404	2	Email	1	Santini	Hector	1.25 hrs	Closed	18.75
3/5/2012	14405	1	Password	3	Listowel	Terri	0.25 hrs	Closed	3.75
3/6/2012	14407	2	Email	4	Benton	Jamie	1.00 hrs	Closed	15.00
3/8/2012	14408	3	Internet	4	Benton	Jamie	0.50 hrs	Closed	7.50
3/8/2012	14409	3	Internet	2	Rubin	Jane	0.50 hrs	Closed	7.50
3/9/2012	14410	1	Hardware	2	Rubin	Jane		Closed	48.75
3/9/2012	14411	3	Email	1	Santini	Hector	1.00 hrs	Closed	15.00
3/12/2012	14412	3	Email	1	Santini	Hector	0.50 hrs	Closed	7.50
3/13/2012	14413	2	Internet	3	Listowel	Terri	0.75 hrs	Closed	11.25
3/15/2012	14414	2	Internet	3	Listowel	Terri	1.25 hrs	Closed	18.75
3/20/2012	14415	3	Password	2	Rubin	Jane	0.50 hrs	Closed	7.50
3/28/2012	14420	2	Hardware	3	Listowel	Terri	1.25 hrs	Closed	18.75
3/28/2012	14421	1	OS	1	Santini	Hector		Closed	33.75
3/30/2012	14425	2	Password	4	Benton	Jamie	0.25 hrs	Closed	3.75
Total							17.50 hrs		262.50

RSR Computer Services
Help Desk Status Report

Operator Summary

ID	Calls	Total Time	Avg Time
1	7	10.75	1.54
2	7	6.50	0.93
3	4	3.50	0.88
4	5	6.00	1.20

Operators	1	2	3	4		Number of calls in March:	23
Last Name	Santini	Rubin	Listowel	Benton		Number of Active calls:	7
First Name	Hector	Jane	Terri	Jamie		Number of Closed calls:	16

Date	Ticket No.	Priority	Type of Call	Operator ID	Last Name	First Name	Time Spent	Status
3/1/2012	14401	1	Hardware	1	Santini	Hector		Closed
3/1/2012	14402	1	Password	2	Rubin	Jane	0.25 hrs	Closed
3/2/2012	14403	1	OS	2	Rubin	Jane	0.50 hrs	Closed
3/2/2012	14404	2	Email	1	Santini	Hector	1.25 hrs	Closed
3/5/2012	14405	1	Password	3	Listowel	Terri	0.25 hrs	Closed
3/5/2012	14406	2	Hardware	4	Benton	Jamie	1.75 hrs	Active
3/6/2012	14407	2	Email	4	Benton	Jamie	1.00 hrs	Closed
3/8/2012	14408	3	Internet	4	Benton	Jamie	0.50 hrs	Closed
3/8/2012	14409	3	Internet	2	Rubin	Jane	0.50 hrs	Closed
3/9/2012	14410	1	Hardware	2	Rubin	Jane		Closed
3/9/2012	14411	3	Email	1	Santini	Hector	1.00 hrs	Closed
3/12/2012	14412	3	Email	1	Santini	Hector	0.50 hrs	Closed
3/13/2012	14413	2	Internet	3	Listowel	Terri	0.75 hrs	Closed
3/15/2012	14414	2	Internet	3	Listowel	Terri	1.25 hrs	Closed
3/20/2012	14415	3	Password	2	Rubin	Jane	0.50 hrs	Closed
3/22/2012	14416	2	Email	2	Rubin	Jane	0.75 hrs	Active
3/25/2012	14417	1	Email	1	Santini	Hector	1.25 hrs	Active
3/26/2012	14418	1	Hardware	1	Santini	Hector		Active
3/27/2012	14419	3	OS	4	Benton	Jamie	1.75 hrs	Active
3/28/2012	14420	2	Hardware	3	Listowel	Terri	1.25 hrs	Closed
3/28/2012	14421	1	OS	1	Santini	Hector		Closed
3/29/2012	14422	3	Internet	2	Rubin	Jane	0.75 hrs	Active
3/29/2012	14423	1	Hardware	4	Benton	Jamie	1.00 hrs	Active

RSR Computer Services
Help Desk Status Report

EL2-U1-A3-RSRHelpDeskRpt(Step15).xlsx

Operator Summary

ID	Calls	Total Time	Avg Time
1	7	10.75	1.54
2	7	6.50	0.93
3	5	4.25	0.85
4	6	6.25	1.04

Operators	1	2	3	4		
Last Name	Santini	Rubin	Listowel	Benton	Number of calls in March:	25
First Name	Hector	Jane	Terri	Jamie	Number of Active calls:	8
					Number of Closed calls:	17

Date	Ticket No.	Priority	Type of Call	Operator ID	Last Name	First Name	Time Spent	Status	Cost
3/1/2012	14401	1	Hardware	1	Santini	Hector		Closed	33.75
3/1/2012	14402	1	Password	2	Rubin	Jane	0.25 hrs	Closed	3.75
3/2/2012	14403	1	OS	2	Rubin	Jane	0.50 hrs	Closed	7.50
3/2/2012	14404	2	Email	1	Santini	Hector	1.25 hrs	Closed	18.75
3/5/2012	14405	1	Password	3	Listowel	Terri	0.25 hrs	Closed	3.75
3/5/2012	14406	2	Hardware	4	Benton	Jamie	1.75 hrs	Active	26.25
3/6/2012	14407	2	Email	4	Benton	Jamie	1.00 hrs	Closed	15.00
3/8/2012	14408	3	Internet	4	Benton	Jamie	0.50 hrs	Closed	7.50
3/8/2012	14409	3	Internet	2	Rubin	Jane	0.50 hrs	Closed	7.50
3/9/2012	14410	1	Hardware	2	Rubin	Jane		Closed	48.75
3/9/2012	14411	3	Email	1	Santini	Hector	1.00 hrs	Closed	15.00
3/12/2012	14412	1	Email	1	Santini	Hector	0.50 hrs	Closed	7.50
3/13/2012	14413	2	Internet	3	Listowel	Terri	0.75 hrs	Closed	11.25
3/15/2012	14414	1	Internet	3	Listowel	Terri	1.25 hrs	Closed	18.75
3/20/2012	14415	3	Password	2	Rubin	Jane	0.50 hrs	Closed	7.50
3/22/2012	14416	2	Email	2	Rubin	Jane	0.75 hrs	Active	11.25
3/25/2012	14417	1	Email	1	Santini	Hector	1.25 hrs	Active	18.75
3/26/2012	14418	1	Hardware	1	Santini	Hector		Active	33.75
3/27/2012	14419	3	OS	4	Benton	Jamie	1.75 hrs	Active	26.25
3/28/2012	14420	2	Hardware	3	Listowel	Terri	1.25 hrs	Closed	18.75
3/28/2012	14421	1	OS	1	Santini	Hector		Closed	33.75
3/29/2012	14422	3	Internet	2	Rubin	Jane	0.75 hrs	Active	11.25
3/29/2012	14423	1	Hardware	4	Benton	Jamie	1.00 hrs	Active	15.00
3/30/2012	14424	2	Email	3	Listowel	Terri	0.75 hrs	Active	11.25
3/30/2012	14425	2	Password	4	Benton	Jamie	0.25 hrs	Closed	3.75
Total							27.75 hrs		416.25

RSR Computer Services
Help Desk Status Report

EL2-U1-A3-RSRHelpDeskRpt(Step13).xlsx

Operator Summary

ID	Calls	Total Time	Avg Time
1	7	10.75	1.54
2	7	6.50	0.93
3	5	4.25	0.85
4	6	6.25	1.04

Operators	1	2	3	4		
Last Name	Santini	Rubin	Listowel	Benton	Number of calls in March:	25
First Name	Hector	Jane	Terri	Jamie	Number of Active calls:	8
					Number of Closed calls:	17

Date	Ticket No.	Priority	Type of Call	Operator ID	Last Name	First Name	Time Spent	Status	Cost
3/1/2012	14402	1	Password	2	Rubin	Jane	0.25 hrs	Closed	3.75
3/5/2012	14405	1	Password	3	Listowel	Terri	0.25 hrs	Closed	3.75
3/20/2012	14415	3	Password	2	Rubin	Jane	0.50 hrs	Closed	7.50
3/30/2012	14425	2	Password	4	Benton	Jamie	0.25 hrs	Closed	3.75
Total							1.25 hrs		18.75

RSR Computer Services
Help Desk Status Report

Operators	1	2	3	4		Number of calls in March:		25
Last Name	Santini	Rubin	Listowel	Benton		Number of Active calls:		8
First Name	Hector	Jane	Terri	Jamie		Number of Closed calls:		17

Operator Summary

ID	Calls	Total Time	Avg Time
1	7	10.75	1.54
2	7	6.50	0.93
3	5	4.25	0.85
4	6	6.25	1.04

Date	Ticket No.	Priority	Type of Call	Operator ID	Last Name	First Name	Time Spent	Status	Cost
3/29/2012	14423	1	Hardware	4	Benton	Jamie	1.00 hrs	Active	15.00
3/6/2012	14407	2	Email	4	Benton	Jamie	1.00 hrs	Closed	15.00
3/5/2012	14406	2	Hardware	4	Benton	Jamie	1.75 hrs	Active	26.25
3/30/2012	14425	2	Password	4	Benton	Jamie	0.25 hrs	Closed	3.75
3/8/2012	14408	3	Internet	4	Benton	Jamie	0.50 hrs	Closed	7.50
3/27/2012	14419	3	OS	4	Benton	Jamie	1.75 hrs	Active	26.25
				Benton Total			0		93.75
3/5/2012	14405	1	Password	3	Listowel	Terri	0.25 hrs	Closed	3.75
3/30/2012	14424	2	Email	3	Listowel	Terri	0.75 hrs	Active	11.25
3/28/2012	14420	2	Hardware	3	Listowel	Terri	1.25 hrs	Closed	18.75
3/13/2012	14413	2	Internet	3	Listowel	Terri	0.75 hrs	Closed	11.25
3/15/2012	14414	2	Internet	3	Listowel	Terri	1.25 hrs	Closed	18.75
				Listowel Total			0		63.75
3/9/2012	14410	1	Hardware	2	Rubin	Jane		Closed	48.75
3/2/2012	14403	1	OS	2	Rubin	Jane	0.50 hrs	Closed	7.50
3/1/2012	14402	1	Password	2	Rubin	Jane	0.25 hrs	Closed	3.75
3/22/2012	14416	2	Email	2	Rubin	Jane	0.75 hrs	Active	11.25
3/8/2012	14409	3	Internet	2	Rubin	Jane	0.50 hrs	Closed	7.50
3/29/2012	14422	3	Internet	2	Rubin	Jane	0.75 hrs	Active	11.25
3/20/2012	14415	3	Password	2	Rubin	Jane	0.50 hrs	Closed	7.50
				Rubin Total			0		97.50
3/25/2012	14417	1	Email	1	Santini	Hector	1.25 hrs	Active	18.75
3/1/2012	14401	1	Hardware	1	Santini	Hector		Closed	33.75
3/26/2012	14418	1	Hardware	1	Santini	Hector		Active	33.75
3/28/2012	14421	1	OS	1	Santini	Hector		Closed	33.75
3/2/2012	14404	2	Email	1	Santini	Hector	1.25 hrs	Closed	18.75
3/9/2012	14411	3	Email	1	Santini	Hector	1.00 hrs	Closed	15.00
3/12/2012	14412	3	Email	1	Santini	Hector	0.50 hrs	Closed	7.50
				Santini Total			0		161.25
				Grand Total			0		416.25

EL2-U1-A4-RSRHelpDeskRpt(Step8).xlsx

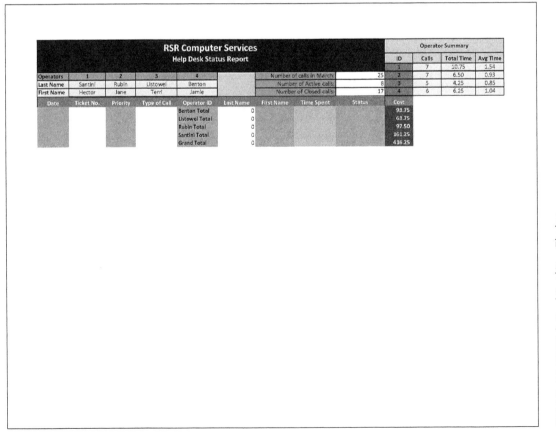

EL2-U1-A4-RSRHelpDeskRpt(Step7).xlsx

Category	(All)			
Row Labels	Sum of North	Sum of South	Sum of East	Sum of West
Cortez	96,351	122,633	62,505	75,406
Hinton	248,871	220,030	237,038	211,133
Kellerman	285,229	232,204	216,420	266,428
Grand Total	630,451	574,867	515,963	552,967

EL2-U1-A6-PrecisionBulkSales(Step5).xlsx

AllClaims Insurance Brokers
Proposed Office Relocation to One Downtown Square
Loan Payment and Interest Cost Analysis

	NEWFUNDS TRUST	DELTA CAPITAL	
LOAN COMPANY:			
LOAN APPLICATION NUMBER:	9834DV1299-Y	DC-983XY345-L6	
Interest Rate	8.14%	9.30%	annual rate
Amortization	20	16	years for repayment
Loan Amount	$ 475,000	$ 475,000	principal amount borrowed
Monthly Payment	($4,014.58)	($4,763.05)	includes principal and interest
Monthly Principal Payment (1st payment)	($792.49)	($1,081.80)	payment on principal for the first month of the loan
Total Loan Payments	($963,498.37)	($914,505.14)	

NOTE:
Both payments are calculated based on a constant interest rate and a constant payment.

Recommendation for source of capital funds to relocate office: Delta Capital
Loan application number: dc-983xy345-l6

EL2-U1-A5-AllClaimsLoan.xlsx

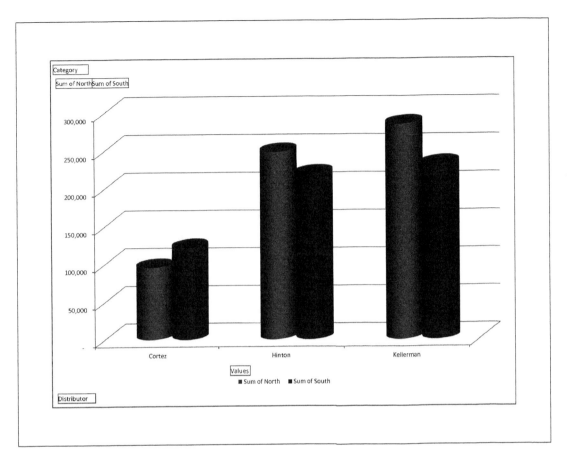

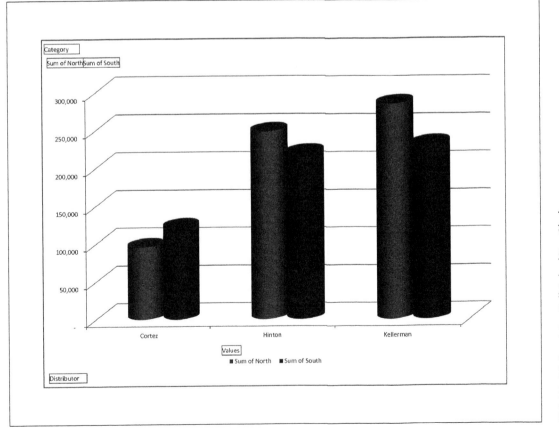

Benchmark Excel 2010 Level 2 Model Answers

Precision Design and Packaging
Bulk Container Sales

Model	Description	Distributor	Category	REGION				Total
				North	South	East	West	
PD-1140	Gaylord with lid	Hinton	A	73,100	67,856	46,875	33,415	221,246
PD-2185	Premium Gaylord with lid	Kellerman	C	67,850	36,248	24,541	36,412	165,051
PD-1150	Gaylord bottom	Kellerman	B	24,584	26,486	19,524	24,854	95,448
PD-1155	Gaylord lid	Hinton	D	25,865	36,846	66,234	24,854	153,799
PD-3695	Telescoping top and bottom	Kellerman	A	51,536	56,236	46,825	47,853	202,450
PD-3698	Telescoping bottom	Kellerman	A	72,253	35,158	48,125	35,568	191,104
PD-3699	Telescoping top	Kellerman	A	32,523	64,528	42,253	85,523	224,827
PD-4100	Additional lids for telescoping containers	Hinton	D	57,842	24,584	36,842	36,214	155,482
PD-4200	"D" 4 piece container	Cortez	A	14,578	39,452	19,563	23,458	97,051
PD-4415	"EO" container	Hinton	A	36,486	39,452	43,158	51,245	170,341
PD-5367	"EH" container	Cortez	A	65,125	67,325	29,457	35,125	197,032
PD-6418	"E" container	Kellerman	A	36,483	13,548	35,152	36,218	121,401
PD-7459	Economy R.S.C.	Hinton	E	35,685	34,526	28,458	51,124	149,793
PD-8854	Premium R.S.C.	Cortez	C	16,648	15,856	13,485	16,823	62,812
PD-9101	Corrugated pads 15 x 15	Hinton	E	3,668	2,454	3,641	6,623	16,386
PD-9105	Corrugated pads 20 x 12	Hinton	E	6,954	6,335	3,585	1,348	18,222
PD-9110	Corrugated pads 24 x 18	Hinton	E	2,648	3,752	4,687	1,354	12,441
PD-9115	Corrugated pads 30 x 30	Hinton	E	6,623	4,225	3,558	4,956	19,362
TOTAL				630,451	574,867	515,963	552,967	2,274,248

EL2-U1-A6-PrecisionBulkSales(Step11).xlsx (3 of 4)

Category	(All)	
Row Labels	Sum of North	Sum of South
Cortez	96,351	122,633
Hinton	248,871	220,030
Kellerman	285,229	232,204
Grand Total	630,451	574,867

EL2-U1-A6-PrecisionBulkSales(Step11).xlsx (2 of 4)

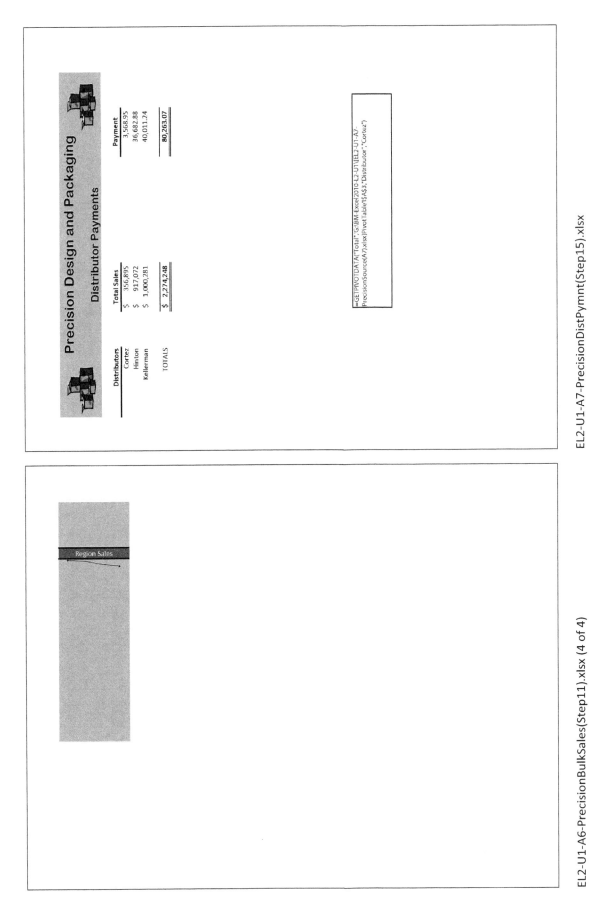

Precision Design and Packaging

Distributor Payments

Distributors	Total Sales	Payment
Cortez	$ 356,895	3,568.95
Hinton	$ 917,072	36,682.88
Kellerman	$ 1,000,281	40,011.24
TOTALS	$ 2,274,248	80,263.07

EL2-U1-A7-PrecisionDistPymnt(Step17).xlsx

National Online Marketing Inc.
Computing Services Department

Wages and benefits	371,875	8,230	380,105
Computer supplies	150,350	2,255	152,605
Training and development	63,850	6,385	70,235
Other administrative costs	49,576	2,479	52,055
Total costs:	635,651		655,000

EL2-C5-A2-NationalCSDeptBdgt.xlsx

Category	Compact	Mid-size	SUV	Cost Per Car	Shipping	Warranty	Finance Rate	Number of Cars
Ford	345,500	289,275	199,776	8,096	15,500	60	3.25%	105
Chrysler	324,200	213,490	176,600	7,679	15,200	48	3.00%	95
Toyota	376,200	256,675	213,450	7,705	16,650	60	2.25%	112
Honda	389,400	249,970	206,490	7,833	15,775	60	2.50%	110
GM	351,700	231,550	200,675	7,133	15,000	48	3.25%	112

EL2-C5-A1-CutRateCars.xlsx

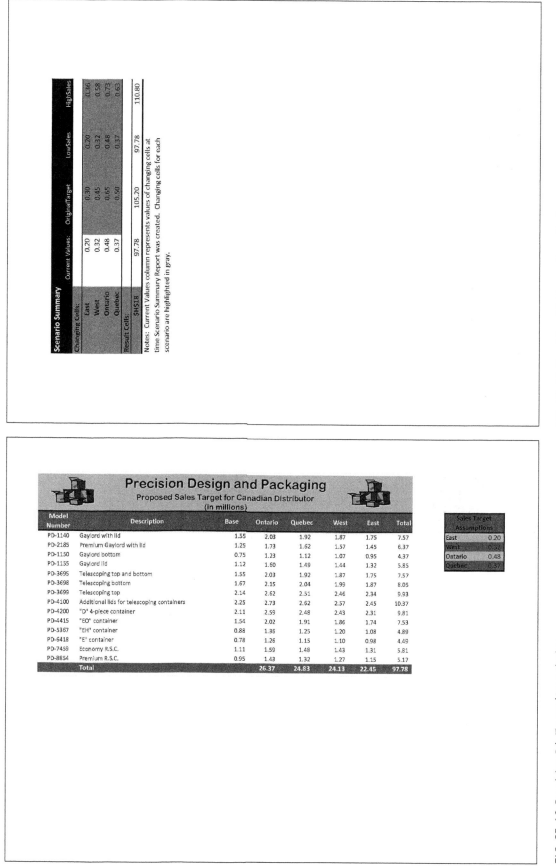

National Online Marketing Inc.
Computing Services Department

Hardware	Quantity	Unit Price	Extended Cost
Cisco 2950 switch	66	2,395.00	158,070.00
Cisco 3550 switch	10	4,590.00	45,900.00
Cisco 2621 router	18	3,195.00	57,510.00
Pix firewall	1	4,720.00	4,720.00
PowerEdge 2850 server	10	7,278.00	72,780.00
PowerEdge 1800 server	5	8,663.00	43,315.00
Total Hardware			$ 382,295.00
Software			
Office suite 2010	1,151	320.00	368,320.00
Exchange 2010 server	1	1,399.00	1,399.00
Anti-malware suite	1,151	45.00	51,795.00
Total Software			$ 421,514.00
Total Hardware and Software			$ 803,809.00

EL2-C5-A5-NationalICSDeptCapital.xlsx

National Online Marketing Inc.
Computing Services Department

		Variable minutes and cost per minute impact on cost			
Tier 1 support	2,648				
Tier 2 support	1,688				
Tier 3 support	774	1.81	0.525	0.575	0.600
Total calls	5,110	15,000.00	1.54	1.69	1.76
		15,300.00	1.57	1.72	1.80
Total call minutes logged	16,100.00	15,500.00	1.59	1.74	1.82
		15,800.00	1.62	1.78	1.86
		15,900.00	1.63	1.79	1.87
Average time per call (mins)	3.15	16,100.00	1.65	1.81	1.89
Average cost per minute	0.575	16,300.00	1.67	1.83	1.91
Average cost per call	$ 1.81	16,500.00	1.70	1.86	1.94

EL2-C5-A4-NationalICSDeptHlpDs.xlsx

Monthly revenue for each lesson assuming no change in number

	18.00	20.00	22.00
	180.00	200.00	220.00
	270.00	300.00	330.00
	176.00	192.00	208.00
	104.00	112.00	120.00
	324.00	360.00	396.00
	220.00	240.00	260.00
	396.00	440.00	484.00
	270.00	300.00	330.00
	352.00	384.00	416.00
	2,292.00	2,528.00	2,764.00

Notes: Current Values column represents values of changing cells at time Scenario Summary Report was created. Changing cells for each scenario are highlighted in green.

Class	Hourly Rate	Registered Students	Monthly Revenue
Basic Drum Theory	21.00	10	209.96
Beginner Rock Drumming	21.00	15	314.94
Intermediate Rock Drumming	25.00	8	199.97
Advanced Rock Drumming	29.00	4	115.98
Beginner Jazz Drumming	21.00	18	377.92
Developing Jazz Style	25.00	10	249.96
Single Pedal Drum Beats	21.00	22	461.91
Single Pedal Drum Fills	21.00	15	314.94
Bass Drum Doubles	25.00	16	399.93
TOTAL			2,645.50

Base hourly rate for all lessons: 21.00

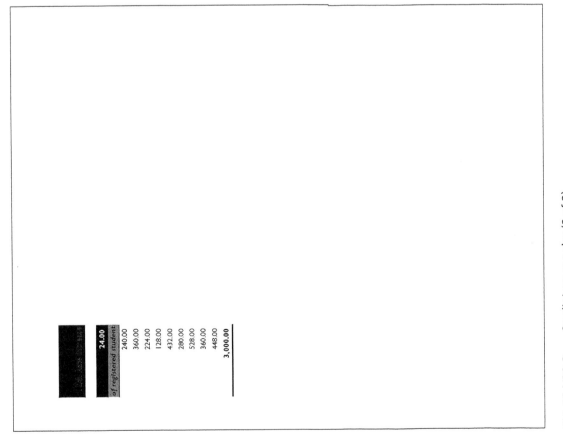

EL2-C5-VB2-DrumStudioLessons.xlsx (2 of 2)

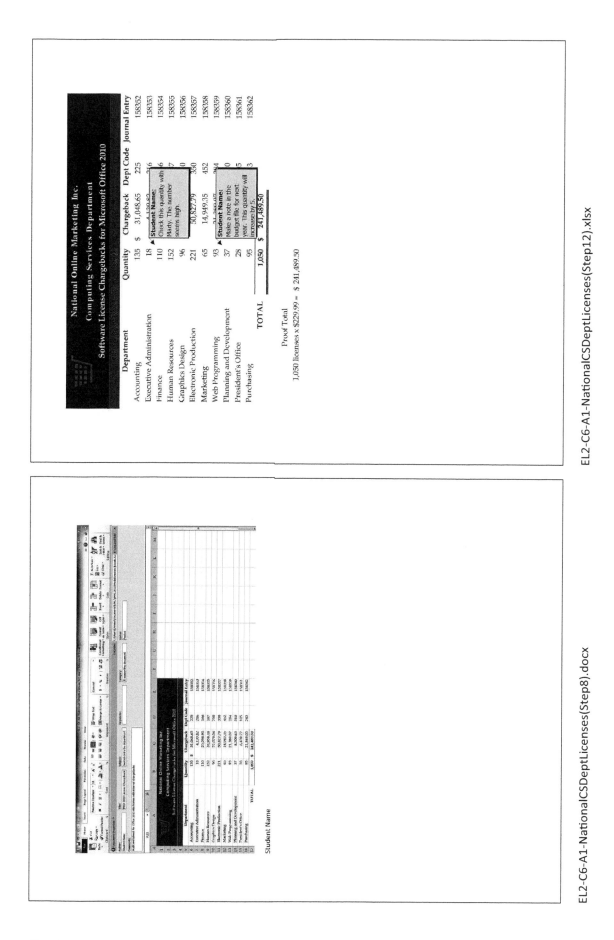

Action Number	Date	Time	Who	Change	Sheet	Range	New Value	Old Value	Action Type	Losing Action
1	3/6/2012	12:02 PM	Grant Antone	Cell Change	2014MfgTargets	D4	3,755.00	3,251.00		
2	3/6/2012	12:02 PM	Grant Antone	Cell Change	2014MfgTargets	D17	6,176.00	5,748.00		
3	3/6/2012	12:03 PM	Jean Kocsis	Cell Change	2014MfgTargets	E6	5,748.00	6,145.00		
4	3/6/2012	12:03 PM	Jean Kocsis	Cell Change	2014MfgTargets	E11	3,417.00	2,214.00		

The history ends with the changes saved on 3/6/2012 at 12:03 PM.

EL2-C6-A6-PrecisionMfgTargets(Step9-HistoryWkst).xlsx

Action Number	Date	Time	Who	Change	Sheet	Range	New Value	Old Value	Action Type	Losing Action
1	3/6/2012	11:17 AM	Lorne Moir	Cell Change	Sheet1	C11	5,520.00	4,352.00		
2	3/6/2012	11:17 AM	Lorne Moir	Cell Change	Sheet1	C18	15,960.00	15,241.00		
3	3/6/2012	11:18 AM	Gerri Gonzales	Cell Change	Sheet1	F4	5,126.00	3,845.00		
4	3/6/2012	11:18 AM	Gerri Gonzales	Cell Change	Sheet1	F9	9,320.00	7,745.00		

The history ends with the changes saved on 3/6/2012 at 11:18 AM.

EL2-C6-A2-PrecisionMfgTargets-HistoryWkst.xlsx

Action Number	Date	Time	Who	Change	Sheet	Range	New Value	Old Value	Action Type	Losing Action
1	3/6/2012	10:46 AM	Erin Haviland	Cell Change	Sheet1	C4	$17.25	$16.50		
2	3/6/2012	10:46 AM	Erin Haviland	Cell Change	Sheet1	C7	$8.50	$8.25		
3	3/6/2012	10:46 AM	Erin Haviland	Cell Change	Sheet1	C10	$22.50	$20.00		
4	3/6/2012	10:46 AM	Erin Haviland	Cell Change	Sheet1	C14	$27.50	$28.50		
5	3/6/2012	10:46 AM	Erin Haviland	Cell Change	Sheet1	B7	25 minute trail walk	30 minute trail walk		

The history ends with the changes saved on 3/6/2012 at 10:46 AM.

Precision Design and Packaging
Bulk Container 2014 Manufacturing Units
(in thousands)

Model Number	Description	East	West	North	South	Total
PD-1140	Gaylord with lid	2,531	3,755	4,215	3,845	14,346
PD-2185	Premium Gaylord with lid	2,251	3,157	4,185	3,214	12,807
PD-1150	Gaylord bottom	5,234	5,584	6,145	4,832	21,795
PD-1155	Gaylord lid	5,234	5,584	6,145	4,832	21,795
PD-3695	Telescoping top and bottom	10,253	12,458	11,254	14,853	48,818
PD-3698	Telescoping bottom	8,532	8,863	9,145	7,745	34,285
PD-3699	Telescoping top	7,541	8,651	8,842	7,652	32,686
PD-4100	Additional lids for telescoping containers	4,352	3,487	3,417	4,832	16,088
PD-4200	"D" 4-piece container	3,475	4,278	5,513	4,862	18,128
PD-4415	"EO" container	3,251	4,577	5,914	5,142	18,884
PD-5367	"EH" container	2,534	3,014	4,437	5,684	15,669
PD-6418	"E" container	6,523	6,988	7,214	6,348	27,073
PD-7459	Economy R.S.C.	6,325	6,942	6,845	6,512	26,624
PD-8854	Premium R.S.C.	5,214	5,748	6,145	6,327	23,434
PD-9101	Corrugated pads 15 x 15	15,241	18,241	16,854	17,458	67,794
PD-9105	Corrugated pads 20 x 12	16,325	19,652	22,418	20,463	78,858
PD-9110	Corrugated pads 24 x 18	12,453	15,874	17,698	18,496	64,521
PD-9115	Corrugated pads 30 x 30	8,653	8,846	9,154	7,763	34,416
	Total	125,922	145,699	155,540	150,860	578,021

Proof of Total   578,021

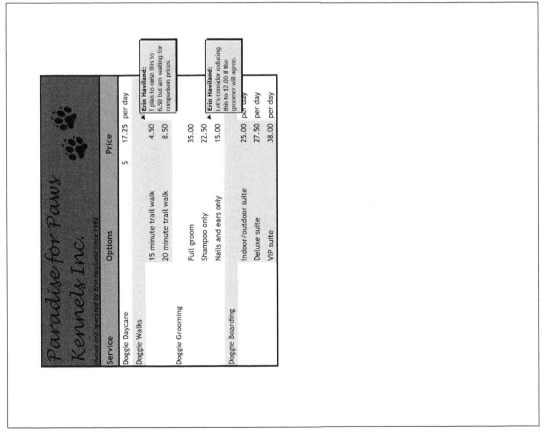

Paradise for Paws Kennels Inc.

Owned and operated by Erin Haviland since 1992

Service	Options	Price	
Doggie Daycare		$ 17.25	per day
Doggie Walks			
	15 minute trail walk	4.50	
	20 minute trail walk	8.50	
Doggie Grooming			
	Full groom	35.00	
	Shampoo only	22.50	
	Nails and ears only	15.00	
Doggie Boarding			
	Indoor/outdoor suite	25.00	per day
	Deluxe suite	27.50	per day
	VIP suite	38.00	per day

Erin Haviland: I plan to raise this to 6.50 but am waiting for comparison prices.

Erin Haviland: Let's consider reducing this to 12.00 if the groomer will agree.

EL2-C6-VB-PawsParadise(Step5).xlsx

```
Module1 - 1

Sub FormulaBarOff()
' FormulaBarOff Macro
' Turns off formula bar and protects worksheet. Created by [Student Name] on [Date].
' Keyboard Shortcut: Ctrl+Shift+M
    Application.DisplayFormulaBar = False
    ActiveSheet.Protect DrawingObjects:=True, Contents:=True, Scenarios:=True
End Sub
Sub FormulaBarOn()
' FormulaBarOn Macro
' Turns on formula bar and unprotects worksheet. Created by [Student Name] on [Date].
' Keyboard Shortcut: Ctrl+Shift+N
    Application.DisplayFormulaBar = True
    ActiveSheet.Unprotect
End Sub
```

EL2-C7-A4-PrintMacros(Step3).xlsx

National Online Marketing Inc.
Accounting Department
General Ledger Journal Entry Documentation

Internal Chargeback for Computing Services Department
Batch Technical Service Requests (TSRs)

	Parts	Labor	Total	CSDept-TSR	Dept Code	GL Account Number	Journal Entry Number
Accounting	$ 557.45	$ 820.00	$ 1,377.45	CS-4020	225	010501	159021
Executive Administration	1,057.45	1,550.00	2,607.45	CS-4021	216	010510	159022
Finance	355.22	225.00	580.22	CS-4022	166	010542	159023
Human Resources	187.42	85.50	272.92	CS-4023	187	010553	159024
Graphics Design	637.54	265.75	903.29	CS-4024	210	010555	159025
Electronic Production	857.00	355.00	1,212.00	CS-4025	350	010560	159026
Marketing	14.00	275.50	289.50	CS-4026	452	010575	159027
Web Programming	72.47	65.75	138.22	CS-4027	284	010582	159028
Planning and Development	65.84	55.50	121.34	CS-4028	310	010585	159029
President's Office	154.75	65.50	220.25	CS-4029	105	010590	159030
Purchasing	346.85	255.50	602.35	CS-4030	243	010596	159031
			$ 8,324.99				

EL2-C7-A2-NationalAcctgDeptCS.xlsx

```
Module1 - 1

Sub Landscape()
'
' Landscape Macro
' Changes to landscape, changes margins, and centers worksheet horizontally. Created by [Student Name]
' on [Date].
'
' Keyboard Shortcut: Ctrl+Shift+Q
'
    Application.PrintCommunication = False
    With ActiveSheet.PageSetup
        .PrintTitleRows = ""
        .PrintTitleColumns = ""
    End With
    Application.PrintCommunication = True
    ActiveSheet.PageSetup.PrintArea = ""
    Application.PrintCommunication = False
    With ActiveSheet.PageSetup
        .LeftHeader = ""
        .CenterHeader = ""
        .RightHeader = ""
        .LeftFooter = ""
        .CenterFooter = ""
        .RightFooter = ""
        .LeftMargin = Application.InchesToPoints(0.5)
        .RightMargin = Application.InchesToPoints(0.5)
        .TopMargin = Application.InchesToPoints(1)
        .BottomMargin = Application.InchesToPoints(0.5)
        .HeaderMargin = Application.InchesToPoints(0.3)
        .FooterMargin = Application.InchesToPoints(0.3)
        .PrintHeadings = False
        .PrintGridlines = False
        .PrintComments = xlPrintNoComments
        .PrintQuality = 1200
        .CenterHorizontally = True
        .CenterVertically = False
        .Orientation = xlLandscape
        .Draft = False
        .PaperSize = xlPaperLetter
        .FirstPageNumber = xlAutomatic
        .Order = xlDownThenOver
        .BlackAndWhite = False
        .Zoom = 100
        .PrintErrors = xlPrintErrorsDisplayed
        .OddAndEvenPagesHeaderFooter = False
        .DifferentFirstPageHeaderFooter = False
        .ScaleWithDocHeaderFooter = True
        .AlignMarginsHeaderFooter = True
        .EvenPage.LeftHeader.Text = ""
        .EvenPage.CenterHeader.Text = ""
        .EvenPage.RightHeader.Text = ""
        .EvenPage.LeftFooter.Text = ""
        .EvenPage.CenterFooter.Text = ""
        .EvenPage.RightFooter.Text = ""
        .FirstPage.LeftHeader.Text = ""
        .FirstPage.CenterHeader.Text = ""
        .FirstPage.RightHeader.Text = ""
        .FirstPage.LeftFooter.Text = ""
        .FirstPage.CenterFooter.Text = ""
        .FirstPage.RightFooter.Text = ""
    End With
    Application.PrintCommunication = True
End Sub

Sub Technic()
'
' Technic Macro
' Changes theme to Technic and turns off display of gridlines. Created by [Student Name] on [Date].
'
' Keyboard Shortcut: Ctrl+t
'
    ActiveWorkbook.ApplyTheme ( _
        "C:\Program Files\Microsoft Office\Document Themes 14\Technic.thmx")
```

EL2-C7-A4-PrintMacros(Step8).xlsx (1 of 2)

```
Module1 - 2

    ActiveWindow.DisplayGridlines = False
End Sub
```

EL2-C7-A4-PrintMacros(Step8).xlsx (2 of 2)

Benchmark Excel 2010 Level 2 Model Answers

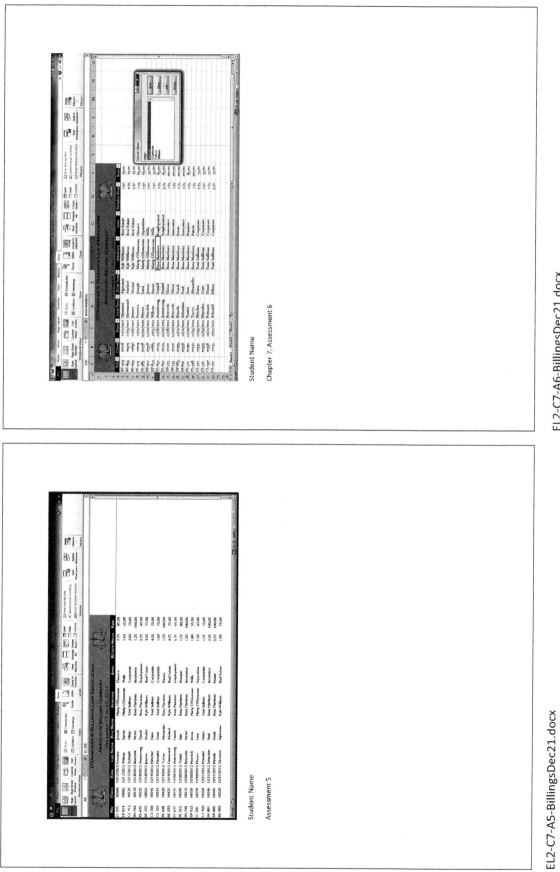

Student Name

Chapter 7, Assessment 6

EL2-C7-A6-BillingsDec21.docx

Student Name

Assessment 5

EL2-C7-A5-BillingsDec21.docx

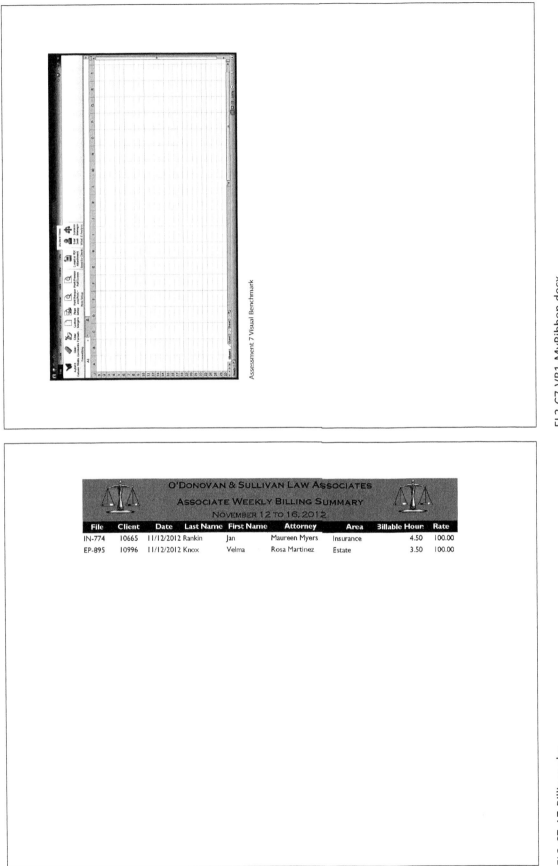

Assessment 7 Visual Benchmark

EL2-C7-VB1-MyRibbon.docx

EL2-C7-A7-Billings.xlsx

Audennita Music

SALES INVOICE

Date: December 18, 2012

Sold to: Jamie Vanderwyst
P. O. Box 24
259 Harlow Street
Bangor, Maine 04401

Ship to: Same

Telephone: 207 555 3745

Code	Description	Quantity	Price	Extended Total
AM205799	Four Piece Cymbal Package with Cymbal Bag & 18" Crash	1	$ 654.95	654.95
AM208000	5A Wood Tip Drumsticks Natural (pair)	1	$ 6.86	6.86
			Total	661.81
			Tax1 5%	33.09
			Tax2 8%	52.94
			Amount Due	747.85

Terms: *Due upon receipt of invoice.*
Cash, Check, Visa, and Mastercard accepted.

Hillsdale Financial Services

Research Services Department
Three-year unemployment data for the State of Michigan
http://data.bls.gov/cgi-bin/surveymost?rs
Series ID:LASST26000003

Year	Period	Labor Force	Employment	Unemployment	Unemployment Rate
2007	Jan	5071959(B)	4725640(B)	346319(B)	6.8(B)
2007	Feb	5064878(B)	4721172(B)	343706(B)	6.8(B)
2007	Mar	5055577(B)	4712852(B)	342725(B)	6.8(B)
2007	Apr	5046029(B)	4701839(B)	344190(B)	6.8(B)
2007	May	5037838(B)	4689400(B)	348438(B)	6.9(B)
2007	Jun	5032100(B)	4677860(B)	354240(B)	7.0(B)
2007	Jul	5028750(B)	4668695(B)	360055(B)	7.2(B)
2007	Aug	5027523(B)	4662968(B)	364555(B)	7.3(B)
2007	Sep	5027545(B)	4660900(B)	366645(B)	7.3(B)
2007	Oct	5027392(B)	4661088(B)	366304(B)	7.3(B)
2007	Nov	5024655(B)	4661781(B)	362874(B)	7.2(B)
2007	Dec	5018688(B)	4661113(B)	357575(B)	7.1(B)
2008	Jan	5010441(B)	4657217(B)	353224(B)	7.0(B)
2008	Feb	5001598(B)	4649316(B)	352282(B)	7.0(B)
2008	Mar	4993950(B)	4637085(B)	356865(B)	7.1(B)
2008	Apr	4988399(B)	4621012(B)	367387(B)	7.4(B)
2008	May	4984647(B)	4602236(B)	382411(B)	7.7(B)
2008	Jun	4981998(B)	4582910(B)	399088(B)	8.0(B)
2008	Jul	4978529(B)	4563683(B)	414846(B)	8.3(B)
2008	Aug	4972756(B)	4543400(B)	429356(B)	8.6(B)
2008	Sep	4965056(B)	4519433(B)	445623(B)	9.0(B)
2008	Oct	4956697(B)	4489675(B)	467022(B)	9.4(B)
2008	Nov	4948301(B)	4454047(B)	494254(B)	10.0(B)
2008	Dec	4940397(B)	4414491(B)	525906(B)	10.6(B)
2009	Jan	4932968(B)	4373714(B)	559254(B)	11.3(B)
2009	Feb	4926706(B)	4334442(B)	592264(B)	12.0(B)
2009	Mar	4921341(B)	4298897(B)	622444(B)	12.6(B)
2009	Apr	4915492(B)	4267686(B)	647806(B)	13.2(B)
2009	May	4908118(B)	4239995(B)	668123(B)	13.6(B)
2009	Jun	4899307(B)	4216022(B)	683285(B)	13.9(B)
2009	Jul	4889126(B)	4196182(B)	692944(B)	14.2(B)
2009	Aug	4878061(B)	4180350(B)	697711(B)	14.3(B)
2009	Sep	4866356(B)	4167176(B)	699180(B)	14.4(B)
2009	Oct	4855043(B)	4155358(B)	699685(B)	14.4(B)
2009	Nov	4844674(B)	4144829(B)	699845(B)	14.4(B)
2009	Dec	4836079(B)	4136416(B)	699663(B)	14.5(B)

EL2-C8-A1-HillsdaleResearchServices(Step9).xlsx

Hillsdale Financial Services

Research Services Department
CPI data from U.S. Department of Labor, Bureau of Labor Statistics
http://data.bls.gov/cgi-bin/surveymost?bls
Price Indexes: CPI for all urban consumers CPI-U 1982-84=100 (Unadjusted) CUUR0000SA0

Year	Jan	Feb	Mar	Apr	May	Jun	Jul	Aug	Sep	Oct	Nov	Dec
2000	168.8	169.8	171.2	171.3	171.5	172.4	172.8	172.8	173.7	174.0	174.1	174.0
2001	175.1	175.8	176.2	176.9	177.7	178.0	177.5	177.5	178.3	177.7	177.4	176.7
2002	177.1	177.8	178.8	179.8	179.8	179.9	180.1	180.7	181.0	181.3	181.3	180.9
2003	181.7	183.1	184.2	183.8	183.5	183.7	183.9	184.6	185.2	185.0	184.5	184.3
2004	185.2	186.2	187.4	188.0	189.1	189.7	189.4	189.5	189.9	190.9	191.0	190.3
2005	190.7	191.8	193.3	194.6	194.4	194.5	195.4	196.4	198.8	199.2	197.6	196.8
2006	198.3	198.7	199.8	201.5	202.5	202.9	203.5	203.9	202.9	201.8	201.5	201.8
2007	202.4	203.5	205.4	206.7	207.9	208.4	208.3	207.9	208.5	208.9	210.2	210.0
2008	211.1	211.7	213.5	214.8	216.6	218.8	220.0	219.1	218.8	216.6	212.4	210.2
2009	211.1	212.2	212.7	213.2	213.9	215.7	215.4	215.8	216.0	216.2	216.3	215.9

EL2-C8-A1-HillsdaleResearchServices(Step5).xlsx

HILLSDALE REALTORS
OCTOBER SALES

NEW SALES RECORD

October exceeded goal
Annual sales will surpass last
$1 million!
2012 sales to exceed $____ million,
last year $____ million

COMMISSIONS BY SALES AGENT

October Sales Commissions by Sales Agent

EL2-C8-A3-HillsdaleOctRpt.pptx

Hillsdale Realtors

October Sales Report

October was another record-breaking month for Hillsdale Realtors. Sales exceeded the target by 8% and if the trend continues, our annual sales will surpass last year by over $1 million! Below is an itemized list of sales by date for the month.

Date	ID	Agent	Type	City	Price	Commission
10/1/2012	282715	Fernandez	Single family home	Phoenix	$ 525,000	$ 18,375.00
10/2/2012	315825	O'Brien	Townhome	Phoenix	$ 212,000	$ 7,420.00
10/4/2012	458215	O'Brien	Single family home	Mesa	$ 225,500	$ 7,892.50
10/7/2012	351245	Youngblood	Single family home	Chandler	$ 325,500	$ 11,392.50
10/10/2012	312548	Williamson	Townhome	Mesa	$ 165,800	$ 5,803.00
10/10/2012	291524	Fernandez	Single family home	Phoenix	$ 425,800	$ 14,903.00
10/12/2012	263412	Youngblood	Single family home	Phoenix	$ 375,800	$ 13,153.00
10/14/2012	254853	O'Brien	Townhome	Chandler	$ 341,500	$ 11,952.50
10/15/2012	302154	Fernandez	Townhome	Chandler	$ 225,600	$ 7,896.00
10/15/2012	311452	Youngblood	Condominium	Phoenix	$ 349,900	$ 12,246.50
10/18/2012	302785	O'Brien	Single family home	Glendale	$ 425,675	$ 14,898.63
10/19/2012	268457	O'Brien	Condominium	Glendale	$ 225,400	$ 7,889.00
10/21/2012	316548	Youngblood	Condominium	Phoenix	$ 345,100	$ 12,078.50
10/21/2012	315863	Fernandez	Single family home	Glendale	$ 455,700	$ 15,949.50
10/22/2012	294563	O'Brien	Condominium	Glendale	$ 415,000	$ 14,525.00
10/24/2012	288451	Fernandez	Townhome	Chandler	$ 385,000	$ 13,475.00
10/25/2012	275143	Fernandez	Single family home	Mesa	$ 275,500	$ 9,642.50
10/25/2012	311148	Youngblood	Single family home	Mesa	$ 345,750	$ 12,101.25
10/29/2012	325984	Youngblood	Condominium	Chandler	$ 285,900	$ 10,006.50
10/30/2012	246845	Youngblood	Single family home	Phoenix	$ 545,200	$ 19,082.00
10/30/2012	334567	O'Brien	Single family home	Phoenix	$ 475,800	$ 16,653.00
10/31/2012	266845	Fernandez	Condominium	Chandler	$ 325,000	$ 11,375.00
10/31/2012	254836	Youngblood	Condominium	Mesa	$ 275,800	$ 9,653.00

EL2-C8-A2-HillsdaleOctRpt.docx

Compatibility Report for EL2-C8-A5-Hillsdale2012Sales.xlsx
Run on 7/31/2012 13:47

The following features in this workbook are not supported by earlier versions of Excel. These features may be lost or degraded when opening this workbook in an earlier version of Excel or if you save this workbook in an earlier file format.

Significant loss of functionality	# of occurrences	
This object will no longer be editable.	1	2012Sales'!A1: G17
One or more cells in this workbook contain a conditional formatting type that is not supported in earlier versions of Excel, such as data bars, color scales, or icon sets.	1	2012Sales'!G4: G15
One or more cells in this workbook contain a data bar rule that uses a "Negative Value" setting. These data bars will not be supported in earlier versions of Excel.	1	2012Sales'!G4: G15

Minor loss of fidelity	# of occurrences	
Some cells or styles in this workbook contain formatting that is not supported by the selected file format. These formats will be converted to the closest format available.	3	
One or more cells in this workbook contain a data bar rule that uses a fill, border, or "bar direction" setting. These data bars will not be supported in earlier versions of Excel.	1	2012Sales'!G4: G15

Student Name

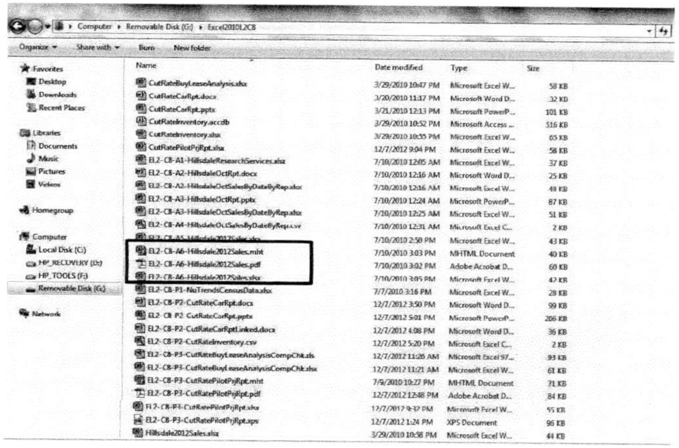

Student Name

Excel Level 2, Chapter 8, Assessment 6, Step 7

EL2-C8-A6-PrintScreen(Step7).docx

Version

Excel 97-2003

Excel 97-2003

Excel 97-2003

Excel 2007

Excel 97-2003

Excel 97-2003

Excel 2007

EL2-C8-A5-Hillsdale2012Sales(Step10).xlsx (2 of 2)

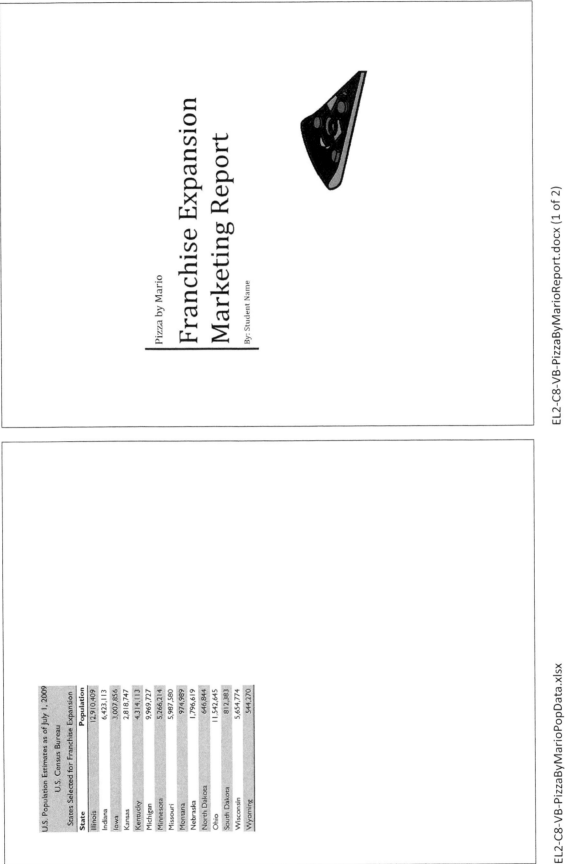

Pizza by Mario

Franchise Expansion
Marketing Report

By: Student Name

U.S. Population Estimates as of July 1, 2009	
U.S. Census Bureau	
States Selected for Franchise Expansion	
State	**Population**
Illinois	12,910,409
Indiana	6,423,113
Iowa	3,007,856
Kansas	2,818,747
Kentucky	4,314,113
Michigan	9,969,727
Minnesota	5,266,214
Missouri	5,987,580
Montana	974,989
Nebraska	1,796,619
North Dakota	646,844
Ohio	11,542,645
South Dakota	812,383
Wisconsin	5,654,774
Wyoming	544,270

Pizza by Mario Franchise Expansion

Selected States for New Franchises

The states selected for franchise expansions are located geographically adjacent to states in which existing franchises are located. This decision was made in consultation with the NuTrends Market Research consultant for the following reasons:

- Minimize travel area for head office personnel
- Provide for lower distribution costs of supplies from the head office warehouse
- Lower cost of travel for franchisees to training and meetings at head office

NuTrends Market Research provided the latest population estimates from the U.S. Census Bureau for the target states. The following chart depicts these estimates.

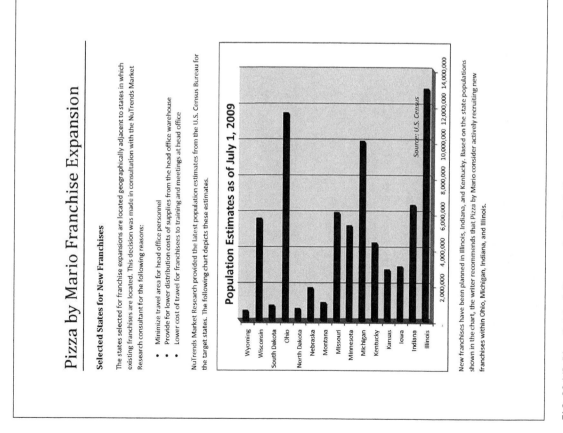

New franchises have been planned in Illinois, Indiana, and Kentucky. Based on the state populations shown in the chart, the writer recommends that Pizza by Mario consider actively recruiting new franchises within Ohio, Michigan, Indiana, and Illinois.

EL2-C8-VB-PizzaByMarioReport.docx (2 of 2)

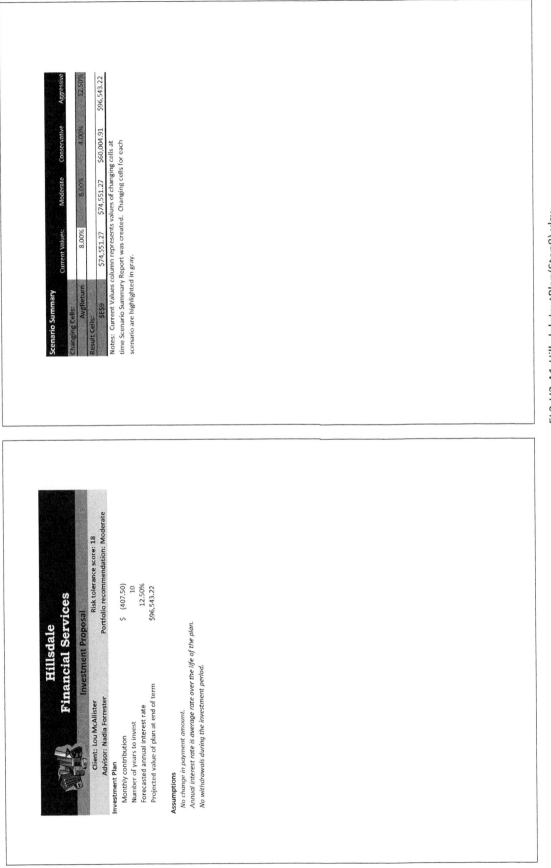

Scenario Summary

	Current Values:	Moderate	Conservative	Aggressive
Changing Cells:				
AvgReturn	8.00%	8.00%	4.00%	12.50%
Result Cells:				
$E$9	$74,551.27	$74,551.27	$60,004.91	$96,543.22

Notes: Current Values column represents values of changing cells at time Scenario Summary Report was created. Changing cells for each scenario are highlighted in gray.

EL2-U2-A1-HillsdaleInvtPlan(Step8).xlsx

Hillsdale Financial Services

Investment Proposal

Client: Lou McAllister
Advisor: Nadia Forrester

Risk tolerance score: 18
Portfolio recommendation: **Moderate**

Investment Plan

Monthly contribution	$ (407.50)
Number of years to invest	10
Forecasted annual interest rate	12.50%
Projected value of plan at end of term	$96,543.22

Assumptions

No change in payment amount.
Annual interest rate is average rate over the life of the plan.
No withdrawals during the investment period.

EL2-U2-A1-HillsdaleInvtPlan(Step6).xlsx

Benchmark Excel 2010 Level 2 Model Answers

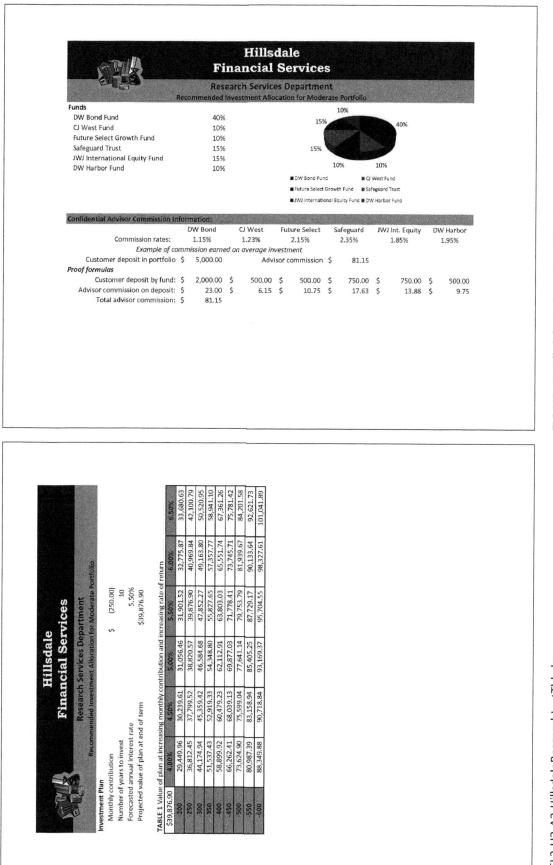

Action Number	Date	Time	Who	Change	Sheet	Range	New Value	Old Value	Action Type	Losing Action
1	7/13/2010	3:26 PM	Carey Winters	Cell Change	ModeratePortfolio	B7	15%	10%		
2	7/13/2010	3:26 PM	Carey Winters	Cell Change	ModeratePortfolio	B8	10%	15%		
3	7/13/2010	3:27 PM	Jodi VanKemenade	Cell Change	ModeratePortfolio	D17	2.32%	2.15%		
4	7/13/2010	3:27 PM	Jodi VanKemenade	Cell Change	ModeratePortfolio	E17	2.19%	2.35%		

The history ends with the changes saved on 7/13/2010 at 3:27 PM.

Student Name

EL2-U2-A4-HillsdaleModeratePortfolio, Step 4

EL2-U2-A4-HillsdaleModeratePortfolio(Step4).docx

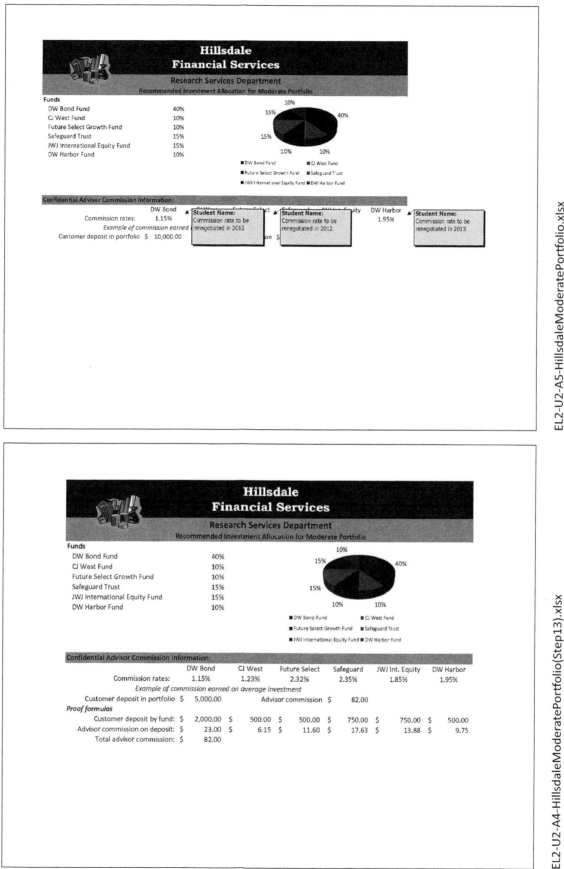

Hillsdale Financial Services

Research Services Department
Recommended Investment Allocation for Moderate Portfolio

Funds
DW Bond Fund	40%
CJ West Fund	10%
Future Select Growth Fund	10%
Safeguard Trust	15%
JWJ International Equity Fund	15%
DW Harbor Fund	10%

Confidential Advisor Commission Information:

	DW Bond			DW Harbor
Commission rates:	1.15%			1.95%

Example of commission earned
Customer deposit in portfolio $ 10,000.00

Student Name:
Commission rate to be renegotiated in 2012

Student Name:
Commission rate to be renegotiated in 2012

Student Name:
Commission rate to be renegotiated in 2013

Hillsdale Financial Services

Research Services Department
Recommended Investment Allocation for Moderate Portfolio

Funds
DW Bond Fund	40%
CJ West Fund	10%
Future Select Growth Fund	10%
Safeguard Trust	15%
JWJ International Equity Fund	15%
DW Harbor Fund	10%

Confidential Advisor Commission Information:

	DW Bond	CJ West	Future Select	Safeguard	JWJ Int. Equity	DW Harbor
Commission rates:	1.15%	1.23%	2.32%	2.35%	1.85%	1.95%

Example of commission earned on average investment

Customer deposit in portfolio $	5,000.00		Advisor commission $	82.00	

Proof formulas

Customer deposit by fund: $	2,000.00 $	500.00 $	500.00 $	750.00 $	750.00 $	500.00
Advisor commission on deposit: $	23.00 $	6.15 $	11.60 $	17.63 $	13.88 $	9.75
Total advisor commission: $	82.00					

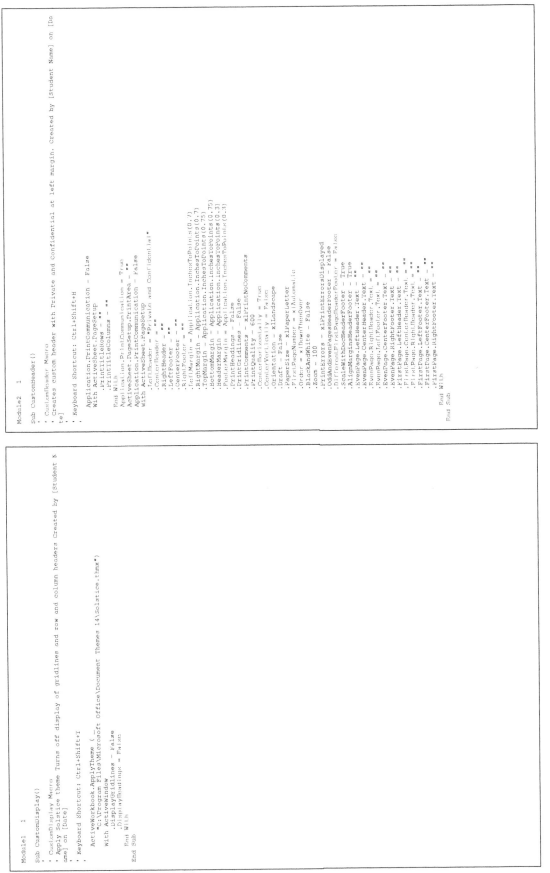

```
Module1    1

Sub CustomDisplay()
'
' CustomDisplay Macro
' Apply Solstice theme Turns off display of gridlines and row and column headers Created by [Student N
ame] on [Date]
'
' Keyboard Shortcut: Ctrl+Shift+T
'
    ActiveWorkbook.ApplyTheme ( _
        "C:\Program Files\Microsoft Office\Document Themes 14\Solstice.thmx")
    With ActiveWindow
        .DisplayGridlines = False
        .DisplayHeadings = False
    End With
End Sub
```

EL2-U2-A6-HillsdaleModeratePortfolio(Step6,Macros).xlsx (1 of 2)

```
Module2    1

Sub CustomHeader()
'
' CustomHeader Macro
' Creates custom header with Private and Confidential at left margin. Created by [Student Name] on [Da
te]
'
' Keyboard Shortcut: Ctrl+Shift+H
'
    Application.PrintCommunication = False
    With ActiveSheet.PageSetup
        .PrintTitleRows = ""
        .PrintTitleColumns = ""
    End With
    Application.PrintCommunication = True
    ActiveSheet.PageSetup.PrintArea = ""
    Application.PrintCommunication = False
    With ActiveSheet.PageSetup
        .LeftHeader = "Private and Confidential"
        .CenterHeader = ""
        .RightHeader = ""
        .LeftFooter = ""
        .CenterFooter = ""
        .RightFooter = ""
        .LeftMargin = Application.InchesToPoints(0.7)
        .RightMargin = Application.InchesToPoints(0.7)
        .TopMargin = Application.InchesToPoints(0.75)
        .BottomMargin = Application.InchesToPoints(0.75)
        .HeaderMargin = Application.InchesToPoints(0.3)
        .FooterMargin = Application.InchesToPoints(0.3)
        .PrintHeadings = False
        .PrintGridlines = False
        .PrintComments = xlPrintNoComments
        .PrintQuality = 600
        .CenterHorizontally = True
        .CenterVertically = False
        .Orientation = xlLandscape
        .Draft = False
        .PaperSize = xlPaperLetter
        .FirstPageNumber = xlAutomatic
        .Order = xlDownThenOver
        .BlackAndWhite = False
        .Zoom = 100
        .PrintErrors = xlPrintErrorsDisplayed
        .OddAndEvenPagesHeaderFooter = False
        .DifferentFirstPageHeaderFooter = False
        .ScaleWithDocHeaderFooter = True
        .AlignMarginsHeaderFooter = True
        .EvenPage.LeftHeader.Text = ""
        .EvenPage.CenterHeader.Text = ""
        .EvenPage.RightHeader.Text = ""
        .EvenPage.LeftFooter.Text = ""
        .EvenPage.CenterFooter.Text = ""
        .EvenPage.RightFooter.Text = ""
        .FirstPage.LeftHeader.Text = ""
        .FirstPage.CenterHeader.Text = ""
        .FirstPage.RightHeader.Text = ""
        .FirstPage.LeftFooter.Text = ""
        .FirstPage.CenterFooter.Text = ""
        .FirstPage.RightFooter.Text = ""
    End With
End Sub
```

EL2-U2-A6-HillsdaleModeratePortfolio(Step6,Macros).xlsx (2 of 2)

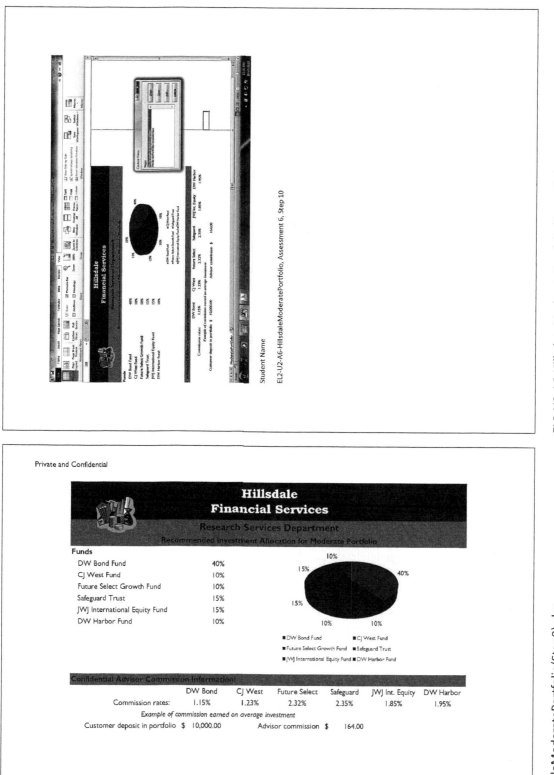

Hillsdale
Financial Services

Research Services Department
Recommended Investment Allocation for Moderate Portfolio

Funds	
DW Bond Fund	40%
CJ West Fund	10%
Future Select Growth Fund	10%
Safeguard Trust	15%
JWJ International Equity Fund	15%
DW Harbor Fund	10%

■ DW Bond Fund ■ CJ West Fund
■ Future Select Growth Fund ■ Safeguard Trust
■ JWJ International Equity Fund ■ DW Harbor Fund

Confidential Advisor Commission Information

	DW Bond	CJ West	Future Select	Safeguard	JWJ Int. Equity	DW Harbor
Commission rates:	1.15%	1.23%	2.32%	2.35%	1.85%	1.95%

Example of commission earned on average investment

Customer deposit in portfolio	$	10,000.00	Advisor commission	$	164.00

Student Name

EL2-U2-A6-HillsdaleModeratePortfolio(Step10).docx

EL2-U2-A6-HillsdaleModeratePortfolio(Step9).xlsx

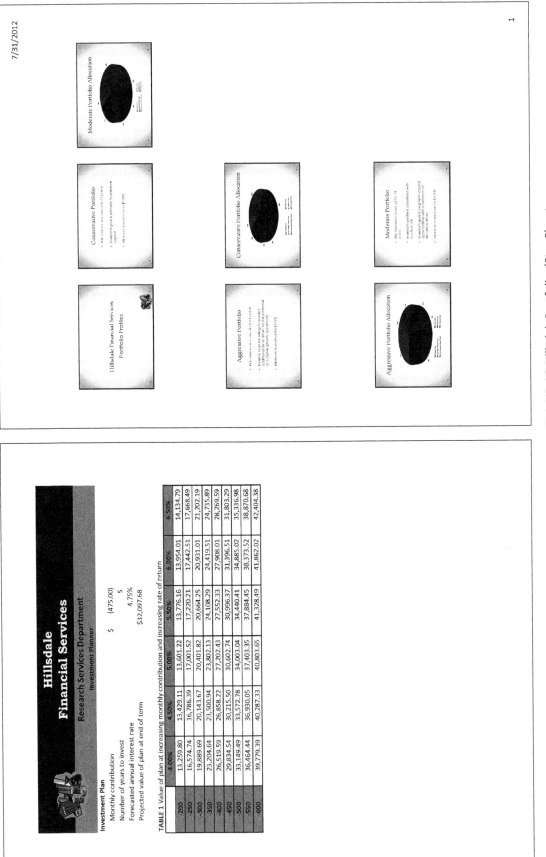

EL2-U2-A8-HillsdalePortfolios(Step6).pptx

Benchmark Excel 2010 Level 2 Model Answers

EL2-U2-A7-HillsdaleInvPlan.xlsx

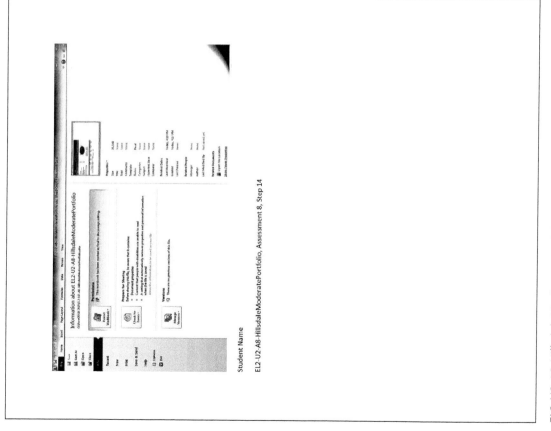

Student Name

EL2-U2-A8-HillsdaleModeratePortfolio, Assessment 8, Step 14

EL2-U2-A8-HillsdaleModeratePortfolio(Step14).docx

Rubrics

Note that the following are suggested rubrics. Instructors should feel free to customize the rubric to suit their grading standards and/or to adjust the point values.

Suggested Scoring Distribution: Above average = student completes 80% or more of task(s); average = student completes 70–79% of task(s); below average = student completes 69% or less of task(s)

Excel Level 1, Chapter 1

Skills Check

Assessment 1: Create a Worksheet using AutoComplete
File: **EL1-C1-A1-Plan.xlsx**

Steps	Tasks	Criteria	Value	Score
1	Typing, Accuracy, Formatting	At a blank workbook, create worksheet shown in Fig. 1.12 as follows: a. To create © symbol in A1, type **(c)**. b. Type misspelled words as shown, letting AutoCorrect correct them; then use AutoComplete to insert second occurrence of *Category, Available,* and *Balance.* c. Merge and center A1 and B1.	7	
2-3	Organization, Finishing	Save as **EL1-C1-A1-Plan**, print, then close workbook.	3	
		TOTAL POINTS	10	

Assessment 2: Create and Format a Worksheet
File: **EL1-C1-A2-Exp.xlsx**

Steps	Tasks	Criteria	Value	Score
1	Typing, Formatting, Formulas	At a blank workbook, create worksheet shown in Fig. 1.13 as follows: a. Merge and center A1 through C1. b. After typing, automatically adjust width of column A. c. Insert in B8 sum of B3 through B7, and in C8 sum of C3 through C7. d. Apply Accounting Number Format style, decrease decimal point by two positions in B3, C3, B8, and C8. e. Apply Comma Style, decrease decimal point two times in B4 through C7. f. For number amounts shown as (###), automatically adjust width of appropriate columns.	7	
2-3	Organization, Finishing	Save as **EL1-C1-A2-Exp**, print, then close workbook.	3	
		TOTAL POINTS	10	

Assessment 3: Create a Worksheet Using the Fill Handle
File: **EL1-C1-A3-Invest.xlsx**

Steps	Tasks	Criteria	Value	Score
1	Typing, Accuracy, Formatting	At a blank workbook, create worksheet shown in Fig. 1.14 as follows: a. Type **Monday** in B2, then use fill handle to fill in remaining days of week. b. Type **350** in B3, then use fill handle to fill in remaining numbers in row. c. Merge and center A1 through G1.	3	
2	Formulas	Insert in G3 the sum of cells B3 through F3, insert in G4 the sum of B4 through F4.	2	
3-4	Formatting	After typing the data, select B3 through G4; then change to Accounting Number Format, two decimal points. If necessary, adjust column widths.	2	
5-6	Organization, Finishing	Save as **EL1-C1-A3-Invest**, print, then close workbook.	3	
		TOTAL POINTS	10	

Assessment 4: Insert Formulas in a Worksheet
File: **EL1-C1-A4-DIAnalysis.xlsx**

Steps	Tasks	Criteria	Value	Score
1	Organization, Accuracy	Open **DIAnalysis.xlsx**, Save As **EL1-C1-A4-DIAnalysis.xlsx.**	3	
2, 4	Formulas	Insert formula in B15 that totals amounts in B4 through B14. Insert formula in D4 that finds average of B4 and C4.	4	
3, 5	Editing	Use fill handle to copy relatively formula in cell B15 to cell C15 and to copy relatively formula in cell D4 down to cells D5 through D14.	3	
6	Formatting	Select D5 through D14, then apply Comma Style with zero decimals.	2	
7	Organization, Finishing	Resave, print, then close workbook.	3	
		TOTAL POINTS	15	

Visual Benchmark

Create, Format, and Insert Formulas in a Worksheet
File: **EL1-C1-VB-PersExps.xlsx**

Steps	Tasks	Criteria	Value	Score
1	Typing, Editing, Formulas, Formatting	At a blank workbook, create worksheet shown in Fig. 1.15 as follows: a. Type data as shown in the figure. Use fill handle when appropriate, merge and center *Personal Expenses – July through December*, automatically adjust column widths. b. Insert formulas to determine averages and totals. c. Apply Accounting Number Format style, zero decimal places, to amounts in B4 through H4 and B12 through H12. d. Apply Comma Style, zero decimals, to amounts in B5 through G11.	7	
2-3	Organization, Finishing	Save as **EL1-C1-VB-PersExps**, print, then close workbook.	3	
		TOTAL POINTS	10	

Case Study

Part 1

File: **EL1-C1-CS-DICalendar.xlsx**

Steps	Tasks	Criteria	Value	Score
1	Organization, Typing, Editing	Open **DICalendar.xlsx**, then do the following: • Insert *October, 2012* in cell A2, then days of the week (*Sunday*, *Monday*, *Tuesday*, *Wednesday*, *Thursday*, *Friday*, and *Saturday*) in A3 through G3. (Fill handle may be used.) • Insert number *1* in B4, *2* in C4, *3* in D4, *4* in E4, *5* in F4, and *6* in G4. • Insert remaining numbers of days (*7* through *13* in A6 through G6, *14* through *20* in A8 through G8, *21* through *27* in A10 through G10, and *28* through *31* in A12 through D12). If fill handle used, fill should not have formatting. • Insert text *Excel training will be held Thursday, October 4, from 9-11 a.m.* in cell E5, using Alt + Enter to put on two lines. • Insert text *A staff meeting is held the second and fourth Monday of each month from 9-10 a.m.* in cells B7 and B11. • Insert text *Time cards are due the first and third Fridays of the month* in cells F5 and F9. • Insert text *A production team meeting is scheduled for Tuesday, October 23, from 1-3 p.m.* in cell C11.	12	
2	Organization, Finishing	Save as **EL1-C1-CS-DICalendar**, print, then close workbook.	3	
		TOTAL POINTS	15	

Part 2

File: **EL1-C1-CS-DIExpenditures.xlsx**

Steps	Tasks	Criteria	Value	Score
1	Accuracy, Typing, Formulas	Open **DIExpenditures.xlsx**, insert data shown in Fig. 1.16, then insert formulas to calculate averages and totals.	7	
2	Organization, Finishing	Save workbook as **EL1-C1-CS-DIExpenditures**, print, then close.	3	
		TOTAL POINTS	10	

Part 3

File: **EL1-C1-CS-DINotetoJS.docx**

Steps	Tasks	Criteria	Value	Score
1	Typing	At a blank document, type a note to Jennifer Strauss explaining an Excel worksheet has been prepared with Purchasing Department expenditures. Included are cells from the worksheet containing the expenditure information.	6	
2	Organization, Editing, Formatting	In Excel, open **EL1-C1-CS-DIExpenditures.xlsx**, copy cells A3 through F9, then paste them in Word document. Make corrections to the table so information is readable.	5	
3	Organization, Finishing	Save document as **EL1-C1-CS-DINotetoJS.docx**, print, then close. Close **EL1-C1-CS-DIExpenditures.xlsx**.	4	
		TOTAL POINTS	15	

Part 4

File: **EL1-C1-CS-Copiers.xlsx**

Steps	Tasks	Criteria	Value	Score
1	Research, Typing	After using the Internet to research three companies that sell copiers (different copier models), open **DICopiers.xlsx**, then type the companies, model numbers, and prices in the designated cells.	7	
2	Organization, Finishing	Save as **EL1-C1-CS-Copiers**, print, then close workbook.	3	
		TOTAL POINTS	10	

Excel Level 1, Chapter 2

Skills Check

Assessment 1: Insert AVERAGE, MAX, and MIN Functions

File: **EL1-C2-A1-DISalesAnalysis.xlsx**

Steps	Tasks	Criteria	Value	Score
1-2	Organization, Accuracy	Open **DISalesAnalysis.xlsx**, Save As **EL1-C2-A1-DIAnalysis**.	3	

Steps	Tasks	Criteria	Value	Score
3, 5-7	Functions, Formulas	3. Use AVERAGE function to determine monthly sales (H4 through H9). 5. Total each monthly column including Average column (B10 through H10). 6–7. Use MAX function to determine highest monthly total (for B10 through G10), then insert amount in B11. 7. Use MIN function to determine lowest monthly total (for B10 through G10), then insert amount in B12.	7	
4	Formatting	Format H4 to Accounting Number, no decimal places.	2	
8	Organization, Finishing	Save, print, then close workbook.	3	
		TOTAL POINTS	15	

Assessment 2: Insert PMT Function

File: EL1-C2-A2-CMRefiPlan.xlsx

Steps	Tasks	Criteria	Value	Score
1-2	Organization, Accuracy	Open **CMRefiPlan.xlsx**, Save As **EL1-C2-A2-CMRefiPlan.**	3	
3	Functions, Editing	In cell E5, insert a formula with following specifications: (Use Insert Function button to) insert formula using PMT with following information: Rate = **C5/12** Nper = **D5** Pv = **-B5** Copy formula in E5 down to cells E6 through E8.	5	
4, 6	Formulas	Insert formula in F5 that multiplies amount in E5 by amount in D5, then insert a formula in G5 that subtracts amount in B5 from the amount in F5.	2	
5, 7	Editing	Copy formula in cell F5 down to F6 through F8. Copy formula in G5 down to G6 through G8.	2	
8	Organization, Finishing	Save, print, then close workbook.	3	
		TOTAL POINTS	15	

Assessment 3: Insert FV Function

File: EL1-C2-A3-RPInvest.xlsx

Steps	Tasks	Criteria	Value	Score
1-2	Organization, Accuracy	Open **RPInvest.xlsx**, Save As **EL1-C2-A3-RPInvest.**	3	

Steps	Tasks	Criteria	Value	Score
3	Formatting, Typing, Function	a. Change percentage in B3 from *9%* to *10%*. b. Change number in B4 from *36* to *60*. c. Change amount in B5 from *($1,200)* to *-500*. d. Use FV function to insert formula that calculates future value of the investment.	4	
4	Organization, Finishing	Save, print, then close workbook.	3	
		TOTAL POINTS	10	

Assessment 4: Write IF Statement Formulas
File: **EL1-C2-A4-DISalesBonuses.xlsx**

Steps	Tasks	Criteria	Value	Score
1-2	Organization, Accuracy	Open **DISalesBonuses.xlsx**, Save As **EL1-C2-A4-DISalesBonuses.xlsx**.	3	
3-4	Functions, Editing, Formulas	Insert formula in cell C4 that inserts *YES* if the amount in B4 is greater than 99999 and inserts *NO* if amount is not greater than 99999. Copy formula down to C5 through C14. In D4 insert formula **=IF(C4="YES",B4*0.05,0)**. Copy formula down to D5 through D14.	7	
5	Formatting	Format D4 with Accounting Number Format, no decimal places.	2	
6	Organization, Finishing	Resave and print worksheet.	3	
7-8	Editing, Finishing	Display formulas in the worksheet, then print. Turn off the display of formulas.	3	
9	Organization	Save and close workbook.	2	
		TOTAL POINTS	20	

Assessment 5: Write Formulas with Absolute Cell References
File: **EL1-C2-A5-CCQuotas.xlsx**

Steps	Tasks	Criteria	Value	Score
1-2	Organization, Accuracy	Open **CCQuotas.xlsx**, Save As **EL1-C2-A5-CCQuotas.**	3	
3	Formulas, Organization, Finishing	a. Insert a formula using an absolute reference to determine projected quotas with 10% increase from current quotas. b. Save, then print. c. Determine projected quotas with a 15% increase from current quota, by changing A15 to *15% Increase* and B15 to *1.15*. d. Save, then print. e. Determine projected quotas with a 20% increase from current quota.	8	

Steps	Tasks	Criteria	Value	Score
4	Formatting	Format C4 with Accounting Number Format, no decimal places.	2	
5	Organization	Resave, then close workbook.	2	
		TOTAL POINTS	15	

Assessment 6: Use Help to Learn About Excel Options

File: EL1-C2-A6-DisplayOptions.xlsx

Steps	Tasks	Criteria	Value	Score
1	Research, Accuracy, Writing	a–b. At a blank workbook, display Excel Options dialog box by clicking File tab, then clicking Options button. At Excel Options dialog box, click *Advanced* option. c. Scroll down and look for section *Display options for this workbook,* read the information, then read information that displays in *Display options for this worksheet* section. d. Write down check box options available *Display options for this workbook* section and *Display options for this worksheet* section, then identify whether or not check box contains a check mark (recording only check box options).	6	
2	Typing, Formulas, Formatting	Using info written down, create Excel spreadsheet with the following information: a–b. In column C, type each option written down, including an appropriate heading. In column B, insert an X in the cell that precedes any option containing a check mark in the check box. (Include an appropriate heading.) c. In column A, write a formula with the IF function that inserts *ON* in the cell if cell in column B contains an X, and inserts *OFF* if it does not. Include an appropriate heading. d. Apply formatting to improve visual appeal.	6	
3	Organization	Save workbook as **EL1-C2-A6-DisplayOptions**.	2	
4-6	Editing, Finishing	Display formulas in worksheet, then print. Turn off the display of formulas.	3	
7	Organization	Resave, print, then close workbook.	3	
		TOTAL POINTS	20	

Visual Benchmark

Create a Worksheet and Insert Formulas

File: **EL1-C2-VB-Formulas.xlsx**

Steps	Tasks	Criteria	Value	Score
1	Typing, Accuracy, Formulas	At a blank workbook, type the data indicated in Fig. 2.4, but **not** in following cells—instead insert formulas as indicated (results of formulas should match results seen in the figure): • In D3 through D9, insert formula that calculates salary. • In D14 through D19, insert formula that calculates differences. • In D24 through D27, insert dates as serial numbers. • In F24 through F27, insert formula that calculates due date. • In B37 through D37, insert formula that calculates averages. • In E32 through E36, insert formula that calculates weighted average of test scores.	12	
2	Formatting	Apply any other formatting so worksheet looks similar to the one shown in Fig. 2.4.	3	
3-4	Organization, Finishing	Save workbook as **EL1-C2-VB-Formulas**, then print.	2	
5-6	Editing, Finishing, Organization	Display formulas in worksheet, print, turn off the display of formulas, then close workbook.	3	
		TOTAL POINTS	20	

Case Study

Part 1

File: **EL1-C2-CS-DWMortgages.xlsx**

Steps	Tasks	Criteria	Value	Score
1	Organization, Typing, Editing	Open **DWMortgages.xlsx**, then complete the home mortgage by inserting the following formulas: • Add $400,000 to worksheet with a 5%, 10%, 15%, and 20% down payment. • In column C, insert formula that determines down payment amount. • In column D, insert formula determining loan amount. • In column G, insert formula using PMT function. (Monthly payment will display as a negative number.)	8	
2	Organization, Finishing	Save as **EL1-C2-CS-DWMortgages**.	2	
		TOTAL POINTS	10	

Part 2

File: **EL1-C2-CS-DWMortgages.xlsx**

Steps	Tasks	Criteria	Value	Score
1	Formulas, Accuracy	With **EL1-C2-CS-DWMortgages.xlsx** open, insert an IF statement in the cells in column H that inserts *No* if the percentage in column B is equal to or greater than 20% or inserts *Yes* if the percentage in column B is less than 20%.	7	
2	Organization, Finishing	Resave the workbook, then print.	3	
		TOTAL POINTS	10	

Part 3

File: **EL1-C2-CS-DWMortgages.xlsx**

Steps	Tasks	Criteria	Value	Score
1	Research, Editing	Using available resources, student determines a current interest rate in area. Delete interest rate of 7% in the Dollar Wise worksheet, then insert the current interest rate.	7	
2	Organization, Finishing	Resave the workbook, then print.	3	
		TOTAL POINTS	10	

Part 4

File: **EL1-C2-CS-DWMortgage.xlsx**

Steps	Tasks	Criteria	Value	Score
1	Research, Typing, Accuracy	Use Help feature to learn about creating hyperlinks in Excel, then use the Internet to locate a helpful website that specializes in private mortgage insurance. Create a hyperlink in worksheet that will display the website.	7	
2	Organization, Finishing	Resave workbook, print, then close.	3	
		TOTAL POINTS	10	

Part 5

File: **EL1-C2-CS-DWLetter.docx**

Steps	Tasks	Criteria	Value	Score
1	Feature, Typing, Editing, Accuracy	Use letter template in Word to create a letter to be sent to client to tell client loan has been approved. Copy and link data from **EL1-C2-CS-DWMortgage.xlsx** worksheet to the letter.	7	
2	Organization, Finishing	Save document as **DWLetter**, print, then close.	3	
		TOTAL POINTS	10	

Excel Level 1, Chapter 3

Skills Check

Assessment 1: Format a Sales and Bonuses Worksheet
File: **EL1-C3-A1-NSPSales.xlsx**

Steps	Tasks	Criteria	Value	Score
1-2	Organization, Accuracy	Open **NSPSales.xlsx**, Save As **EL1-C3-A1-NSPSales.**	3	
3-5, 7-10	Formatting	3. Change the width of columns as follows: Column A = 14.00, Columns B–E = 10.00, Column F = 6.00 4. Select row 2 and then insert a new row 5. Merge and center A2 through F2. 7–9. Increase height of row 1 to 33.00, row 2 to 21.00, and row 3 to 18.00. 10. Make formatting changes to worksheet: a. In A1, change font size to 18 points, bold. b. In A2, change font size to 14 points, bold. c. Select A3 through F3, click Bold, then click Center. d. Select A1 through F3, change vertical alignment to Middle Align.	12	
6	Typing	Type **Sales Department** in A2 and then press Enter.	2	
11	Formulas	Insert the following formulas: a. In D4, a formula that adds amounts in B4 and C4, then copy it down to D5 through D11. b. In E4, a formula that averages amounts in B4 and C4, then copy it down to E5 through E11. c. In F4, an IF statement that says if amount in E4 is greater than 74999, insert the word *Yes* and if amount is not greater than 74999, insert *No*. Copy formula down to F5 through F11.	7	

Steps	Tasks	Criteria	Value	Score
12	Formatting	Make the following changes to the worksheet: a. Select F4 through F1, then click Center button. b. Select B4 through E4, then change number formatting to Accounting with 0 decimal places and a dollar sign. c. Select B5 through E11, click Comma Style button, then click twice on Decrease Decimal button. d. Add double-line border around A1 through F11. e. Select A1 and A2, then apply light orange fill color. f. Select A3 through F3, then apply orange fill color.	7	
13-15	Organization, Finishing, Formatting	Resave and print the worksheet. Apply Verve theme. Resave, print, then close worksheet.	4	
		TOTAL POINTS	35	

Assessment 2: Format an Overdue Accounts Worksheet

File: **EL1-C3-A2-CCorpAccts.xlsx**

Steps	Tasks	Criteria	Value	Score
1-2	Organization, Accuracy	Open **CCorpAccts.xlsx**, Save As **EL1-C3-A2-CCorpAccts.**	3	
3-9, 12	Formatting, Accuracy, Typing	3. Change the width of columns as follows: Column A = 21.00; Column B ≈ 10.00; Column C = 10.00; Column D = 12.00; Column E ≈ 7.00; Column F = 12.00 4. Make cell A1 active, then insert a new row. 5. Merge and center A1 through F1. 6. Type **Compass Corporation** in A1, press Enter. 7–8. Increase height of row 1 to 42.00, then height of row 2 to 24.00. 9a–9c. Select A1 through F11, then change font to 10-point Cambria; make A1 active, change font size to 24 points, turn on bold; make A2 active, change font size to 18 points, turn on bold. d. Select A3 through F3, click Bold button, then click Center button in Alignment group. e. Select A1 through F3, click Middle Align button. f–g. Select B4 through B11, then click Center; select E4 through E11 and then click Center button. 12. Apply following borders and fill color: a. Add a thick line border around A1 through F11. b–c. Make A2 active, then add double-line border at top and bottom of cell; select A3 through F3, then add a single line border to bottom of cells. d. Select A1 and A2 and then apply a light blue fill color.	24	

Steps	Tasks	Criteria	Value	Score
10-11	Functions, Formulas	10. Use DATE function in following cells to enter a formula that returns serial number for following dates: D4 = October 1, 2012; D5 = October 3, 2012; D6 = October 8, 2012; D7 = October 10, 2012; D8 = October 15, 2012; D9 = October 30, 2012; D10 = November 6, 2012; D11 = November 13, 2012 11. Enter a formula in F4 that inserts due date (purchase date plus number of days in Terms column). Copy formula down to F5 through F11.	10	
13	Organization, Finishing	Save, print, then close workbook.	3	
		TOTAL POINTS	40	

Assessment 3: Format a Supplies and Equipment Worksheet
File: **EL1-C3-A3-OEBudget.xlsx**

Steps	Tasks	Criteria	Value	Score
1-2	Organization, Accuracy	Open **OEBudget.xlsx**, Save As **EL1-C3-A3-OEBudget.**	3	
3-4 10, 13	Formatting	3. Select and then merge across A1 through D2. 4. With A1 and A2 selected, click Middle Align button, then click Center button. 10. Select A3 through A17, turn on bold, then click Wrap Text button. 13. Automatically adjust width of column B.	6	
5-6	Formatting	5–6. Make A1 active, then change font size to 22 points and turn on bold; make A2 active, then change font size to 12 points and turn on bold.	4	
7-9	Formatting	7–8. Change height of row 1 to 36.00; change height of row 2 to 21.00. 9. Change width of column A to 15.00.	3	
11-12	Formatting	11–12. Make B3 active, then change number formatting to Currency with no decimal places; select C6 through C19, then change number formatting to Percentage with one decimal place.	4	
14	Formulas, Editing	Make D6 active, then type a formula that multiplies absolute reference $B$3 with percentage in C6. Copy formula down to cells D7 through D19.	3	
15	Formatting	With D6 through D19 selected, change number formatting to Currency, no decimal places.	2	
16	Formatting, Editing	Make D8 active, then clear contents. Use Repeat command to clear contents from D11, D14, and D17.	5	
17	Formatting	Select A1 through D19, change font to Constantia, then change font color to dark blue.	2	

Steps	Tasks	Criteria	Value	Score
18-19	Formatting	18. Add light green fill color to following cells: A1, A2, A5–D5, A8–D8, A11–D11, A14–D14, and A17–D17. 19. Add borders and/or additional shading (user-chosen) to enhance visual appeal of worksheet.	5	
20	Organization, Finishing	Save, print, then close workbook.	3	
		TOTAL POINTS	40	

Assessment 4: Format a Financial Analysis Worksheet

File: **EL1-C3-A4-FinAnalysis.xlsx**

Steps	Tasks	Criteria	Value	Score
1	Research	At a blank workbook, display Format Cells dialog box with Alignment tab selected, then experiment with options in *Text control* section.	3	
2-3	Organization, Accuracy	Open **FinAnalysis.xlsx**, Save As **EL1-C3-A4-FinAnalysis.xlsx**.	3	
4	Formulas, Editing	Make B9 active, then insert formula that averages percentages in B3 through B8. Copy formula to C9 and D9.	4	
5-8	Formatting	5. Select B3 through D9, display Format dialog box, Alignment tab, change horizontal alignment to *Right (Indent)* and indent to *2*, then close dialog box. 6–8. Select A1 through D9, then change font size to 14; select B2 through D2, then change orientation to 45 degrees; with B2 through D2 selected, shrink font size to show all data in cells.	7	
9	Organization, Finishing	Resave, print, then close workbook.	3	
		TOTAL POINTS	20	

Visual Benchmark

Create a Worksheet and Insert Formulas

File: **EL1-C3-VB-BonusAmounts.xlsx**

Steps	Tasks	Criteria	Value	Score
1	Typing, Accuracy, Formulas	At a blank workbook, type data indicated in Fig. 3.11, but **not** in following cells—instead insert formulas as indicated (results of formulas should match results seen in figure): • In C4 through C14, insert formula with an IF statement that inserts *Yes* if sales amount is greater than $114,999 and *No* if sales amount is not greater than $114,999. • In D4 through D14, insert formula with an IF statement that, if content of previous is *Yes*, multiplies amount in column B by 0.05, but if previous cell does not contain word *Yes*, then inserts a zero.	12	
2	Formatting	Apply formatting so worksheet looks similar to Fig. 3.11.	3	
3-4	Organization, Finishing	Save as **EL1-C3-VB-BonusAmounts**, then print.	2	
5-6	Editing, Finishing, Organization	Display formulas in worksheet, print, turn off display of formulas, then close workbook.	3	
		TOTAL POINTS	20	

Case Study

Part 1

File: **EL1-C3-CS-HFCDues-1.xlsx** and **EL1-C3-CS-HFCDues-2.xlsx**

Steps	Tasks	Criteria	Value	Score
1	Organization	Open **HFCDues.xlsx**, Save As **EL1-C3-CS-HFCDues-1.xlsx**.	3	
2	Formatting, Typing, Formulas, Editing	Select B3 through D8, then change number formatting to Accounting, two decimal places, and dollar sign. • In B3, insert *500.00*. • In B4, insert formula that adds amount in B3 with product (multiplication) of B3 multiplied by 10%. (Formula looks like this: **=B3+(B3*10%)**. Copy formula in B4 down to B5 through B8. • Insert formula in C3 that divides amount in B3 by 4, then copy formula down to C4 through C8. • Insert formula in D3 that divides amount in B3 by 12, then copy formula down to D4 through D8. • Apply formatting to enhance visual display of worksheet.	12	
3	Organization, Finishing	Resave, then print worksheet.	2	

Steps	Tasks	Criteria	Value	Score
4	Organization	With **EL1-C3-CS-HFCDues-1.xlsx** open, Save As **EL1-C3-CS-HFCDues-2.xlsx**.	3	
5	Formatting, Typing, Formulas, Editing	The base rate for yearly dues has increased from $500.00 to $600.00, so change this amount in B3. • Add late fee information to the worksheet by inserting new column to right of Column C, typing Late Fees in D2 and F2. Insert formula in D3 that multiplies amount in C3 by 5%. Copy formula down to D4 through D8. • Insert formula in F3 that multiplies amount in E3 by 7%, then copy formula down to F4 through F8. (If necessary, change number formatting for F3 through F8 to Accounting with two decimal places and dollar sign.) • Apply any additional formatting to enhance visual display of worksheet.	7	
6	Organization, Finishing	Resave, print, then close worksheet.	3	
		TOTAL POINTS	30	

Part 2

File: **EL1-C3-CS-HFCPayroll.xlsx**

Steps	Tasks	Criteria	Value	Score
1	Typing, Accuracy	At a blank workbook, prepare a payroll worksheet (as shown in-line, in Part 2 on page 104).	5	
2	Formulas, Formatting, Finishing, Editing	Insert formula in *Weekly Salary* column that multiplies hourly wage by number of hours. Insert an IF statement in *Benefits* column that states if number in *Hours* column is greater than 19, insert *Yes*, but if not, insert *No*. Apply formatting to enhance visual display of worksheet. Save as **EL1-C3-CS-HFCPayroll**, then print. Turn on display of formulas, print worksheet again, then turn off display of formulas.	10	
3	Typing, Editing	Change hourly wage for Amanda Turney to *$22.00;* increase hours for Emily Dugan to *20*; remove row for Grant Baker; insert row between Jean Overmeyer and Bonnie Haddon, type following in cells in new row: Employee: **Tonya McGuire**; Hourly Wage: **$17.50**; Hours: **15.**	6	
4	Editing, Finishing, Organization	Resave and print worksheet. Turn on display of formulas, print worksheet again, then turn off display of formulas. Resave then close workbook.	4	
		TOTAL POINTS	25	

Part 3

File: **EL1-C3-CS-HFCEquip.xlsx**

Steps	Tasks	Criteria	Value	Score
1	Research, Writing	Use Internet to research/search for: • Elliptical machines for sale, locating two different models and, and if possible, at least two companies that sell each model. Make a note of company names, model numbers, and prices. • Recumbent bikes for sale, locating two different models and if possible, at least two companies that sell each model. Make notes as above. • Upright bikes for sale, locating two different models and if possible, at least two companies that sell each model. Make notes as above.	10	
2	Typing, Formulas, Formatting	Prepare an Excel worksheet with the following information: • Equipment name; Equipment model; Price • A column that multiplies the price by the number required (which is 3). Include fitness center name, HealthWise Fitness Center, and any other information determined necessary. Apply formatting to enhance visual display of worksheet.	7	
3	Organization, Finishing	Save as **EL1-C3-CS-HFCEquip**, print, then close.	3	
		TOTAL POINTS	20	

Part 4

File: **EL1-C3-CS-HFCLetter.docx**

Steps	Tasks	Criteria	Value	Score
1	Feature, Typing, Editing, Accuracy	Use letter template in Word to create a letter to be sent to prospective client (user-chosen) on information about the fitness center, plans offered, and dues amounts. Copy data from **EL1-C2-CS-HFCDues-02.xlsx** worksheet to the letter. Make any formatting changes to make data more readable.	7	
2	Organization, Finishing	Save document as **HFCLetter**, print, then close.	3	
		TOTAL POINTS	10	

Excel Level 1, Chapter 4

Skills Check

Assessment 1: Format a Sales and Bonuses Worksheet

File: **EL1-C4-A1-DISemiSales.xlsx**

Steps	Tasks	Criteria	Value	Score
1-2	Organization, Accuracy	Open **DISemiSales.xlsx**, Save As **EL1-C4-A1-DISemiSales.**	3	
3	Formulas, Formatting, Editing	Make changes to worksheet: a. Insert formula in H4 that averages amounts in cells B4 through G4. b. Copy formula in H4 down to H5 through H9. c. Insert formula in B10 adding amounts in B4 through B9. d. Copy formula in B10 to C10 through H10. (Use *Fill Without Formatting*.) e. Apply Accounting Number Format style to H4. f. Change orientation of worksheet to landscape. g. Change top margin to 3 inches, left margin to 1.5 inches.	8	
4, 6	Organization, Finishing	Resave and print (settings in force in Step 3, including landscape); resave, print, then close (after Step 5 changes).	5	
5	Formatting	Change orientation to portrait. Change top margin to 1 inch, left margin to 0.7 inch. Horizontally and vertically center worksheet on the page. Scale worksheet so it fits on one page.	4	
		TOTAL POINTS	20	

Assessment 2: Format a Test Results Worksheet

File: **EL1-C4-A2-CMTests.xlsx**

Steps	Tasks	Criteria	Value	Score
1-2	Organization, Accuracy	Open **CMTests.xlsx**, Save As **EL1-C4-A2-CMTests.**	3	
3, 7-8	Formulas, Editing, Typing, Formatting	3a–3f. Insert a formula in cell N4 that averages test scores in B4 through M4. Copy formula in N4 down to N5 through N21. Type **Average** in A22. Insert formula in B22 that averages test scores in B4 through B21. Copy formula in B22 to C22 through N22. Insert a page break between columns G and H. 7–8. Create header that prints page number at right side of page. Create footer that prints student name at left side of page and workbook file name at right side of page.	12	

Steps	Tasks	Criteria	Value	Score
4-6, 9-11	Finishing, Organization	4–5. View worksheet in Page Break Preview, then change back to Normal view. 6. Specify column titles (A3 through A22) to print on each page. 9. Save, then print worksheet. 10–11. Set print area for N3 through N22, then print those cells. Clear print area.	8	
12	Organization, Finishing	Resave, then close workbook.	2	
		TOTAL POINTS	25	

Assessment 3: Format an Equipment Rental Worksheet
File: **EL1-C4-A3-HERInvoices.xlsx**

Steps	Tasks	Criteria	Value	Score
1-2	Organization, Accuracy	Open **HERInvoices.xlsx**, Save As **EL1-C4-A3-HERInvoices**.	3	
3-4	Formulas, Editing	Insert formula in H3 that multiplies rate in cell G3 by hours in F3. Copy formula down to cells H4 through H16. Insert formula in H17 that sums amounts in H3 through H16.	5	
5	Editing	Complete the following find and replaces: a. Find all occurrences of cells containing *75*, replace with *90*. b. Find all occurrences of cells containing *55* replace with *60*. c. Find all occurrences of *Barrier Concrete*, replace with *Lee Sand and Gravel*. d. Find all occurrences of 11-point Calibri, replace with 10-point Cambria. After completing, clear all formatting from Format buttons.	5	
6-7	Formatting	Insert header that prints date at left side of page and time at right side of page, then insert footer that prints student name at left side of page and workbook file name at right side of page.	4	
8-9	Organization, Finishing	Resave, print, then close workbook.	3	
		TOTAL POINTS	20	

Assessment 4: Format an Invoices Worksheet
File: **EL1-C4-A4-RPInvoices.xlsx**

Steps	Tasks	Criteria	Value	Score
1-2	Organization, Accuracy	Open **RPInvoices.xlsx**, Save As **EL1-C4-A4-RPInvoices**.	3	

Steps	Tasks	Criteria	Value	Score
3-9	Formulas, Editing	3–4. Insert formula in G4 that multiplies amount in E4 with percentage in F4, then adds product to E4. (Result should display as *$488.25*.) Copy formula in G4 down to G5 through G17, click Auto Fill Options button, then click *Fill Without Formatting*. 5. Complete a spelling check. 6. Find all occurrences of *Picture* and replace with *Portrait*. (Goal is to find occurrences that end with an *s. Match entire contents* check box should not contain check mark.) 7–9. Sort records by invoice number in ascending order (smallest to largest); complete new sort that sorts records by client number in ascending order (A to Z); complete new sort that sorts date in ascending order (oldest to newest).	12	
10-11	Formatting	10. Insert footer in the worksheet that prints student name at left side of page and current date at right side. 11. Center worksheet horizontally and vertically.	5	
12	Organization, Finishing	Resave, then print.	2	
13	Enhancement	Select cells A3 through G3, then turn on filter feature and complete following filters: a. Filter, then print list of rows containing client number 11-279, then clear the filter. b. Filter, then print list of rows containing top three highest amounts due, then clear the filter. c. Filter, then print list of rows containing amounts due that are less than $500, then clear the filter.	6	
14	Organization, Finishing	Resave, then close workbook.	2	
		TOTAL POINTS	30	

Assessment 5: Create a Worksheet Containing Keyboard Shortcuts
File: EL1-C4-A5-KeyboardShortcuts.xlsx

Steps	Tasks	Criteria	Value	Score
1	Research, Typing, Formatting	After using Excel Help feature to learn about keyboard shortcuts, create a worksheet with the following features: • A worksheet title. • Include at least 10 keyboard shortcuts along with an explanation of each shortcut. • Set the data in cells in a typeface other than Calibri and change the color. • Add borders to cells, add color shading (both are user-selected, shading should be complementary to data color.) • Create header that prints date at right margin; create footer that prints student name at left margin and file name at right margin.	12	

Steps	Tasks	Criteria	Value	Score
2-3	Organization, Finishing	Save as **EL1-C4-A5-KeyboardShortcuts**, print, then close.	3	
		TOTAL POINTS	15	

Visual Benchmark

Create and Format an Expense Worksheet

File: **EL1-C4-VB-HERExpenses.xlsx**

Steps	Tasks	Criteria	Value	Score
1	Typing, Accuracy, Formulas	At a blank workbook, type data indicated in Fig. 4.13, but **not** in following cells—instead insert formulas as indicated (results of formulas should match results seen in figure). In N3 through N8, insert formula that sums monthly expenses for the year. In B9 through N9, insert formula that sums the monthly expenses for each month and for entire year.	10	
2-3	Formatting	2. Change left and right margins to 0.45, and change top margin to 1.5. 3. Apply formatting so worksheet looks similar to the one shown in figure (heading in 26-point Cambria, remaining data in 10-point Cambria, bold formatting as shown.)	5	
4, 6-7	Organization, Finishing	After Step 3, Save as **EL1-C4-VB-HERExpenses**. After Step 5, resave, print, then close (should be on 2 pages).	5	
5	Formatting	After examining Fig. 4.14, make following changes: Insert page break between columns G and H; insert headers and footer as shown; specify column titles print on second page as shown in Fig. 4.14.	5	
		TOTAL POINTS	25	

Case Study

Part 1

File: **EL1-C4-CS-MRMortgages-01.xlsx** and **EL1-C4-CS-MRMortgages-02.xlsx**

Steps	Tasks	Criteria	Value	Score
1	Organization	Open **MRMortgages.xlsx**, Save As **EL1-C4-CS-MRMortgages-01.xlsx**.	3	

Steps	Tasks	Criteria	Value	Score
2	Formulas, Functions, Formatting, Editing	• In column C, insert formula that determines down payment amount; in column D, insert formula that determines loan amount; in column G, insert formula using PMT function. (*Pv* is entered as a negative.) • Insert date and time as a header, student name and workbook name as footer. • Find 11-point Calibri formatting and replace with 11-point Candara. • Scale the worksheet so it prints on one page.	12	
3	Organization, Finishing	Resave, then print worksheet.	2	
4	Editing, Typing, Formatting	• Sort the *Price of Home* column from smallest to largest. • Change percentage amount in column E from 6% to 7%. • Shade cells in row 4 in light yellow color that matches the fill in A2. Copy shading to every other row of cells in worksheet (stopping at row 46).	4	
5	Typing, Organization, Finishing	Save As **EL1-C4-CS-MRMortgages-02**. Edit the footer to reflect workbook name change. Resave, print, then close (print on one page).	4	
		TOTAL POINTS	25	

Part 2

File: **EL1-C4-CS-MRIRA-01.xlsx** and **EL1-C4-CS-MRIRA-02.xlsx**

Steps	Tasks	Criteria	Value	Score
1	Organization	Open **MRIRA.xlsx**, Save As **EL1-C4-CS-MRIRA-01.xlsx**.	3	
2	Formulas, Functions, Editing, Formatting, Typing	• Insert in cell C6 a formula that calculates future value of an investment; use FV function to write formula. Use absolute and mixed references for formula. When entering *Rate* (percentage), column letter is variable but row number is fixed; but when entering *Nper* (years), column letter is fixed but row number is variable. When entering *Pmt* (contribution amount), both column letters and row numbers are absolute. • Copy formula in C6 down to C7 through C19; copy formula in C6 across to D6 through K6. Continue until amounts are entered in all appropriate cells. • Select, then merge and center A6 through A19. Type text **Number of Years,** then rotate text up. (Make sure text is centered in merged cells.) Apply 12-point Calibri bold formatting to text. • Adjust column widths so all text is visible in cells. • Change page orientation to landscape, then vertically and horizontally center worksheet. • Include header that prints page number, then insert footer that prints student name.	16	

Steps	Tasks	Criteria	Value	Score
3	Organization, Finishing	Resave, then print (row titles print on both pages).	2	
4	Editing, Formatting	• Remove the header containing page number. Edit footer so date prints at left margin and name prints at the right. • Scale worksheet so it prints on one page.	4	
5	Typing, Organization, Finishing	Save As **EL1-C4-CS-MRIRA-02**. Change amount in D3 to *$3,000*, then print again. Resave, then close worksheet.	5	
		TOTAL POINTS	30	

Part 3

File: **EL1-C4-CS-CanadaPrices.xlsx**

Steps	Tasks	Criteria	Value	Score
1	Research, Writing, Accuracy, Typing, Formatting, Formulas, Functions	Use Internet to search for MS MoneyCentral Investor Currency Rate site, determining current exchange rate for Canada, then create a worksheet with following specs: • Apply formatting similar to formatting in first two parts of case study. • Create the following columns: 　Column for home price in American dollars. 　Column for home price in Canadian dollars. 　Column for amount of down payment. 　Column for loan total. 　Column for monthly payment. • In column for home prices, insert home amounts beginning with $100,000, incrementing every $50,000 and ending with $1,000,000. • Insert formula in home price in Canadian dollars column that displays home price in Canadian dollars; insert formula in down payment column that multiplies Canadian home price by 20%; insert formula in loan total column that subtracts down payment from Canadian home price. • Insert formula in monthly payment column that determines monthly payment using PMT function. Use 6% as rate (divide by 12 months), 360 as number of payments, loan, and loan amount as a negative as present value. • Apply any other formatting necessary to improve worksheet.	25	
2	Organization, Editing, Finishing	Save as **EL1-C4-CS-CanadaPrices**. Display formulas, then print. Redisplay formulas, then close workbook.	5	
		TOTAL POINTS	30	

Excel Level 1, Unit 1
Performance Assessment

Assessing Proficiency

Assessment 1: Create Sales Bonuses Workbook

File: **EL1-U1-A1-SBASales.xlsx**

Steps	Tasks	Criteria	Value	Score
1	Typing, Accuracy, Formatting	At a blank workbook, create the Excel worksheet shown in Fig. U1.1, formatting cells as seen in the figure.	5	
2, 4-5	Functions, Formulas	2. Insert an IF statement in cell C4 that inserts *7%* if B4 is greater than 99999, *3%* if B4 is not greater than 99999. 4. Insert a formula in D4 that multiplies amount in B4 with percentage in C4. Copy formula down to D5 through D11. 5. Insert sum of cells B4 through B11 in B12, then insert sum of D4 through D11 in D12.	6	
3, 6-7	Formatting, Editing	3. Format number in C4 for percentage, no decimal places; copy it down to cells C5 through C11. Center percents in C4 through C11. 6. Apply Accounting Number Format style, two decimal places, to B4, B12, D4, D12. Apply Comma style, two decimal places, to B5 through B11 and D5 through D11. 7. Insert footer that contains student first and last names and current date.	10	
8-10	Finishing, Organization	Print worksheet horizontally/vertically centered on page. Save as **EL1-U1-A1-SBASales**, then close workbook.	4	
		TOTAL POINTS	25	

Assessment 2: Format Equipment Purchases Plan Worksheet

File: **EL1-U1-A2-HERPurPlans.xlsx**

Steps	Tasks	Criteria	Value	Score
1	Organization, Accuracy	Open **HERPurPlans.xlsx**, Save As **EL1-U1-A2-HERPurPlans**.	3	
2-6	Formulas, Editing	2. Insert formula in cell E4 that uses PMT function to calculate monthly payments. Copy down to E5 and E6. 3. Insert formula in F4 that multiplies amount in E4 by amount in D4, then copy it down to cells F5 and F6. 5-6. Insert formula in G4 that subtracts amount in B4 from amount in F4. Formula should return a positive number. Copy formula down to G5 and G6.	12	
7-8	Formatting	Change vertical alignment of A2 to Middle Align, then change the vertical alignment of A3 through G3 to Bottom.	2	

Steps	Tasks	Criteria	Value	Score
9	Finishing, Organization	Resave workbook, print, then close.	3	
		TOTAL POINTS	20	

Assessment 3: Format Accounts Due Worksheet
File: **EL1-U1-A3-RPAccts.xlsx**

Steps	Tasks	Criteria	Value	Score
1	Organization, Accuracy	Open **RPAccts.xlsx**, Save As **EL1-U1-A3-RPAccts.**	3	
2-4, 6	Functions, Formulas, Editing	2. Use DATE function to enter formula in each of specified cells that returns serial numbers for specified dates: C4 = October 29, 2012; C5 = October 30, 2012; C6 = October 30, 2012; C7 = November 1, 2012; C8 = November 5, 2012; C9 = November 7, 2012; C10 = November 7, 2012; C11 = November 14, 2012; C12 = November 14, 2012 3. Enter formula in E4 that inserts due date (date of service plus number of days in *Terms* column), then copy it down to cells E5 through E12. 6. In A15, use NOW function to insert current date and time as a serial number.	12	
5	Typing	In A14, type student name.	2	
7	Organization, Finishing	Resave, print, then close workbook.	3	
		TOTAL POINTS	20	

Assessment 4: Format First Quarter Sales Workbook
File: **EL1-U1-A4-PSQtrlySales.xlsx**

Steps	Tasks	Criteria	Value	Score
1	Organization, Accuracy	Open **PSQtrlySales.xlsx**, Save As **EL1-U1-A4-PSQtrlySales.**	3	
2-4	Formulas, Formatting, Functions	2. Insert formula in E4 that totals amounts in B4, C4, D4; then copy it down to E5 through E18. Apply Accounting Number Format style, no decimal places, to E4. 3. Insert IF statement in F4 that inserts *5%* if E4 is greater than 74999, but *0%* if E4 is not greater than 74999. 4. Make sure result of IF formula displays in F4 as a percentage, no decimal points; then copy down to F5 through F18. Center percent amounts in F4 through F18.	10	

Steps	Tasks	Criteria	Value	Score
5	Formatting	Select A5 through F5; apply same yellow fill as in A2; then apply same fill to A7 through F7, A9 through F9, A11 through F11, A13 through F13, A15 through F15, and cells A17 through F17.	5	
6	Editing	Insert footer that prints student name at left, current date at middle, and current time at right.	3	
7-8	Finishing, Organization	Print worksheet centered horizontally and vertically on page, resave, print, then close workbook.	4	
		TOTAL POINTS	25	

Assessment 5: Format Weekly Payroll Workbook
File: **EL1-U1-A5-CCPayroll.xlsx**

Steps	Tasks	Criteria	Value	Score
1	Organization, Accuracy	Open **CCPayroll.xlsx**, Save As **EL1-U1-A4-CCPayroll.**	3	
2-5	Formulas, Editing	2. Insert formula in E3 that multiplies hourly rate by hours, then adds that to multiplication of hourly rate by overtime pay rate (1.5), then overtime hours. (Use parentheses in formula and use an absolute reference for overtime pay rate (1.5). Refer to Chapter 2, Project 5c.) Copy formula down to cells E4 through E16. 3. Insert formula in F3 that multiplies gross pay by withholding tax rate (W/H Rate). (Use an absolute reference for containing withholding rate. Refer to Chapter 2, Project 5c.) Copy formula down to cells F4 through F16. 4. Insert formula in G3 that multiplies gross pay by Social Security rate (SS Rate). Use an absolute reference for cells containing Social Security rate. (Refer to Chapter 2, Project 5c.) Copy formula down to cells G4 through G16. 5. Insert formula in H4 that adds together Social Security tax and withholding tax and subtracts that from gross pay. (Refer to Chapter 2, Project 5c.) Copy formula down to cells H4 through H16.	18	
6, 8	Editing	6. Sort employee last names alphabetically in ascending order (A to Z). 8. Insert footer that prints student name at left side of page and file name at right side.	4	
7	Formatting	Center worksheet horizontally and vertically on page.	2	
9	Organization, Finishing	Resave, print, then close workbook.	3	
		TOTAL POINTS	30	

Assessment 6: Format Customer Sales Analysis Workbook

File: **EL1-U1-A6-DIAnnualSales.xlsx**

Steps	Tasks	Criteria	Value	Score
1	Organization, Accuracy	Open **DIAnnualSales.xlsx**, Save As **EL1-U1-A6-DIAnnualSales.**	3	
2-3	Formulas, Editing, Accuracy, Functions	2. Insert formulas and drag them to complete worksheet. After dragging total formula in row 10, specify to fill without formatting. (This retains right border in N10.) Use AutoFill Options button. 3. Insert in B11 highest total from cells B10 through M10, then in B12 lowest total from B10 through M10.	8	
4, 7	Formatting	4. Change orientation to landscape. 7. Horizontally and vertically center worksheet.	2	
5-6, 8	Editing	5–6. Insert header that prints page number at right side of page, then a footer that prints student name at right side. 8. Specify that column headings in A3 through A12 print on both pages.	4	
9	Organization, Finishing	Resave, print, then close workbook.	3	
		TOTAL POINTS	20	

Assessment 7: Format Invoices Workbook

File: **EL1-U1-A7-RPInvoices.xlsx**

Steps	Tasks	Criteria	Value	Score
1	Organization, Accuracy	Open **RPInvoices.xlsx**, Save As **EL1-U1-A7-RPInvoices.**	3	
2-3	Formulas	Insert formula in cell G4 that multiplies amount in E4 by percentage in F4, then adds that total to amount in E4. (Use parentheses in formula.) Copy formula G5 through G18.	4	
4-6	Editing	4. Find all occurrences of cells containing *11-279* and replace with *10*-005; then find all occurrences of cells containing *8.5* and replace with *9.0*. Search for Calibri font, then replace with Cara font. (Font size not specified.)	5	
7-10	Enhancement, Finishing	7. Print worksheet. 8–10. Filter, then print list of rows containing only client number 04-*325*. (After printing, return to *(Select All)*.) Filter, then print list of rows containing only service *Development*. (Return to *(Select All)*.) Filter, then print list of rows containing top three highest totals in *Amount Due* column, and after printing, turn off filter feature.	6	
11	Organization	Resave, then close workbook.	2	
		TOTAL POINTS	20	

Writing Activities

Activity 1: Plan and Prepare Orders Summary Workbook

File: **EL1-U1-Act1-OrdersSumm.xlsx**

Steps	Tasks	Criteria	Value	Score
1	Accuracy, Typing, Formatting	Plan and prepare worksheet with the information shown in Fig. U1.2. Apply formatting (user-chosen) to worksheet.	12	
2	Organization, Finishing	Save as **EL1-U1-Act1-OrdersSumm**, print, then close.	3	
		TOTAL POINTS	15	

Activity 2: Prepare Depreciation Workbook

File: **EL1-U1-Act2-DepMethods.xlsx**

Steps	Tasks	Criteria	Value	Score
1	Research, Typing, Functions, Formatting	Use Excel Help feature to learn about two depreciation methods—straight-line and double-declining (the straight-line depreciation function, SNL, and double-declining depreciation function, DDB, are located in Financial category.) Create an Excel worksheet with following information: • An appropriate title • A heading for straight-line depreciation, and one for the straight-line depreciation function • The name and description for each straight-line depreciation function argument category • A heading for double-declining depreciation, double-declining depreciation function, and name and description for each double-declining depreciation function argument category Apply formatting (user-chosen) to worksheet.	11	
2	Organization, Finishing	Save as **EL1-U1-Act2-DepMethods**, print (with worksheet horizontally/vertically/centered on page), then close.	4	
		TOTAL POINTS	15	

Activity 3: Insert Straight-Line Depreciation Formula

File: **EL1-U1-Act3-RPDepreciation.xlsx** and **EL1-U1-Act3-DepReport.docx**

Steps	Tasks	Criteria	Value	Score
1	Organization, Accuracy	Open **RPDepreciation.xlsx**, Save As **EL1-U1-Act3-RPDepreciation.**	3	

Steps	Tasks	Criteria	Value	Score
2	Functions, Editing, Formatting	Insert function to determine straight-line depreciation in cell E3. Copy formula down to E4 through E10. Apply formatting (user-chosen) to worksheet.	5	
3	Finishing, Organization	Save as **EL1-U1-Act3-RPDepreciation**, print (worksheet horizontally/vertically/centered on page), then close.	4	
4	Research, Writing	[OPTIONAL EXERCISE] Use Internet or school library to research topic of straight-line and double-declining depreciation, to learn why businesses depreciate their assets. What purpose does it serve? Use Word 2010 to write a half-page, single-spaced report explaining financial reasons for using depreciation methods.	10	
5	Organization, Finishing	[OPTIONAL EXERCISE] Save document as **EL1-U1-Act3-DepReport**, print, then close.	3	
		TOTAL POINTS	25	

Internet Research

Activity 4: Create a Travel Planning Worksheet

File: **EL1-U1-Act4-TrvWksht.xlsx**

Steps	Tasks	Criteria	Value	Score
1	Research, Typing, Formulas, Formatting	After using Internet (user-chosen search engine) to research info on traveling to specific country of interest, find sites providing cost info for airlines, hotels, meals, entertainment, and car rentals. Create travel planning worksheet for country chosen that includes: • An appropriate title and appropriate headings • Airline costs, hotel costs (off-season and in-season rates if available), estimated meal costs, entertainment costs, and car rental costs.	12	
3	Organization, Finishing	Save as **EL1-U1-Act4-TrvlWksht**, print, then close.	3	
		TOTAL POINTS	15	

Excel Level 1, Chapter 5

Skills Check

Assessment 1: Copy and Paste Data Between Worksheets in a Sales Workbook
File: **EL1-C5-A1-EPSales.xlsx**

Steps	Tasks	Criteria	Value	Score
1	Organization, Accuracy	Open **EPSales.xlsx**, Save As **EL1-C5-A1-EPSales.xlsx**.	3	
2-3	Editing, Accuracy, Typing	2. Turn on display of the Clipboard task pane, click Clear All button, then complete the following: a–c. Select and copy cells A7 through C7; select and copy A10 through C10; then select and copy A13 through C13. d–f. Display second worksheet, make A7 active, then paste the *Avalon Clinic* cells; make A10 active, then paste *Stealth Media* cells; then make A13 active and paste the *Danmark Contracting* cells. g. Make the third worksheet active, then complete similar steps to paste the cells in same location as second worksheet. h. Clear contents of Clipboard task pane, then close. 3. Change names of Sheet1 tab to *2010 Sales*, Sheet2 tab to *2011 Sales*, and Sheet3 tab to *2012 Sales*.	18	
4, 7	Formatting	4. Change colors of 2010 Sales tab to blue, 2011 Sales tab to green, and 2012 Sales tab to yellow. 7. Apply the Accounting Number Format style with no decimal places to D4 (on all three worksheets).	4	
5-6	Formulas	5. Display 2010 Sales worksheet, select all three tabs, then insert a formula in D4 that sums amounts in cells B4 and C4. Copy formula down to cells D5 through D14. 6. Make D15 active, then insert a formula that sums amounts in cells D4 through D14.	4	
8	Editing	Insert footer on all three worksheets that prints student name at left side and current date at right.	3	
9-10	Organization, Finishing	Resave, print all 3 worksheets, then close.	3	
		TOTAL POINTS	35	

Assessment 2: Copy, Paste, and Format Worksheets in an Income Statement Workbook
File: **EL1-C5-A2-CMJanIncome.xlsx**

Steps	Tasks	Criteria	Value	Score
1	Organization, Accuracy	Open **CMJanIncome.xlsx**, Save As **EL1-C5-A2-CMJanIncome.xlsx**.	3	

Steps	Tasks	Criteria	Value	Score
2	Editing	Copy cells A1 through B17 in Sheet1, paste into Sheet2. (Using Paste Options button, keep Source Column Widths.)	3	

3, 5-6	Formatting, Typing	3. Make changes to the Sheet2 worksheet:
		    a. Adjust row heights so they match heights in Sheet1.
		    b. Change the month from January to February.
		    c–e. Change amount in B4 to 97,655; the amount in B5 to 39,558; then the amount in B11 to *1,105.*
		5. Change name of Sheet1 tab to *January* and name of Sheet2 tab to February.
		6. Change color of January tab to blue and color of February tab to red.
			8	

4	Formulas	Select both sheet tabs, insert the following formulas: A formula in B6 that subtracts *Cost of Sales* from *Sales Revenue* (*=B4-B5*); a formula in B16 that sums amounts in B8 through B15; then a formula in B17 that subtracts *Total Expenses* from the *Gross Profit* (*=B6-B16*).	5	
7	Editing	Insert custom header on both worksheets that prints student name at left, date in the middle, and file name at right.	3	
8	Organization, Finishing	Resave, print, then close workbook.	3	
		TOTAL POINTS	25	

Assessment 3: Freeze and Unfreeze Window Panes in a Test Scores Workbook
File: **EL1-C5-A3-CertTests.xlsx**

Steps	Tasks	Criteria	Value	Score
1	Organization, Accuracy	Open **CertTests.xlsx**, Save As **EL1-C5-A3-CertTests.xlsx.**	3	
2-4 7-8	Customization, Accuracy	2. Make cell A1 active, split window by clicking View tab, then clicking Split button in Window group. (Window splits into four panes.) 3. Drag horizontal and vertical gray lines up and to left until horizontal gray line is immediately below second row and vertical gray line is immediately to right of first column. 4. Freeze window panes. 7–8. After Step 6, unfreeze window panes, remove split.	6	
5	Editing, Typing	Add two rows immediately above row 18, then type text shown (in Step 5, on page 191) in specified cells.	8	
6	Formulas, Editing	Insert formula in cell N3 that averages percentages in cells B3 through M3; copy down to N4 through N22.	3	
9	Formatting	Change orientation to *Landscape,* then scale worksheet to print on one page (using *Width* option in the Scale to Fit group in Page Layout tab).	2	

Steps	Tasks	Criteria	Value	Score
10	Organization, Finishing	Resave, print, then close workbook.	3	
		TOTAL POINTS	25	

Assessment 4: Create, Copy, Paste, and Format Cells in an Equipment Usage Workbook

File: **EL1-C5-A4-HCMachRpt.xlsx**

Steps	Tasks	Criteria	Value	Score
1-2	Typing, Formatting, Organization	At a blank workbook, create worksheet shown in Fig. 5.10, changing width of column A to 21. Save as **EL1-C5-A4-HCMachRpt**.	5	
3-4	Organization, Editing	3. With EL1-**C5-A4-HCMachRpt.xlsx** open, open **HCEqpRpt.xlsx**. 4. Select and copy following cells from **HCEqpRpt.xlsx** to **EL1-C5-A4-HCMachRpt.xlsx**: a–b. Copy A4 through G4 in **HCEqpRpt.xlsx**, paste into **EL1-C5-A4-**HCMachRpt**.xlsx** beginning with cell A12; copy A10 through G10 in **HCEqpRpt.xlsx**, paste into **EL1-C5-A4-HCMachRpt.xlsx** beginning with cell A13.	5	
5-11	Formatting, Finishing	5. With **EL1-C5-A4-HCMachRpt.xlsx** active, make cell A1 active, then apply following formatting: a. Change height of row 1 to 25.50. b. Change font size of text in cell A1 to 14 points. c. Insert Olive Green, Accent 3, Lighter 60% fill in A1. 6–10. Select cells A2 through G2, insert Olive Green, Accent 3, Darker 50% fill color; select B2 through G2, change text color to white and turn on italics. (Text in these cells is right-aligned.) Select A3 through G3, insert Olive Green, Accent 3, Lighter 80% fill color; select A7 through G7, insert Olive Green, Accent 3, Lighter 80% fill color; select A11 through G11, insert Olive Green, Accent 3, Lighter 80% fill color. 11. Print worksheet centered horizontally and vertically.	12	
12-13	Organization, Finishing	Resave, then close workbook. Close **HCEqpRpt.xlsx**.	3	
		TOTAL POINTS	25	

Assessment 5: Copying and Linking Data in a Word Document
File: **EL1-C5-A5-DWLtr.docx** and **EL1-C5-A5-DWMortgages.xlsx**

Steps	Tasks	Criteria	Value	Score
1-2	Organization, Accuracy	In Word, open **DWLtr.docx**, Save As **EL1-C5-A5-DWLtr**. In Excel, open **DWMortgages.xlsx**, Save As **EL1-C5-A5-DWMortgages**.	6	
3	Formulas, Functions, Formatting	In Excel, in column G, insert a formula using PMT function, then automatically adjust width of column G.	4	
4-8	Editing, Accuracy	4. Select cells A2 through G10, then click the Copy button. 5–8. Click Word button on Taskbar, move insertion point between two paragraphs of text, click Paste button arrow, then click *Paste Special* at drop-down list; at Paste Special dialog box, click *Paste link* option, click *Microsoft Excel Worksheet Object* in *As* list box, then click OK.	5	
9	Formatting	Click Center button in Paragraph group in Home tab.	2	
10,13, 16-17	Organization, Finishing	10. Save, print, then close **EL1-C5-A5-DWLtr.docx**. 13. Save, print, then close **EL1-C5-A5-DWMortgages.xlsx**. 16. Save, print, then close **EL1-C5-A5-DWLtr.docx**. 17. Exit Word.	10	
11-12	Editing, Typing	In Excel button, make cell A3 active, then change the number from *$300,000* to *$400,000*; copy the number in cell A3 down to cells A4 through A10.	4	
14-15	Organization, Accuracy	Click Word button on Taskbar, then open **EL1-C5-A5-DWLtr.docx**. At message about updating, click Yes.	4	
		TOTAL POINTS	35	

Visual Benchmark

Create and Format a Sales Worksheet Using Formulas
File: **EL1-C5-VB-CMSemiSales.xlsx**

Steps	Tasks	Criteria	Value	Score
1	Typing, Editing, Formulas, Formatting	At a blank workbook, create worksheet shown in Fig. 5.11 as follows: • Do not type data in cells D4 through D9; instead enter a formula that totals first-half and second-half yearly sales. • Apply formatting shown in the figure, including changing font sizes, column widths, row heights, shading, and borders. • Rename sheet tab, change tab color as shown in figure.	12	
2	Editing	Copy A1 through D9, then paste the cells in Sheet2.	3	

Steps	Tasks	Criteria	Value	Score
3	Editing, Typing, Formatting	Edit the cells and apply formatting, matching worksheet shown in Fig. 5.12. Rename sheet tab and change tab color as shown in the figure.	5	
4-6	Organization, Finishing	Save completed workbook as **EL1-C5-VB-CMSemiSales**. Print both worksheets, then close **EL1-C5-VB-CMSemiSales. xlsx**.	5	
		TOTAL POINTS	25	

Case Study

Part 1

File: **EL1-C5-CS-GGExp.xlsx**

Steps	Tasks	Criteria	Value	Score
1	Typing, Editing, Formatting, Formulas	At a blank workbook, create a worksheet as follows: • Company name is Gateway Global and the title is *January Expenditures*. • Create columns and type info (see Part 1, page 194). • Insert formula in *Total* column that sums amounts in *supplies* and *equipment* columns, then insert formula in *total* row that sums supplies amounts, equipment amounts, and total amounts. • Apply formatting (fill color, borders, font color, shading) to enhance visual appeal of worksheet.	15	
2	Editing, Typing	After creating and formatting worksheet, do the following: Copy worksheet data to Sheet2 and then to Sheet3. Make following changes to data in Sheet2: • Change *January Expenditures* to *February Expenditures*. • Change Production department supplies to *$38,550* and equipment amount to *$88,500*. • Change Technical Support department equipment amount to *$44,250* and Finance department supplies to *$7,500*. Make the following changes to data in Sheet3: • Change *January Expenditures* to *March Expenditure*. • Change Research and Development department supplies to *$65,000* and equipment amount to *$150,000*. • Change Technical Support department supplies amount to *$21,750* and equipment amount to *$43,525*. • Change Facilities department equipment amount to *$18,450*.	10	

Steps	Tasks	Criteria	Value	Score
3	Typing, Formatting, Editing	Create a new worksheet that summarizes supplies and equipment totals for January, February, and March. Apply same formatting to worksheet as applied to other three. Change tab name for Sheet1 to *Jan. Expenditures*, for Sheet2 to *Feb. Expenditures*, for Sheet3 to *Mar. Expenditures*, and for Sheet4 to *Qtr. Summary*. Change color of each tab (user-determined). Insert header that prints student name at left side of each worksheet and current date at right side.	7	
4	Organization, Finishing	Save as **EL1-C5-CS-GGExp**, print, then close workbook.	3	
		TOTAL POINTS	35	

Part 2

File: **EL1-C5-CS-GGStats.xlsx**

Steps	Tasks	Criteria	Value	Score
1	Formulas, Typing, Formatting, Editing	Open **CGStats.xlsx**, change both worksheets as follows: • Insert formula that calculates a player's batting average (Hits ÷ At Bats); then a formula that calculates player's on-base percentage: (Walks + Hits) ÷ (At Bats + Walks). • Select E5 through F15, then specify three decimal places. • Insert company name. • Apply formatting to enhance visual appeal of worksheets; then horizontally and vertically center worksheets. • Insert footer that prints on both worksheets, with student name at left of worksheet and date at right.	12	
2	Research, Enhancement	After using Help feature and/or experimenting, apply *Good* cell style to any cell in *Batting Average* column with average over .400; apply same style to cells in both worksheets.	5	
3	Organization, Finishing	Resave, print, then close workbook.	3	
		TOTAL POINTS	20	

Part 3

File: **EL1-C5-CS-GGConv.xlsx**

Steps	Tasks	Criteria	Value	Score
1	Research, Typing, Accuracy	After using the Internet for research, create a conversion worksheet in a blank workbook as follows: • Include length conversions: 1 inch to centimeters; 1 foot to centimeters; 1 yard to meters; 1 mile to kilometers. • Include weight conversions: 1 ounce to grams; 1 pound to kilograms; 1 ton to metric tons. • Include volume conversions: 1 fluid ounce to milliliters; 1 pint to liters; 1 quart to liters; 1 gallon to liters.	15	
2	Research, Formulas, Editing	Locate a site on the Internet that provides formula for converting Fahrenheit temperatures to Celsius, then create another worksheet in workbook with the following: Insert Fahrenheit temperatures beginning with zero, continuing to 100, and incrementing by 5 (for example, 0, 5, 10, 15); then insert formula converting Fahrenheit temperatures to Celsius.	8	
3	Typing, Formatting	Include company name *Gateway Global* in both worksheets. Apply additional formatting to improve the visual appeal of worksheets. Rename both sheet names, then apply a color to each tab (name and color are user-chosen).	8	
4	Organization, Finishing	Save as **EL1-C5-CS-GGConv**. Print both worksheets centered horizontally and vertically, then close the workbook.	4	
		TOTAL POINTS	35	

Part 4

File: **EL1-C5-CS-GGLtrhd.docx** and **EL1-C5-CS-GGConvLtr.docx**

Steps	Tasks	Criteria	Value	Score
1	Typing, Formatting, Organization	At a blank document in Word, create letterhead containing the following: The company name *Gateway Global*, the address including street address, city, state, and ZIP code, or street address, city, province, and postal code (user-determined); and the telephone number (user-determined). Apply formatting to improve visual appeal of the letterhead. Save as **EL1-C5-CS-GGLtrhd**; then save again as **EL1-C5-CS-GGConvLtr**.	10	
2	Organization, Editing, Formatting	In Excel, open **EL1-C5-CS-GGConv.xlsx**. In first worksheet, copy the cells containing data, then paste into **EL1-C5-CS-GGConvLtr.docx** as a picture object. Center the picture object between left and right margins.	5	
3	Organization, Finishing	Save, print, then close **EL1-C5-CS-ConvLtr.docx**. Exit Word, then in Excel, close **EL1-C5-CS-GGConv.xlsx**.	5	
		TOTAL POINTS	20	

Excel Level 1, Chapter 6

Skills Check

Assessment 1: Manage Workbooks

File: **N/A**

Steps	Tasks	Criteria	Value	Score
1-7	Folder and Workbook Management, Accuracy	1. Display Open dialog box with Excel2010L1C6 as the active folder. 2–6. Create new folder named *O'Rourke* in the active folder. Copy **OEBudget.xlsx**, **OEPayroll.xlsx**, and **OEPlans.xlsx** to O'Rourke folder. Display contents of O'Rourke folder, rename **OEBudget.xlsx** to **OEEquipBudget.xlsx**; then rename **OEPlans.xlsx** to **OEPurchasePlans.xlsx**. Change the active folder back to Excel2010L1C6. 7. Close Open dialog box.	10	
		TOTAL POINTS	10	

Assessment 2: Move and Copy Worksheets Between Sales Analysis Workbooks

File: **EL1-C6-A2-DISales.xlsx**

Steps	Tasks	Criteria	Value	Score
1, 3, 6-7, 9	Organization, Accuracy	Open **DISales.xlsx**, Save As **EL1-C6-A2-DISales.xlsx**; open **DIQtrs.xlsx**; after Step 5, make **DIQtrs.xlsx** active, then close it without saving; open **DI4thQtr.xlsx**; after Step 8, make **DI4thQtr.xlsx** active, close without saving.	7	
2, 4-5, 8	Editing, Typing	Rename Sheet1 to *1st Qtr*. Rename Sheet1 to *2nd Qtr*, then copy it to **EL1-C6-A2-DISales.xlsx** following 1st Qtr worksheet. Make **DIQtrs.xlsx** active, rename Sheet 2 to *3rd Qtr*, then copy it to **EL1-C6-A2-DISales.xlsx** following 2nd Qtr tab. Rename Sheet1 to *4th Qtr*, then move it to **EL1-C6-A2-DISales.xlsx** following 3rd Qtr worksheet.	7	
10	Editing, Formulas, Formatting	With **EL1-C6-A2-DISales.xlsx** open, make the following changes to all four quarterly worksheets at same time: a–b. Make 1st Qtr active worksheet, then hold down Shift key and click 4th Qtr tab (selecting all four worksheets). c–d. Insert in cell E4 a formula to calculate average of cells B4 through D4, then copy formula down to cells E5 through E9. Insert in B10 formula to calculate sum of cells B4 through B9, then copy formula to C10 through E10. e. Make E4 active, apply Accounting Number Format with no decimal places.	7	

Steps	Tasks	Criteria	Value	Score
11-13	Editing, Formatting	11. Insert footer on all worksheets that prints student name at left, page number in middle, current date at right. 12. Horizontally and vertically center all worksheets. 13. Delete Sheet2 and Sheet3 tabs.	5	
14-15	Organization, Finishing	Resave, print all four worksheets, then close workbook.	4	
		TOTAL POINTS	30	

Assessment 3: Define and Apply Styles to a Projected Earnings Workbook
File: **EL1-C6-A3-Styles.xlsx** and **EL1-C6-A3-ProjEarnings.xlsx**

Steps	Tasks	Criteria	Value	Score
1-3	Organization, Formatting, Enhancement	1. At a blank worksheet, define a style named *C06Heading* with following formatting: a–d. 14-point Cambria bold in dark blue color; horizontal alignment of Center; top and bottom border in dark red color; and light purple fill. 2. Define a style named *C06Subheading* that contains following formatting: a–d. 12-point Cambria bold in dark blue color; horizontal alignment of Center; top and bottom border in dark red color; and light purple fill. 3. Define style named *C06Column* with the following formatting: a–c. At Style dialog box, click *Number* check box to remove check mark; 12-point Cambria in dark blue color; and light purple fill.	13	
4-6, 9, 11	Organization	4. Save workbook and name it **EL1-C6-A3-Styles**. 5–6. With **EL1-C6-A3-Styles.xlsx** open, open **ProjEarnings.xlsx**, Save As **EL1-C6-A3-ProjEarnings**. 9. Copy styles from **EL1-C6-A3-Styles.xlsx** into **EL1-C6-A3-ProjEarnings.xlsx**. 11. Save again, then print **EL1-C6-A3-ProjEarnings.xlsx**.	10	
7	Formulas	Make C6 active, insert a formula that multiplies content of B6 with amount in B3. (Cell B3 is an absolute reference.) Copy formula down to cells C7 through C17.	3	
8, 10	Formatting, Enhancement	8. Make C6 active, click Accounting Number Format. 10. Apply following styles: a–c. Select A1 and A2, apply C06Heading style; select A5 through C5, apply C06Subheading style; then select A6 through A17, apply C06Column style.	4	

Steps	Tasks	Criteria	Value	Score
12	Formatting, Enhancement	With **EL1-C6-A3-ProjEarnings.xlsx** open, modify styles: a–c. Modify C06Heading so it changes font color to dark purple, vertical alignment to Center, and inserts top and bottom border in dark purple. Modify C06Subheading so it changes font color to dark purple and inserts a top and bottom border in dark purple. Modify C06Column so it changes font color to dark purple, but leaves all of other formatting attributes.	6	
13-14	Organization, Finishing	Resave, print **EL1-C6-A3-ProjEarnings**, then close both workbooks without saving them.	4	
		TOTAL POINTS	40	

Assessment 4: Insert Hyperlinks in a Book Store Workbook
File: **EL1-C6-A4-BGSpecials.xlsx**

Steps	Tasks	Criteria	Value	Score
1	Organization, Accuracy	Open **BGSpecials.xlsx**, Save As **EL1-C6-A4-BGSpecials.xlsx**.	3	
2-6	Editing, Typing, Accuracy	2–5. Make cell E3 active, then hyperlink it to www.microsoft.com; make E4 active, then hyperlink to www.symantec.com; make E5 active, then hyperlink to www.nasa.gov; then make E6 active, hyperlink to www.cnn.com website. 6. Make A8 active, type **Weekly specials!**, then create a hyperlink to workbook named **BGWklySpcls.xlsx**.	10	
7-9	Accuracy, Research	Click hyperlink to the Microsoft website, explore the site, then close the web browser. Click hyperlink to NASA site, explore it, then close browser. Click the Weekly specials! hyperlink, view workbook, then close workbook.	4	
10	Organization, Finishing	Resave, print, then close original workbook.	3	
		TOTAL POINTS	20	

Assessment 5: Apply Conditional Formatting to a Sales Workbook
File: **EL1-C6-A5-PSSales.docx**

Steps	Tasks	Criteria	Value	Score
1-2	Research, Organization, Accuracy	After using Excel Help feature to learn about conditional formatting or after experimenting, open **PSSales.xlsx**, then Save As **EL1-C6-A5-PSSales**.	5	
3	Enhancement	Select cells D5 through D19, then use conditional formatting to display amounts as data bars.	3	
4	Editing	Insert header that prints student name, page number, and current date.	3	

Steps	Tasks	Criteria	Value	Score
5	Organization, Accuracy	Resave, print, then close workbook.	4	
		TOTAL POINTS	15	

Visual Benchmark

Fill In an Expense Report Form

File: **EL1-C6-VB-OEExpRpt.xlsx**

Steps	Tasks	Criteria	Value	Score
1	Accuracy	Display New tab Backstage view, click Sample templates button, then double-click *Expense Report* template.	3	
2-3, 5	Enhancement	2. With the expense report open, apply the Paper theme. 3, 5. Select J1 through L1, then apply Note cell style. Make L18 active and apply Bad cell style.	4	
4	Typing, Accuracy	4. Type information in cells as indicated in Fig. 6.9.	10	
6-7	Organization, Finishing	Save as **EL1-C6-VB-OEExpRpt**, print, then close.	3	
		TOTAL POINTS	20	

Case Study

Part 1

File: **EL1-C6-CS-LMExpSummary.xlsx**

Steps	Tasks	Criteria	Value	Score
1	Organization, Accuracy	Open **LMEstExp.xlsx**, Save As **EL1-C6-CS-LMExpSummary.xlsx**. Open **LMActExp.xlsx**.	4	
2	Editing, Organization	With **LMActExp.xlsx** open, copy the worksheet into **EL1-C6-CS-LMExpSummary.xlsx**, make **LMActExp.xlsx** the active workbook, then close.	4	
3	Formatting, Typing, Enhancement	Apply appropriate formatting to numbers, insert necessary formulas in each worksheet. (Use Clear to clear contents of cells N8, N9, M13, M14 in both worksheets.) Include company name *Leeward Marine* in worksheets. Create styles, then apply the styles to cells in each worksheet to maintain consistent formatting. Automatically adjust widths of columns to accommodate the longest entry.	15	

Steps	Tasks	Criteria	Value	Score
4	Organization	Resave workbook.	2	
		TOTAL POINTS	**25**	

Part 2
File: **N/A**

Steps	Tasks	Criteria	Value	Score
1	Organization, Editing, Accuracy	With **EL1-C6-CS-LMExpSummary.xlsx** open, open **LMExpVar.xlsx**, then copy worksheet into **EL1-C6-CS-LMExpSummary.xlsx**. Make **LMExpVar.xlsx** the active workbook, then close.	5	
2	Editing, Typing, Formatting	Rename sheet tab containing estimated expenses to *Estimated Exp*, rename tab with actual expenses to *Actual Exp*, rename tab containing variances to *Summary*. Select yearly estimated expense amounts (column N) in Estimated Exp, then paste amounts in appropriate cells in Summary worksheet; click Paste Options button, then click Values & Number Formatting button in *Paste Values* section of drop-down list. Select yearly actual expense amounts (column N) in Actual Exp worksheet, then paste amounts in appropriate cells in Summary worksheet; click Paste Options button, then click Values & Number Formatting button in *Paste Values* section of drop-down list. Recolor three sheet tabs just renamed.	12	
3	Formatting, Formulas, Enhancement	Apply appropriate formatting to numbers, then insert a formula to insert variances (differences) of estimated and actual expenses. Clear contents of cells D8, D9, D13, D14. Apply styles to Summary worksheet so formatting is similar to Estimated Exp and Actual Exp worksheets.	10	
4	Editing, Formatting	Insert an appropriate header or footer in each worksheet. Scale worksheets so each prints on one page.	4	
5	Organization, Finishing	Resave, print all worksheets, then close workbook.	4	
		TOTAL POINTS	**35**	

Part 3

File: **EL1-C6-CS-LMProdList.xlsx**

Steps	Tasks	Criteria	Value	Score
1	Research, Accuracy, Typing	Display New tab Backstage view, click *Lists* option in *Office.com Templates* section, click Business folder, then double-click Product price list template. (Steps may vary.) Use information below to fill in the form in the appropriate locations: Leeward Marine 4500 Shoreline Drive Ketchikan, AK 99901 (907) 555-2200 (907) 555-2595 (fax) www.emcp.com/lmarine Insert worksheet information in the appropriate columns (this data is in Part 3, on page 237).	12	
2	Organization, Finishing	Save as **EL1-C6-CS-LMProdList**, print, then close.	3	
		TOTAL POINTS	15	

Part 4

File: **EL1-C6-CS-LMProducts.docx**

Steps	Tasks	Criteria	Value	Score
1	Organization, Typing, Editing	In Word, open **LMLtrd.docx**. Press Enter four times. Make Excel active program, then open **EL1-C6-CS-LMProdList.xlsx**. Copy cells A2 through E11, then paste them into **LMLtrhd.docx** as a picture object.	7	
2	Organization, Finishing	Save document as **EL1-C6-CS-LMProducts**, print, then close. Close Excel document.	3	
		TOTAL POINTS	10	

Excel Level 1, Chapter 7

Skills Check

Assessment 1: Create a Company Sales Column Chart

File: **EL1-C7-A1-CMSales.xlsx**

Steps	Tasks	Criteria	Value	Score
1	Organization, Accuracy	Open **CMSales.xlsx**, Save As **EL1-C7-A1-CMSales.xlsx**.	3	

Steps	Tasks	Criteria	Value	Score
2	Graphing, Formatting	Select cells A3 through C15, then create a Column chart with these specifications: a. Choose *3-D Clustered Column* chart at Chart button drop-down list. b. At Chart Tools Design tab, click *Layout 3* option in Chart Layouts group. c. Change chart style to *Style 26*. d. Select text *Chart Title* and then type **Company Sales**. e. Move location of chart to a new sheet.	9	
3-4	Finishing, Organization	Print only the worksheet containing the chart, save, then close workbook.	3	
		TOTAL POINTS	15	

Assessment 2: Create Quarterly Domestic and Foreign Sales Bar Chart
File: **EL1-C7-A2-CMPQtrlySales.xlsx**

Steps	Tasks	Criteria	Value	Score
1	Organization, Accuracy	Open **CMPQtrlySales.xlsx**, Save As **EL1-C7-A2-CMPQtrlySales.xlsx**.	3	
2	Graphing, Formatting	Select A3 through E5, then create Bar chart with following: a. Click *Clustered Bar in 3-D* option at Bar button drop-down list. b. At Chart Tools Design tab choose *Layout 2* option in Chart Layouts group. c. Choose *Style 23* option in Chart Styles group. d. Select text *Chart Title*, type **Quarterly Sales**, and then click in chart, but outside any chart elements. e. Display Chart Tools Layout tab, then insert primary vertical minor gridlines. f–i. Display Chart Tools Format tab, then apply to chart *Subtle Effect - Olive Green, Accent 3* option in Shape Styles group; select *Domestic* series, then apply purple fill (*Purple, Accent 4, Darker 25%*) using Shape Fill button; select Foreign series, then apply dark aqua fill (*Aqua, Accent 5, Darker 25%*) using Shape Fill button; select chart title, then apply *Gradient Fill - Purple, Accent 4, Reflection* option with WordArt Styles button. j. Increase height of chart to 4 inches, width to 6 inches. k. Move chart below cells containing data, make sure chart fits on the page with the data.	14	
3-4	Organization, Finishing	Print only worksheet, save, then close workbook.	3	
		TOTAL POINTS	20	

Assessment 3: Create and Format a Corporate Sales Column Chart
File: EL1-C7-A3-CorpSales.xlsx

Steps	Tasks	Criteria	Value	Score
1	Organization, Accuracy	Open **CorpSales.xlsx**, Save As **EL1-C7-A3-CorpSales.xlsx**.	3	
2	Graphing, Formatting, Accuracy	Create a column chart, then format it so it displays as shown in Fig. 7.12.	9	
3	Organization, Finishing	Resave, print, then close workbook.	3	
		TOTAL POINTS	15	

Assessment 4: Create a Fund Allocations Pie Chart
File: EL1-C7-A4-Funds.xlsx

Steps	Tasks	Criteria	Value	Score
1	Typing, Accuracy	At blank workbook, create a worksheet with the following: Fund Allocations Fund Percentage Annuities 23% Stocks 42% Bonds 15% Money Market 20%	5	
2	Graphing, Formatting, Enhancement	Using data above, create a pie chart as a separate worksheet with the following specifications: a–b. Create a title for the pie chart, then add data labels to the chart. c. Add other enhancements that will improve the visual presentation of the data.	7	
3-5	Organization, Finishing	Save as **EL1-C7-A4-Funds**, print only the worksheet containing chart, then close workbook.	3	
		TOTAL POINTS	15	

Assessment 5: Create an Actual and Projected Sales Chart
File: EL1-C7-A5-StateSales.docx

Steps	Tasks	Criteria	Value	Score
1	Organization, Accuracy	Open **StateSales.xlsx**, Save As **EL1-C7-A5-StateSales.xlsx**.	3	
2	Graphing, Formatting, Enhancement	Look at data in the worksheet, then create chart to represent it. Ad a title to the chart, add enhancements to improve visual display of the chart.	8	

Steps	Tasks	Criteria	Value	Score
3-4	Organization, Finishing	Resave, print chart, then close workbook.	4	
		TOTAL POINTS	**15**	

Assessment 6: Create a Chart
File: **EL1-C7-A6-CMPerSales.docx**

Steps	Tasks	Criteria	Value	Score
1	Research, Typing, Graphing, Formatting	After using Excel Help feature to learn more about chart types, specifically stacked 3-D column charts, create a worksheet with the data shown in Fig. 7.13. Create a 100% stacked cylinder chart in a separate sheet, an appropriate title for the chart; then apply other formatting to enhance the appearance of the chart.	6	
2-4	Organization, Finishing	Save as **EL1-C7-A6-CMPerSales**, print both sheets of the workbook (sheet containing data in cells and sheet containing chart), then close workbook.	4	
		TOTAL POINTS	**10**	

Visual Benchmark

Create and Format a Pie Chart
File: **EL1-C7-VB-CMFebExp.xlsx**

Steps	Tasks	Criteria	Value	Score
1	Typing, Graphing, Accuracy, Formatting	At a blank workbook, enter data, then create a pie chart in a separate sheet as shown in Fig. 7.14, using the information shown in the pie chart to create the data. Format chart so it appears similar to the figure.	7	
2-4	Organization, Finishing	Save as **EL1-C7-VB-CMFebExp**, print both worksheets, then close the workbook.	3	
		TOTAL POINTS	**10**	

Case Study

Part 1

File: **EL1-C7-CS-DWQtrSales.xlsx**

Steps	Tasks	Criteria	Value	Score
1	Typing, Graphing, Enhancement	At a blank workbook, create two charts based on data provided (shown in Part 1 on page 269). (Type and style of chart, layout, formatting, are user-chosen.) In Commercial Loans chart containing the text *All-time High,* insert a shape pointing to the second quarter amount (*$6,785,250*).	12	
2	Organization, Finishing	Save as **EL1-C7-CS-DWQtrSales**, print only the chart, then close workbook.	3	
		TOTAL POINTS	15	

Part 2

File: **EL1-C7-CS-DWBudgetPercentages.xlsx**

Steps	Tasks	Criteria	Value	Score
1	Typing, Accuracy, Formulas, Graphing	At a blank workbook, using the information provided (see Part 2 page 269), calculate the percentage of the budget for each item, then create a pie chart with it. (Chart style, layout, and formatting is user-determined.)	12	
2	Organization, Finishing	Save as **EL1-C7-CS-DWBudgetPercentages**, print only the chart, then close workbook.	3	
		TOTAL POINTS	15	

Part 3

File: **EL1-C7-CS-DWStocks.xlsx**

Steps	Tasks	Criteria	Value	Score
1	Research, Typing, Graphing	After using Excel Help feature to learn about stock charts, create a stock chart with the following information: IDE POE QRR High $23.75 $18.55 $34.30 Low $18.45 $15.00 $31.70 Close $19.65 $17.30 $33.50	7	
2	Organization, Finishing	Save as **EL1-C7-CS-DWStocks**, print only the chart, then close workbook.	3	
		TOTAL POINTS	10	

Part 4

File: **EL1-C7-CS-DWRates.docx**

Steps	Tasks	Criteria	Value	Score
1	Research, Accuracy, Typing, Formulas, Graphing	After using the Internet to search for historical data on the national average for mortgage rates, determine the average mortgage rate for a 30-year FRM (fixed-rate mortgage) for each January and July beginning with the year 2008 and continuing to the current year. Include the current average rate. Use this information to create a chart.	12	
2	Organization, Finishing	Save document as **EL1-C7-CS-DWRates**, print, then close. Close Excel document.	3	
		TOTAL POINTS	15	

Excel Level 1, Chapter 8

Skills Check

Assessment 1: Insert a Clip Art Image and WordArt in an Equipment Purchase Workbook
File: **EL1-C8-A1-ASPurPlans.xlsx**

Steps	Tasks	Criteria	Value	Score
1	Organization, Accuracy	Open **ASPurPlans.xlsx**, Save As **EL1-C8-A1-ASPurPlans.xlsx**.	3	
2-7	Formulas, Functions, Editing	2–3. Insert formula in E4 using PMT function that calculates monthly payments. Hint: Refer to Chapter 2, Project 3a, then copy it to cells E5 and E6. 4–5. Insert formula in F4 that calculates total amount of payments, then copy it to F5 and F6. 6–7. Insert a formula in cell G4 that calculates total amount of interest paid, then copy it to G5 and G6.	10	
8-10	Formatting	8. Insert clip art image shown in Fig. 8.10 with the following specifications: • Search for it using search word *movies*. (Colors of this clip art image are yellow and black.) • Change its image color to *Blue, Accent color 1 Light*. • Apply *Brightness: 0% (normal), Contrast: +40%*, then apply *Reflected Rounded Rectangle* picture style. • Size and move image to position as shown in the figure. 9. Insert company name *Azure Studios* in A1 as WordArt. Use *Fill - Blue, Accent 1, Metal Bevel, Reflection* option to create it. 10. Change worksheet orientation to landscape.	9	
11	Finishing, Organization	Resave, print, then close workbook.	3	
		TOTAL POINTS	25	

Assessment 2: Insert Formulas and Format a Travel Company Workbook
File: **EL1-C8-A2-TSGEVacs.xlsx**

Steps	Tasks	Criteria	Value	Score
1	Organization, Accuracy	Open **TSGEVacs.xlsx**, Save As **EL1-C8-A2-TSBEVacs.xlsx**.	3	

2, 4, 6	Formatting	2. Apply shading to data in cells as shown in Fig. 8.11. (Use options in Aqua column.)
		4. Format image of airplane position as shown in figure, with following specs:
		  a. Use Remove Background button to remove a portion of yellow background so image displays similar to figure.
		  b. Rotate image.
		  c. Apply *Brightness: +20%, Contrast: +20%* correction.
		  d. Position image as shown in figure.
		6. Change orientation to landscape.
			8	

3	Formulas	Insert appropriate formulas to calculate prices based on 10 percent and 20 percent discounts, then apply appropriate number formatting.	4	
5	Organization, Enhancement	Open Word, then open **TSAirfare.docx** located in Excel2010L1C8 folder. Click Excel button on Taskbar, then use Screenshot button (*Screen Clipping* option) to select and insert airfare information in **EL1-C8-A2-TSGEVacs.xlsx**, positioning the info at right side of the data in the worksheet.	6	
7-9	Organization, Finishing	Making sure data and airfare info displays on one page, print worksheet, save, close workbook, then exit Word.	4	
		TOTAL POINTS	25	

Assessment 3: Insert and Format Shapes in a Company Sales Workbook
File: **EL1-C8-A3-MSSales.xlsx**

Steps	Tasks	Criteria	Value	Score
1	Organization, Accuracy	Open **MSSales.xlsx**, Save As **EL1-C8-A3-MSSSales.xlsx**.	3	
2-6	Typing, Formatting, Editing	2. In cell A1, type **Mountain**, press Alt + Enter, then type **Systems**. 3. Select *Mountain Systems,* change font to 26-point Calibri bold. 4. Change horizontal alignment of cell A1 to left and vertical alignment to middle. 5. Display Format Cells dialog box with Alignment tab selected, then change *Indent* measurement to *2*. 6. Click outside cell A1.	7	

Steps	Tasks	Criteria	Value	Score
7,11	Enhancement, Formatting	7. Use *Isosceles Triangle* shape located in *Basic Shapes* section of Shapes drop-down to draw triangle as shown in Figure 8.12. 11. Insert arrow pointing to $97,549 using left arrow shape, apply olive green fill to shape, then remove shape outline. Set text in 10-point Calibri bold. Position arrow as shown in figure.	6	
8-9	Editing, Formatting	8. Copy triangle three times. Add olive green fill and dark olive green outline color (user-chosen) to triangles so they appear similar to triangles in figure, then position triangles as shown in figure. 9. Apply shading to cells as shown in the figure (using colors in Olive Green column).	7	
10	Typing, Accuracy	Insert total amounts in cells B10 through D10.	4	
12	Organization, Finishing	Resave, print, then close workbook.	3	
		TOTAL POINTS	30	

Assessment 4:

File: **EL1-C8-A4-PS2ndQtrSales.xlsx**

Steps	Tasks	Criteria	Value	Score
1	Organization, Accuracy	Open **PS2ndQtrSales.xlsx**, Save As **EL1-C8-A4-PS2ndQtrSales.xlsx**.	3	

2-4	Enhancement, Typing, Formatting	2. Change orientation to landscape.
		3. Insert a pyramid shape at right side of worksheet data using *Pyramid List* diagram with the following specs:
		  a. Change color to *Gradient Loop - Accent 3*.
		  b. Apply *Cartoon* SmartArt style.
		  c–e. In bottom text box, type **Red Level**, press Enter, then type **$25,000 to $49,999**. In middle text box, type **Blue Level**, press Enter, then type **$50,000 to $99,999**. In top text box, type **Gold Level**, press Enter, then type **$100,000+**.
		  f. Apply fill to each text box to match level color.
		4. Size or move diagram so it displays attractively at right side of worksheet data. (Make sure entire diagram will print on same page as worksheet data.)
			14	

5	Organization, Finishing	Resave, print, then close workbook.	3	
		TOTAL POINTS	20	

Assessment 5: Create and Insert a Screenshot
File: **EL1-C8-A5-PMTFormula.docx**

Steps	Tasks	Criteria	Value	Score
1	Organization, Accuracy	Open **RPRefiPlan.xlsx**, then display formulas (Ctrl + `).	3	
2	Enhancement, Formatting	Insert arrow shape shown in Fig. 8.13, then add fill to shape, remove shape outline, bold text in shape, then figure out how to rotate it rotation handle. Rotate, size, and position arrow as shown in figure.	8	
3-4	Organization, Editing	Open Word. At a blank document, press Ctrl + E to center insertion point, press Ctrl + B to turn on bold, type **Excel Worksheet with PMT Formula**, then press Enter twice.	6	
5	Enhancement	Click Insert tab, click Screenshot button, then click the thumbnail of the Excel worksheet.	4	
6-8	Organization, Finishing	Save Word document as **EL1-C8-A5-PMTFormula**, print, then close, exit Word. In Excel, close **RPRefiPlan.xlsx** without saving changes.	4	
		TOTAL POINTS	25	

Visual Benchmark

Insert Formulas, WordArt, and Clip Art in a Worksheet
File: **EL1-C8-VB-TSYrlySales.xlsx**

Steps	Tasks	Criteria	Value	Score
1	Organization, Accuracy	Open **TSYrlySales.xlsx**, Save As **EL1-C8-VB- TSYrlySales. xlsx**.	3	
2	Formulas, Functions	Insert following formulas, as indicated in Fig. 8.14: (*Do not type data in following cells—insert formulas instead. Results of formulas should match results in figure.*) • Cells C4 through C14: Insert formula with IF function that inserts *5%* if amount in cell in column B is greater than $249,999 or *2%* if amount is not greater than $249,999. • Cells D4 through D14: Insert formula that multiplies amount in column B with amount in column C.	6	

Steps	Tasks	Criteria	Value	Score
3, 5	Enhancement, Typing, Formatting	3. Insert company name *Target Supplies* as WordArt with following specifications: • Use *Gradient Fill - Black, Outline - White, Outer Shadow* WordArt option. • To type WordArt text, press Ctrl + L (this changes to left text alignment), type **Target**, press Enter, type **Supplies**. • Change text outline color to *Orange, Accent 6, Darker 25%*. • Move WordArt to position as shown in the figure. 5. Draw shape displaying below data with following specs: • Use *Bevel* shape. • Type text in shape, apply bold, change to center and middle alignment. • Change shape fill color to *Red, Accent 2, Darker 50%*, then shape outline color to *Orange, Accent 6, Darker 25%*.	12	
4	Formatting	Insert target clip art image (use word *target* to search) with following specs: • Change color to *Red, Accent color 2 Dark*. • Change correction to *Brightness: 0% (Normal), Contrast: +40%*. • Apply *Drop Shadow Rectangle* picture style. • Size position clip art image as shown in figure.	5	
6-8	Organization, Finishing	Save and then print worksheet. Press Ctrl + ` to turn on display of formulas, print worksheet again. Turn off display of formulas, close workbook.	4	
		TOTAL POINTS	30	

Case Study

Part 1

File: **EL1-C8-CS-OTSales.xlsx**

Steps	Tasks	Criteria	Value	Score
1	Organization, Accuracy	Open **OTSales.xlsx**, Save As **EL1-C8-CS-OTSales.xlsx**.	3	
2	Formatting	Apply formatting to improve appearance of the worksheet, then insert at least one clip art (use *truck* or *ocean*).	9	
3	Organization, Finishing	Resave, then print worksheet.	3	
		TOTAL POINTS	15	

Part 2

File: **EL1-C8-CS-OTSalesF&C.xlsx**

Steps	Tasks	Criteria	Value	Score
1	Organization, Accuracy	With **EL1-C8-CS-OTSales.xlsx** open, Save As **EL1-C8-CS-OTSalesF&C.xlsx**	3	
2	Editing	Divide workbook into two worksheets with one worksheet containing all Ford vehicles, the other containing all Chevrolets. Rename worksheet tabs to reflect contents. Sort each worksheet by price, most expensive to least.	6	
3	Enhancement	Insert in first worksheet a SmartArt diagram (user-chosen) that contains the following information: Small-sized truck = $100 2WD Regular Cab = $75 SUV 4x4 = $50	4	
4	Editing, Formatting	Copy diagram in first worksheet, then paste into the second one. Change the orientation to landscape.	3	
5	Organization, Finishing	Resave, print, then close workbook.	4	
		TOTAL POINTS	20	

Part 3

File: **EL1-C8-CS-OTSales-WebPage.mht**

Steps	Tasks	Criteria	Value	Score
1	Organization, Accuracy	Open **EL1-C8-CS-OTSales.xlsx**. Display Save As dialog box, click *Save as type* option, determine how to save the workbook as a single file web page (*.mht, *.mhtml), then save as one with the name **EL1-CS-OTSales-WebPage.**	6	
2	Accuracy	Open Internet browser, then open the web page. Look at the information in the file, then close the Internet browser.	4	
		TOTAL POINTS	10	

Part 4

File: **N/A**

Steps	Tasks	Criteria	Value	Score
1	Organization, Accuracy	Open **EL1-C8-CS-OTSalesF&C.xlsx,** then open PowerPoint.	3	
2	Formatting, Editing	Change slide layout in PowerPoint to Blank. Copy diagram in first worksheet, then paste it into the PowerPoint blank slide. Increase and/or move diagram so it better fills slide.	4	

Steps	Tasks	Criteria	Value	Score
3	Finishing, Organization	Print the slide, then close PowerPoint without saving the presentation. Close **EL1-C8-CS-OTSalesF&C.xlsx**.	3	
		TOTAL POINTS	10	

Excel Level 1, Unit 2
Performance Assessment

Assessing Proficiency

Assessment 1: Copy and Paste Data and Insert WordArt in a Training Scores Workbook
File: **EL1-U2-A1-RLTraining.xlsx**

Steps	Tasks	Criteria	Value	Score
1	Organization, Accuracy	Open **RLTraining.xlsx**, Save As **EL1-U2-A1-RLTraining.**	3	
2, 4-13	Editing, Typing	2. Delete row 15. 4. After Step 3, copy formula in cell D4 to D5 through D20. 5. Make A22 active, turn on bold, type **Highest Averages**. 6. Display Clipboard task pane, making sure it is empty. 7. Select then copy each of following rows (individually): row 7, 10, 14, 16, 18. 8–12. Make A23 cell active, then paste row 14 (*Jewett, Troy*); make A24 active, then paste row 7 (*Cumpston, Kurt*); make A25 active, then paste row 10 (*Fisher-Edwards, Theresa*); make A26 active, then paste row 16 (*Mathias, Caleb*); then make cell A27 active and paste row 18 (the row for *Nyegaard, Curtis*). 13. Click Clear All in Clipboard task pane, then close it.	14	
3	Formulas	3. Insert a formula in cell D4 that averages percentages in cells B4 and C4.	2	
14	Enhancement, Formatting	Insert in cell A1 the text *Rosel* as WordArt. Format the WordArt to add visual appeal to worksheet.	3	
15	Organization, Finishing	Resave, print, then close workbook.	3	
		TOTAL POINTS	25	

Assessment 2: Manage Multiple Worksheets in a Projected Earnings Workbook
File: **EL1-U2-A2-RLProjEarnings.xlsx**

Steps	Tasks	Criteria	Value	Score
1	Organization, Accuracy	Open **RLProjEarnings.xlsx**, Save As **EL1-U2-A2-RLProjEarnings.**	3	
2-9, 11	Editing, Formatting, Typing	2. Delete *Roseland* in cell A1. Open **EL1-U2-A1-RLTraining.xlsx**, then copy the *Rosel* WordArt text and paste it into A1 in **EL1-U2-A2-RLProjEarnings.xlsx**. If necessary, increase height of row 1 to accommodate the WordArt. 3. Notice fill color in cells in **EL1-U2-A1-RLTraining.xlsx**, apply same fill color to cells of data in **EL1-U2-A2-RLProjEarnings.xlsx**, then close **EL1-U2-A1-RLTraining.xlsx**. 4. Select cells A1 through C11, then copy and paste to Sheet2, keeping source column widths. 5. With Sheet2 displayed, make following changes: a. Increase height of row 1 to accommodate WordArt. b. Delete contents of cell B2. c. Change contents of following cells: A6: Change *January* to *July;* A7: Change *February* to *August;* A8: Change *March* to *September;* A9: Change *April* to *October;* A10: Change *May* to *November;* A11: Change *June* to *December;* B6: Change *8.30%* to *8.10%;* B8: Change *9.30%* to *8.70%.* 6. Make Sheet1 active, then copy cell B2 and paste (linking it) to cell B2 in Sheet2. 7. Rename Sheet1 to *First Half* and rename Sheet2 to *Second Half.* 8. Make First Half worksheet active, then determine effect on projected monthly earnings if projected yearly income is increased by 10% by changing number in B2 to *$1,480,380.* 9. Horizontally and vertically center both worksheets. Insert a custom header with student name at left, current date in center, and sheet name (use Sheet Name button) at right. 11. Determine effect on projected monthly earnings if projected yearly income is increased by 20%, by changing number in cell B2 to *$1,614,960.*	23	
10, 12-13	Finishing, Organization	After Step 9, print both worksheets. After Step 11, resave, print both worksheets, then close workbook.	4	
		TOTAL POINTS	30	

Assessment 3: Create Charts in Worksheets in a Sales Totals Workbook
File: **EL1-U2-A3-EPYrlySales.xlsx**

Steps	Tasks	Criteria	Value	Score
1	Organization, Accuracy	Open **EPYrlySales.xlsx**, Save As **EL1-U2-A3-EPYrlySales.**	3	

Steps	Tasks	Criteria	Value	Score
2	Editing, Accuracy	Rename Sheet1 to *2010 Sales*, Sheet2 to *2011 Sales*, and Sheet3 to *2012 Sales*.	3	
3	Formatting, Typing, Formulas	Select all three sheet tabs, make cell A12 active, click Bold, then type **Total**. In B12, insert formula to total amounts in B4 through B11. In C12, insert formula to total amounts in C4 through C11.	5	
4-6	Graphing, Formatting	Make 2010 Sales worksheet active, select cells A3 through C11 (not the totals in row 12), then create a column chart. Click Switch Row/Column button at Chart Tools Design tab. Apply formatting to increase visual appeal of chart, then drag it below worksheet data. (Fit on one page.) Make the 2011 Sales worksheet active, then create the same type of chart done in previous step. Make 2012 Sales worksheet active, then create same type of chart you created in previous steps.	16	
7-8	Organization, Finishing	Resave, print entire workbook, then close.	3	
		TOTAL POINTS	30	

Assessment 4: Create and Format a Line Chart

File: **EL1-U2-A4-CtrySales.xlsx**

Steps	Tasks	Criteria	Value	Score
1	Typing, Accuracy	At blank workbook, type the following in a worksheet: **Country** **Total Sales** Denmark $85,345 Finland $71,450 Norway $135,230 Sweden $118,895	5	
2, 5	Graphing, Formatting	2. Using data just entered, create line chart with the following specs: a. Apply a chart style (user-chosen). b. Insert major/minor primary vertical gridlines. c. Insert drop lines (using Lines button in Analysis group). d. Apply other formatting to improve visual appeal of chart. e. Move chart to a new sheet. 5. After Step 4, change line chart to bar chart (user-chosen).	10	
3-4, 6-7	Organization, Finishing	3. After Step 2, save workbook as **EL1-U2-A4-CtrySales**, then print only the sheet containing chart. 6. After Step 5, resave, print only the sheet containing chart, then close workbook.	5	
		TOTAL POINTS	20	

Assessment 5: Create and Format a Pie Chart

File: **EL1-U2-A5-EPProdDept.xlsx**

Steps	Tasks	Criteria	Value	Score
1	Organization, Accuracy	Open **EPProdDept.xlsx**, Save As **EL1-U2-A5-EPProdDept.**	3	
2	Graphing, Formatting	Create a pie chart as a separate sheet, with the data in cells A3 through B10. Student determines type of pie. Include an appropriate title and percentage labels.	9	
3-4	Organization, Finishing	Resave, print, then close workbook.	3	
		TOTAL POINTS	15	

Assessment 6: Insert a Text Box in and Save a Travel Workbook as a Web Page

File: **EL1-U2-A6-TravDest.xlsx**

Steps	Tasks	Criteria	Value	Score
1	Organization, Accuracy	Open **TravDest.xlsx**, Save As **EL1-U2-A6-TravDest.**	3	
2	Enhancement, Formatting, Typing	Insert a text box, with the following specs: a. Draw text box at right side of clip art image. b. Remove fill in text box outline around text box. c. Type **Call 1-888-555-1288 for last-minute vacation specials!** d. Select text, change font to 24-point Forte in blue color. e. Size and position text box so it appears visually balanced with travel clip art image.	7	
3-5	Research, Accuracy	3. Use Internet to search for sites that might be of interest to tourists for each of cities in worksheet. Write down web addresses for best web pages you find for each city. 4–5. Create a hyperlink for each city to the web address written down in Step 3, then select each hyperlinked text and change font size to 18 points. Test hyperlinks to make sure web addresses were entered correctly. Close web browser when done.	12	
6	Organization, Finishing	Resave, print, then close workbook.	3	
		TOTAL POINTS	25	

Assessment 7: Insert Clip Art Image and SmartArt Diagram in a Projected Quotas Workbook

File: **EL1-U2-A7-SalesQuotas.xlsx**

Steps	Tasks	Criteria	Value	Score
1	Organization, Accuracy	Open **SalesQuotas.xlsx**, Save As **EL1-U2-A7-SalesQuotas.**	3	
2-3	Formulas, Formatting	Insert formula in C3 using absolute reference to determine projected quotas at a 10% increase of current quotas. Copy formula to cells C4 through C12. Apply Accounting Number Format style to cell C3.	5	
4-6, 8	Formatting, Enhancement	4. Insert clip art image in row 1 related to money (size and position is user-determined). 5–6. Insert a SmartArt diagram at right side of data that contains the three shapes, then insert following quota ranges in the shapes and apply specified fill color: $50,000 to $99,999 (apply green color) $100,000 to $149,999 (apply blue color) $150,000 to $200,000 (apply red color) Apply formatting to SmartArt to improve visual appeal. 8. Change orientation to landscape, make sure diagram fits on the page.	11	
7	Editing	7. Insert a custom header that prints student name at left, current date in middle, and file name at right.	3	
9	Organization	Resave, print, then close workbook.	3	
		TOTAL POINTS	25	

Assessment 8: Insert Symbol, Clip Art, and Comments in a Sales Workbook

File: **EL1-U2-A8-CISales.xlsx**

Steps	Tasks	Criteria	Value	Score
1	Organization, Accuracy	Open **CISales.xlsx**, Save As **EL1-U2-A8-CISales.**	3	
2-4	Editing, Typing, Accuracy	2. Delete *Lower Company* in A7, then type **Económico**. 3. Insert new row at beginning of worksheet. 4. Select and merge cells A1 through D1.	4	
5-7	Formatting, Enhancement	5. Increase height of row 1 to approximately 141.00. 6. Insert *Custom Interiors* as WordArt in cell A1 (formatting user-determined). Move and size WordArt to fits in cell A1. 7. In Word, open **CICustomers.docx** located in Excel2010L1U2 folder. Click Excel button with **EL1-U2-A8-CISales.xlsx** open, make a screenshot (use *Screen Clipping*) of customer information in Word document, then position screenshot image below data in cells.	7	
8	Editing	Insert a custom footer that prints student name at left and file name at right.	3	

Steps	Tasks	Criteria	Value	Score
9-10	Organization	Make sure data in cells and screenshot display on same page, then print worksheet. Resave, then close workbook.	3	
		TOTAL POINTS	20	

Assessment 9: Insert and Format a Shape in a Budget Workbook

File: **EL1-U2-A9-SEExpenses.xlsx**

Steps	Tasks	Criteria	Value	Score
1	Organization, Accuracy	Open **SEExpenses.xlsx**, Save As **EL1-U2-A9-SEExpenses**.	3	
2	Editing, Formatting, Typing, Accuracy, Enhancement	Make changes, so it displays as shown in Fig. U2.1: a. Select and merge cells A1 through D1. b. Add fill to cells as shown in the figure. c. Increase height of row 1 to approximate size shown. d. Type **SOLAR ENTERPRISES** in cell A, 20-point Calibri bold, center and middle aligned, aqua (*Aqua, Accent 5, Darker 25%*). e. Insert sun shape (from *Basic Shapes* section), then apply orange shape fill and change shape outline to aqua (*Aqua, Accent 5, Darker 25%*).	9	
3	Organization	Resave, print, then close workbook.	3	
		TOTAL POINTS	15	

Writing Activities

Activity 1: Prepare a Projected Budget

File: **EL1-U2-Act1-MFBudget.xlsx** and **EL1-U2-Act1-MFMemo.docx**

Steps	Tasks	Criteria	Value	Score
1	Accuracy, Typing, Formatting	Create a departmental budget worksheet (department has a budget of $1,450,00) with the following information that shows the projected yearly budget, the budget items in the department, the percentage of the budget, and the amount for each item. The percentages for the proposed budget items are: Salaries, 45%; Benefits, 12%; Training, 14%; Administrative Costs, 10%; Equipment, 11%; Supplies, 8%.	10	
2	Organization, Finishing	Save as **EL1-U2-Act1-MFBudget**, print, then close.	3	
3	Writing	[OPTIONAL EXERCISE] In Word 2010, write a memo to McCormack Funds Finance Department explaining that proposed annual department budget is attached for their review. Comments and suggestions are to be sent within one week.	4	

Steps	Tasks	Criteria	Value	Score
4	Organization, Finishing	Save the Word document as **EL1-U2-Act1-MFMemo**, print, then close document.	3	
		TOTAL POINTS	20	

Activity 2: Create a Travel Tours Bar Chart
File: **EL1-U2-Act2-CTTours.xlsx**

Steps	Tasks	Criteria	Value	Score
1	Accuracy, Typing, Formatting	At a blank workbook, prepare a worksheet including the following information: **Scandinavian Tours** **Country** **Tours** **Booked** Norway 52 Sweden 62 Finland 29 Denmark 38	6	
2	Graphing, Formatting	Use the information in the worksheet to create and format a bar chart as a separate sheet.	5	
3	Organization, Finishing	Save as **EL1-U2-Act2-CTTours**, print only the sheet containing the chart, then close workbook.	4	
		TOTAL POINTS	15	

Activity 3: Prepare a Ski Vacation Worksheet
File: **EL1-U2-Act3-CTSkiTrips.xlsx**

Steps	Tasks	Criteria	Value	Score
1	Typing, Enhancement, Formatting, Formulas	At a blank workbook, prepare worksheet for Carefree Travels that advertises snow skiing trip. Include the following information in the announcement: • At the beginning of the worksheet, create company logo that includes company name *Carefree Travels* and a clip art image related to travel. • Include heading *Whistler Ski Vacation Package* in the worksheet. • Include the following below the heading: Round-trip air transportation: $395 Seven nights hotel accommodations: $1,550 Four all-day ski passes: $425 Compact rental car with unlimited mileage: $250 Total price of the ski package: (calculated) • Include the following somewhere in the worksheet: Book your vacation today at special discount prices. Two-for-one discount at many local ski resorts.	12	

Steps	Tasks	Criteria	Value	Score
2	Organization, Finishing	Save as **EL1-U2-Act3-CTSkiTrips**, print, then close.	3	
		TOTAL POINTS	15	

Internet Research

Find Information on Excel Books and Present the Data in a Worksheet
File: **EL1-U2-DR-Books.xlsx**

Steps	Tasks	Criteria	Value	Score
1	Research, Accuracy, Typing	Use the Internet to locate two companies that sell new books. At the first new book company site, locate three books on Microsoft Excel. Record title, author, and price for each book. At the second new book company site, locate the same three books and record the prices.	5	
2	Accuracy, Typing, Formatting	Create Excel worksheet that includes the following: Name of each new book company; title and author of the three books; prices for each book from the two sites. Create a hyperlink for each book company to the website on the Internet.	7	
3	Organization, Finishing	Save as **EL1-U2-DR-Books**, print, then close workbook.	3	
		TOTAL POINTS	15	

Job Study

Create a Customized Time Card for a Landscaping Company
File: **EL1-U2-JS-TimeCard.xlsx**

Steps	Tasks	Criteria	Value	Score
1	Accuracy	Locate the time card template available with *Sample templates* selected at the New tab Backstage view.	3	
2	Editing, Enhancement, Formatting	With template open, insert additional blank rows to increase spacing above the Employee row. Insert a clip art image related to landscaping or gardening, then position and size it attractively in the form. Include a text box with the text *Lawn* and *Landscaping Specialists* inside the box, then format, size, and position the text attractively in the form.	7	

Steps	Tasks	Criteria	Value	Score

3		Fill in the form for the current week with the following employee information:
		Employee = Jonathan Holder
		Address = 12332 South 152nd Street
		           Baton Rouge, LA 70804
		Manager = (Student name)
		Employee phone = (225) 555-3092
		Employee email = None
		Regular hours = 8 hours for Monday,
		           Tuesday, Wednesday, Thursday
		Overtime = 2 hours on Wednesday
		Sick hours = None
		Vacation = 8 hours on Friday
		Rate per hour = $20.00
		Overtime pay = $30.00
			12	

4	Organization, Finishing	Save as **EL1-U2-JS-TimeCard**, print, then close workbook.	3	
		TOTAL POINTS	25	

Excel Level 2, Chapter 1

Skills Check

Assessment 1: Use Conditional and Fraction Formatting
File: **EL2-C1-A1-RSRServRpt.xlsx**

Steps	Tasks	Criteria	Value	Score
1-2	Opening, Saving	Open **RSRServRpt.xlsx**. Save As **EL2-C1-A1-RSRServRpt**.	1	
3	Formatting	Apply the following formatting changes to worksheet: • Format C6:C23 to fractions using type *As quarters (2/4)* • Format rate codes in D6:D22 with icon set *3 Traffic Lights (Rimmed)* • Format parts values in F6:F22 to color cell with *Light Red Fill* for cells equal to zero • Bold values in G6:G22 • Format total invoice values in G6:G22 using *Red Data Bar* option in *Gradient Fill* section of Data Bars side menu.	8	
4	Saving, Printing	Save, print, and close **EL2-C1-A1-RSRServRpt.xlsx**.	1	
		TOTAL POINTS	10	

Assessment 2: Apply Custom Number Formatting
File: **EL2-C1-A2-RSRServRpt.xlsx**

Steps	Tasks	Criteria	Value	Score
1-2	Opening, Saving	Open **EL2-C1-A1-RSRServRpt.xlsx**. Save As **EL2-C1-A2-RSRServRpt**.	1	
3	Creating, Applying Custom Number Formats	Create and apply the following custom number formats: • Create custom number format that displays *hrs* one space after the values in C6:C23 • Create custom number format that displays *RSR-* in front of each work order number in B6:B22	8	
4	Saving, Closing	Save, print, and close **EL2-C1-A2-RSRServRpt.xlsx**. Print and close document.	1	
		TOTAL POINTS	10	

Assessment 3: Use Custom AutoFilter; Filter and Sort by Color
File: **EL2-C1-A3-RSRServRpt.xlsx**

Steps	Tasks	Criteria	Value	Score
1-2	Opening, Saving	Open **EL2-C1-A2-RSRServRpt**. Save As **EL2-C1-A3-RSRServRpt**.	1	

Steps	Tasks	Criteria	Value	Score
3-5	Filtering	Select A5:G22 and turn on Filter feature. Filter worksheet as follows: • Use filter arrow button in *Hours Billed* column, display invoices where hours billed is between 1.75 and 3.75 hours • Print filtered worksheet • Clear filter from *Hours Billed* column • Filter *Parts* column by color to show only those invoices for which no parts were billed • Print filtered worksheet • Clear filter from *Parts* column • Filter worksheet by icon associated with rate code **3** • Print filtered worksheet • Clear filter from *Rate Code* column Remove filter arrow buttons from worksheet	10	

6	Defining Custom Sort	Define custom sort to sort invoices by rate code icon set as follows:
		• Make any cell active within invoice list
		• Open Sort Dialog box
		• Define three sort levels as follows:
		  ○ *Sort by* Rate Code, *Sort On* Cell Icon, *Order* Red Traffic Light (On Top)
		  ○ *Sort by* Rate Code, *Sort On* Cell Icon, *Order* Yellow Traffic Light (On Top)
		  ○ *Sort by* Rate Code, *Sort On* Cell Icon, *Order* Green Traffic Light (On Top)
			3	

7-8	Printing, Saving	Print sorted worksheet. Save and close **EL2-C1-A3-RSRServRpt.xlsx**.	1	
		TOTAL POINTS	15	

Assessment 4: Create, Edit, and Delete Formatting Rules
File: **EL2-C1-A4-VantagePay-Oct27.xlsx**

Steps	Tasks	Criteria	Value	Score
1-2	Opening, Saving	Open **VantagePay-Oct27.xlsx**. Save As **EL2-C1-A4-VantagePay-Oct27**.	1	
3	Creating, Applying Formatting Rules	Create and apply two formatting rules for values in *Pay Rate* column as follows: • Apply light purple fill color to values from 7.50 to 8.00 • Apply light green fill color to values greater than 8.00	4	
4	Creating, Applying Formatting Rules	Create formatting rule for *Gross Pay* column that will format values in red bold font color if employee has worked overtime hours.	4	
5	Printing	Print worksheet.	1	

Steps	Tasks	Criteria	Value	Score
6-7	Editing Formatting	Edit formatting rule for *Cell Value > 8* by changing fill color to orange and applying bold to font. Delete formatting rule for *Cell Value between 7.50 and 8.00.*	4	
8-9	Printing, Saving	Print revised worksheet. Save then close **EL2-C1-A4-VantagePay-Oct27.xlsx**.	1	
		TOTAL POINTS	15	

Visual Benchmark

Format a Billing Summary

File: **EL2-C1-VB-BillingsOct8to12.xlsx**

Steps	Tasks	Criteria	Value	Score
1-2	Opening, Saving	Open **BillingsOct8to12.xlsx**. Save As **EL2-C1-VB-BillingsOct8to12**.	1	
3	Formatting	Format the worksheet to match Figure 1.9 using the following information: • Data in *Billing Code* column formatted to add text *Amicus #-* in front of code number in blue font color • Icon sets are used in *Attorney Code* column and same icon set should be applied in Attorney Code Table section of worksheet • Data bars added to values in *Legal Fees* column edited to change bar appearance to *Turquoise, Accent 3* gradient fill • Values below1500.00 in *Total Due* column are conditionally formatted and worksheet sorted by font color used for conditional format	8	
4	Saving, Printing	Save, print, and close **EL2-C1-VB-BillingsOct8to12.xlsx**.	1	
		TOTAL POINTS	10	

Case Study

Part 1

File: **EL2-C1-CS-P1-USIncomeStats.xlsx**

Steps	Tasks	Criteria	Value	Score
1	Opening, Saving	Open **USIncomeStats.xlsx**. Save As **EL2-C1-CS-P1-USIncomeStats.xlsx**.	1	

Steps	Tasks	Criteria	Value	Score
2	Formatting	Format data using color to differentiate income levels. Apply color formatting to: *Average Median Income Range* • Less than 45,000 • Between 45,00 and 55,000 • Great than 55,000 Use color formats to distinguish from each other.	6	
3	Creating Reference Table	Create reference table starting in E3 that provides a legend to read the colors.	2	
4	Saving, Printing	Save and close **EL2-C1-CS-P1-USIncomeStats.xlsx**.	1	
		TOTAL POINTS	10	

Part 2

File: **EL2-C1-CS-P2-USIncomeStats.xlsx**

Steps	Tasks	Criteria	Value	Score
1	Saving	In order to keep original file, **EL2-C1-CS-P1-USIncomeStats.xlsx** intact, save worksheet as **EL2-C1-CS-P2-USIncomeStats**.	1	
2	Sorting	Sort in descending order from highest income level to lowest. Do not include Entries in row 3 for United States average in sort operation.	4	
3	Filtering	After sorting, filter median incomes to display the top 20 states.	3	
4	Creating List	Add contact telephone list next to Top 20 state data. Create list using telephone numbers provided below in a suitable location: Yolanda (cell) 800 555 3117 Yolanda (office) 800 555 4629 Yolanda (home) 800 555 2169 Yolanda (fax) 800 555 6744 Apply special number format for phone numbers to ensure data is displayed consistently.	6	
5	Saving, Printing	Save and print **EL2-C1-CS-P2-USIncomeStats.xlsx**.	1	
		TOTAL POINTS	15	

Part 3

File: **EL2-C1-CS-P3-USIncomeStats.xlsx**

Steps	Tasks	Criteria	Value	Score
1	Applying Conditional Formatting	With **EL2-C1-CS-P2-USIncomeStats.xlsx** still open, apply conditional formatting using either a two-color or three-color scale to the filtered cells in Colum C (exclude the United States median income at top of column).	8	
2	Saving, Printing	Save As **EL2-C1-CS-P3-USIncomeStats.xlsx**. Print worksheet. *If color printer not available, student should write on printout the two- or three-color scale conditional formatting option applied to filtered values in Column C.*	2	
		TOTAL POINTS	10	

Part 4

File: **EL2-C1-CS-P4-USIncomeStats.xlsx**

Steps	Tasks	Criteria	Value	Score
1	Gathering Information	Using the Internet, go to URL www.census.gov/ and find page that describes the history of the Census Bureau.	1	
2	Typing Text	In new sheet in same file as median income data, type in column A five to seven interesting facts student learned about the bureau from the website.	6	
3	Formatting	Adjust width of column A. Apply wrap text or shrink to fit formatting to improve the appearance.	2	
4	Saving, Printing	Save revised workbook as **EL2-C1-CS-P4-USIncomeStats. xlsx**. Print worksheet and close workbook.	1	
		TOTAL POINTS	10	

Excel Level 2, Chapter 2

Skills Check

Assessment 1: Create Range Names and Use the Lookup Function

File: **EL2-C2-A1-RSROctLaborCost.xlsx**

Steps	Tasks	Criteria	Value	Score
1-2	Opening, Saving	Open **RSROctLaborCost.xlsx**. Save As **EL2-C2-A1-RSROctLaborCost**.	1	

Steps	Tasks	Criteria	Value	Score
3	Creating Range Names	Create the following range names: • C7:C22 *Hours* • D7:D22 *TechCode* • F7:F22 *LaborCost* • I3:J5 *RateChart*	3	
4-5	Creating VLOOKUP	In E7 create VLOOKUP formula to return correct hourly rate based on technician code in D7. Use range name *RateChart* within formula to reference hourly rate chart. Make sure Excel returns values for exact matches only. Copy VLOOKUP formula in E7 and past to E8:E22.	6	
6-7	Creating Formula	In F7 create formula to extend labor cost by multiplying hours in C7 times hourly rate in E7. Copy formula in F7 and paste to F8:F22.	2	
8	Creating Formula	Create formula in F23 to sum column.	1	
9	Printing	Preview and print worksheet.	1	
10	Saving, Printing	Save and close **EL2-C2-A1-RSROctLaborCost.xlsx**.	1	
		TOTAL POINTS	15	

Assessment 2: Use Conditional Statistical and Math Functions
File: **EL2-C2-A2-RSROctLaborCost.xlsx**

Steps	Tasks	Criteria	Value	Score
1-2	Opening, Saving	Open **EL2-C2-A1-RSROctLaborCost.xlsx**. Save As **EL2-C2-A2-RSROctLaborCost**.	1	
3	Creating COUNTA Formula	In I23 create a COUNTA formula to count number of calls made in October using dates in column A as source range.	4	
4	Creating COUNTIF Formula	Create COUNTIF formulas in cells as indicated below: I9: Count number of calls made by Technician 1 I10: Count number of calls made by Technician 2 I11: Count number of calls made by Technician 3	4	
5	Creating COUNTIFS Formulas	In I14 create COUNTIFS formula to count number of calls made by Technician 3 where hours logged were greater than 3.	2	
6	Creating SUMIF Formulas	Create SUMIF formulas in cells as indicated below: J9: Add labor cost for calls made by Technician 1 J10: Add labor cost for calls made by Technician 2 J11: Add labor cost for calls made by Technician 3	4	
7	Formatting	Format J9:J11 to Comma Style number format.	1	
8	Creating SUMIFS Formula	In J14 create SUMIFS formula to add labor cost for calls made by Technician 3 where hours logged were greater than 3.	2	

Steps	Tasks	Criteria	Value	Score
9	Formatting	Format J14 to Comma Style number format.	1	
10	Creating AVERAGEIF Formulas	Create AVERAGEIF formulas in cells indicated below: J18: Average the labor cost for calls made by Technician 1 J19: Average the labor cost for calls made by Technician 2 J20: Average the labor cost for calls made by Technician 3	4	
11	Formatting	Format J18:J20 to Comma Style number format.	1	
12	Saving, Printing	Save, print, and close **EL2-C2-A2-RSROctLaborCost.xlsx**.	1	
		TOTAL POINTS	25	

Assessment 3: Use Financial Functions PMT and PPMT
File: **EL2-C2-A3-PrecisionWarehouse.xlsx**

Steps	Tasks	Criteria	Value	Score
1-2	Opening, Saving	Open **PrecisionWarehouse.xlsx**. Save As **EL2-C2-A3-PrecisionWarehouse.xlsx**.	1	
3	Creating Formula	Create PMT formula in D8 to calculate monthly loan payment for proposed loan from New Ventures Capital Inc.	2	
4	Creating Formula	Find principal portion to loan payment for first loan payment in D10 and last loan payment in D11 using PPMT formulas.	2	
5	Creating Formula	In D13 create formula to calculate total cost of loan by multiplying monthly loan payment times 12 times the amortization period in years.	2	
6	Creating Formula	In D14 create formula to calculate interest cost of loan by entering formula =**d13+d6**.	2	
7-8	Printing, Saving	Print worksheet. Save and close **EL2-C2-A3-PrecisionWarehouse.xlsx**.	1	
		TOTAL POINTS	10	

Assessment 4: Use Logical Functions
File: **EL2-C2-A4-AllClaimsPremiumReview.xlsx**

Steps	Tasks	Criteria	Value	Score
1-2	Opening, Saving	Open **AllClaimsPremiumReview.xlsx**. Save As **EL2-C2-A4-AllClaimsPremiumReview.xlsx**.	1	
3	Creating Range Names	Create the following range names: B4:B23 *Claims* C4:C23 *AtFault* D4:D23 *Rating* E4:E23 *Deductible*	3	

Steps	Tasks	Criteria	Value	Score
4	Creating Formula	Create formula in G4 to display *Yes* if number of At Fault Claims is greater than 1 and Current Rating is greater than 2. Both conditions must test true to display *Yes*; otherwise display *No* in cell. *Hint: Use a nested IF and AND formula.*	3	
5	Formatting, Copying	Center result in G4. Copy formula in G5:G23.	2	
6	Creating Formula	Create formula in H4 to display *Yes* if either number of claims is greater than 2 or current deductible is less than $1,000.00; otherwise, display *No* in cell. *Hint: Use a nested IF and OR formula.*	3	
7	Formatting, Copying	Center result in H4. Copy formula in H5:H23. Deselect range after copying.	2	
8	Printing, Saving	Print, save, and close **EL2-C2-A4-AllClaimsPremiumReview. xlsx**.	1	
		TOTAL POINTS	15	

Assessment 5: Use the HLOOKUP Function
File: **EL2-C2-A5-JanelleTutoringProgressRpt.xlsx**

Steps	Tasks	Criteria	Value	Score
1-2	Opening, Saving	Open **JanelleTutoringProgressRpt.xlsx**. Save As **EL2-C2-A5-JanelleTutoringProgressRpt.xlsx**.	1	
3-4	Creating Range	Review layout of lookup table in ProgressComments sheet. Data is organized in rows with score in row 1 and grade comment in row 2. Select A1:G2 and create range name *GradeTable*.	3	
5-6	Creating Formula	Deselect range and make StudentProgress the active sheet. Create formula in G4 that will look up student's total score in range named *GradeTable* and return appropriate progress comment.	3	
7	Copying	Copy formula in G4 and paste to G5:G12.	2	
8	Printing, Saving	Print, save, and close **EL2-C2-A5-JanelleTutoringProgressRpt. xlsx**.	1	
		TOTAL POINTS	10	

Visual Benchmark

Use Lookup, Statistical, and Math Functions in a Billing Summary

File: **EL2-C2-VB1-BillableHrsOctober8to12.xlsx**

Steps	Tasks	Criteria	Value	Score
1-2	Opening, Saving	Open **BillingsOct8to12.xlsx**.Save As **EL2-C2-VB1-BillingsOct8to12**.	1	
3	Creating Formulas	Use the following information to create the required formulas. Create range names to use in all of the formulas so that readers can easily interpret the formula. • In column F, create a formula to look up attorney's hourly rate from the table located at the bottom right of the worksheet • In column G, calculate legal fees billed by multiplying billable hours times the hourly rate • In J6:J9 calculate total legal fees billed by attorney • In J13:J16 calculate average hours bill by attorney	8	
4	Saving, Printing	Save, print, and close **EL2-C2-VB1-BillingsOct8to12.xlsx**.	1	
		TOTAL POINTS	10	

Use Lookup and Logical Functions to Calculate Cardiology Costs

File: **EL2-C2-VB2-WPMCCardiologyCosts.xlsx**

Steps	Tasks	Criteria	Value	Score
1-2	Opening, Saving	Open **WPMCCardiologyCosts.xlsx**. Save As **EL2-C2-VB2-WPMCCardiologyCosts**.	1	
3-4	Creating Formulas	Review range names and cells each name references to become familiar with the worksheet. Review worksheet shown in Figure 2.9 and complete the worksheet to match the one shown by creating formulas using the following information: • In column G, create a formula to look up surgery fee in the table located at bottom of worksheet. Specify in formula to return result for exact matches only. • In column H insert aortic or mitral valve cost if cardiac surgery required a replacement valve; otherwise place a zero in the cell. *The surgery codes for surgery codes for surgeries that include a replacement valve are* ART *and* MRT. • In column I, calculate postoperative hospital cost by multiplying number of days patient was in hospital by postoperative cost per day. • In column J, calculate total cost as sum of surgery fee, valve cost, and postoperative hospital cost. • Calculate total cost for each column in row 22.	18	

Steps	Tasks	Criteria	Value	Score
5	Saving, Printing	Save, print, and close **EL2-C2-VB2-WPMCCardiologyCosts.xlsx**.	1	
		TOTAL POINTS	20	

Case Study

Part 1

File: **EL2-C2-CS-P1-PizzaByMarioSales.xlsx**

Steps	Tasks	Criteria	Value	Score
1	Opening, Saving	Open **PizzaByMarioSales.xlsx**. Save As **EL2-C2-CS-P1-PizzaByMarioSales.xlsx**.	1	
2	Creating Formulas	Create formulas in rows 3 to 16 in columns H and I. Create range names for data to easily understand formulas. Use the following specifications: • A count of number of stores with gross sales greater than $500,000 • A count of number of stores location in Michigan with sales greater than $500,000 • Average sales for Detroit, Michigan stores • Average sales for Michigan stores established prior to 2004 • Total sales for stores established prior to 2010 • Total sales for Michigan stores established prior to 2010	12	
3	Formatting	Student determines layout, labels, and other formats for statistics section.	6	
4	Saving, Printing	Save and print **EL2-C2-CS-P1-PizzaByMarioSales.xlsx**.	1	
		TOTAL POINTS	20	

Part 2

File: **EL2-C2-CS-P2-PizzaByMarioSales.xlsx**

Steps	Tasks	Criteria	Value	Score
1	Saving	Continue working with the **EL2-C2-CS-P1-PizzaByMarioSales.xlsx** worksheet. Save as **EL2-C2-CS-P2-PizzaByMarioSales.xlsx**.	1	
2	Creating Formulas	Use the following specifications: • Create range name for royalty rate table. • Create lookup formula to insert correct royalty percentage for each store in column F. • Create formula to calculate dollar amount of royalty payment based on store's sales times percent value in column F.	7	

Steps	Tasks	Criteria	Value	Score
3	Formatting	Format royalty percent and royalty fee columns appropriately.	5	
4	Saving, Printing	Print worksheet making sure printout fits on one page. Adjust if necessary. Save revised workbook **EL2-C2-CS-P2-PizzaByMarioSales.xlsx**.	2	
		TOTAL POINTS	15	

Part 3

File: **EL2-C2-CS-P3-PizzaByMarioSales.xlsx**

Steps	Tasks	Criteria	Value	Score
1	Opening, Saving	Continue working with the **EL2-C2-CS-P2-PizzaByMarioSales.xlsx** worksheet. Save As **EL2-C2-CS-P3-PizzaByMarioSales.xlsx**.	1	
2	Using Help, Copying	Using the Help feature to learn about MEDIAN and STDEV functions. Copy A2:E29 to Sheet 2 keeping source column widths.	2	
3	Creating Formulas	Using sales data in column E, calculate the following statistics: • Average sales • Maximum store sales • Minimum store sales • Median store sales • Standard deviation of sales data	10	
3	Formatting	Student determines layout, labels, and other formats.	6	
4	Creating Text Box	Create text below statistics. Write explanation in each box explaining what median and standard deviation numbers mean based on what was learned in Help.	4	
5	Saving, Printing	Print worksheet making sure printout fits on one page. Adjust if necessary. Save and close revised workbook **EL2-C2-CS-P3-PizzaByMarioSales.xlsx**.	2	
		TOTAL POINTS	25	

Part 4

File: **EL2-C2-CS-P4-PizzaByMarioSales.xlsx**

Steps	Tasks	Criteria	Value	Score
1	Researching	Select two states that in close proximity to Michigan, Ohio, Wisconsin, and Iowa. Research statistics on the Internet. Within each state find population and income statistics for two cities.	4	
2	Opening, Saving	Open **EL2-C2-CS-P3-PizzaByMarioSales.xlsx**. Save as **EL2-C2-CS-P4-PizzaByMarioSales.xlsx**.	1	

Steps	Tasks	Criteria	Value	Score
3	Creating Worksheet	Create new worksheet within Pizza By Mario franchise worksheet. Prepare summary of research findings. Include URLs of sites from which data was obtained.	8	
4	Saving, Printing	Save as **EL2-C2-CS-P4-PizzaByMarioSales.xlsx**. Print worksheet making sure printout fits on one page. Adjust if necessary. Save and close workbook.	2	
		TOTAL POINTS	15	

Excel Level 2, Chapter 3

Skills Check

Assessment 1: Create and Format a Table
File: **EL2-C3-A1-VantageClassics.xlsx**

Steps	Tasks	Criteria	Value	Score
1-2	Opening, Saving	Open **VantageClassics.xlsx**. Save As **EL2-C3-A1-VantageClassics**.	1	
3	Creating Table	Select A4:L30 and create table using *Table Style Medium 12*.	2	
4	Adding Formulas	Add a calculated column to table in column M. Type the label **Total Cost** as column heading. Create formula in first record that multiplies number of copies in column G times cost price in Column L.	6	
5-7	Formatting	Adjust three rows above table to merge and center across columns A through M. Adjust all column widths to AutoFit. Band columns instead of rows. Emphasize last column in table.	4	
8	Insert Row, Adding Functions	Add Total row to table. Add Average functions that calculate average number of copies and average cost price of classic video.	3	
9-11	Formatting, Deleting	Format average value in *Copies* column of Total row to zero decimals. Delete video *Blue Hawaii* record. Delete row in table for record with Stock No. CV-1015.	3	
10	Saving, Printing	Save, print, and close **EL2-C3-A1-VantageClassics.xlsx**.	1	
		TOTAL POINTS	20	

Assessment 2: Use Data Tools
File: EL2-C3-A2-VantageClassics.xlsx

Steps	Tasks	Criteria	Value	Score
1-2	Opening, Saving	Open **EL2-C3-A1-VantageClassics.xlsx**. Save As **EL2-C3-A2-VantageClassics**.	1	
3-4	Banding, Inserting Column	Remove banding on columns and band the rows. Insert new blank column to right of column containing director names.	2	
5-6	Editing	Split director names into two columns. Edit column headings to **DirectorFName** and **DirectorLName**, respectively.	2	
7	Creating Validation Rules	Create the following validation rules: • Create validation rule for *Stock No.* column that ensures all new entries are seven characters in length. Add input message to column to advise user that stock numbers need to be seven characters. Student determines title and message text. Use default error alert options. • Create validation rule that restricts entries in copies column to number than six. Add appropriate input and error message. Use default Stop error alert. • Create drop-down list for the *Genre* column with entries provided. Do not enter an input message and use default error alert settings. **Action,Comedy,Drama,Family,History,Horror, Musical,Thriller,War**	6	
8	Adding Record	Add the following record to table to test data validation rules. Initially enter incorrect values in *Stock No., Genre,* and *Copies* columns to make sure rule and messages work correctly. *Stock No.* **CV-1026** *Title* **The Philadelphia Story** *Year* **1940** *Genre* **Comedy** *Stock Date* **12/12/2011** *Director FName* **George** *Director LName* **Cukor** *Copies* **3** *VHS* **No** *DVD* **Yes** *Blu-ray* **Yes** *Category* **7-day rental** *Cost Price* **10, 15**	3	
12	Saving, Printing	Save, print, and close **EL2-C3-A2-VantageClassics.xlsx**.	1	
		TOTAL POINTS	15	

Assessment 3: Subtotal Records
File: **EL2-C3-A3-VantageClassics.xlsx**

Steps	Tasks	Criteria	Value	Score
1-2	Opening, Saving	Open **EL2-C3-A2-VantageClassics.xlsx**. Save As **EL2-C3-A3-VantageClassics.xlsx**.	1	
3-5	Formatting	Remove Total row, remove row banding, and remove emphasis from last column in table. Convert table to normal range. Adjust all column widths to AutoFit.	5	
6	Sorting	Sort the list first by genre, then by director's last name, and then by title of video. Use default sort values and sort order for each level.	3	
7	Inserting Subtotals	Add subtotals using the Subtotal button in Outline group of Data tab to *Total Cost* column to calculate sum and average total costs of videos by genre.	3	
8-9	Displaying Level, Showing Details	Display worksheet at Level 2 of outline. Show details for Comedy, Drama, and Family genres.	2	
10-11	Printing, Saving	Print worksheet. Save and close **EL2-C3-A3-VantageClassics. xlsx**.	1	
		TOTAL POINTS	15	

Visual Benchmark

1: Using Table and Data Tools in a Call List
File: **EL2-C3-VB1-WPMCNurseCallList.xlsx**

Steps	Tasks	Criteria	Value	Score
1-2	Opening, Saving	Open **WPMCNurseCallList.xlsx**. Save As **EL2-C3-VB1-WPMCNurseCallList**.	1	
3	Formatting	Format and apply data tools as required to duplicate worksheet in Figure 3.9 using the following information: • Worksheet has *Table Style Medium 5* applied to table range • Table is sorted by three levels using fields *Designation, Hourly Rate,* and *Hire Date* • Shift cost multiplies hourly rate times 8 hours • Split names into two columns • Include Total row and apply appropriate banded options	8	
4	Saving, Printing	Save, print, and close **EL2-C3-VB1-WPMCNurseCallList. xlsx**.	1	
		TOTAL POINTS	10	

2: Using Subtotals in a Call List
File: **EL2-C3-VB2-WPMCNurseCallList.xlsx**

Steps	Tasks	Criteria	Value	Score
1-2	Opening, Saving	Open **EL2-C3-VB1-WPMCNurseCallList.xlsx**. Save As **EL2-C3-VB2-WPMCNurseCallList.xlsx**.	1	
3-4	Creating Subtotals	Create subtotals and view revised worksheet at appropriate level to display as shown in Figure 3.10.	3	
5	Saving, Printing	Save, print, and close **EL2-C3-VB2-WPMCNurseCallList. xlsx**.	1	
		TOTAL POINTS	5	

Case Study

Part 1
File: **EL2-C3-CS-P1-NuTrendsMktPlans.xlsx**

Steps	Tasks	Criteria	Value	Score
1	Opening, Saving	Open **NuTrendsMktPlans.xlsx**. Save As **EL2-C3-CS-P1-NuTrendsMktPlans.xlsx**.	1	
2	Sorting	Sort table first by consultant's last name, then by marketing campaign's start date, both in ascending order. Split consultant names into two columns.	6	
3	Formatting	Format using the following specifications: • Improve formatting of dollar values. • Add Total row to sum the columns containing dollar amounts. • Add formatting to titles above table that are suited to colors in table style student selected. • Make other formatting changes to improve appearance of worksheet.	5	
4	Saving, Printing	Save **EL2-C3-CS-P1-NuTrendsMktPlans.xlsx**. Print worksheet in landscape orientation with width scaled to 1 page.	3	
		TOTAL POINTS	15	

Part 2
File: **EL2-C3-CS-P2-NuTrendsMktPlans.xlsx**

Steps	Tasks	Criteria	Value	Score
1	Saving	With **EL2-C3-CS-P1-NuTrendsMktPlans.xlsx** open save as **EL2-C3-CS-P2-NuTrendsMktPlans.xlsx**.	1	

Steps	Tasks	Criteria	Value	Score
2	Creating Formulas	Include the following information: • Total marketing plan budget values managed by each consultant as well as total planned expenditures by month. • Average marketing plan budget managed by each consultant as well as average planned expenditures by month.	6	
3	Saving, Printing	Save **EL2-C3-CS-P2-NuTrendsMktPlans**. Set printout to display only the total and average values for each consultant as well as grand average and grand total. Print and close worksheet.	3	
		TOTAL POINTS	10	

Part 3

File: **EL2-C3-CS-P3-NuTrendsMktPlans.xlsx**

Steps	Tasks	Criteria	Value	Score
1	Opening, Saving	Open **NuTrendsMktPlans.xlsx**. Save As **EL2-C3-CS-P3-NuTrendsMktPlans**.	1	
2	Using Help, Inserting	Use the Help feature to learn how to filter a range of cells using Advanced Filter button in Sort & Filter group of Data tab and how to copy rows that meet filter criteria to another area of worksheet. Printout request needs to show original data at top of worksheet and few blank rows below. Marketing plan details for Yolanda Robertson's clients with a campaign starting after January 31, 2012. Using the information, insert three new rows above worksheet and use these rows to create criteria range.	2	
3	Filtering, Copying	Filter list as specified above. Rows that meet criteria should be copied below worksheet starting in A22.	5	
4	Inserting Title	Add appropriate title to describe copied data inA21.	2	
5	Formatting	Make formatting changes to improve appearance of worksheet.	4	
6	Saving, Printing	Save revised workbook. Print and close **EL2-C3-CS-P3-NuTrendsMktPlans**.	1	
		TOTAL POINTS	15	

Part 4
File: **EL2-C3-CS-P4-NuTrendsSalaryAnalysis.xlsx**

Steps	Tasks	Criteria	Value	Score
1	Researching	Use the Internet to find information on current salary ranges for a market researcher in the United States. If possible, find salary information that is regional to student's state for a minimum of three cities. Find a low salary and a high salary for a market research in each city. Find a minimum of three resources and a maximum of five.	4	
2	Creating Worksheet	Create worksheet that summarizes results of research with the following specifications: • Include Web site addresses as hyperlinked cells next to salary range information. • Organize data as a table. • Apply table formatting options so data is attractively presented and easy to read. • Add Total row to table. • Include Average function to find average salary from three cities.	10	
3	Saving, Printing	Save As **EL2-C3-CS-P4-NuTrendsSalaryAnalysis.xlsx**. Print worksheet and close workbook.	1	
		TOTAL POINTS	15	

Excel Level 2, Chapter 4

Skills Check

Assessment 1: Summarize Data in Multiple Worksheets Using Range Names
File: **EL2-C4-A1-NewAgeDentalQ1Fees.xlsx**

Steps	Tasks	Criteria	Value	Score
1-2	Opening, Saving	Open **NewAgeDentalQ1Fees.xlsx**. Save As **EL2-C4-A1-NewAgeDentalQ1Fees**.	1	
3	Creating Range Names	Create a range name in F13 of each worksheet to reference the total fees earned by the dentist for the quarter as follows: • Name F13 in the Popovich worksheet *Popovich Total* • Name F13 in the Vanket worksheet *Vanket Total* • Name F13 in the Jovanovic worksheet *Jovanovic Total*	3	
4	Adding Label	In the FeeSummary worksheet, type the following label in A6: **Quarter 1 fees for Popovich, Vanket, and Jovanovic.**	1	
5	Inserting Formula	In F6, create a Sum formula to add the total fees earned by each dentist using the range names created in Step 3.	2	
6	Formatting	Format F6 to Accounting Number Format style and adjust column width to AutoFit.	2	

Steps	Tasks	Criteria	Value	Score
7-8	Saving, Printing	Print FeeSummary worksheet. Save and close **EL2-C4-A1-NewAgeDentalQ1Fees.xlsx**.	1	
		TOTAL POINTS	10	

Assessment 2: Summarize Data Using Linked External References
File: **EL2-C4-A2-PremiumFitnessSalesSummary.xlsx**

Steps	Tasks	Criteria	Value	Score
1-2	Opening, Saving	Open **PremiumFitnessSalesSummary.xlsx**. Save As **EL2-C4-A2-PremiumFitnessSalesSummary**.	1	
3-4	Opening, Inserting Titles	Open **PremiumFitnessQ1.xlsx, PremiumFitnessQ2.xlsx, PremiumFitnessQ3.xlsx,** and **PremiumFitnessQ4.xlsx**. Title all open workbooks.	2	
5-7	Creating Formulas	Starting in cell B5 in the **EL2-C4-A2-PremiumFitnessSalesSummary.xlsx** workbook, create formulas to populate cells in column B by linking to appropriate source cell in **PremiumFitnessQ1.xlsx**. *Hint: After creating first formula, edit entry in B5 to use a relative reference to the source cells (instead of absolute) so formula can be copied and pasted in B5 to B6:B9.* Create formulas to link to appropriate source cells for second, third, and fourth quarter sales. Close four quarterly sales workbooks. Click Don't Save when prompted to save changes.	6	
8-10	Saving, Printing	Maximize **EL2-C4-A2-PremiumFitnessSalesSummary.xlsx**. Print and close workbook.	1	
		TOTAL POINTS	10	

Assessment 3: Break Linked References
File: **EL2-C4-A2-PremiumFitnessSalesSummary.xlsx**

Steps	Tasks	Criteria	Value	Score
1	Opening	Open **EL2-C4-A2-PremiumFitnessSalesSummary.xlsx**. Click Enable Content button in Message bar if Security Warning appears saying Automatic update of links has been disabled.	1	
2	Converting Formulas	Convert formulas to their existing values by breaking the links to external references in the four quarterly sales workbooks.	3	
3	Printing, Saving	Save, print and close **EL2-C4-A2-PremiumFitnessSalesSummary.xlsx**.	1	
		TOTAL POINTS	5	

Assessment 4: Summarize Data Using 3-D References
File: EL2-C4-A4-MayParkEntries.xlsx

Steps	Tasks	Criteria	Value	Score
1	Opening, Saving	Open **MayParkEntries.xlsx**. Save As **EL2-C4-A4-MayParkEntries**.	1	
2	Using 3-D References	With AttendanceSummary worksheet active, summarize data in the three park worksheets using 3-D references as follows: • Delete label in A7. • Copy A6:A22 from any of the park worksheets and paste to A6:A22 in AttendanceSummary worksheet. • Copy D6:D21 from any of the park worksheets and paste to D6:D21 in AttendanceSummary worksheet. • Type label **Entries** right-aligned in B6 and E6. • Make B7 the active cell and create a 3-D formula to sum attendance values in the three park worksheets for Day 1. Copy and paste formula to remaining cells in column B to complete summary to Day 16. • Make E7 the active cell and create a 3-D formula to sum attendance values in three park worksheets for Day 17. Copy and paste formula to remaining cells in column E to complete summary to Day 31. • Type label **Total Vehicle and Individual Entrances** in A24. • Create Sum formula in E24 to computer grand total. • Apply formatting options to grand total to make total stand out.	18	
3	Printing, Saving	Print AttendanceSummary worksheet. Save and close **EL2-C4-A4-MayParkEntries.xlsx**.	1	
		TOTAL POINTS	20	

Assessment 5: Summarize Data in a PivotTable and PivotChart
File: EL2-C4-A5-NewAgeDental2012Fees.xlsx

Steps	Tasks	Criteria	Value	Score
1-2	Opening, Saving	Open **NewAgeDental2012Fees.xlsx**. Save As **EL2-C4-A5-NewAgeDental2012Fees.xlsx**	1	
3	Creating PivotTable Report	Create PivotTable report in a new worksheet as follows: • Display range named *FeeSummary* and insert a PivotTable in a new worksheet • Add the *Service Provided* field as row labels • Add the *Dentist* field as column labels • Sum the *FeesBilled* field	3	

Steps	Tasks	Criteria	Value	Score
4-6	Formatting, Printing	Format values to Comma Style number format with zero decimals and right-align dentist names. Name worksheet *PivotTable*. In rows 1 and 2 above the table enter an appropriate title and subtitle merged and centered across the PivotTable report. Print PivotTable report.		
7	Creating, Filtering PivotChart	Create a PivotChart from PivotTable using the Clustered Column chart type. Move chart to its own sheet named *PivotChart*. Filter PivotChart by dentist name *Jovanovic*.		
8-9	Printing, Saving	Print the PivotChart. Save and close **EL2-C4-A5-NewAgeDental2012Fees.xlsx**		
		TOTAL POINTS	5	

Assessment 6: Filtering a PivotTable Using Slicers
File: **EL2-C4-A6-NewAgeDental2012Fees.xlsx**

Steps	Tasks	Criteria	Value	Score
1-2	Opening, Saving	Open **EL2-C4-A5-NewAgeDental2012Fees.xlsx**. Save As **EL2-C4-A6-DentalFeesFiltered.xlsx**.	1	
3-5	Viewing Report, Inserting Slicer Panes	View PivotTable report in PivotTable sheet. Insert Slicer panes for *Dentist* and *Service Provided* fields. Move Slice panes below PivotTable Report.	18	
6	Filtering	Use Dentist Slicer pane to filter PivotTable by *Popovich*.		
7	Filtering	Use Service Provided Slicer pane to filter PivotTable report by *Crown and Bridges*		
8-9	Printing, Saving	Print PivotTable report. Save and close **EL2-C4-A6-DentalFeesFiltered.xlsx**.	1	
		TOTAL POINTS	20	

Assessment 7: Creating and Customizing Sparklines
File: **EL2-C4-A4-MayParkEntries.xlsx**

Steps	Tasks	Criteria	Value	Score
1-2	Opening, Saving	Open **EL2-C4-A2-PremiumFitnessSalesSummary.xlsx**. Save As **EL2-C4-A7-PremiumFitnessSalesSummary.xlsx**.	1	

Steps	Tasks	Criteria	Value	Score
3-7	Creating, Customizing Sparklines	Create and customize using the following specifications: • Select H5-H9 and insert Line Sparklines referencing data range B5:E9. • Show high point and markers on each line. • Change Sparkline color to *Dark Blue*. • Change width of column H to 19. • Type label **Region Sales by Quarter** in H4.	12	
8-9	Printing, Saving	Change page orientation to landscape and print worksheet. Save and close **EL2-C4-A7-PremiumFitnessSalesSummary. xlsx**.	2	
		TOTAL POINTS	15	

Visual Benchmark

1: Summarizing Real Estate Sales and Commission Data

File: **EL2-C4-VB-HillsdaleOctSales.xlsx**

Steps	Tasks	Criteria	Value	Score
1-2	Opening, Saving	Open **HillsdaleOctSales**. Save As **EL2-C4-VB-HillsdaleOctSales**.	1	
3	Creating PivotTable	Create PivotTable report shown in Figure 4.12 in new worksheet named *PivotTable*. Use *Pivot Style Medium 11* and set column widths to 18.	8	
4	Creating PivotChart Report	Create PivotChart report shown in Figure 4.12 in new worksheet named *PivotChart*. Use 3-D Clustered Column chart and *Style 26*.		
5-6	Saving, Printing	Print PivotTable and PivotChart sheets. Save and close **EL2-C4-VB-HillsdaleOctSales.xlsx**.	1	
		TOTAL POINTS	10	

Case Study

Part 1

File: **EL2-C4-CS-P1-PizzaByMarioRpt.xlsx**

Steps	Tasks	Criteria	Value	Score
1	Opening, Saving	Open **PizzaByMarioSales&Profits.xlsx**. Save As **EL2-C4-CS-P1-PizzaByMarioRpt.xlsx**.	1	

Steps	Tasks	Criteria	Value	Score
2	Creating PivotTable Report	Create PivotTable report using the following specifications: • Include average gross sales and average net income by city by state. • Organize layout of report *(Hint: Add more than one numeric field to* Values *list box).* • Remove grand totals at right of report so that grand total row appears only at bottom of PivotTable. *(Hint: Use Grand Totals button in Layout group of PivotTable Tools Design tab).*	8	
3	Formatting	Apply formatting options to improve appearance and to be sure report will print on one page.	4	
4	Saving, Printing	Print report in landscape orientation. Rename worksheet containing report *PivotTable*. Save **EL2-C4-CS-P1-PizzaByMarioRpt.xlsx**.	2	
		TOTAL POINTS	15	

Part 2

File: **EL2-C4-CS-P2-PizzaByMarioRpt.xlsx**

Steps	Tasks	Criteria	Value	Score
1	Opening, Saving	With **EL2-C4-CS-P1-PizzaByMarioRpt.xlsx** open save as **EL2-C4-CS-P2-PizzaByMarioRpt.xlsx**.	1	
2	Creating PivotChart	Include the following information to create a PivotChart: • Create PivotChart in new sheet named *PivotChart* • Graph the average net income data for state of Michigan only • Determine appropriate chart style and elements. • Be sure chart is of professional quality	8	
3	Saving, Printing	Print chart. Save and **EL2-C4-CS-P2-PizzaByMarioRpt.xlsx**.	1	
		TOTAL POINTS	10	

Part 3

File: **EL2-C4-CS-P3-PizzaByMarioRpt.xlsx**

Steps	Tasks	Criteria	Value	Score
1	Opening, Saving	Open **EL2-C4-CS-P1-PizzaByMarioRpt.xlsx**. Save As **EL2-C4-CS-P4-PizzaByMarioRpt**.	1	

Steps	Tasks	Criteria	Value	Score
2	Using Help, Changing Display	Use the Help feature to learn how to modify a numeric field setting to show values as ranked numbers from largest to smallest. Change display of average sales to show the values ranked from largest to smallest using *City* as the base field. Remove *Net Income* field from PivotTable. Remove grand total row at bottom of PivotTable.	9	
3	Formatting	Make formatting changes to improve appearance of worksheet.	4	
4	Saving, Printing	Print PivotTable. Save and close **EL2-C4-CS-P4-PizzaByMarioRpt.xlsx**.	1	
		TOTAL POINTS	15	

Part 4
File: **EL2-C4-CS-P4-PizzaFranchiseComparison.xlsx**

Steps	Tasks	Criteria	Value	Score
1	Researching	Use the Internet to research sales and net income information of a pizza franchise with which student is familiar.	4	
2	Creating Worksheet	Create worksheet that summarizes results of research with the following specifications: • Compare total annual sales and net income values of pizza franchise researched with the Pizza By Mario Information in the **EL2-C4-CS-P1-PizzaByMarioRpt.xlsx**. • Provide URL of website used to obtain the competitive data.	10	
3	Creating Chart	Create chart that visually presents comparison data.	4	
4	Saving, Printing	Save As **EL2-C4-CS-P4-PizzaFranchiseComparison.xlsx**. Print comparison data and chart. Close workbook.	2	
		TOTAL POINTS	20	

Excel Level 2, Unit 1
Performance Assessment

Assessing Proficiency

Assessment 1: Conditionally Format and Filter a Help Desk Worksheet
File: **EL2-U1-A1-RSRHelpDeskRpt.xlsx**

Steps	Tasks	Criteria	Value	Score
1-2	Opening, Saving	Open **RSRHelpDeskRpt.xlsx**. Save As **EL2-U1-A1-RSRHelpDeskRpt**.	1	
3	Formatting	Apply conditional formatting to display the *3 Flags* icon set to values in *Priority* column. Calls with priority code of 1 should display a red flag, priority 2 calls should display a yellow flag, and priority 3 calls should display a green flag.	3	
4	Creating Custom Format	Create custom format for values n *Time Spent* column. Format should display leading zeroes, two decimal places, and text *hrs* at end of entry separate by one space from number.	3	
5	Creating Conditional Formatting Rules	Create two conditional formatting rules for values in *Time Spent* column as follows: • For all entries where time spent is less than 1 hour, apply bold and a pale green fill color. • For all entries where time spent is more than 2 hours, apply a bright yellow fill color.	4	
6	Filtering	Filter worksheet by the bright yellow fill color applied in *Time Spent* column. If necessary delete clip art image if image overlaps the data.	2	
7	Printing	Print filtered worksheet.	1	
8-9	Clearing Filter, Printing, Saving	Clear filter and filter arrow buttons. Print worksheet. Save and close **EL2-U1-A1-RSRHelpDeskRpt.xlsx**.	1	
		TOTAL POINTS	15	

Assessment 2: Use Conditional Logic Formulas in a Help Desk Worksheet
File: **EL2-U1-A2-RSRHelpDeskRpt.xlsx**

Steps	Tasks	Criteria	Value	Score
1-2	Opening, Saving	Open **EL2-U1-A1-RSRHelpDeskRpt.xlsx**. Save As **EL2-U1-A2-RSRHelpDeskRpt.xlsx**.	1	

Steps	Tasks	Criteria	Value	Score
3	Creating Range Names	Create range names for the following ranges: • Name cells in A4:E6, which will be used in a lookup formula • Name entries in *Operator ID* column • Name values in *Time Spent* column • Name cells in *Status* column Student determines appropriate names.	2	
5-11	Creating Formulas	Creating formulas with the following specifications: • Create COUNTA formula in I4 to count number of help desk calls in March using column A as the source range. • Create COUNTIF formulas in I5 and I6 to count number of active calls (I5) and number of closed calls (I6). • Create COUNTIF formulas in K3 through K6 to count calls assigned to Operator ID 1, 2, 3, and 4, respectively. Use range names in formulas. • Create SUMIF formulas in L3 through L6 to calculate total time spent on calls assigned to Operator ID 1, 2, 3, and 4, respectively. Use range names in formulas. Format results to display two decimal places. • Create AVERAGEIF formulas in M3 through M6 to find average time spent on calls assigned to Operator ID 1, 2, 3, and 4, respectively. Use range names in formulas. Format results to display two decimal places. • Create HLOOKUP formula with exact match in F8 to return last name for operator assigned to the call. Use the range name for lookup table in formula. • Create HLOOKUP formula with exact match in G8 to return first name for operator assigned to call. Use range name for lookup table in formula. • Copy HLOOKUP formulas in F8:G8 and past to remaining rows in list.	16	
12	Saving, Printing	Save, print, and close **EL2-U1-A2-RSRHelpDeskRpt.xlsx**.	1	
		TOTAL POINTS	20	

Assessment 3: Use Table and Data Management Features in a Help Desk Worksheet
File: EL2-U1-A3-RSRHelpDeskRpt.xlsx

Steps	Tasks	Criteria	Value	Score
1	Opening, Saving	Open **EL2-U1-A2-RSRHelpDeskRpt.xlsx**. Save as **EL2-U1-A3-RSRHelpDeskRpt.xlsx**.	1	
2	Formatting	Format A7:I30 as table using *Table Style Medium 20*.	2	

Steps	Tasks	Criteria	Value	Score
3-7	Inserting, Formatting	Insert the following as specified: • Add calculated column to table in column J that multiplies the time spent times 15.00. Use column heading *Cost* in J7. Format results to display Comma Style number format. • Add a total row to table. Display sum total in columns H and J. • Add emphasis to last column in table and band the columns instead of the rows. • Create drop-down list for *Operator ID* column that displays the entries 1, 2, 3, 4.	8	
8	Creating Validation Rule	Create validation rule in the *Times Spent* column that ensures no value greater than 3 is entered. Create appropriate input and error messages.	2	
9	Adding Records	Add two records to the table as shown for Ticket No. 14424 and 14425.	2	
10-11	Filtering, Printing	Filter table to display only those calls with a *closed* status. Print filtered list.	2	
12-13	Filtering, Printing	Filter worksheet to display only those calls with a *Closed* status where type of call was *Password*. Print filtered list.	2	
14-15	Clearing, Printing, Saving	Clear both filters. Save, print, and close **EL2-U1-A3-RSRHelpDeskRpt.xlsx**.	1	
		TOTAL POINTS	20	

Assessment 4: Add Subtotals and Outline a Help Desk Worksheet
File: **EL2-U1-A4-RSRHelpDeskRpt.xlsx**

Steps	Tasks	Criteria	Value	Score
1-2	Opening, Saving	Open **EL2-U1-A3-RSRHelpDeskRpt.xlsx**. Save As **EL2-U1-A4-RSRHelpDeskRpt.xlsx**.	1	
3-4	Editing	Remove Total row from table. Convert table to a normal range.	2	
5	Sorting	Sort list first by operator's last name, then by operator's first name, then by call priority, and finally by type of call; all in ascending order.	5	
6	Inserting	Add subtotal to list at each change in operator last name to calculate the total cost of calls by operator.	2	
7-8	Displaying, Printing	Display outlined worksheet at level 2 and print worksheet. Display outlined worksheet at level 3 and print worksheet.	4	
9	Saving	Save and close **EL2-U1-A4-RSRHelpDeskRpt.xlsx**.	1	
		TOTAL POINTS	15	

Assessment 5: Use Financial and Text Functions to Analyze Data for a Project
File: **EL2-U1-A5-AllClaimsLoan.xlsx**

Steps	Tasks	Criteria	Value	Score
1-2	Opening, Saving	Open **AllClaimsLoan.xlsx**. Save As **EL2-U1-A5-AllClaimsLoan.xlsx**.	1	
3	Creating Formulas	Create formulas to analyze cost of loan from NEWFUNDS TRUST and DELTA CAPITAL as follows: • In C10 and E10, calculate monthly loan payment from each lender • In C12 and E12, calculate principal portion of each payment for first loan payment • In C14 and E14, calculate total loan payments that will be made over the life of the loan from each lender	9	
4-5	Using Text Functions	In E20, use text function =*PROPER* to return loan company for loan that represents the lowest total cost to AllClaims Insurance. In E21, use text function =*LOWER* to return loan application number for loan company name displayed in E20.	4	
8-9	Saving, Printing	Save, print, and close **EL2-U1-A5-AllClaimsLoan.xlsx**.	1	
		TOTAL POINTS	15	

Assessment 6: Analyze Sales Using a PivotTable, a PivotChart, and Sparklines
File: **EL2-U1-A6-PrecisionBulkSales.xlsx**

Steps	Tasks	Criteria	Value	Score
1-2	Opening, Saving	Open **PrecisionBulkSales.xlsx**. Save As **EL2-U1-A6-PrecisionBulkSales.xlsx**.	1	
3	Creating PivotTable	Select A4:I22 and create a PivotTable in a new worksheet named *PivotTable* as follows: • Add *Category* field as report filter field • Add *Distributor* field as row labels • Sum North, South, East, and West sales values.	6	
4-5	Formatting, Printing	Apply formatting options to PivotTable to make data easier to read and interpret. Print PivotTable.	3	
6-9	Creating PivotChart, Printing	Create PivotChart in separate sheet named *PivotChart* that graphs data from PivotTable in a Clustered Cylinder chart. Edit chart fields to display only sum of North and South values. Print chart.	6	
10	Creating Sparklines	Make Sheet1 active and create Sparklines in J5:J22 that show North, South, East, and West sales in a line chart. Set width of column J to 18. Customize Sparklines by changing Sparkline color and adding data points. Student determines data points and colors. Type appropriate label in J4 and add additional formatting to improve appearance.	8	

Steps	Tasks	Criteria	Value	Score
8-9	Printing, Saving	Save, print, and close **EL2-U1-A6-PrecisionBulkSales.xlsx**.	1	
		TOTAL POINTS	25	

Assessment 7: Link to an External Data Source and Calculate Distributor Payments
File: **EL2-U1-A7-PrecisionDistPymnt.xlsx** and **EL2-U1-A7-PrecisionSource.xlsx**

Steps	Tasks	Criteria	Value	Score
1-4	Opening, Saving	Open **PrecisionDistPymnt.xlsx**. Save As **EL2-U1-A7-PrecisionDistPymnt.xlsx**. Open **EL2-U1-A6-PrecisionBulkSales.xlsx**. Save As **EL2-U1-A7-PrecisionSource.xlsx**.	1	
5-7	Editing, Saving	Make PivotTable worksheet active. Edit PivotTable Field List so that *Sum of Total* is only numeric field displayed in table. Save **EL2-U1-A7-PrecisionSource.xlsx**. Arrange display of two workbooks vertically.	4	
8-9	Creating Linked External References	Create linked external references starting in D6 in **EL2-U1-A7-PrecisionDistPymnt.xlsx** to appropriate sources cells in PivotTable in **EL2-U1-A7-PrecisionSource.xlsx** so that distributor payment worksheet displays total sales for each distributor. Close **EL2-U1-A7-PrecisionSource.xlsx**.	4	
10-11	Formatting	Maximize **EL2-U1-A7-PrecisionDistPymnt.xlsx**. Format D6:D8 to Accounting Number format style with zero defaults.	2	
12	Calculating	Using data in illustrated chart, calculate payment owed for distributors in H6:H8. Perform calculation using either one of the following two methods: • Create a nested IF statement; OR • Create a lookup table in worksheet that contains sales ranges and three percentage values. Next, add a column next to each distributor with a lookup formula to return correct percentage and then calculate payment using total sales times percent value.	4	
13	Formatting	Format H6:H8 to Comma Style number format.	2	
14	Creating Formulas, Formatting	Add label *TOTALS* in B10. Create formulas in D10 and H10 to calculate total sales and total payments respectively. Format totals and adjust column widths as necessary.	6	
15	Printing	Print worksheet. Write the GETPIVOTDATA formula for D6 at bottom of printout.	2	
16	Breaking link	Break link to external references. Convert formulas to their existing values.	3	

Steps	Tasks	Criteria	Value	Score
17	Printing, Saving	Save, print, and close **EL2-U1-A7-PrecisionDistPymnt.xlsx**.	2	
		TOTAL POINTS	30	

Writing Activities

Activity 1: Create a Worksheet to Track Video Rental Memberships

File: **EL2-U1-Act01-VantageMemberships.xlsx**

Steps	Tasks	Criteria	Value	Score
1	Creating Worksheet	Worksheet needs to provide in list format the following information: • Date annual membership needs to be renewed • Customer name • Customer telephone number • Membership level • Annual membership fee • Discount on video rentals • Table U.1 provides the three memberships levels and discounts	6	
2	Adding Formulas	Use lookup table to populate cells containing membership fee and discount level. Create drop-down list for cell containing membership level that restricts the data entered to three membership categories. Use special number format for telephone number column so all telephone numbers include area code and are displayed in consistent format.	9	
3	Adding Records	Enter a minimum of five sample records to test worksheet with student settings. Format enough rows with data features to include at least 35 memberships.	4	
5-6	Saving, Printing	Save As **EL2-U1-Act01-VantageMemberships.xlsx**. Print and close worksheet.	1	
		TOTAL POINTS	20	

Activity 2: Create a Worksheet to Log Hours Walked in a Company Fitness Contest
File: **EL2-U1-Act02-FitnessProgram.xlsx**

Steps	Tasks	Criteria	Value	Score
1	Creating Worksheet	Worksheet needs to total each department's totals by month and summarize data to show total distance walked for entire company at end of year as follows: • Create separate worksheets for each department: Accounting, Human Resources, Purchasing, and Marketing • Enter miles or kilometers walked by day • Calculate statistics by department to show total distance walked, average distance walked, number of days in month in which employees walked during their lunch hour • When calculating average and number of days, include only those days in which employees logged a distance (do not include days in which employees did not log any distance) • Create summary worksheet that calculates total of all miles or kilometers walked for all four departments	10	
2	Adding Information	Enter at least five days of sample data in each worksheet to test settings.	4	
3	Saving, Printing	Save As **EL2-U1-Act02-FitnessProgram.xlsx**. Print entire workbook and close workbook.	1	
		TOTAL POINTS	20	

Activity 2A: Optional Create a Worksheet to Log Hours Walked in a Company Fitness Contest
File: **EL2-U1-Act02-FitnessProgram.docx**

Steps	Tasks	Criteria	Value	Score
1	Researching, Writing	Use the Internet or other sources to find information on health benefits of walking. Write a memo from Human Resources announcing the contests and provide a summary of information on health benefits of walking.	9	
3	Saving, Printing	Save As **EL2-U1-Act02-FitnessProgram.docx**. Print memo and close file.	1	
		TOTAL POINTS	5	

Internet Research

Create a Worksheet to Compare Online Auction Listing Fees
File: **EL2-U1-Act03-AuctionAnalysis.xlsx**

Steps	Tasks	Criteria	Value	Score
1	Researching	Research at least two Internet auction sites for all selling and payment fees associated with selling online. Find out costs for the following activities involved in an auction sale: • Listing fees (insertion fees) • Option features that can be attached to an ad such as reserve bid fees, picture fees, listing upgrades, etc. • Fees paid when item is sold based on sale value • Fees paid to third part to accept credit card payments (such as PayPal)	4	
2	Creating Worksheet	Create worksheet comparing fees for each auction site researched. Include two sample transactions and calculate total fees that would be paid. Add optional features to listing such as picture and/or reserve bid. Assume in both sample transactions the buyer pays by credit card using a third party service.	10	
3	Formatting	Based on your analysis, decide which auction site is a better choice from a cost perspective. Apply formatting options to make worksheet easy to read and explain your recommendation for the lower cost auction site.	5	
4	Saving, Printing	Save As **EL2-U1-Act03-AuctionAnalysis.xlsx**. Print and close worksheet.	1	
		TOTAL POINTS	20	

Excel Level 2, Chapter 5

Skills Check

Assessment 1: Convert Columns to Rows; Add Source Cells to Destination Cells; Filter
File: **EL2-C5-A1-CutRateCars.xlsx**

Steps	Tasks	Criteria	Value	Score
1-2	Opening, Saving	Open **CutRateCars.xlsx**. Save As **EL2-C5-A1-CutRateCars**.	1	
3-4	Editing	Copy and paste A4:F12 below worksheet, converting data arrangement to that columns become rows and rows become columns. Delete original source data rows from worksheet.	4	

Steps	Tasks	Criteria	Value	Score
5	Formatting	Adjust merge and centering of title rows across top of worksheet, adjust column widths, and change formatting options to improve appearance of revised worksheet.	4	
6-8	Copying	Copy values in *Shipping* column. Paste values to *Total Cost* values using Add operation so that Total Cost includes shipping fee. Copy values in *Number of Cars* column. Paste values to *Total Cost* values using Divide operation. Change column heading from *total Cost* to *Cost Per Car*. Adjust column width as needed. Copy *Compact* values and past only validation rule to *Mid-Size* and *SUV* columns.	5	
7-8	Saving, Printing	Save, print, and close **EL2-C5-A1-CutRateCars.xlsx**.	1	
		TOTAL POINTS	15	

Assessment 2: Use Goal Seek
File: **EL2-C5-A2-NationalCSDeptBdgt.xlsx**

Steps	Tasks	Criteria	Value	Score
1-2	Opening, Saving	Open **NationalCSDeptBdgt.xlsx**. Save As **EL2-C5-A2-NationalCSDeptBdgt**.	1	
3-5	Editing	Make D8 the active cell and open Goal Seek dialog box. Find projected increase for *Wages and benefits* that will make total cost of new budge equal $655,000. Accept the solution Goal Seek calculates.	3	
6	Saving, Printing	Save, print, and close. **EL2-C5-A2-NationalCSDeptBdgt.xlsx**.	1	
		TOTAL POINTS	5	

Assessment 3: Use Scenario Manager
File: **EL2-C5-A3-PrecisionCdnTarget.xlsx**

Steps	Tasks	Criteria	Value	Score
1-2	Opening, Saving	Open **PrecisionCdnTarget.xlsx**. Save As **EL2-C5-A3-PrecisionCdnTarget**.	1	

Steps	Tasks	Criteria	Value	Score

3	Creating Scenarios	Create scenarios to save various percentage data sets for four regions using the following information:
		• A scenario named *OriginalTarget* that stores current values in K4:K7
		• A scenario named *LowSales* with the following values:
		   East .20
		   West .32
		   Ontario .48
		   Quebec .37
		• A scenario named *HighSales* with the following values:
		   East .36
		   West .58
		   Ontario .77
		   Quebec .63
			6	

4	Applying Scenario, Printing	Apply *LowSales* scenario and print worksheet.	2	
5	Editing	Edit *HighSales* scenario to change Ontario value from *0.77* to *.73*.	2	
6-8	Creating Report, Printing, Saving	Create scenario summary report displaying H18 as the result cell. Print Scenario Summary sheet. Save and close **EL2-C5-A3-PrecisionCdnTarget.xlsx**.	4	
		TOTAL POINTS	15	

Assessment 4: Create a Two-Variable Data Table
File: **EL2-C5-A4-NationalCSDeptHlpDsk.xlsx**

Steps	Tasks	Criteria	Value	Score
1	Opening, Saving	Open **NationalCSDeptHlpDsk.xlsx**. Save As **EL2-C5-A4-NationalCSDeptHlpDsk**.	1	
2	Creating Two-Variable Data Table	Create a two-variable data table that will calculate the average cost per call in data table for each level of total call minutes logged and at each average cost per minute.	6	
3	Formatting	Format average costs to display two decimal places.	2	
4	Printing, Saving	Save, print, and close **EL2-C5-A4-NationalCSDeptHlpDsk.xlsx**.	1	
		TOTAL POINTS	10	

Assessment 5: Find and Correct Formula Errors
File: **EL2-C5-A5-NationalCSDeptCapital.xlsx**

Steps	Tasks	Criteria	Value	Score
1-2	Opening, Saving	Open **NationalCSDeptCapital.xlsx**. Save As **EL2-C5-A5-NationalCSDeptCapital.xlsx**	1	
3-6	Correcting Errors	Make D19 the active cell and use Trace Error feature to draw red tracer arrows to find source cell creating the *#N/A* error. The cost of a Pix firewall is $4,720.00. Enter this data in appropriate cell to correct the *#N/A* error. Remove tracer arrows. Find and correct the logic error in one of the formulas.	8	
7	Printing, Saving	Save, print, and close **EL2-C5-A5-NationalCSDeptCapital.xlsx**	1	
		TOTAL POINTS	10	

Visual Benchmark

1: Find the Base Hourly Rate for Drum Lessons
File: **EL2-C5-VB1-DrumStudioLessons.xlsx**

Steps	Tasks	Criteria	Value	Score
1-2	Opening, Saving	Open **DrumStudioLessons.xlsx**. Save As **EL2-C5-VB1-DrumStudioLessons**.	1	
3-4	Using Goal Seek	The current hourly rates in B5:B13 are linked to cell named *BaseRate* located in B16. Intermediate-level and advanced-level lessons have $4 and $8 added to hourly base rate. Drum teacher wants to earn $2,645.50 per month from drum lessons instead of current total of $2,292.00. Use Goal Seek to change base hourly rate to required value needed to reach drum teacher's target.	3	
5	Saving, Printing	Save, print, and close **EL2-C5-VB1-DrumStudioLessons.xlsx**.	1	
		TOTAL POINTS	5	

2: Create Scenarios for Drum Lesson Revenue
File: **EL2-C5-VB2-DrumStudioLessons.xlsx**

Steps	Tasks	Criteria	Value	Score
1-2	Opening, Saving	Open **DrumStudioLessons.xlsx**. Save As **EL2-C5-VB2-DrumStudioLessons**.	1	
3	Creating Scenarios	Examine Scenario Summary report shown in Figure 5.12. Create three scenarios to save the hourly base rates shown: **Low Rate Increase, Mid Rate Increase,** and **High Rate Increase**.	6	

Steps	Tasks	Criteria	Value	Score
4	Generating Report	Generate Scenario Summary report to show monthly revenue for all classes at the three hourly base rates.		
5	Formatting	Format report by changing fill color and font color. Add descriptive text in row 7. Student should try to match colors shown in Figure 5.12.	5	
6	Editing	Edit Notes text in B20 so that the sentence correctly references the highlighted color for changing cells.	2	
7-8	Printing, Saving	Print Scenario Summary worksheet. Save and close **EL2-C5-VB2-DrumStudioLessons**.	1	
		TOTAL POINTS	15	

Case Study

Part 1
File: **EL2-C5-CS-P1-PizzaByMarioStartup.xlsx**

Steps	Tasks	Criteria	Value	Score
1	Opening, Saving	Open **PizzaByMarioStartup.xlsx**. Save As **EL2-C5-CS-P1-PizzaByMarioStartup.xlsx**.	1	
2	Applying What-If Analysis	Apply what-if analysis to find out the value that is needed for project sales in Year 1 in order to pay back the initial investment in 12 months (instead of 17). Accept proposed solution.	8	
3	Saving, Printing	Print worksheet. Save **EL2-C5-CS-P1-PizzaByMarioStartup.xlsx**.	1	
		TOTAL POINTS	10	

Part 2
File: **EL2-C5-CS-P2-PizzaByMarioStartup.xlsx**

Steps	Tasks	Criteria	Value	Score
1	Opening, Saving	With **EL2-C5-CS-P1-PizzaByMarioStartup.xlsx** open, save as **EL2-C5-CS-P2-PizzaByMarioStartup.xlsx**.	1	
2	Editing	Restore sales for year to the original value of $485,000.	3	
3	Creating Worksheets	Using the information illustrated, set up worksheet to save each model *(Conservative, Optimistic,* and *Aggressive)*. Use comma to separate two cell references as the changing cells.	5	
4	Creating Report	Create report that shows the input variables for each model and the impact of each on the number of months to recoup the initial investment.	4	

Steps	Tasks	Criteria	Value	Score
5	Saving, Printing	Save the revised workbook. Print the summary report	2	
6	Editing	Switch to worksheet and show model that reduces the number of months to recoup the initial investment to the lowest value.	4	
7	Printing, Saving	Print the worksheet. Save **EL2-C5-CS-P2-PizzaByMarioStartup.xlsx**	1	
		TOTAL POINTS	20	

Part 3

File: **EL2-C5-CS-P3-PizzaByMarioRpt.xlsx**

Steps	Tasks	Criteria	Value	Score
1	Using Help, Editing	Use the Help feature to find out how to select cells that contain formulas. With **EL2-C5-CS-P2-PizzaByMarioStartup.xlsx** open and using information learned in Help, select cells within worksheet that contain formulas. Review each formula cell in Formula bar to ensure formula is logically correct. Type the name of the feature used in a blank cell below the worksheet.	4	
2	Printing, Saving	Print and save as **EL2-C5-CS-P3-PizzaByMarioRpt.xlsx**.	1	
		TOTAL POINTS	5	

Part 4

File: **EL2-C5-CS-P4-PizzaByMarioStartup.xlsx**

Steps	Tasks	Criteria	Value	Score
1	Researching	Use the Internet to research current lending rates for secured credit lines at a bank.	2	
2	Creating Worksheet	Create worksheet with the following specifications: • Document the current loan rate found on the Internet and the URL of the bank website from which the rate was obtained. • Add two percentage points to lending rate to compensate the owners for the higher risk associated with financing the startup. • Create linked cell in the new worksheet to th3 Total Estimated Initial Investment in Sheet 1. • Calculate monthly loan payment for a term of five years.	8	
3	Formatting	Add appropriate labels to describe the date. Format worksheet to improve the appearance of the worksheet.	4	

Steps	Tasks	Criteria	Value	Score
4	Saving, Printing	Save As **EL2-C5-CS-P4-PizzaByMarioStartup.xlsx**. Print loan worksheet.	1	
		TOTAL POINTS	15	

Excel Level 2, Chapter 6

Skills Check

Assessment 1: Enter and Display Workbook Properties; Insert Comments
Files: **EL2-C6-A1-NationalCSDeptLicenses.xlsx; EL2-C6-A1-NationalCSDeptLicenses.docx**

Steps	Tasks	Criteria	Value	Score
1-2	Opening, Saving	Open **NationalCSDeptLicenses.xlsx**. Save As **EL2-C6-A1-NationalCSDeptLicenses**.	1	
3-4	Editing Properties	Type following text in appropriate workbook properties: • *Add an Author:* **Student's Name** • *Title:* **MSO 2010 License Chargeback** • *Subject:* **Journal entry by department** • *Category:* **JE supporting document** • *Status:* **Posted** • *Comments:* **Audit worksheet for Office 2010 site license with internal chargebacks** Remove existing author *Paradigm Publishing Inc.*	5	
5-6	Creating Word Document	Display the Document Information Panel. Insert screen image of the worksheet showing Document Information Panel in a new Word document using either Print Screen with Past, the Screenshot feature, or the Windows Snipping tool. Student's name typed a few lines below the screen image.	3	
7-8	Saving, Printing	Save the Microsoft Word document as **EL2-C6-A1-NationalCSDeptLicenses.docx**. Print document and exit Word.	1	
9-11	Inserting Comments	At Microsoft Excel worksheet, close Document Information Panel. Make B8 the active cell and insert a new comment. Type in the comment box: **Check this quantity with Marty. The number seems high.** Make B14 the active cell and insert a new comment. Type in the comment box: **Make a note in the budget file for next year. This quantity will increase by 5.**	4	
12-13	Saving, Printing	Print worksheet with comments displayed on sheet. Save and close **EL2-C6-A1-NationalCSDeptLicenses.xlsx**.	1	
		TOTAL POINTS	15	

Assessment 2: Share a Workbook; Edit a Shared Workbook; Print a History Sheet
File: **EL2-C6-A2-PrecisionMfgTargets.xlsx**

Steps	Tasks	Criteria	Value	Score
1-2	Opening, Saving	Open **PrecisionMfgTargets.xlsx**. Save As **EL2-C6-A2-PrecisionMfgTargets**.	1	
3-7	Sharing, Editing	Share the workbook. Change user name to *Lorne Moir* and edit the following cells: C11 from *4,352* to *5520* C18 from *15,241* to *15960* Save the workbook. Change user name to *Gerri Gonzales* and edit the following cells: F4 from *3,845* to *5126* F9 from *7,745* to *9320* Save the workbook.	6	
8-9	Creating, Printing History Sheet	Create History sheet with a record of changes made to the data by all users. Print History sheet.	2	
10-11	Saving, Changing Name	Save and close **EL2-C6-A2-PrecisionMfgTargets.xlsx**. Change user name back to original user name for the computer student used.	1	
		TOTAL POINTS	10	

Assessment 3: Remove Shared Access
File: **EL2-C6-A3-PrecisionMfgTargets.xlsx**

Steps	Tasks	Criteria	Value	Score
1-2	Opening, Saving	Open **EL2-C6-A2-PrecisionMfgTargets.xlsx**. Save As **EL2-C6-A3-PrecisionMfgTargets**.	0	
3	Removing Shared Access	Remove shared access to workbook.	1	
4	Closing	Close **EL2-C6-A3-PrecisionMfgTargets.xlsx**.	0	
		TOTAL POINTS	1	

Assessment 4: Protect an Entire Worksheet; Add a Password to a Workbook
File: **EL2-C6-A1-NationalCSDeptLicenses.xlsx**

Steps	Tasks	Criteria	Value	Score
1-2	Opening, Saving	Open **EL2-C6-A1-NationalCSDeptLicenses.xlsx**. Save As **EL2-C6-A4-NationalCSDeptLicenses.xlsx**.	1	

Steps	Tasks	Criteria	Value	Score
3-5	Protecting Worksheet	Protect entire worksheet using password *L$07j* to unprotect. Add password *J07$e* to open workbook. Save and close **EL2-C6-A4-NationalCSDeptLicenses.xlsx**.	6	
6-8	Testing	Open **EL2-C6-A4-NationalCSDeptLicenses.xlsx** and test password to open workbook. Unprotect worksheet to test password to unprotect. Close **EL2-C6-A4-NationalCSDeptLicenses.xlsx**. Click Don't Save when prompted to save changes.	3	
		TOTAL POINTS	10	

Assessment 5: Unlock Cells and Protect a Worksheet; Protect Workbook Structure
File: **EL2-C6-A5-PrecisionMfgTargets.xlsx**

Steps	Tasks	Criteria	Value	Score
1-2	Opening, Saving	Open **PrecisionMfgTargets.xlsx**. Save As **EL2-C6-A5-PrecisionMfgTargets.xlsx**	1	
3-7	Protecting Worksheet	Select range C4:F21 and unlock cells. Deselect range and then protect worksheet using password *Mt14#* to unprotect. Rename Sheet 1 to *2014MfgTargets*. Delete Sheet2 and Sheet3. Protect workbook structure to prevent users from inserting, deleting, or renaming sheets using the password *Mt14!shts* to unprotect.	8	
8	Saving	Save **EL2-C6-A5-PrecisionMfgTargets.xlsx**.	1	
		TOTAL POINTS	10	

Assessment 6: Track Changes; Accept/Reject Changes; Print a History Sheet
File: **EL2-C6-A6-PrecisionMfgTargets.xlsx**

Steps	Tasks	Criteria	Value	Score
1-2	Opening, Saving	Open **EL2-C6-A5-PrecisionMfgTargets.xlsx**. Save As **EL2-C6-A6-PrecisionMfgTargets.xlsx**	1	

Steps	Tasks	Criteria	Value	Score
3-7	Editing	Unprotect workbook structure so that new sheets can be added, deleted, renamed, or copied. Turn on Track Changes feature. Change user name to *Grant Antone* and edit the following cells: D4 from *3,251* to *3755* D17 from *5,728* to *3417* Save workbook, change user name to *Jean Kocsis*, and edit the following cells: E6 from *6,145* to *5748* E11 from *2,214* to *3417* Save workbook and change user name back to original user name for computer student used.	9	
8	Accepting, Rejecting Changes	Accept and Reject changes as follows: Accept D4 Reject D17 Reject E6 Accept E11	2	
9	Creating History Sheet, Printing	Create and print History sheet of changes made to worksheet.	2	
10-11	Printing, Saving	Print the 2014MfgTargets worksheet. Save and close **EL2-C6-A6-PrecisionMfgTargets.xlsx**.	1	
		TOTAL POINTS	15	

Visual Benchmark

Track Changes; Insert Comments

File: **EL2-C6-VB-PawsParadise.xlsx**

Steps	Tasks	Criteria	Value	Score
1-2	Opening, Saving	Open **PawsParadise.xlsx**. Save As **EL2-C6-VB-PawsParadise**.	1	
3	Making Changes	Make changes as illustrated in Figure 6.16 and Figure 6.17 making sure changes are associated with the owner's name.	6	
4	Creating History Worksheet, Printing	Create and print a History worksheet scaled to fit on one page. *Note: If work is submitted electronically, create a copy of History worksheet in new workbook since History worksheet is automatically deleted when file is saved.*	2	

Steps	Tasks	Criteria	Value	Score
5-7	Saving, Printing	Print worksheet with changes highlighted and the comments as displayed on the worksheet. Save and close **EL2-C6-VB-PawsParadise.xlsx**. Change user name back to original user name for computer student used.	1	
		TOTAL POINTS	10	

Case Study

Part 1

File: **EL2-C6-CS-P1-PizzaByMarioNewFranchises.xlsx**

Steps	Tasks	Criteria	Value	Score
1	Opening, Saving	Open **PizzaByMarioNewFranchises.xlsx**. Save As **EL2-C6-CS-P1-PizzaByMarioNewFranchises**.	1	
2	Inserting Properties	Add appropriate title and subject to workbook's properties. Include comment text explain that the draft workbook was created in consultation with Nicola Carlucci.	3	
3	Protecting Workbook	Protect workbook to prevent accidental data modifications or erasure when workbook is shared with others. City, state, and store numbers should be protected. Month new store is planned to open and names of prospective franchises can be changed. Share the workbook. Password to unprotect worksheet is *U14@s*. Password to open workbook is *SbM@14*.	5	
4	Saving	Save **EL2-C6-CS-P1-PizzaByMarioNewFranchises.xlsx**.	1	
		TOTAL POINTS	10	

Part 2

File: **EL2-C6-CS-P2-PizzaByMarioNewFranchises.xlsx**

Steps	Tasks	Criteria	Value	Score
1	Saving	With **EL2-C6-CS-P1-PizzaByMarioNewFranchises.xlsx** open, save as **EL2-C6-CS-P2-PizzaByMarioNewFranchises.xlsx**.	1	
2	Editing	Make sure the user name is correct and make the following changes: Store 138 Franchisee is Jae-Don Han Store 149 Franchisee is Leslie Posno Save workbook.	2	

Steps	Tasks	Criteria	Value	Score

3	Editing	Make sure the user name is correct and make the following changes:
		     Store 135, Open in February
		     Store 141, Open in December
		Save workbook.
		Display worksheet with all changes highlighted.
			2	

4	Creating History Sheet, Printing	Create History sheet. Print worksheet with cells highlighted. Print history sheet. Restore worksheet to exclusive use. Close **EL2-C6-CS-P2-PizzaByMarioNewFranchises.xlsx**. Change user name back to original user name for computer used by student.	5	
		TOTAL POINTS	10	

Part 3

File: **EL2-C6-CS-P3-PizzaByMario-LScriver.xlsx**

Steps	Tasks	Criteria	Value	Score
1	Opening, Unprotecting, Saving	Open **EL2-C6-CS-P3-PizzaByMarioNewFranchises.xlsx**. Unprotect worksheet and remove password to open workbook. Save as **EL2-C6-CS-P3-PizzaByMario-LScriver.xlsx**.	2	
2	Making Changes	Make sure user name is correct so that the comment boxes display Leonard's name: • Store 136: Opening a second store in Chicago is more likely to occur in April • Store 144: Move this opening to June as resources at head office will be stretched in May • Store 152: Try to open this franchise at the same time as store 151 Show all comments within worksheet.	6	
3	Printing, Saving	Print worksheet with comments printed as displayed. Save and close **EL2-C6-CS-P3-PizzaByMario-LScriver.xlsx**. Change user name back to original name for computer used by student.	2	
		TOTAL POINTS	10	

Part 4

File:**EL2-C6-CS-P4-PizzaByMarioPasswords.xlsx** and
EL2-C6-CS-P4-PizzaByMarioPasswords.docx

Steps	Tasks	Criteria	Value	Score
1	Researching	Use the Internet to research guidelines for creating strong passwords.	2	

Steps	Tasks	Criteria	Value	Score
2	Creating Word Document	Create a Microsoft Word document that highlights the components of a strong password. Include a table of do's and don'ts for creating strong passwords in a user-friendly easy-to-understand format. Create a minimum of three examples that show a week password improved by a stronger password. Include a suggestion for how to use the phrasing technique to create strong passwords to they are easier to remember.	12	
3	Saving, Printing	Save the Word documents as **EL2-C6-CS-P4-PizzaByMarioPasswords**. Print and close **EL2-C6-CS-P4-PizzaByMarioPasswords.docx**.	1	
		TOTAL POINTS	15	

Excel Level 2, Chapter 7

Skills Check

Assessment 1: Create Macros
Files: **MyMacros-StudentName.xlsm**

Steps	Tasks	Criteria	Value	Score
1	Creating Macros	At a new blank workbook, create the following two macros: • Create a macro named *Landscape* that changes page orientation to landscape, sets custom margins at top = 1 inch; bottom, left, and right = 0.5 inch; and centers worksheet horizontally. Assign macro the shortcut key Ctrl + Shift + Q. Enter appropriate description that includes student's name and date macro was created. • Create a macro named *Technic* that applies the theme named *Technic* and turns off the display of gridlines in the active worksheet. Assign macro the shortcut key Ctrl + t. Enter an appropriate description that includes student's name and date macro was created.	9	
2-3	Saving	Save workbook as a macro-enabled workbook named **MyMacros-Student Name**. Leave **MyMacros-Student Name.xlsm** workbook open for next assessment.	1	
		TOTAL POINTS	10	

Assessment 2: Run Macros
File: **EL2-C7-A2-NationalAcctgDeptCS.xlsx**

Steps	Tasks	Criteria	Value	Score
1-2	Opening, Saving	Open **NationalAcctgDeptCS.xlsx**. Save As **EL2-C7-A2-NationalAcctgDeptCS**.	1	
3-4	Running Macros	Press Ctrl + t to run the Technic macro. Press Ctrl + Shift + Q to run the Landscape macro.	3	
5-6	Saving, Printing	Save, print, and close **EL2-C7-A2-NationalAcctgDeptCS.xlsx**. Close **MyMacros-Student Name.xlsm**.	1	
		TOTAL POINTS	5	

Assessment 3: Create Macros; Save as a Macro-Enabled Workbook
File: **EL2-C7-A3-NationalAcctgDeptCS.xlsm**

Steps	Tasks	Criteria	Value	Score
1-3	Opening, Creating Macros	Open **EL2-C7-A2-NationalAcctgDeptCS.xlsx**. Create the following two macros within the current workbook: • Create a macro named *FormulaBarOff* that turns off the display of the Formula bar and protects the worksheet. Do not enter a password to unprotect the sheet. Assign the macro to the shortcut key Ctrl + Shift + M. Enter an appropriate description that includes student's name and date macro was created. • Create a macro names *FormulaBarOn* that turns on display of the Formula bar and unprotects the worksheet. Assign the macro to the shortcut key Ctrl + Shift + B. Enter an appropriate description that includes student's name and date macro was created. Test each macro to make sure shortcut key runs the correct commands.	9	
4-5	Saving	Save revised workbook as a macro-enabled workbook and name it **EL2-C7-A3-NationalAcctgDeptCS**. Close **EL2-C7-A3-NationalAcctgDeptCS.xlsm**.	1	
		TOTAL POINTS	10	

Assessment 4: Print Macros
File: **EL2-C7-A3-NationalAcctgDeptCS.xlsm**

Steps	Tasks	Criteria	Value	Score
1-2	Opening	Open **EL2-C7-A3-NationalAcctgDeptCS.xlsm** and enable content. Open Macro dialog box and edit the FormulaBarOff macro.	1	

Steps	Tasks	Criteria	Value	Score
3-5	Printing	At Microsoft Visual Basic Application Window, click *Print,* and then Print + VBAProject dialog box, click OK. Click on File on Menu bar and click *Close and Return to Microsoft Excel.* Close **EL2-C7-A3-NationalAcctgDeptCS.xlsm**	2	
6-10	Printing	Open **MyMacros-StudentName.xlsm** and enable content. Open dialog box Macro dialog box and edit Landscape macro. At Microsoft Visual Basic Application Window, click *Print,* and then Print + VBAProject dialog box, click OK. Click on File on Menu bar and click *Close and Return to Microsoft Excel.* Close **MyMacros-StudentName.xlsm**	2	
		TOTAL POINTS	5	

Assessment 5: Customize the Excel Environment
File: **EL2-C7-A5-BillingsDec21.xlsx**

Steps	Tasks	Criteria	Value	Score
1-2	Opening, Saving	Open **BillingsDec21.xlsx**. Save As **EL2-C7-A5-BillingsDec21.xlsx**	1	
3-5	Formatting	Make the following changes to the Display options: • Turn off the horizontal scroll bar • Turn off sheet tabs • Turn off row and column headers • Turn off gridlines Change current them to Origin. Freeze first four rows in worksheet.	7	
6-9	Creating Screen Image, Saving, Printing	Create screen image of worksheet with the modified display options and paste image into a new Word document. Type student name a few lines below screen image. Save Word document as **EL2-C7-A5-BillingsDec21**. Print **EL2-C7-A5-BillingsDec21.docx** and exit Word. Save and close **EL2-C7-A5-BillingsDec21.xlsx**.	2	
		TOTAL POINTS	10	

Assessment 6: Create Custom Views
File: **EL2-C7-A6-BillingsDec21.xlsx**

Steps	Tasks	Criteria	Value	Score
1-2	Opening, Saving	Open **BillingsDec21.xlsx**. Save As **EL2-C7-A6-BillingsDec21.xlsx**	1	

Steps	Tasks	Criteria	Value	Score
3-12	Creating Custom Views	• Select A4:I23 and custom sort in ascending order by *Attorney* and then by client's *Last Name*. • With A4:I23 selected turn on filter arrows. • Deselect range and then filter the Attorney column to show only those rows with the attorney name *Kyle Williams*. • Create custom view names *Williams* to save filter settings. • Clear filter in the *Attorney* column. • Filter list by *Attorney* named *Marty O'Donovan*. • Create a custom view named *O'Donovan* to save filter settings. • Clear filter in *Attorney* column. • Create custom view named *Martinez* and clear filter from *Attorney* column. • Create custom view named *Sullivan* and clear filter from *Attorney* column.	12	
13-16	Creating Screen Image, Printing	Open Custom Views dialog box. Create screen image of worksheet with dialog box open and past image into a new Word document. Type student name a few lines below screen image. Save Word document as **EL2-C7-A6-BillingsDec21**. Print **EL2-C7-A6-BillingsDec21.docx** and exit Word. Close Custom Views dialog box; save and close **EL2-C7-A6-BillingsDec21.xlsx**.	2	
		TOTAL POINTS	15	

Assessment 7: Create and Use a Template
File: **EL2-C7-A7-Billings.xlsx** and **Billings-StudentName.xltx**

Steps	Tasks	Criteria	Value	Score
1	Opening	Open **EL2-C7-A5-BillingsDec21.xlsx**. Turn on display of row and column headers.	1	
2-4	Revising Workbook	Make the following changes to workbook: • Select and delete all of the data below the column headings in row 4 • Delete text in A3 • Edit subtitle in A2 to *Associate Weekly Billing Summary*. Save revised workbook as template named **Billings-StudentName**. Close **Billings-StudentName.xltx**.	4	
5-7	Creating Workbook	Start new workbook based on the **Billings-StudentName.xltx** template. Type dates for Monday to Friday of current week in A3 in the format *November 12 to 16, 2012*. Enter two billings using Monday's date of current week. Enter dates in format mm/dd/yyyy.	8	

Steps	Tasks	Criteria	Value	Score
8-12	Saving, Printing	Save As **EL2-C7-A7-Billings**. Print **EL2-C7-A7-Billings.xlsx**. Display New dialog box and right-click template **billings-StudentName.xltx** and Copy. Open a Computer window and navigate to Excel2010L2C7 folder and past template. Close Window. At New dialog box, delete custom template named **Billings-StudentName.xltx**. Close New dialog box and click Home tab.	2	
		TOTAL POINTS	15	

Visual Benchmark

1: Customize the Ribbon

File: **EL2-C7-VB1-MyRibbon.docx**

Steps	Tasks	Criteria	Value	Score
1-2	Creating Custom Tab, Inserting Screen Image	Create custom tab including groups and buttons shown in Figure 7.12. Insert a screen image in a new Word document that shows the ribbon with custom tab displayed in Microsoft Excel.	4	
3-5	Saving, Printing	Save Word document as **EL2-C7-VB1-MyRibbon**. Print **EL2-C7-VB1-MyRibbon.docx** and exit Word. Restore ribbon in Excel to its original settings.	1	
		TOTAL POINTS	5	

2: Customize a Custom Template

File: **EL2-C7-VB2-AudennitaSalesInv.xltm** and
EL2-C7-VB2-AudennitaInvToVanderwyst.xlsx

Steps	Tasks	Criteria	Value	Score
1-2	Creating Custom Template	Create custom template that could be used to generate a sales invoice similar to Figure 7.13. Match column widths, row heights, and color formatting. Font in A1 is *Footlight MT Light 36-point* and *Garamond* for remaining cells (18-point in A2 and 12-point elsewhere). Save workbooks as a template and name it **EL2-C7-VB2-AudennitaSalesInv**.	5	

Steps	Tasks	Criteria	Value	Score
3-7	Completing Invoice, Printing, Saving	Use the template to fill out sale invoice using data shown in Figure 7.13. Save completed invoice as **EL2-C7-VB2-AudennitaInvToVanderwyst.** Print invoice and close **EL2-C7-VB2-AudennitaInvToVanderwyst.xlsx.** Make copy of custom template and save copy to storage medium in the Excel2010L2C7 folder. Delete custom template from computer.	5	
		TOTAL POINTS	10	

Case Study

Part 1

File: **EL2-C7-CS-P1-NuTrendMacros.xlsm**

Steps	Tasks	Criteria	Value	Score
1	Creating Macros	Delete Sheet 2 and Sheet 3 form workbook. Rename Sheet1 to *MacroDocumentation*. Document macros with macro names, shortcut keys assigned, and descriptions of actions each macro performs. Create a separate macro for each of the following tasks: • Apply theme named *Equity* and show all comments. • Set active column's width to 20. • Apply conditional formatting to highlight top 10 in a selected list. Accept the default formatting options. • Apply Accounting format with zero decimals. • Create a footer that prints student's name centered at bottom of worksheet.	9	
2	Printing, Editing	Print MacroDocumentation worksheet. Open Macro dialog box and edit first macro. Print the macros in the VBAProject. Close Visual Basic for Applications windo2. Save **EL2-C7-CS-P1-NuTrendsMacros.xlsm**.	1	
		TOTAL POINTS	10	

Part 2

File: **EL2-C7-CS-P2-PizzaByMarioNewFranchiseRev.xlsx**

Steps	Tasks	Criteria	Value	Score
1	Opening, Saving	Open **PizzaByMarioNewFranchiseRev.xlsx**. Save As **EL2-C7-C2-PS- PizzaByMarioNewFranchiseRev**.	1	

Steps	Tasks	Criteria	Value	Score
2	Running Macros	Run each macro created in 1 using the following information: • Set all of the column widths to 20 except column C. • Run the number formatting and the conditional formatting with the values in column E selected. • Run the theme and footer macros.	8	
3	Printing, Saving	Print the worksheet making sure comments print as displayed. Save and close **EL2-C7-C2-PS-PizzaByMarioNewFranchiseRev.xlsx**. Close **EL2-C7-CS-P1-NuTrendsMacros.xlsm**.	1	
		TOTAL POINTS	10	

Part 3

File: **EL2-C7-CS-P3-CustomizeQATMemo.docx**

Steps	Tasks	Criteria	Value	Score
1	Using Help	Use Excel Help to learn how to add a button to the Quick Access toolbar directly from the ribbon. Test information learned by adding Orientation button and New Comment button.	1	
2	Creating Memo	Using Microsoft Word, compose a memo that describes steps to add a button to Quick Access toolbar directly from ribbon. Insert screen image of Quick Access toolbar in Excel that display the buttons that were added. Place image below the memo text.	8	
3	Printing, Saving	Save, print, and close Word memo as **EL2-C7-C3-P3-CustomizeQATMemo.docx**. Exit Word. Remove two buttons added to Quick Access toolbar.	1	
		TOTAL POINTS	10	

Part 4

File: **EL2-C7-CS-P4-DocRecovery.docx**

Steps	Tasks	Criteria	Value	Score
1	Researching	Use Help and the Internet to research Document Recovery messages in Excel.	2	
2	Creating Word Document	Create a Microsoft Word document explaining in student's own words the AutoRecover and AutoSave features. Include explanation that Document Recovery task pane appears after Excel has not been properly closed. Provide advice on how to review files in the pane to make sure data has not been lost.	7	
3	Saving, Printing	Save As **EL2-C7-CS-P4-DocRecovery**. Print and close **EL2-C7-CS-P4-DocRecovery.docx**.	1	
		TOTAL POINTS	10	

Excel Level 2, Chapter 8

Skills Check

Assessment 1: Import Data From Access and a Text File

Files: **EL2-C8-A1-HillsdaleResearchServices.xlsx**

Steps	Tasks	Criteria	Value	Score
1-2	Opening, Saving	Open **HillsdaleResearchServices.xlsx**. Save As **EL2-C8-A1-HillsdaleResearchServices**.	1	
3	Importing	Make A6 of CPIData worksheet the active cell. Import table named CPI from Access database **NuTrendsCensusData.accdb**.	2	
4	Editing	Make the following changes to worksheet: • Apply *Table Style Medium 15* to imported cells. • Format values in all columns *except* column A to one decimal place. • Remove the filter arrow buttons and then center column headings. • If necessary, adjust column widths to accommodate data.	4	
5	Printing	Print CPIData worksheet.	1	
6-7	Importing	Make UIRateMI the active worksheet. Make A6 the active cell. Import comma delimited text file named **UIRateMI.csv**.	2	
8	Editing	Make the following changes to data: • Change width of column B to 8.00 (61 pixels). • Change width of columns C to F to 15.00 (110 pixels). • Change width of column G to 5.00 (40 pixels). • Center the months in column B.	4	
9-10	Printing, Saving	Print the UIRate-MI worksheet. Save **EL2-C8-A1-HillsdaleResearchServices.xlsx** and close.	1	
		TOTAL POINTS	15	

Assessment 2: Link Data to a Word Document

File: **EL2-C8-A2-HillsdaleOctSalesByDateByRep.xlsx and EL2-C8-P2-HillsdaleOctRpt.docx**

Steps	Tasks	Criteria	Value	Score
1-2	Opening, Saving	Open **HillsdaleOctSalesByDateByRep.xlsx**. Save As **EL2-C8-A2-HillsdaleOctSalesByDateByRep**.	1	
3-5	Linking to Word, Formatting	With SalesByDate the active worksheet, link A3:G27 a double-space below the paragraph in the Word document **HillsdaleOctRpt.docx**. Change margins in Word document to *Narrow* (Top, Bottom, Left, and Right to 0.5 inch). Save As **EL2-C8-A2-HillsdaleOctRpt.docx**.	5	

Steps	Tasks	Criteria	Value	Score
6-9	Editing Excel	Switch to Excel. Deselect range. Change value in F4 to *525000*. Change value in F5 to *212000*. Save **EL2-C8-A2-HillsdaleOctSalesByDateByRep.xlsx**.	2	
10-14	Updating Link, Printing, Saving	Switch to Word, *Update Link*. Print Word document. Break link in Word document. Save **EL2-C8-A2-HillsdaleOctRpt.docx** and exit Word. Save and close **EL2-C8-A2-HillsdaleOctSalesByDateByRep.xlsx**.	2	
		TOTAL POINTS	10	

Assessment 3: Embed Data in a PowerPoint Presentation

File: **EL2-C8-A2-HillsdaleOctSalesByDateByRep.xlsx** and **HillsdaleOctRpt.pptx**

Steps	Tasks	Criteria	Value	Score
1-2	Opening, Saving	Open **HillsdaleOctSalesByDateByRep.xlsx**. Save As **EL2-C8-A3-HillsdaleOctSalesByDateByRep**.	9	
3-5	Creating Column Chart	Make SalesByRep the active worksheet. Display worksheet at outline level 2 (only sales agent names, sale prices, and commissions display). Create column chart in separate sheet to graph sales commissions earned by each sales agent. Student determines appropriate chart style, title, and other chart elements.	1	
6-7	Opening, Saving	Open **HillsdaleOctRpt.pptx**. Save As **EL2-C8-A3-HillsdaleOctRpt.pptx**.		
8	Embedding Chart	Embed chart created in step 5 on Slide 3.		
9-11	Printing, Saving	Print presentation as Handouts with three slides per page. Save **EL2-C8-A3-HillsdaleOctRpt.pptx** and exit PowerPoint. Save and close **EL2-C8-A3-HillsdaleOctSalesByDateByRep.xlsx**.		
		TOTAL POINTS	10	

Assessment 4: Export Data as a Text File
File: **EL2-C8-A4-HillsdaleOctSalesByDateByRep.csv**

Steps	Tasks	Criteria	Value	Score
1-3	Opening, Saving	Open **HillsdaleOctSalesByDateByRep.xlsx**. With SalesByDate the active worksheet, save as a CSV (Comma delimited) (*.csv) text file named **EL2-C8-A4-HillsdaleOctSalesByDateByRep**. Close (if prompted do not save changes) **EL2-C8-A4-HillsdaleOctSalesByDateByRep.csv**.	1	
4-6	Editing	Start Notepad and open **EL2-C8-A4-HillsdaleOctSalesByDateByRep.csv**. Delete first three rows at beginning of file. Delete bottom row in file that contains the total commission value and the ending commas.	3	
7-8	Printing, Saving	Print document. Save **EL2-C8-A4-HillsdaleOctSalesByDateByRep.csv** and exit Notepad.	1	
		TOTAL POINTS	5	

Assessment 5: Prepare a Workbook for Distribution
File: **EL2-C8-A5-Hillsdale2012Sales.xlsx**

Steps	Tasks	Criteria	Value	Score
1-2	Opening, Saving	Open **Hillsdale2012Sales.xlsx**. Save As **EL2-C8-A5-Hillsdale2012.xlsx**	1	
3-9	Reading Information, Changing Settings, Inserting Screen Shot, Printing	Read information in properties and comments as instructed. Check for header or footer. Use Document Inspector for private and hidden information. Remove all items displayed with a red exclamation mark. Turn off Show All Comments feature. Paste a screen image into a new Word document using the PrintScreen key, the Screenshot feature, or the Window Snipping tool. Type student name a few lines below screen image. Print Word document and exit Word without saving.	2	
10-12	Running Compatibility Feature, Marking as Final	Run Compatibility Feature to check for loss of functionality or fidelity in workbook if saved in earlier Excel version. Save Summary report to new sheet. Print Compatibility Report sheet. Mark workbook as final. Close **EL2-C8-A5-Hillsdale2012.xlsx**.	2	
		TOTAL POINTS	5	

Assessment 6: Prepare and Distribute a Workbook

File: **EL2-C8-A6-Hillsdale2012Sales.xlsx**; **EL2-C8-A6-Hillsdale2012Sales.pdf**; and
EL2-C8-A6-Hillsdale2012Sales.mht

Steps	Tasks	Criteria	Value	Score
1-2	Opening, Saving	Open **Hillsdale2012Sales.xlsx**. Save As **EL2-C8-A6-Hillsdale2012Sales**.	1	
3-6	Publishing, Saving	Use Document Inspector feature to remove comments and annotations only from worksheet. Publish worksheet as PDF file named **EL2-C8-A6-Hillsdale2012Sales.pdf**. Publish worksheet as single file web page named **EL2-C8-A6-Hillsdale2012Sales.mht** with a page title *Hillsdale Realtors*. Save and close **EL2-C8-A6-Hillsdale2012Sales.xlsx**.	3	
7	Displaying File Extensions, Printing	Display contents of Excel2010L2C8 folder and display file extensions. Paste screen image of folder's content into new Word document. Type student's name a few lines below screen image. Print Word document and exit Word without saving.	1	
		TOTAL POINTS	5	

Assessment 6: Option 1

Steps	Tasks	Criteria	Value	Score
1	Opening, Sending Email	With **EL2-C8-A6-Hillsdale2012Sales.xlsx** open, email workbook to student's email account. Compose appropriate message within message window. Open message from Inbox and print message. Close message window and exit email program.	5	
		TOTAL POINTS	5	

Assessment 6: Option 2

Steps	Tasks	Criteria	Value	Score
1	Opening, Uploading Files, Pasting, Printing	With **EL2-C8-A6-Hillsdale2012Sales.xlsx** open, sign into Windows Live and create a new folder in student's SkyDrive folder. Upload three files created in this assessment into the Excel20120L2C8 folder. Paste screen image showing three files into new Word document. Type student name a few lines below screen image. Print Word document and exit Word. Sign out of Windows Live. Close **EL2-C8-A6-Hillsdale2012Sales.xlsx**.	5	
		TOTAL POINTS	5	

Visual Benchmark

1: Import, Analyze, and Export Population Data

File: **EL2-C8-VB-PizzaByMarioReport.docx; EL2-C8-VB-PizzaByMarioReportPopData.xlsx**

Steps	Tasks	Criteria	Value	Score
1	Importing Table from Access, Formatting	Create the worksheet shown in Figure 8.8 by importing PopByState table from the Access database ***NuTrendsCensusData.accdb***. Worksheet has *Table Style Light 2* style and Solstice theme. Add title rows and change title in B4 as shown. Match other formatting characteristics such as column width, row height, number formatting, alignment, and fill color.	6	
2	Renaming, Printing	Rename worksheet *PopulationTable*. Print worksheet.	1	
3-4	Creating Chart, Saving	Select A4:B19 and create chart as shown in Figure 8.9 in a new sheet named *PopulationChart*. Chart has *Style 36* style applied. Match other chart options and formatting with chart shown. Save As **EL2-C8-VB-PizzaByMarioPopData**.	4	
5-6	Copying, Pasting, Printing	Open **PizzaByMarioReport.docx**. Use Save As to name **EL2-C8-VB-PizzaByMarioPopData**. Change *Student Name* on page 1 to student's name. Copy and paste Excel chart, positioning the chart between last two paragraphs on page 2. Make formatting adjustments to chart as needed. Save, print, and close Word document **EL2-C8-VB-PizzaByMarioPopData.docx**. Close **EL2-C8-VB-PizzaByMarioPopData.xlsx**.	4	
		TOTAL POINTS	15	

Case Study

Part 1

File: **EL2-C8-CS-P1-PizzaByMarioResearch.xlsx**

Steps	Tasks	Criteria	Value	Score
1	Creating Worksheets	Start new workbook and set up three worksheets named using the state names *Illinois, Indiana*, and *Kentucky*. In each sheet use New Web Query feature, display the web page http://quickfacts.census.gov/qfd/ , and import People Quickfacts for the state. Delete column A. Add appropriate title merged and centered above imported data and apply formatting to improve appearance of column headings.	9	
2	Saving, Printing	Save As **EL-C8-CS-P1-PizzaByMarioResearch**. Print all three worksheets.	1	
		TOTAL POINTS	10	

Part 2

File: **EL2-C8-CS-P2-PizzaByMarioExpansionResearch.docx**

Steps	Tasks	Criteria	Value	Score
1	Opening, Saving	Open **PizzaByMarioExpansionResearch.docx**. Save As **EL2-C8-C2-PS- PizzaByMarioExpansionResearch**.	1	
2	Copying, Pasting	Copy and Paste to Word document the following data from Excel worksheet created in Part 1 for each state (do not include data in USA column). Do not embed or link data: Households Persons per household Median household income At bottom of document, create a reference for data from U.S. Census Bureau. Check with instructor for preferred format for reference.	8	
3	Saving, Printing	Save, print, and close Word document **EL2-C8-C2-PS- PizzaByMarioExpansionResearch**. Close **EL-C8-CS-P1-PizzaByMarioResearch.xlsx**.	1	
		TOTAL POINTS	10	

Part 3

File: **EL2-C8-CS-P3-PizzaByMarioResearch.xlsx** and
EL2-C8-CS-P3-DataConnectionsMemo.docx

Steps	Tasks	Criteria	Value	Score
1	Using Help	Use Excel Help to learn how to manage connections to external data using Workbook Connections dialog box.	1	
2	Opening, Removing Connections	Open **EL-C8-CS-P1-PizzaByMarioResearch.xlsx**. Open Workbook Connections dialog box and using information learned in Help, remove all of the connections.	4	
3	Saving	Save revised workbook as **EL-C8-CS-P3-PizzaByMarioResearch.xlsx** and close workbook.	1	
4	Composing Memo	Use Word and compose memo that provides brief explanation of why security warning message about data connections appears when a workbook is opened that contains external content. Base memo on information learned in Help. Be sure memo is composed in student's own words. Include explanation that student created a new copy of workbook with the connections removed.	8	
5-6	Saving, Printing	Save Word memo as **EL2-C8-CS-P3-DataConnectionsMemo. docx**. Print and close document.	1	
		TOTAL POINTS	15	

Part 4

File: **EL2-C8-CS-P4-InternetFaxMemo.docx**

Steps	Tasks	Criteria	Value	Score
1	Researching	Use Excel Help to learn how to use the Internet Fax feature. Search the Internet to research for at least two fax service providers.	2	
2	Creating Word Document	Using Microsoft Word compose a memo that briefly explains how to use the Internet Fax feature in Excel. Student uses own words. Include in memo the URL of two fax service providers visited and add own recommendation for provider.	7	
3	Saving, Printing	Save As **EL2-C8-CS-P4-InternetFaxMemo**. Print and close **EL2-C8-CS-P4-InternetFaxMemo.docx**.	1	
		TOTAL POINTS	10	

Excel Level 2, Unit 2
Performance Assessment

Assessing Proficiency

Assessment 1: Use Goal Seek and Scenario Manager to Calculate Investment Proposals

File: **EL2-U2-A1-HillsdaleInvtPlan.xlsx**

Steps	Tasks	Criteria	Value	Score
1-2	Opening, Saving	Open **HillsdaleInvtPlan.xlsx**. Save As **EL2-U2-A1-HillsdaleInvtPlan**.	1	
3	Using Goal Seek	Use Goal Seek to find monthly contribution amount client must make in order to increase projected value of the plan to $65,000 at end of the term. Accept solution Goal Seek calculates.	4	
4-5	Assigning Range Name, Creating Scenarios	Assign range name *AvgReturn* to E8. Create three scenarios for changing E8 as follows: *Scenario Name* *Interest Rate* Moderate 5.5% Conservative 4.0% Aggressive 12.5%	5	
6	Applying Scenario, Printing	Apply *Aggressive* scenario. Print worksheet.	2	
7-9	Editing, Creating Report, Printing, Saving	Edit *Moderate* scenario's interest rate to 8.0% and apply the scenario. Create and print a Scenario Summary report. Save and close **EL2-U2-A1-HillsdaleInvtPlan.xlsx**.	3	
		TOTAL POINTS	15	

Assessment 2: Calculate Investment Outcomes for a Portfolio Using a Two-Variable Data Table

File: **EL2-U2-A2-HillsdaleResearchInvtTbl.xlsx**

Steps	Tasks	Criteria	Value	Score
1-2	Opening, Saving	Open **HillsdaleResearchInvtTbl.xlsx**. Save As **EL2-U2-A2-HillsdaleResearchInvtTbl.xlsx**.	1	
3	Creating Two-Variable Data Table	Create two-variable data table that calculates projected value of investment at end of term for each monthly contribution payment and at each interest rate in the range A11:G20.	7	
4-7	Formatting	Apply Comma Style format to projected values in table and adjust column widths if necessary. Make E8 the active cell and display precedent arrows. Make A11 the active cell and display precedent arrows. Remove the arrows.	2	
8	Saving, Printing	Save, print, and close **EL2-U2-A2-HillsdaleResearchInvtTbl.xlsx**.	1	
		TOTAL POINTS	10	

Assessment 3: Solve an Error and Check for Accuracy in Investment Commission Formulas

File: **EL2-U2-A3-HillsdaleModeratePortfolio.xlsx**

Steps	Tasks	Criteria	Value	Score
1-2	Opening, Saving	Open **HillsdaleModeratePortfolio.xlsx**. Save as **EL2-U2-A3-HillsdaleModeratePortfolio.xlsx**.	1	
3	Solving Error	Solve the #VALUE! Error in E19. Use formula auditing tools to help find source cell containing the invalid entry.	4	
4	Checking Logic Accuracy	Check logic accuracy of formula in E19 by creating proof formulas below worksheet as follows: • In row 2, calculate amount from customer's deposit that would be deposited into each of the six funds based on the percentages in column B. Example: In B21 create formula to multiply customer's deposit in B19 times percentage recommended for investment in DW Bond fund in B5. Create similar formula for remaining funds in C21:G21. • In row 22, multiply amount deposited to each fund by fund's commission rate. Example: in B22, create formula to multiply value in B2 times the commission rate paid by DW Bond fund in B17. Create similar formula for remaining funds in C22:G22. • In B23, create a SUM function to calculate the total of the commissions for the six funds in B22:G22. Add appropriate labels next to the values created in rows 21 to 23.	9	
5	Saving, Printing	Save, print, and close **EL2-U2-A3-HillsdaleModeratePortfolio.xlsx**.	1	
		TOTAL POINTS	15	

Assessment 4: Document and Share a Workbook and Manage Changes in an Investment Portfolio Worksheet

File: **EL2-U2-A4-HillsdaleModeratePortfolio.xlsx**

Steps	Tasks	Criteria	Value	Score
1-2	Opening, Saving	Open **EL2-U2-A3-HillsdaleModeratePortfolio.xlsx**. Save As **EL2-U2-A4-HillsdaleModeratePortfolio**.	1	
3	Entering Data	Enter following data into workbook properties: *Author:* Logan Whitmore *Title:* Recommended Moderate Portfolio *Comments:* Proposed moderate fund *Subject:* Moderate Investment Allocation	2	
4-5	Creating Word Document, Sharing	Paste screen image of Info tab Backstage view showing all properties into a new Word document. Type student name a few blank lines below image, print document, and exit without saving. Click Review tab and share workbook.	2	
6-7	Editing, Saving	Change user name to *Carey Winters* and edit the following cells: B7 to *15%* B8 to *10%* Save **EL2-U2-A4-HillsdaleModeratePortfolio.xlsx**.	2	
8-9	Editing, Saving	Change user name to *Jodi VanKemenade* and edit the following cells: D17 to *2.32%* E17 to *2.19%* Save **EL2-U2-A4-HillsdaleModeratePortfolio.xlsx**.	2	
10	Creating, Printing	Create and print a History sheet.	1	
11-12	Accepting, Rejecting Changes	Change user name back to original name on computer. Accept and reject changes made to ModeratePortfolio worksheet as follows: Reject B7 Reject B8 Accept D17 Reject E17	4	
13	Saving, Printing	Save, print, and close **EL2-U2-A4-HillsdaleModeratePortfolio.xlsx**.	1	
		TOTAL POINTS	15	

Assessment 5: Insert Comments and Protect a Confidential Investment Portfolio Workbook

File: **EL2-U2-A5-HillsdaleModeratePortfolio.xlsx**

Steps	Tasks	Criteria	Value	Score
1-2	Opening, Saving	Open **EL2-U2-A4-HillsdaleModeratePortfolio.xlsx**. Save As **EL2-U2-A5-HillsdaleModeratePortfolio.xlsx**.	1	

Steps	Tasks	Criteria	Value	Score
3-10	Formatting	Make the following changes to workbook: • Remove shared access to workbook. • Hide rows 20 to 23. • Make B17 the active cell and insert a comment. Type **Commission rate to be renegotiated in 2012** in comment box. • Copy comment in B17 and paste it to D17 and G17. • Edit comment in G17 to change year from *2012* to *2013*. • Protect worksheet with password *Mod%82* • Save and close **EL2-U2-A5-HillsdaleModeratePortfolio.xlsx**.	8	
11-14	Editing, Printing, Saving	Complete the following: • Test security features added to work by opening **EL2-U2-A5-HillsdaleModeratePortfolio.xlsx** using password *Mod%82* (created in step 9). Try to change one of the values in range B5:B10 and B17:G17. • Make B19 active cell and change value to *10000*. • Display all comments in worksheet and print worksheet with comments *As displayed on sheet* and with worksheet scaled to fit on 1 page. • Save and close **EL2-U2-A5-HillsdaleModeratePortfolio.xlsx**.	6	
		TOTAL POINTS	15	

Assessment 6: Automate and Customize an Investment Portfolio Workbook
File: **EL2-U2-A6-HillsdaleModeratePortfolio.xlsx**

Steps	Tasks	Criteria	Value	Score
1-2	Opening, Unprotecting Workbook, Deleting Comments	Open **EL2-U2-A5-HillsdaleModeratePortfolio.xlsx**. Unprotect worksheet. Turn off display of all comments. Delete comments in B17, D17, and G17.	2	
3	Deleting Custom Views	Display Custom Views dialog box. Delete all custom views in dialog box. Add a new custom view named *ModeratePortfolioOriginalView*.	3	

Steps	Tasks	Criteria	Value	Score
4-5	Creating and Testing Macros	Create two macros stored in active workbook as follows: • A macro named *CustomDisplay* that applies *Solstice* theme and turns off display of gridlines and row and column headers in current workbook. Assign macro the shortcut key Ctrl + Shift + T. Enter appropriate description that includes student name and date macro was created. • A macro named *CustomHeader* that prints text *Private and Confidential*. Assign macro the shortcut key Ctrl + Shift + H. Enter appropriate description that includes student name and date macro was assigned. Test macros by opening **EL-U2-A1-HillsdaleInvtPlan.xlsx**. Make InvestmentPlanProposal the active worksheet. Run two macros created in the assessment. View worksheet in Print Preview. Close Print Preview and close without saving **EL-U2-A1-HillsdaleInvtPlan.xlsx**.	6	
6	Printing Visual Basic Code	Print Visual Basic program code for the two macros and close Microsoft Visual Basic window. Return to Excel.	2	
7	Creating Custom View	Create custom view *ModeratePortfolioTemplateView*.	3	
8-9	Printing, Saving	Save revised workbook as macro-enabled named **EL2-U2-A6-HillsdaleModeratePortfolio.xlsm**. Remove password to open workbook. Print worksheet.	2	
10-11	Creating, Printing Word Document	Paste screen image of worksheet with the Custom Views dialog box in a new Word document. Type student name a few lines below image. Print document and exit Word without saving. Close Custom Views dialog box and then close **EL2-U2-A6-HillsdaleModeratePortfolio.xlsm**.	2	
		TOTAL POINTS	20	

Assessment 7: Create and Use an Investment Planner Template
File: EL2-U2-A7-HillsdaleInvPlan-StudentName.xltx and EL2-U2-A7-HillsdaleInvPlan.xlsx

Steps	Tasks	Criteria	Value	Score
1-4	Opening, Editing, Saving	Open **EL2-U2-A2-HillsdaleResearchInvtTbl.xlsx**. Make the following changes: • Change label in A3 to *Investment Planner*. • Change font color of A11 to white (cell will appear to be empty). • Clear contents of E5:E7. • Protect worksheet allowing editing to E5:E7 only. Assign password *H$pl@n* to unprotect worksheet. Save revised workbook as template named **HillsdaleInvPlan-StudentName.xltx** and close template.	8	

Steps	Tasks	Criteria	Value	Score

5-8	Creating, Saving, Printing	Start new workbook based on template **HillsdaleInvPlan-StudentName.xltx**.
		Enter the following information in appropriate cells:
		   Monthly Contribution *-475*
		   Number of years to invest *5*
		   Forecasted annual interest rate *4.75%*
		Save As and print workbook named **EL2-U2-A7-HillsdaleInvPlan.xlsx**.
			5	

9-10	Copying, Deleting	Display New dialog box. Copy template created in this assessment to Excel20120L2U2 folder. Delete custom template created in this assessment from hard disk drive on computer.	2	
		TOTAL POINTS	15	

Assessment 8: Export a Chart and Prepare and Distribute an Investment Portfolio Worksheet

File: **EL2-U2-A8-HillsdaleModeratePortfolio.xlts** and **EL2-U2-A8-HillsdalePortfolios.pptx**

Steps	Tasks	Criteria	Value	Score
1-3	Opening, Saving	Open **EL2-U2-A6-HillsdaleModeratePortfolio.xlsm** and enable content if security warning message bar appears. Start PowerPoint and open **HillsdalePortfolios.pptx**. Save As **EL2-U2-A8-HillsdalePortfolios**.	2	
4-7	Copying, Printing, Saving	Copy pie chart from Excel to Slide 7 in PowerPoint presentation. Resize chart on slide and edit legend if necessary to make chart consistent with other charts in presentation. Print presentation as *9 Slides Horizontal Handouts*. Save **EL2-U2-A8-HillsdalePortfolios.pptx** and exit PowerPoint.	4	
8-12	Inspecting, Editing	Deselect chart. Inspect document, leaving all items checked at Document Inspector dialog box. Remove all items that display with red exclamation mark and close dialog box. Change file to type to *.xlsx* and name it **EL2-U2-A6-HillsdaleModeratePortfolio**. Click Yes when prompted that file cannot be save with VBA Project. Click OK at privacy warning message box. Mark workbook as final. Click OK if privacy warning message box reappears.	2	

Steps	Tasks	Criteria	Value	Score
13-15	Composing and Sending Email, Printing	Send workbook as XPS document to student in email initiated from Excel. Include appropriate message. Open message window from Inbox in email program and print message. Close message window and exit email. Display Info tab Backstage view showing all properties. Paste a screen image into a new Word document. Type student name a few blank lines below image. Print document and exit Word without saving. Close **EL2-U2-A6-HillsdaleModeratePortfolio.xlsx**.	7	
		TOTAL POINTS	15	

Writing Activities

Activity: Create a Computer Maintenance Template

File: **EL2-U1-Act1-NationalCMForm.xltx**

Steps	Tasks	Criteria	Value	Score
1	Creating Template	In a new workbook, create a template that can be used to complete the maintenance form electronically. The template should information that identifies the workstation by asset ID number, department in which computer is located, name of employee using computer, name of technician that performs maintenance, date maintenance is perform. Include a column next to each task with a drop-down list with options: *Completed, Not Completed, Not Applicable*. Next to this column include a column in which technician can type notes. At bottom of template include text box with message text: **Save using the file naming standard CM-StationID##-yourinitials where ## is the asset ID. Example CM-StationID56-JW**	10	
2	Protecting, Saving	Protect worksheet, leaving cells unlocked that technician will fill in. Do not include password for unprotecting sheet. Save template as **NationalCMForm-StudentName**.	3	
3	Creating Workbook	Start new workbook based on custom template. Fill out form as if student was technician working on computer to test template's organization and layout.	5	
4	Saving, Printing	Save As **EL2-U2-Act1-NationalCMForm**. Print form scaled to fit one page in height and width. Copy **NationalCMForm-StudentName.xltx** to storage medium and delete template from computer.	2	
		TOTAL POINTS	20	

Internet Research

Activity 1: Apply What-If Analysis to a Planned Move

File: **EL2-U2-Act2-MyFirstYearBudget.xlsx**

Steps	Tasks	Criteria	Value	Score
1	Researching, Creating Workbook	After researching create a workbook based on the following: • Research typical rents for apartments in city of student's choice. • Estimate other living costs in the city include: transportation, food, entertainment, clothes, telephone, cable/satellite, cell phone, Internet, etc. • Calculate total living costs for an entire year. • Research annual starting salaries of student's chosen field of study. Estimate the take home pay at approximately 70% of annual salary. • Use take-home pay and total living costs for the year. Calculate if there will be money left over if will have to borrow money to meet expenses. • Use Goal Seek to find take-home pay needed to earn in order to have $2,000 left over at end of year. Accept solution that Goal Seek provides.	14	
2	Creating Scenarios	Create two scenarios in worksheet as follows: • Scenario named *LowestValues* in which you adjust each value down to lowest amount you think is reasonable. • Scenario named *HighestValues* in which you adjust each value up to highest amount you think is reasonable. Apply each scenario and notice impact on amount left over at end of year.	6	
3	Creating Scenario Summary Report, Printing	Display worksheet in the *HighestValues* scenario and create a scenario summary report. Print worksheet applying print options as necessary to minimize pages required. Print scenario summary report.	4	
4	Saving	Save As **EL2-U2-Act2-MyFirstYearBudget.xlsx**. Close worksheet.	1	
		TOTAL POINTS	25	

Activity 2: Research and Compare Smartphones
File: **EL2-U2-Act2-MyFirstYearBudget.xlsx**

Steps	Tasks	Criteria	Value	Score
1	Researching, Creating Workbook	Research the latest smartphone from three different manufacturers. Features needed include conference calling, email, web browsing, text messaging, and modifying PowerPoint presentations, Word documents, and Excel worksheets. Create a workbook that compares the three smartphones. Organize the worksheet so that main features are along the left side of the page by category and each phone's specifications for those features are set in column. At bottom of each column, provide hyperlink to phone's specifications on the Web. Based on student's perception of best value, provide a brief explanation as to why the phone was selected; place in a comment box in the price cell of selected phone.	18	
2	Saving, Publishing, Printing	Save As **EL2-U2-Act3-Smartphones**. Publish worksheet as single file web page accepting default file name. Change page title to *Smartphone Feature and Price Comparison.* Print web page from Internet Explorer window. Close Internet Explorer and close **EL2-U2-Act3-Smartphones.xlsx**.	2	
		TOTAL POINTS	20	

Job Study

Prepare a Wages Budget and Link the Budget to a Word Document
File: **EL2-U2-JS-GardenviewWageBdgt.xlsx** and **EL2-U2-JS-GardenviewOpBdgt.docx**

Steps	Tasks	Criteria	Value	Score
1	Creating Worksheet	Create worksheet to estimate next year's hourly wages expense using the information provided about hourly paid works and average wage costs in Table U2.1.	14	
2	Formatting	Format worksheet to make use of colors, themes, and/or table features to make budget calculations easy to read.	6	
3	Saving, Printing	Save As **EL2-U2-JS-GardenviewWageBdgt**. Print worksheet adjusting print options as necessary to minimize pages required.	2	
4	Creating Chart	On a separate sheet, create a chart to show the total hourly wages budget by worker category. Student determines chart type and chart options to present information.	4	
5	Opening Word Document, Linking Chart	Open Word document **GardenviewOpBdgt**. Edit year on title page to current year. Edit name and date at bottom of title page to include student's name and current date. Link chart created in Excel to end of Word document.	3	

Steps	Tasks	Criteria	Value	Score
6	Printing, Saving	Save As **EL2-U2-JS-GardenviewOpBdgt.docx**. Print and close document. Deselect chart and close **EL2-U2-JS-GardenviewWageBdgt. xlsx**.	1	
		TOTAL POINTS	30	

Benchmark Excel 2010 Level 1, Unit 1

Supplemental Assessment 1

Instructions

1. A friend has made several visits to the doctor in the past month because of a serious illness and has asked you to calculate what he will owe after the insurance company has paid its part of the bill. The insurance company usually takes about a month to process a claim and your friend is hoping you can help figure the amount right away so he can plan ahead.

2. Create a worksheet to include the following information from the visits to the doctor.

    a. Input the Date of Visit using the date function.

    b. Format the Cost of Visit to Currency.

	A	B	C
1	Date of Visit	Doctor	Cost of Visit
2	8/6/2010	Goodman	$113.00
3	8/8/2010	Goodman	$145.00
4	8/10/2010	Loman	$120.00
5	8/13/2010	Goodman	$110.00
6	8/15/2010	Loman	$140.00
7	8/17/2010	Loman	$175.00
8	8/21/2010	Loman	$135.00
9	8/22/2010	Walker	$215.00
10	8/24/2010	Walker	$235.00
11	8/27/2010	Loman	$120.00
12	8/28/2010	Goodman	$105.00

3. Your friend has a copayment of $25.00 and the insurance will pay 80% of the remaining cost. In Column D create a formula that displays how much the insurance company will pay. In Column E create a formula that displays the amount your friend will have to pay.

4. The insurance company is supposed to respond within 30 days of billing. The doctor's office has said that they will bill 3 days after the visit. In Column F create a formula that calculates the insurance response date.

5. In cell A13, type the word **Total**. In cell C13 insert a formula that calculates the total cost of the visits. Copy this formula to cells D13 and E13.

6. In cell A14, type the word **Average**. In cell C14, input a formula that calculates the Average Cost of Visit.

7. Format the spreadsheet to make it easy to read and visually attractive. Add a footer that includes your name.

8. Save the file with the name **EL1-U1-SA1-DoctorVisits**. Print the worksheet.

Rubric

File: **EL1-U1-SA1-DoctorVisits.xlsx**

Steps	Tasks	Criteria	Value	Score
2	**Typing/Accuracy**	Create worksheet and enter data	2	
2a	**Feature**	Date of Visit – DATE function	2	
2b	**Editing**	Cost of Visit formatted to Currency	1	
3	**Editing**	Insurance Pays – Column D formula =(C2-25)*0.8	3	
3	**Editing**	Friend Pays – Column E formula =25+(C2-25)*.02 OR =C2-D2	3	
4	**Editing**	Insurance Response Date formula – Column F =A2+33	3	
5	**Feature/Editing**	C13 SUM function (copied to D13, E13)	2	
6	**Feature**	C14 AVERAGE function	2	
7	**Feature**	Format the spreadsheet	3	
7	**Feature**	Insert a Footer	2	
8	**Finishing**	Save and print	2	
		TOTAL POINTS	25	

Date of Visit	Doctor	Cost of Visit	Insurance Pays	Friend Pays	Insurance Response Date
8/6/2012	Goodman	$ 113.00	$ 70.40	$ 42.60	9/8/2012
8/8/2012	Goodman	$ 145.00	$ 96.00	$ 49.00	9/10/2012
8/10/2012	Loman	$ 120.00	$ 76.00	$ 44.00	9/12/2012
8/13/2012	Goodman	$ 110.00	$ 68.00	$ 42.00	9/15/2012
8/15/2012	Loman	$ 140.00	$ 92.00	$ 48.00	9/17/2012
8/17/2012	Loman	$ 175.00	$ 120.00	$ 55.00	9/19/2012
8/21/2012	Loman	$ 135.00	$ 88.00	$ 47.00	9/23/2012
8/22/2012	Walker	$ 215.00	$ 152.00	$ 63.00	9/24/2012
8/24/2012	Walker	$ 235.00	$ 168.00	$ 67.00	9/26/2012
8/27/2012	Loman	$ 120.00	$ 76.00	$ 44.00	9/29/2012
8/28/2012	Goodman	$ 105.00	$ 64.00	$ 41.00	9/30/2012
Total		$ 1,613.00	$ 1,070.40	$ 542.60	
Average		$ 146.64			

Student Name

EL1-U1-SA1-DoctorVisits.xlsx

Supplemental Assessment 2

Instructions

1. Use the Save As command and save the worksheet created in Assessment 1 as **EL1-U1-SA2-DoctorVisits**.

2. Sort the worksheet alphabetically by Doctor and then by Cost of Visit.

3. Since your friend already has some money saved, calculate whether or not he will need a loan if the total he has to pay is more than $600. In cell A15 type **Bank Loan**. In cell E15 create an IF statement that will display the words *No Loan* if your friend does not need a loan and *Yes Loan* if your friend needs a loan.

4. Apply any additional necessary formatting. Save the document and print the worksheet.

Rubric

File: **EL1-U1-SA2-DoctorVisits.xlsx**

Steps	Tasks	Criteria	Value	Score
2	**Feature**	Sort by Doctor and then by Cost of Visit	4	
3	**Feature**	IF statement =IF(E13>600, "Yes Loan", "No Loan"). This statement could also be done IF(E13<=600, "No Loan ", "Yes Loan ")	4	
4	**Finishing**	Formatting new information. Save and print.	2	
		TOTAL POINTS	10	

Date of Visit	Doctor	Cost of Visit	Insurance Pays	Friend Pays	Insurance Response Date
8/28/2012	Goodman	$ 105.00	$ 64.00	$ 41.00	9/30/2012
8/13/2012	Goodman	$ 110.00	$ 68.00	$ 42.00	9/15/2012
8/6/2012	Goodman	$ 113.00	$ 70.40	$ 42.60	9/8/2012
8/8/2012	Goodman	$ 145.00	$ 96.00	$ 49.00	9/10/2012
8/10/2012	Loman	$ 120.00	$ 76.00	$ 44.00	9/12/2012
8/27/2012	Loman	$ 120.00	$ 76.00	$ 44.00	9/29/2012
8/21/2012	Loman	$ 135.00	$ 88.00	$ 47.00	9/23/2012
8/15/2012	Loman	$ 140.00	$ 92.00	$ 48.00	9/17/2012
8/17/2012	Loman	$ 175.00	$ 120.00	$ 55.00	9/19/2012
8/22/2012	Walker	$ 215.00	$ 152.00	$ 63.00	9/24/2012
8/24/2012	Walker	$ 235.00	$ 168.00	$ 67.00	9/26/2012
Total		$ 1,613.00	$ 1,070.40	$ 542.60	
Average		$ 146.64			
Bank Loan				No Loan	

Student Name

EL1-U1-SA2-DoctorVisits.xlsx

Benchmark Excel 2010 Level 1, Unit 2

Supplemental Assessment 1

Instructions

1. Create a workbook named **EL1-U2-SA1-StockPortfolio.xlsx** to track your stock portfolio. Create the following on Sheet1:

Utility Companies	Symbol	# Shares	Closing Price 06/21/2012	Total Value 06/21/2012	Closing Price Current Date	Total Value Current Date	Gain/ Loss	% Gain/ Loss
Ameren Corporation	AEE	50	25.32					
Detroit Edison	DTH	144	37.18					
Southern Company	SO	20	33.92					
Dynegy, Inc.	DYN	16	4.85					
Totals								

2. Rename Sheet1 to *Utilities* and change the tab color to *Green*. Change the page orientation to landscape.
3. Use the Internet to find current stock quotes for each of the utilities above; insert them in the *Closing Price Current Date* column.
4. Insert formulas in the first cell in each column listed below; copy the formula to the other three stocks in the column.
   - Total Value 06/21/2012 = # Shares * Closing Price 06/21/2012
   - Total Value Current Date = # Shares * Closing Price Current Date
   - Gain/Loss = Total Value Current Date - Total Value 06/21/2012
5. Insert formulas in the *Totals* row to calculate the totals for columns C, E, G, H
6. Select cell H6 and define it as *UtilityTotalGL*.
7. Insert a formula in cells I2 through I5 as follows:
   % Gain/Loss = Gain/Loss ÷ UtilityTotalGL (the range you just named in Step 6 above)
8. Format D2:H6 as currency and format I2:I5 as a percentage with 2 places after the decimal.
9. In cell A11, insert a hyperlink using the text *Stock Quotes* to the website used in Step 3.
10. Insert a new row above row 1. Adjust the height to 80. Insert an applicable WordArt title in row 1.
11. Apply borders and shading to enhance the worksheet. Do not use a predefined table style to format the worksheet.
12. Create a copy of the worksheet, insert it before Sheet2, and rename it *Cars*. Change the tab color to *Dark Red*. Change the text of the WordArt title appropriately, change the color of the WordArt title, and change the formatting applied in Step 11 to *Accent 2* colors.
13. Delete row 5.

14. Update columns A, B, C, and D as necessary to match the following:

Automobile Companies	Symbol	# Shares	Closing Price 06/21/2012
Ford	F	60	$11.53
Toyota	TM	25	$71.86
Honda	HMC	45	$30.38

15. Use the Internet to find current stock quotes for each of the car companies above; insert them in the *Closing Price Current Date* column. Be sure the rest of the columns are updated.
16. Select cell H6 and define it as a range named *CarTotalGL*.
17. Change the formula in cells I2:I5 to be as follows:
    % Gain/Loss = Gain/Loss ÷ CarTotalGL (the range you just named in Step 16 above)
18. Rename Sheet 2 (it should be empty) to *Stock Portfolio*. Change the tab color to *Blue*.
19. Adjust the height of row 1 to 80. Insert an applicable WordArt title in row 1.
20. Create the following starting in cell A2:

Company	Gain/Loss	%Gain/Loss
Utilities		
Cars		
Total		

21. Insert a formula in cell B3 that links to the Utilities Total Gain/Loss (H7). Insert a formula in cell B4 that links to the Cars Total Gain/Loss (H6).
22. In cell B5, insert a formula to calculate the total for column B.
23. Insert the following formula in cell C3 and copy the formula to cell C4.
    % Gain/Loss = Gain/Loss ÷ Total Gain/Loss
24. Format C3:C4 as a percentage with 2 places after the decimal.
25. Apply borders and shading to enhance the worksheet. Do not use a predefined table style to format the worksheet.
26. Insert a footer on each Worksheet that includes the file name at the left margin, the page number in the center, and your name at the right margin.
27. Save and print the workbook.

Rubric

File: **EL1-U2-SA1-StockPortfolio.xlsx**

Steps	Tasks	Criteria	Value	Score
1	Typing/ Accuracy	Create Utilities worksheet and enter data Students answers will vary	2	
2,12,18	Feature	Rename and color sheet names for all 3 sheets	3	
3,15	Internet Research	Search Internet and enter data	3	
4,5	Editing	Insert and copy formulas for Total Value 6/21/2010, Gain/Loss, and Totals	4	
6,16	Feature	Name a range or cell UtilityTotalGL, CarTotalGL	2	
7	Editing	Insert formula in Column I	1	
8,24	Format	Format to currency and percentage with 2 decimals	2	
9	Feature	Insert hyperlink	2	
10,12,19	Feature	WordArt on all 3 sheets	3	
11,12,25	Feature	Format worksheet – not predefined style	4	
13,14	Editing	Update Cars sheet	2	
17	Editing	Update formula in Column I	1	
20	Editing	Enter data for Stock Portfolio sheet	2	
21	Feature	Insert a formula that is linked to the other sheets	2	
22,23	Editing	Insert a formula for % Gain Loss and copy Insert total formula	2	

26	Feature	Insert a footer on all three sheets as follows:
		    File name on left
		    Page number in center
		    Student name on right
			3	

27,28	Finishing	Save and print Page numbers at bottom of page should be 1, 2, and 3 as it asks them to print as a workbook.	2	
		TOTAL POINTS	40	

Car Stocks

Car Companies	Symbol	# Shares	Closing Price 06/21/2012		Total Value 06/21/2012	Closing Price Current Date		Total Value Current Date	Gain /Loss		%Gain/Loss
Ford	F	60	$	11.53	$ 691.80	$	11.71	$ 702.60	$	10.80	13.06%
Toyota	TM	25	$	71.86	$ 1,796.50	$	68.22	$ 1,705.50	-$	91.00	-110.04%
Honda	HMC	45	$	30.38	$ 1,367.10	$	34.00	$ 1,530.00	$	162.90	196.98%
Totals		**130**						**$ 3,938.10**	**$**	**82.70**	

Stock Quotes

Student Name

Utility Stocks

Utility Companies	Symbol	# Shares	Closing Price 06/21/2012		Total Value 06/21/2012	Closing Price Current Date		Total Value Current Date	Gain /Loss		%Gain/Loss
Ameren Corporation	AEE	50	$	25.32	$ 1,266.00	$	28.46	$ 1,423.00	$	157.00	39.88%
Detroit Edison	DTH	144	$	37.18	$ 5,353.92	$	38.39	$ 5,528.16	$	174.24	44.26%
Southern Company	SO	20	$	33.92	$ 678.40	$	36.84	$ 736.80	$	58.40	14.84%
Dynegy, Inc.	DYN	16	$	4.85	$ 77.60	$	5.10	$ 81.60	$	4.00	1.02%
Totals		**230**			**$ 7,375.92**			**$ 7,769.56**	**$**	**393.64**	

Stock Quotes

Student Name

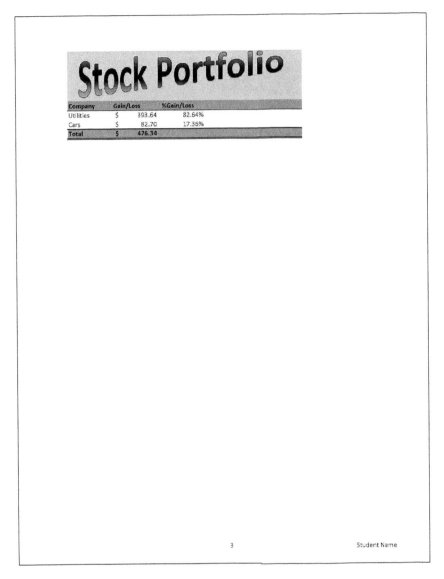

Stock Portfolio

Company	Gain/Loss	%Gain/Loss
Utilities	$ 393.64	82.64%
Cars	$ 82.70	17.36%
Total	$ 476.34	

EL1-U2-SA1-StockPortfolio.xlsx (3 of 3)

Supplemental Assessment 2

Instructions

1. Use a search engine to research roller coaster statistics. Create a worksheet named **EL1-U2-SA2-RollerCoaster.xlsx** that includes the following information for five roller coasters:
   - Name of the coaster
   - Park where it is located
   - State where it is located
   - Length of the ride
   - Top speed
2. Be sure to include an appropriate title and a roller coaster-related clip art image at the top of the worksheet. Format the worksheet with borders and shading.
3. Rename Sheet1 to *Roller Coasters* and change the tab color to *Blue*.
4. Create a pie chart to display the name of the coaster and the length, and a column chart to display the name of the coaster and the top speed. Format both charts to enhance their appearance. Make sure you include an appropriate title. Each chart should appear on its own sheet with an appropriately named tab. On the column chart, draw a thick arrow to the fastest roller coaster. Input appropriate text in the arrow.
5. Insert a footer on each worksheet that includes the file name and sheet name at the left margin, the number of total number of pages in the center, and your name at the right margin.
6. Save and print the workbook.

Rubric

File: **EL1-U2-SA2-RollerCoaster.xlsx**

Steps	Tasks	Criteria	Value	Score
1	**Internet Research**	Research for information on roller coasters, create worksheet and enter data Students answers will vary	4	
2	**Format**	Format the worksheet including borders, shading, and clip art	4	
3,4	**Feature**	Rename and color sheet names	2	
4	**Feature**	Pie chart – create on separate sheet and format	5	
4	**Feature**	Column chart – create on separate sheet and format	5	

5	**Feature**	Insert a footer on all three sheets as follows:
		
		    File name and sheet name on left
		
		    Page number in center
		
		    Student name on right
			3	

6	Finishing	Save and print Page numbers at bottom of page should be 1, 2, and 3 as it asks them to print entire workbook.	2	
		TOTAL POINTS	**25**	

Roller Coasters of America

Name	Park	State	Length	Top Speed
Wicked Twister	Cedar Point	OH	2700	72
Vertical Velocity	Six Flags Great America	IL	630	70
Déjà Vu	Six Flags Great America	IL	1204	65.6
Great Bear	Hersheypark	PA	2800	58
Raptor	Cedar Point	OH	3790	57

EL1-U2-SA2-RollerCoaster-ModelAnswer.xlsxRoller Coaster 1 of 3   Student Name

EL1-U2-SA2-RollerCoaster.xlsx (1 of 3)

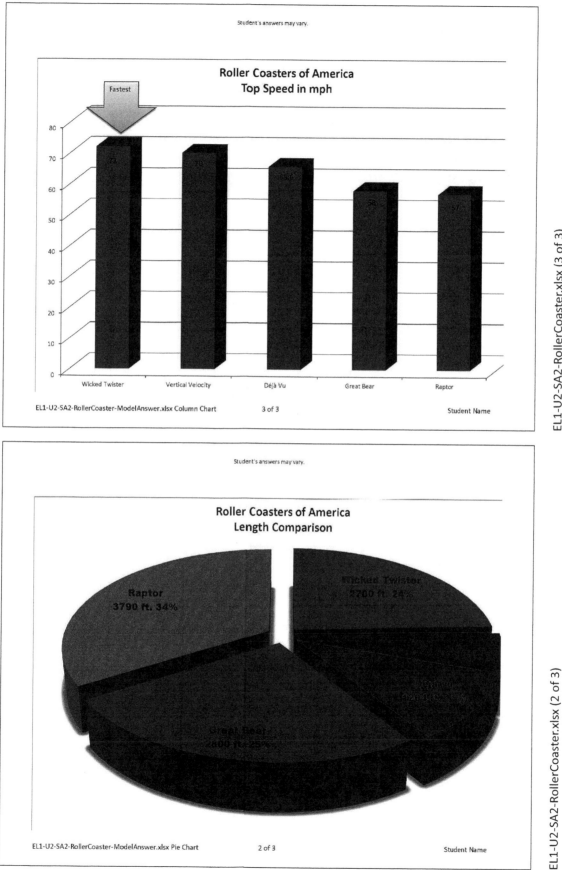

Student's answers may vary.

Roller Coasters of America
Top Speed in mph

Fastest

80
70
60
50
40
30
20
10
0

Wicked Twister   Vertical Velocity   Déjà Vu   Great Bear   Raptor

EL1-U2-SA2-RollerCoaster-ModelAnswer.xlsx Column Chart   3 of 3   Student Name

Student's answers may vary.

Roller Coasters of America
Length Comparison

Raptor
3790 ft. 34%

Wicked Twister
2700 ft. 24%

Great Bear
2800 ft. 25%

EL1-U2-SA2-RollerCoaster-ModelAnswer.xlsx Pie Chart   2 of 3   Student Name

Benchmark Excel 2010, Level 2, Unit 1

Supplemental Assessment 1

Instructions

1. Create a workbook to calculate grades for a computer programming course. Create the following on Sheet1. All column headings should be displayed on one line. Use Merge and Center as shown.

GRADEBOOK										
	Chapter Assignments									
Name	Ch 1	Ch 2	Ch 3	Ch 4	Ch 5	Ch 6	Final	# Missing Assignments	Average	Final Grade
Allister, Roger	85	0	100	0	98	87	54			
Akers, Ann	86	100	92	89	79	89	92			
Cooper, Don	57	98	89	60	99	100	83			
Fredricks, Sandra	78	0	98	84	0	99	86			
Kress, David	0	87	79	87	97	98	92			
Mitchell, Tina	95	94	97	83	87	99	81			
Ortiz, Megan	96	76	86	0	88	79	75			
Sanstein, Joan	87	89	82	90	90	77	80			
Thomas, Jacob	88	94	92	100	95	85	83			
Average										
Distribution of Grades										
A										
B										
C										
D										
F										

2. Rename Sheet1 to *Gradebook*.

3. In column I, calculate the number of missing chapter assignments for each person. An assignment that is missing has a score of 0 entered.

4. In column J, calculate an average for each student's chapter assignments and final. In row 14 for each chapter and final, create an AVERAGEIF function to calculate the average grade for those students who actually received a grade other than 0. Cell J14 should include the average of column J. Format both Row 14 and Column J to show one decimal.

5. In column K, calculate the final grade using a nested IF statement using the guidelines below:

A	93-100
B	85-92
C	77-84
D	70-77
F	69 and below

6. Use conditional formatting in the final grade cell using light red fill with dark red text for any student earning an F.

7. Insert a column after the student names for student numbers. Update the worksheet as follows:

Allister, Roger	546878
Akers, Ann	464548
Cooper, Don	164978
Fredricks, Sandra	312546
Kress, David	335486
Mitchell, Tina	489786
Ortiz, Megan	426927
Sanstein, Joan	513464
Thomas, Jacob	502132

8. In the Distribution of Grades section, use a function to calculate the number of students who have earned each grade. Merge and center the title across the two columns. Add a border around the Distribution of Grades section.

9. Add a header to the worksheet; it should include your name at the left and the sheet name at the right.

10. Add additional formatting to the worksheet as necessary. Do not use a predefined table style to format the worksheet.

11. Save the worksheet as **EL2-U1-SA1-Gradebook**. Print the worksheet so that it fits on one page.

12. Hide all columns except the student number and final grade. Hide rows 14 to 21. Print the worksheet again.

13. Unhide the columns and the rows and save the worksheet again using the same name (**EL2-U1-SA1-Gradebook**).

Rubric

Note: Answers will vary.

File: EL2-U1-SA1-Gradebook.xlsx

Steps	Tasks	Criteria	Value	Score*
1	Editing	Create the worksheet as shown	5	
2	Editing	Rename Sheet 1 to *Gradebook*	1	
3	Feature	***Note: Columns will vary from instructions as a column is added in instruction 7.*** Column J - # of missing assignments =COUNTIF(C4:I4,0)	3	
4	Feature	Column K - Average for chapter assignments and final =AVERAGE(C4:I4)	3	
	Feature	Row 14 – AVERAGEIF to calculate average >0 =AVERAGEIF(C4:C12,">0")	3	
	Editing	Format to Column K and Row 14 to one decimal	2	
5	Feature	Column L, nested IF to calculate grade =IF(K4>=93,"A",IF(K4>=85,"B",IF(K4>=77,"C",IF(K4>=70,"D","F"))))	4	
6	Editing	Conditional formatting Column L – Red fill and text for an F grade	2	
7	Editing	Insert column and add student numbers in Column B	2	
8	Feature	Distribution of Grades. In the next row, the "A" will vary to "B", etc. =COUNTIF($L$4:$L$12,"A")	5	
9	Editing	Header to include name at left and sheet name at right	2	
10	Editing	Additional formatting such as bolding, shading, etc.	2	
11	Editing	Save worksheet and print on one page	2	
12	Editing	Hide all columns except student number and final grade Hide rows Print the worksheet	3	
13	Finishing	Unhide the columns and rows and save.	1	
		TOTAL POINTS	40	

GRADEBOOK

Name	Student Number	Chapter Assignments						Final	# Missing Assignments	Average	Final Grade
		Ch 1	Ch 2	Ch 3	Ch 4	Ch 5	Ch 6				
Allister, Roger	546878	85	0	100	0	98	87	54	2	60.6	F
Akers, Ann	464548	86	100	92	89	79	89	92	0	89.6	B
Cooper, Don	164978	57	98	89	60	99	100	83	0	83.7	C
Fredricks, Sandra	312546	78	0	98	84	0	99	86	2	63.6	F
Kress, David	335486	0	87	79	87	97	98	92	1	77.1	C
Mitchell, Tina	489786	95	94	97	83	87	99	81	0	90.9	B
Ortiz, Megan	426927	96	76	86	0	88	79	75	1	71.4	D
Sanstein, Joan	513464	87	89	82	90	90	77	80	0	85.0	B
Thomas, Jacob	502132	88	94	92	100	95	87	83	0	91.3	B
Average		84.0	91.1	90.6	84.7	91.6	90.6	80.7		79.2	C

Distribution of Grades	
A	0
B	4
C	2
D	1
F	2

GRADEBOOK

Student Number	Final Grade
546878	F
464548	B
164978	C
312546	F
335486	C
489786	B
426927	D
513464	B
502132	B

Supplemental Assessment 2

Instructions

1. Open the file **EL2-U1-SA2-LabRevenue-DataFile.xlsx** that was provided with this project. Save the file as **EL2-U2-SA2-LabRevenue**.

2. Add a header to both worksheets; it should include your name at the left and the sheet name at the right.

3. The *Revenue* worksheet contains information for a diagnostic laboratory. It tracks the doctor's ID, the doctor's name, the location number where patients go to have their testing done, and the monthly revenue received from each location. The Locations worksheet contains the address information for each location number.

4. Search the Internet to find a diagnostic laboratory that is located in your city. Find five different locations around your city for this laboratory. On the Locations worksheet, fill in the missing address information. Print the worksheet.

5. In the Revenue worksheet, convert the laboratory revenue data to a table. Adjust each column width so that the headers can be read.

6. Add a formula in column P to calculate the yearly revenue. Provide an appropriate header and adjust the column width.

7. Create a validation rule, input message, and error alert for locations in the Revenue worksheet. The location must be 1, 2, 3, 4, or 5.

8. Filter the data to show only Location 1. Print page 1.

9. Create a copy of the Revenue worksheet and rename the copy *Revenue Subtotal*. Calculate subtotals for each month and calculate yearly revenue at each change in name. Adjust column widths where needed and then display the second outline level. Print page 1.

10. Create a copy of the Revenue Subtotal worksheet and rename the copy *PivotTable Data*. On the PivotTable Data worksheet, remove the subtotaling. Create a PivotTable report on Sheet2 to summarize the revenue received by each doctor (*Name*) for January, February, and March. Change the sheet name to *PivotTable*.

11. Add a PivotChart below the PivotTable, using a column style. Add an appropriate title to the PivotChart.

12. In Column E of the PivotTable worksheet create an appropriate Sparkline. Show the high point.

13. Add a header to the worksheet; it should include your name at the left and the sheet name at the right.

14. Adjust the worksheet so that it prints on one page and print the worksheet.

15. Save **EL2-U1-SP2-LabRevenue.xlsx**.

Rubric

File: **EL2-U1-SP2-LabRevenue.xlsx**

Steps	Tasks	Criteria	Value	Score*
1	Editing	Open and save the workbook with a different name	1	
2	Editing	Header to include name at left and sheet name at right	2	
4	Research/ Editing	Search Internet to find diagnostic laboratories Insert locations on Locations worksheet and print	3	
5	Feature	Convert laboratory revenue to a table Adjust column widths so all data can be seen	2	
6	Feature/ Editing	Column P – calculate yearly revenue Format and adjust column width	2	
7	Feature	Validation rule, input message and error alert for locations Location must be 1, 2, 3, 4, or 5	3	
8	Feature	Filter data to show only Location 1	3	
	Finishing	Print page 1	1	
9	Editing	Create a copy and name it *Revenue Subtotal*	1	
	Feature	Calculate subtotals for each month and yearly revenue at each change in name	4	
	Feature	Display the second outline level	2	
	Finishing	Print page 1	1	
10	Editing	Create a copy of Revenue Subtotal and rename it *PivotTable Data*	1	
	Feature	Create a PivotTable report on Sheet2 to summarize revenue received by each doctor for Jan, Feb, and Mar	4	
	Editing	Change Sheet Name to *PivotTable*	1	
11	Feature	Create PivotChart below PivotTable Column style Title	3	
12	Feature	Column E of PivotTable, add a Sparkline Show the high point	3	
13	Editing	Header to include student name at left and sheet name at right	2	
14	Finishing	Adjust worksheet to print on one page and print	2	
		TOTAL POINTS	41	

Page 1 of 3

ID	Name	Location	Jan	Feb	Mar
5001	Dr. Jon MacIntre	1	546	678	789
5002	Dr. Bill McGillicudy	1	-	-	13
5003	Dr. Sam Brown	1	-	2	-
5004	Dr. Jill Graham	1	111	116	112
5005	Dr. Jack Blundell	1	543	489	554
5006	Dr. Gertrude Fellder	1	16	-	-
5007	Dr. Anthony James	1	-	-	13
5008	Dr. Rebecca Sullivan	1	543	456	645
5009	Dr. David Merriweather	1	546	678	789
5010	Dr. Samantha Star	1	-	-	13
5011	Dr. William Markus	1	-	2	-
5012	Dr. Alexander Williamson	1	111	116	112
5013	Dr. Noah Webster	1	124	129	125
5014	Dr. Jake Russel	1	503	635	746
5015	Dr. Benjamin Broach	1	208	213	209
5016	Dr. Susan Whitby	1	221	226	222
5017	Dr. Seth O'scope	1	543	456	645
5018	Dr. L. Ivor	1	546	678	789
5019	Dr. Moe Trin	1	-	-	13
5020	Dr. Imma Patient	1	124	129	125

EL2-U1-SA2-LabRevenue-ModelAnswer(Step8).xlsx (Page 1 of 3)

Page 2 of 3

Laboratory Revenue

Apr	May	Jun	Jul	Aug	Sep	Oct
621	487	358	349	299	320	450
-	-	-	-	-	17	-
-	-	-	34	-	-	123
122	136	111	101	136	111	-
576	586	486	489	521	543	554
-	-	-	23	-	-	-
-	-	-	-	-	17	-
437	234	103	100	112	278	299
621	487	358	349	299	320	450
-	-	-	34	-	17	-
-	-	-	-	-	-	123
122	136	111	101	136	111	136
135	149	124	114	149	124	407
578	444	315	306	256	277	220
219	233	208	198	233	208	450
232	487	358	349	299	320	450
437	487	358	349	299	320	-
621	-	-	34	-	17	-
-	-	-	-	-	-	-
135	150	155	151	161	176	181

EL2-U1-SA2-LabRevenue-ModelAnswer(Step8).xlsx (Page 2 of 3)

ID	Name	Location	Laboratory Revenue				
			Jan	Feb	Mar	Apr	May
	Dr. Jon MacIntre Total		722	805	977	841	755
	Dr. Bill McGillicudy Total		761	844	1,029	880	770
	Dr. Sam Brown Total		739	801	971	835	725
	Dr. Jill Graham Total		690	588	713	767	801
	Dr. Jack Blundell Total		952	805	1,013	1,084	1,156
	Dr. Gertrude Feilder Total		842	825	839	881	919
	Dr. Anthony James Total		211	243	209	206	220
	Dr. Rebecca Sullivan Total		1,255	1,124	1,383	1,259	1,132
	Dr. David Merriweather Total		722	805	977	841	755
	Dr. Samantha Star Total		761	844	1,029	880	770
	Dr. William Markus Total		739	801	971	835	725
	Dr. Alexander Williamson Total		690	588	713	767	801
	Dr. Noah Webster Total		847	991	1,092	944	838
	Dr. Jake Russel Total		2,340	2,869	3,312	2,640	2,104
	Dr. Benjamin Broach Total		1,768	2,042	2,256	1,940	1,700
	Dr. Susan Whitby Total		1,351	1,435	1,606	1,470	755
	Dr. Steth O'scope Total		563	521	725	538	755
	Dr. L. Ivor Total		722	805	977	841	770
	Dr. Moe Trin Total		761	844	1,029	880	725
	Dr. Imma Patient Total		1,284	1,298	1,506	1,229	1,211
	Grand Total		18,720	19,878	23,327	20,558	18,387

Nov	Dec	Yearly Revenue
678	765	6,340
-	-	30
-	-	36
112	131	1,422
576	596	6,513
51	-	90
-	-	30
301	587	4,095
678	765	6,340
-	-	30
-	-	36
112	131	1,422
125	96	1,530
635	722	5,824
209	228	2,586
678	765	4,607
-	765	5,787
-	-	2,651
-	-	47
177	187	1,851

PivotTable

Row Labels	Values			Sparkline
	Sum of Jan	Sum of Feb	Sum of Mar	
Dr. Alexander Williamson	690	588	713	
Dr. Anthony James	211	243	209	
Dr. Benjamin Broach	1768	2042	2256	
Dr. Bill McGillicudy	761	844	1029	
Dr. David Merriweather	722	805	977	
Dr. Gertrude Feilder	842	825	839	
Dr. Imma Patient	1284	1298	1506	
Dr. Jack Blundell	952	805	1013	
Dr. Jake Russel	2340	2869	3312	
Dr. Jill Graham	690	588	713	
Dr. Jon MacIntre	722	805	977	
Dr. L. Ivor	722	805	977	
Dr. Moe Trin	761	844	1029	
Dr. Noah Webster	847	991	1092	
Dr. Rebecca Sullivan	1255	1124	1383	
Dr. Sam Brown	739	801	971	
Dr. Samantha Star	761	844	1029	
Dr. Steth O'scope	563	521	725	
Dr. Susan Whitby	1351	1435	1606	
Dr. William Markus	739	801	971	
Grand Total	18720	19878	23327	

Jan - March Doctor Summary

EL2-U1-SA2-LabRevenue-ModelAnswer(Step14).xlsx

Revenue Subtotal

Jun	Jul	Aug	Sep.	Oct	Nov	Dec	Yearly Revenue
477	461	478	496	676	888	1,029	8,605
539	500	517	552	688	927	1,058	9,065
471	510	472	490	643	882	1,008	8,547
576	595	671	690	724	802	816	8,433
781	760	961	964	1,021	1,054	1,171	11,722
769	775	881	826	861	912	971	10,301
218	208	247	212	207	247	272	2,700
701	687	907	990	1,081	1,128	1,537	13,184
477	461	478	496	676	888	1,029	8,605
539	500	517	552	688	927	1,058	9,065
471	510	472	490	643	882	1,008	8,547
576	595	671	690	724	802	816	8,433
659	676	650	621	775	1,071	1,058	10,222
1,588	1,575	1,352	1,436	1,956	2,913	3,216	27,301
1,392	1,354	1,324	1,316	1,600	2,034	2,198	20,924
477	461	478	496	676	888	1,029	11,122
477	461	478	496	676	888	1,029	7,607
539	500	517	552	688	927	1,058	8,896
471	510	472	490	643	882	1,008	8,715
945	948	854	879	1,135	1,654	1,798	14,741
13,143	13,047	13,397	13,734	16,781	21,596	24,167	216,735

EL2-U1-SA2-LabRevenue-ModelAnswer(Step9).xlsx (Page 2 of 2)

Benchmark Excel 2010 Level 2, Unit 2

Supplemental Assessment 1

Instructions

You are considering purchasing a new home with a price of $156,500. From the sale of a previous home and your savings, you plan on a down payment of $30,000.

1. Create a worksheet similar to the one below to calculate your monthly house payment (not including any taxes).

Insert house clip art here	Calculating an Affordable House Payment					
	Selling Price	Down Payment	Interest Rate	Term in Years	Length of Loan in Years	Monthly Payment
	$ 156,500	$ 30,000		10	30	
	$ 156,500	$ 30,000		7	15	

2. Research local mortgage rates to perform the calculations; find a fair rate for a 15-year and a 30-year mortgage and include them in your worksheet.
3. Use a function to calculate the monthly house payment.
4. Assume you decide that, if you take the 30-year mortgage, you cannot afford a monthly payment higher than $850. Use Goal Seek to determine how much of a down payment would be necessary to bring the house payment down to $850.
5. Assume you decide that, if you take the 15-year mortgage, you cannot afford a monthly payment higher than $1,000. Use Goal Seek to determine how low the interest rate must be to bring the house payment down to $1,000.
6. Apply formatting of your choice to the worksheet.
7. Add a header to the worksheet that includes your name in the center.
8. Save the worksheet as **EL2-U2-SA1-HousePayment** with the password *L2U2PMT* to open it. Close the worksheet and exit Excel.
9. Open Excel and then open **EL2-U2-SA1-HousePayment.xlsx** using the correct password. Print the worksheet so that it fits on one page. Save and then close **EL2-U2-SA1-HousePayment**.

Rubric

Notes: Answers will vary.

Supplemental Assessment 1

File name: **EL2-U2-SA1-HousePayment.xlsx**

Steps	Tasks	Criteria	Value	Score*
1	File Management/ Typing	Create worksheet and enter data	5	
	Editing	Insert clip art	2	
2	Research/Typing	Search Internet for 15- and 30-year mortgage interest rates. Input rates into worksheet.	4	
3	Feature	Calculate monthly house payments using PMT function	3	
4	Feature	Goal Seek – 30 yr – monthly payment $850, interest rate stays the same, find down payment.	4	
5	Feature	Goal Seek – 15 yr – monthly payment $1000, find interest rate.	4	
6	Editing	Format worksheet	3	
7	Editing/Typing	Header – name in center	2	
8	Feature	Password protect with *L2U2PMT* as the password	2	
9	Finishing	Open with password; print, save, and close	1	
		TOTAL POINTS	30	

Calculating an Affordable House Payment

Selling Price	Down Payment	Interest Rate	Term	Length of Loan in Years	Monthly Payment
$156,500	$ 40,107	7.95%	10	30	$850.00
$156,500	$ 30,000	4.99%	7	15	$1,000.00

Student answers may vary.

EL2-U2-SA1-HousePayment-ModelAnswer(Step9).xlsx

Supplemental Assessment 2

Instructions

1. At a blank worksheet, in cell A1, create a macro and name it *Font*. Use an appropriate description. The macro should change the font to Bookman Old Style 12 pt, and autofit the column. Assign the macro to the Ctrl + Shift + L shortcut.
2. Import the **EL2-U2-SA-Mileage-DataFile.txt** file into a worksheet.
3. Merge and center the worksheet title over the worksheet.
4. Run the macro in cells A3, B3, C3, D3. Autofit the columns.
5. Use the Internet to determine the mileage between the home city (St. Louis) and each destination. Enter them in Column C.
6. Save the workbook as a macro-enabled workbook with the name **EL2-U2-SA2-Mileage**. Add a header to the worksheet; it should include your name at the left and the sheet name at the right. Print the worksheet.
7. In Cell E3, put the heading *Cost*. Apply the Font macro. If the cost per mile is $.30, calculate the cost for each location. Format the cell to currency with two decimal points.
8. Use the Paste Special function and paste the values (not the formulas) in column E. Autofit the column if necessary. Merge and center the title again.
9. Apply formatting of your choice to the worksheet.
10. Save and print **EL2-U2-SA2-Mileage.xlsm**.
11. Open **EL2-U2-SA2-TravelRoutesMemo-DataFile.docx**. Add your instructor's name and your name as indicated. Update the date to the current date. Save as **EL2-U2-SA2-TravelRoutesMemo**. Embed the data from the Sheet1 worksheet of **EL2-U2-SA2-Mileage.xlsx** at the end of the memo. Remember to go back and enable the macros.
12. Save and print the memo.

Rubric

File names: **EL2-U2-SA2-Mileage.xlsx, EL2-U2-SA2-Travel-Routes-Memo.docx**

Steps	Tasks	Criteria	Value	Score*
1	Feature	Create a macro named *Font* Add appropriate description Ctrl + Shirt + L = Shortcut font = Bookman Old Style 12 pt Autofit the column	5	
2	Feature	Import mileage text file	3	
3	Editing	Merge and center title	1	
4	Feature	Run macro from A3:D3	2	
5	Research/Typing	Determine mileage between St. Louis and each destination. Enter data in Column C.	5	

6	Finishing	Save workbook as macro-enabled Add header with student name at left and sheet name at right Print worksheet	2	
7	Feature/Editing	Column E heading: *Cost*. Apply macro. Calculate cost at $0.30/mile. Format to currency with two decimals.	3	
8	Feature	Use Paste Special to paste values instead of formulas in the column.	3	
9	Editing	Format	3	
10	Finishing	Save and print the worksheet.	1	
11	Editing/Feature	Open TravelRoutesMemo Add names Update date Embed worksheet at end of memo Enable the macros	4	
12	Finishing	Save and print the memo	2	
		TOTAL POINTS	34	

Sheet1

Student Name

Gateway Trucking Travel Routes

	Delivery Day	Mileage	Truck	Cost
Atlanta, GA	Monday	556	A	$ 166.80
Detroit, MI	Monday	648	B	$ 194.40
Philadelphia, PA	Monday	238	D	$ 71.40
Kansas City, MO	Monday	1287	F	$ 386.10
Little Rock, AR	Tuesday	1367	E	$ 410.10
Milwaukee, WI	Tuesday	921	B	$ 276.30
Denver, CO	Tuesday	1814	C	$ 544.20
Detroit, MI	Wednesday	648	I	$ 194.40
Chicago, IL	Wednesday	820	F	$ 246.00
Dallas, TX	Wednesday	1682	E	$ 504.60
San Diego, CA	Wednesday	2898	G	$ 869.40
Philadelphia, PA	Thursday	238	H	$ 71.40
Little Rock, AR	Thursday	1367	A	$ 410.10
Denver, CO	Thursday	1814	D	$ 544.20
Louisville, KY	Friday	830	F	$ 249.00
Milwaukee, WI	Friday	921	B	$ 276.30

EL2-U2-SA2-Mileage-ModelAnswer.xlsx

Memo

To: Instructor Name

From: Student Name

Date: 7/31/2012

Re: Travel Routes

Below you will find the trucking travel routes. The distance has been calculated from our warehouse to the warehouse at each location listed below. If you need further information please contact me.

Gateway Trucking Travel Routes			
	Delivery Day	Mileage	Truck	Cost
Atlanta, GA	Monday	556	A	$166.80
Detroit, MI	Monday	648	B	$194.40
Philadelphia, PA	Monday	238	D	$ 71.40
Kansas City, MO	Monday	1287	F	$386.10
Little Rock, AR	Tuesday	1367	E	$410.10
Milwaukee, WI	Tuesday	921	B	$276.30
Denver, CO	Tuesday	1814	C	$544.20
Detroit, MI	Wednesday	648	I	$194.40
Chicago, IL	Wednesday	820	F	$246.00
Dallas, TX	Wednesday	1682	E	$504.60
San Diego, CA	Wednesday	2898	G	$869.40
Philadelphia, PA	Thursday	238	H	$ 71.40
Little Rock, AR	Thursday	1367	A	$410.10
Denver, CO	Thursday	1814	D	$544.20
Louisville, KY	Friday	830	F	$249.00
Milwaukee, WI	Friday	921	B	$276.30

1

EL2-U2-SA2-TravelRoutesMemo-ModelAnswer.xlsx

Benchmark Excel 2010 Level 1
Final Case Study

Scenario: You are on a temporary work assignment at Body Mechanics & Rehabilitation. BMR provides physiotherapy, massage therapy and accident rehabilitation. Your expertise in Excel has been requested to assist management in preparing some spreadsheets required for an upcoming meeting. As you work through each activity, additional information will be provided as needed.

This case study will allow you to exercise creativity and polish your Excel skills. In each activity, specific step-by-step instructions may not be provided to simulate a more realistic workplace assignment. Some instructions may appear vague or not comprehensive, but they are purposefully open-ended to allow each student to do original work and showcase individual creativity in problem solving.

Part 1

1. Use an Excel template to create a new sales invoice. Name the worksheet **EL1-FCS-Receipt**. Fill in the worksheet with information of your choosing, making sure that you include at least the following information. In Step 1e, replace *Student Name* with your name. Format to enhance the appearance of the invoice.
   a. Name of company
   b. Address, phone number, and email of the clinic
   c. Name and address of the customer
   d. Current date
   e. One 60-minute massage provided by *Student Name* at a price of $74.00
   f. Add 13% sales tax.
   g. Insert the logo called **EL1-FCS-BMRLogo-DataFile.jpg**.
2. Save and print the worksheet.

Part 2

1. Create a new workbook called **EL1-FCS-Treatment.xlsx**.
2. Place the following information on Sheet1.

Week	Number of		
	30-Minute Treatments	45-Minute Treatments	60-Minute Treatments
Wk 1	3	6	0
Wk 2	5	3	6
Wk 3	8	1	2
Wk 4	2	0	7
Schedule of Fees			
60 minutes	$74		
45 minutes	$60		
30 minutes	$50		

3. Rename the sheet to *Treatments*. Change the color of the tab to blue.
4. Determine the following:
    a) The total number of treatments each week
    b) The total number of 30-, 45-, and 60-minute treatments over four weeks
    c) The average number of 30-, 45-, and 60-minute treatments over four weeks
    d) The weekly income
    e) The monthly income
    f) The total number of minutes worked each week
5. Use an IF statement to determine whether the clinic has met its goal of earning at least $480 per week. If the weekly income is $480 or more, the IF statement should return the value *Target met*; if the weekly income is less than $480, the statement should return the value *Target not met*.

Part 3

1. In row 1, insert the name of the company as WordArt.
2. Insert the logo called **EL1-FCS-BMRLogo-DataFile.jpg**.
3. Add an appropriate clip art image.
4. Format the spreadsheet to enhance its appearance including shading and borders.

Part 4

1. Create a pie chart that shows the total number of treatments on a weekly basis. Place the chart on a new sheet. Name the sheet appropriately and color the tab.
2. Add a title and the company logo (**EL1-FCS-BMRLogo-DataFile.jpg**). Format the chart to enhance the appearance. Include week numbers on each piece and what percent of the monthly income each piece represents.

Part 5

1. Copy the Treatments worksheet to a new sheet. Rename the sheet *Increase*. Change the color of the tab.
2. Increase the fees by 10%. Show zero decimals. Make sure the weekly and monthly income formulas change.
3. Change the title to *Tentative 10% Increase*.

Part 6

1. Put your name and the page number as a footer on each worksheet. Ensure that each sheet prints on one page. Print the workbook.
2. Submit all electronic copies of files and folders to your instructor, along with any printouts.

Benchmark Excel 2010 Level 1
Final Case Study Rubric

Files: **EL1-FCS-Receipt.xlsx, EL1-FCS-Treatment.xlsx**

Steps	Tasks	Criteria	Value	Score
		Note: Student's answer may vary.		
Part 1 1	Organization/ Accuracy/ Editing	Create a workbook using a sales invoice template.	3	
a-g	Editing	Add • Name of the company • Address, phone number and email of the clinic • Name and address of the customer • Today's date • One 60-minute massage provided by *Student Name* at a price of $74.00 • Add 13% sales tax • Insert the logo	5	
3	Feature	Print the worksheet	2	
Part 2 1,2	Feature/Editing	Create workbook and enter information	5	
3	Feature	Rename sheet and color tab	2	
4	Feature	Determine the following: • The total number of treatments each week • The total number of 30-, 45-, and 60-minute treatments over 4 weeks • The average number of 30-, 45-, and 60-minute treatments over 4 weeks • The weekly income • The monthly income	10	
5	Feature	IF statement	5	
Part 3 1	Feature	Name of company as WordArt	3	
2	Feature	Insert logo	2	
3	Feature	Clip art	3	
3	Feature	Format to enhance the worksheet Include shading and borders	5	
Part 4 1	Feature	Create a pie chart	5	
1	Feature	Separate sheet Rename sheet and color tab	2	
2	Feature	Add a title and logo Format the chart Add % and week numbers	4	

Steps	Tasks	Criteria	Value	Score
Part 5 **1**	**Feature**	Copy Treatments sheet and rename it *Increase* Change the color of the tab	3	
2	**Feature/Editing**	Increase the fees by 10%	3	
3	**Editing**	Change title	2	
Part 6 **1**	**Feature**	Name and page number as footer	3	
1	**Feature**	Print the workbook Each page should be landscape Check numbering at bottom of page	5	
		TOTAL POINTS	**72**	

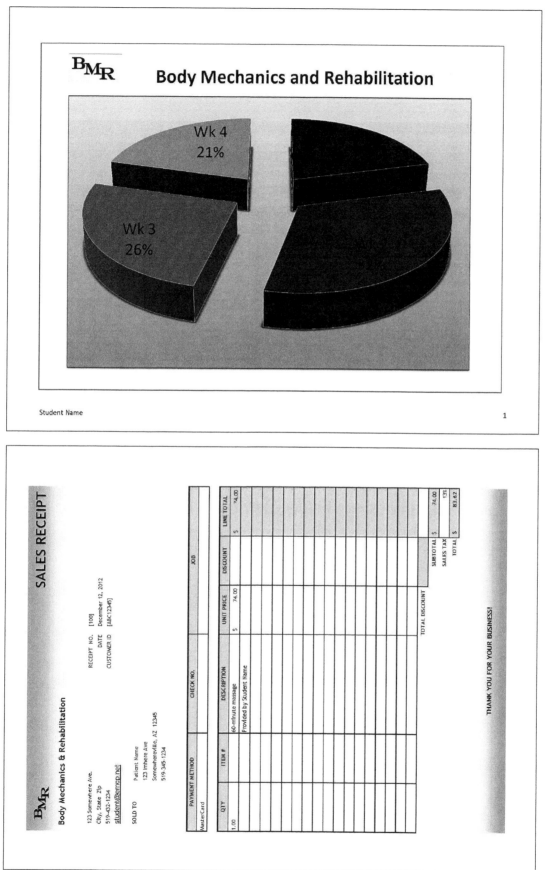

Student Name

1

BM**R**

TENTATIVE 10% INCREASE

Week	Number of			Total Number of Treatments	Weekly Income	
	30-Minute Treatments	45-Minute Treatments	60-Minute Treatments			
Wk 1	3	6	0	9	$ 561	Target not met
Wk 2	5	3	6	14	$ 961	Target met
Wk 3	8	1	2	11	$ 669	Target not met
Wk 4	2	0	7	9	$ 680	Target met
Total Number of Treatments	18	10	15			
Average Number of Treatments	4.5	2.5	3.75			
Total Monthly Income					$ 2,871	

Schedule of Fees	
60 minutes	$ 81
45 minutes	$ 66
30 minutes	$ 55

BM**R**

BODY MECHANICS AND REHABILITATION

Week	Number of			Total Number of Treatments	Weekly Income	
	30-Minute Treatments	45-Minute Treatments	60-Minute Treatments			
Wk 1	3	6	0	9	$ 510	Target not met
Wk 2	5	3	6	14	$ 874	Target met
Wk 3	8	1	2	11	$ 608	Target not met
Wk 4	2	0	7	9	$ 618	Target met
Total Number of Treatments	18	10	15			
Average Number of Treatments	4.5	2.5	3.75			
Total Monthly Income					$ 2,610	

Schedule of Fees	
60 minutes	$ 74
45 minutes	$ 60
30 minutes	$ 50

Benchmark Excel 2010 Level 2
Final Case Study

Scenario: You are on a temporary work assignment at Worldwide Enterprises located in New York. Worldwide Enterprises distributes independent movies to cinemas around the world. Your expertise in Excel has been requested to assist management with various data analysis tasks. As you work through each activity, additional information will be provided as needed.

This case study will allow you to exercise creativity and polish your Excel skills. In each activity, specific step-by-step instructions will not be provided to simulate a more realistic workplace assignment. Some instructions may appear vague or not comprehensive, but they are purposefully open-ended to allow each student to do original work and showcase individual creativity in problem solving.

Activity 1

The manager of Human Resources has downloaded a text file from the company's accounting system. She wants you to create a table. To begin this activity, locate and copy the data file named **EL2-FCS-EmployeeDeptAndSalaryInfo-DataFile.txt**.

a. Import the text file into a new Excel workbook and then adjust column widths as necessary. *Note: This file is in comma-delimited format.*

b. Use Save As to save the workbook in Excel Workbook and name it **EmployeeInfo-Macros.xlsx**.

c. Rename the worksheet **EmployeeDeptAndSalaryInfo**.

d. The human resources manager is concerned about upcoming salary increases. She wants to do some analysis before negotiations begin with each department manager. Using the **EmployeeDeptAndSalaryInfo** worksheet, add statistics to the bottom of the worksheet as follows:

   i) The sum of the salaries for staff in all departments.

   ii) Calculate the total salaries for each department. *Hint: Use the SUMIF function to calculate the total for each department.*

e. In a separate area adjacent to the statistics created in step d, create labels similar to the ones shown below.

Projected Salary Costs for 2012:		
Wage Increase	2.5%	
European Distribution		
North American Distribution		
Overseas Distribution		

Enter formulas to calculate the projected salary costs for each department if a 2.5% wage increase is granted and then calculate the total cost of all salaries at the increased wage. Use an absolute reference for the wage increase.

f. The Human Resources manager is concerned that the wages for the Overseas Distribution department are too high. She wants to know what the wage increase percent would be if she capped the total wages for 2012 for that department at $620,000. Use Goal Seek to find the answer. Do not click OK to change the percent since this salary ceiling affects only one department. Instead, type a note to the manager inside a cell below the projected salary costs in which you state the result that Goal Seek calculated. At this time, the manager is only looking at various wage options; no firm decisions have been made.

g. To further prepare for upcoming wage increase negotiations, the Human Resources manager has asked you to create three versions of projected wage costs for 2012. She wants the three versions stored in scenarios to keep the worksheet uncluttered and avoid confusion. The president has directed the maximum wage increase is 2.5%; however, the company's goal is to settle somewhat lower than this at 1.5%. The manager wants a third scenario calculated that settles the wage increase halfway between the other two rates. Name the three scenarios *Maximum Increase*, *Goal Increase*, and *Compromise Increase*, respectively. Save the revised worksheet with the Goal Increase scenario displayed. Create a scenario summary report.

h. Format the worksheet as necessary to produce a professional appearance. Set print options so that the worksheet fits on one page in landscape orientation in an attractive layout. Exclude any cells used for criteria ranges in the print area. Set up a custom header that identifies the printout as *Projected Salary Costs for 2012*. In a custom footer, add your name, the current date, and any other identifying information you routinely use in the course. Save the revised workbook.

Activity 2

The Human Resources manager has asked you to add the following properties to the workbook:

Author	Student Name
Subject	Your course code
Keywords	Employee, Department, Salary
Comments	Any changes must be authorized by the Human Resources Manager

You also need to create macros with shortcut keys that the Human Resources manager can use to perform the following sorts on the salary records within the worksheet:

a. Ctrl + Shirt + B - Sort all of the salary records first by department in ascending order, then by annual salary in descending order, and then by last name in ascending order.

b. Ctrl + Shirt + C - Sort all of the salary records first by year of hire in descending order, then by department in ascending order, and then by last name in ascending order.

c. Ctrl + Shirt + D - Sort all of the salary records by employee number in ascending order.

Begin each macro with a Go To command that will ensure the active cell is moved to a cell within the list before opening the Sort dialog box. Make sure you put in proper descriptions. Name the macros *SalaryByDept*, *SalaryByYear*, and *SalaryByEmpNo*, respectively.

Save the revised workbook as a macro-enabled workbook.

Activity 3

The workbook you have been editing for the Human Resources manager contains confidential salary information. After discussing security issues with her, you have agreed to secure the data using the following methods:

a. Delete the Scenario Summary worksheet. Make active the EmployeeDeptAndSalaryInfo worksheet. Add a comment to the cell containing the wage increase percentage. The comment should inform the reader that three scenarios for wage increases have been stored and then inform the user how to open the Scenarios dialog box.

b. Use the Save As function and save the workbook as **EmployeeInfo-Password**. Assign the following password to open the workbook: *L2FCS*. ***Note: Passwords are case sensitive. Be sure you type the password as shown.***

c. Assign the following password to protect the worksheet: *L2FCS*. Close the **EmployeeInfo-Password.xlsx** workbook.

Activity 4

The Human Resources manager has asked you to research inflation rates on the Internet. Inflation is measured based on the change in the consumer price index (CPI). You need to find the projected inflation rate for 20XX (use the current year). This information will help management with the upcoming salary negotiations. To begin this activity, locate the student data file **WorldwideLogo.bmp**.

a. Using **EmployeeInfo-Macros.xlsx** insert a new worksheet into the workbook named *InflationProjection* and change the tab color to red. Position the new sheet to the right of the EmployeeDeptAndSalaryInfo sheet. Enter the projected inflation rate for 20XX, describe the source of the information, and include a hyperlink to the website from which you obtained the projection. ***Hint: Make sure you locate inflation predictions for the United States. Government agencies often track and forecast economic data such as inflation rates. Consider starting your search from a government source such as the U.S. Department of Commerce Economics and Statistics Administration.***

b. A few rows below the hyperlink, locate a web page that provides historical data on the consumer price index (CPI). Try to find a site that provides 10 years of historical CPI data. The Human Resources manager can use this historical information to compare current inflation with historical rates and the 20XX projected rate. Import the data from the web page into the worksheet using the Web Query feature if the historical data is presented in table format on the web page. If the data is not in a table, use another method to import the data. Above the imported data, include a description of the source from which you obtained the history and the URL of the source.

c. Embed the company's logo (**WorldwideLogo.bmp**) at the top of the InflationProjection worksheet.

d. Below the imported historical CPI data, create and format a chart that plots the CPI. Depending on your data, decide to plot either the monthly CPI for the most recent 12-month history, or, the annual CPI for the previous five years. Add a trendline to the chart to predict the future CPI.

e. Set print options so that the worksheet fits on one page. You determine if the best output is portrait or landscape orientation. Set up a custom header that identifies the printout as *Inflation Research for Salary Negotiations*. In a custom footer, add your name, the current date, and any other identifying information you routinely use in the course. Save the revised workbook.

Submit the electronic copies of the following files to your instructor:
> EmployeeInfo-Macros.xlsx
> EmployeeInfo-Macros.xlsm
> EmployeeInfo-Password.xlsm

Keep a copy of all files completed in this case study until you have received your grade.

Benchmark Excel 2010 Level 2
Final Case Study Rubric

Note: Answers will vary.

File names: **EmployeeInfo-Macros.xlsx, EmployeeInfo-Macros.xlsm, EmployeeInfo-Password.xlsm**

Step	Tasks	Criteria	Value	Score
1 a, b	File Management/ Feature	File named properly and data imported correctly.	3	
c	Editing	Rename worksheet	1	
d	Feature	Totals calculated – grand total and each department's total salaries (SumIF).	6	
e	Feature	Projected salaries for 2012 labeled and calculated using an absolute reference for the wage increase.	6	
f	Feature	Goal Seek results typed below 2012 projections— entry states a 1.4 % increase to cap at $620,000 for the Overseas Distribution department.	3	
g	Feature	Three scenarios stored—Maximum Increase, Goal Increase, Compromise Increase Wage increase percentage displayed is 1.5% (Goal Increase) Create a scenario summary report	8	
h	Feature/Finishing/ Editing	Worksheet formatted Print options set to exclude criteria range Landscape orientation Custom Header – *Projected Salary Costs for 2012* Custom Footer – *Name, current date*	10	

2	Editing	Add properties to the workbook • Author – Student Name • Subject – Your course code • Keywords – *Employee, Department, Salary* • Comments – *Any changes must be authorized by the Human Resources Manager*	4	
a, b, c	Feature	Each shortcut key/macro performs the correct sort. Ctrl + Shift + B (SalaryByDept) Ctrl + Shift + C (SalaryByYear) Ctrl + Shift + D (SalaryByEmpNo) Each macro begins with a Go To statement or Ctrl + Home to move the active cell within the database list	9	
	File Management	Save the workbook as macro-enabled	2	
3a	Editing	Delete Scenario Summary Worksheet Add comment to cell containing wage increase to inform user how to open the Scenarios dialog box	3	
b	File Management/ Feature	SaveAs **EmployeeInfo-Password** Workbook requires password to open the file—**L2FCS**. *Note: Passwords are case sensitive. If this password doesn't work, try the first letter in lowercase format or the @ instead of the 2. Deduct a point if either of these errors occurs*	4	
c	Feature	Protect the worksheet with *L2FCS*.	2	
4a	Editing	In **EmployeeInfo-Macros.xlsx**, insert new sheet named *InflationProjection* and change tab color to red	2	
a	Research/Typing	Search Internet for information on inflation rate Enter projected inflation rate Include hyperlink to source web page	4	
b	Feature	Historical CPI data imported Include a description of the source data and the URL	5	
c	Editing	Company logo at the top of a worksheet	2	
d	Feature	Chart created and formatted that plots either one year of monthly CPI or five years of annual CPI	5	
	Feature	Trendline added to chart	2	
e	Finishing/Typing	Print options set to print on one page either landscape or portrait Custom Header – *Inflation Research for Salary Negotiations* Custom Footer – *Name, current date*	4	
		TOTAL POINTS	85	